Religious Fundamentalism in the Contemporary World

Religious Fundamentalism in the Contemporary World

Critical Social and Political Issues

Edited by
Santosh C. Saha

LEXINGTON BOOKS
Lanham • Boulder • New York • Toronto • Oxford

BL 238 .R475 2004 c.2

Religious fundamentalism in
the contemporary world

LEXINGTON BOOKS

Published in the United States of America
by Lexington Books
An imprint of The Rowman & Littlefield Publishing Group, Inc.
4501 Forbes Boulevard, Suite 200, Lanham, Maryland 20706

PO Box 317
Oxford
OX2 9RU, UK

Copyright © 2004 by Lexington Books

All rights reserved. No part of this publication may be reproduced,
stored in a retrieval system, or transmitted in any form or by any
means, electronic, mechanical, photocopying, recording, or otherwise,
without the prior permission of the publisher.

British Library Cataloguing in Publication Information Available

Library of Congress Cataloging-in-Publication Data

Religious fundamentalism in the contemporary world : critical social and political issues /
  edited by Santosh C. Saha.
    p. cm.
  Includes bibliographical references (p.) and index.
  ISBN 0-7391-0760-7 (cloth : alk. paper)
  1. Religious fundamentalism. I. Saha, Santosh C.

BL238.R475 2003
306.6—dc22

2003060817

Printed in the United States of America

⊖™ The paper used in this publication meets the minimum requirements of American
National Standard for Information Sciences—Permanence of Paper for Printed Library
Materials, ANSI/NISO Z39.48–1992.

For

*Priyashi
and
Piyali*

our granddaughters

Contents

Introduction   *Anthony J. Parel*   1

Part I: Approaches to Fundamentalisms

Chapter 1:   Religious Fundamentalism and Its "Other": Snapshot View from the Global Information Order
Dipankar Sinha   9

Chapter 2:   Some Priority Variables in the Study of Comparative Religious Politics
Ted G. Jelen   29

Chapter 3:   Fundamentalist Ideology, Institutions, and the State: A Formal Analysis
Graeme Stuart Lang and Vivienne Wee   47

Chapter 4:   Religion between Universal and Particular: Eastern Europe after 1989
Alexander Agadjanian   71

Part II: Regional Fundamentalisms

Chapter 5:   Phases of Political Islam
Tamara Sonn   93

Chapter 6:	Hindu Revivalist Cultural Policies and Programs in India: A Critique *Santosh C. Saha*	127
Chapter 7:	Perceiving Islam: The Cause and Consequences of Islamophobia in Western Media *Zohair Husain and David Rosenbaum*	171
Chapter 8:	Democracy vs. Fundamentalism: Religious Politics of the Bharatiya Janata Party in India *Krishna K. Tummala*	207
Chapter 9:	Ethnicity and Religion in Israeli Politics: Emergence of the Shas Party *Jacob Abadi*	235
Chapter 10:	Contesting Historiographies in South Asia: The Islamization of Pakistani Social Studies Textbooks *Yvette Claire Rosser*	265
Bibliography		309
Index		325
About the Contributors		337

Introduction

Anthony J. Parel

Religious fundamentalism is a very powerful force in world affairs today. It occupies a position not dissimilar to that occupied by Marxism in the twentieth century. Like Marxism, it is not only a belief system but also a plan of action to transform humanity. In addition, the plan in question sometimes involves the use of extreme violence, exercised not only within but also across state boundaries. In academia too, religious fundamentalism has become a subject of teaching and research. And, in North America, the events of 9/11 have added a sense of urgency to what otherwise would have remained a part of the sober study of comparative religion. Whether we like it or not, after 9/11, religious fundamentalism has become an issue of national security as well.

The present volume, ably planned and executed by Dr. Saha, makes a valuable contribution to our understanding of this expanding field of enquiry. Of this volume's many virtues three deserve special commendation: the attention given to the question of a working definition of fundamentalism, the importance of its regional variants, and the damage that it can do to the educational system.

Even though everyone knows that religious fundamentalism is a fact of contemporary life, nobody seems to know how to give a definition of it that is applicable in every case. For the phenomenon varies from religion to religion, and even within the same religion, it takes different form in different countries. The popular media was initially responsible for giving the concept wide circulation. Critical thought, as usual, was slow in submitting it to the scrutiny that it deserved. There was nothing surprising in this, for as Hegel reminds us, the owl Minerva spreads its wings only at the dusk. The phenomenon had to occur first, before philosophers and social scientists are ready to give their verdict. Now that the concept is here, scholars have to define it as best they can.

Part I of this volume tackles the issue of definition or approaches to fundamentalism with great care and circumspection. A wide range of phenomena, some violent, others peaceful, goes under the name of religious fundamentalism: the Shia regime now entrenched in Iran, the Taliban regime recently ousted from Afghanistan, the *Hindutva* movement now gaining ground in India, the Jamaat-e-Islami and Jamiat-e-Ulema-Islam of Pakistan, the Muslim Brotherhood of Egypt, the Communione e Liberazione movement of Italy, the conservative Baptist movement in the United States of the 1920s, the Hamas of Palestine, the Kach movement of Rabbi Kahane in Israel, the rethinking of the social doctrines in the Russian Orthodox Church, and the pancasila in Indonesia. This list is by no means exhaustive. However, it gives us a good idea of the difficulties encountered when trying to apply the same definition to describe them.

A convenient way of resolving the difficulties would be to identify the characteristics commonly associated with religious fundamentalism. Five such characteristics may be listed. First, there is a conscious effort to return to the core beliefs or values of a given religion or culture. We include both religion and culture under the fundamentalist umbrella for the reason that in some instances religion is the center of attention, while in others, culture takes the place of religion. Where religion is the focus of attention, it is appropriate to speak of a return to "beliefs" or "doctrines," and where culture is the focus of attention, it is appropriate to speak of a revival of "values." Second, texts taken to be authoritative are used to justify the return to past beliefs or values. Third, an attitude of ambivalence is exhibited toward modernity or secularism. While some aspects of modernity are rejected, others are cordially endorsed. Fourth, there is normally a self-appointed elite that assumes the leadership role in promoting the fundamentalist agenda. The ultimate aim of this elite is the transformation of society, which, in many instances, includes the capture of state power. Finally, there is the question of violence. While some fundamentalist groups reject it, others make it their main vehicle.

If a group or a movement exhibits a majority of these characteristics, there is good scientific reason for calling it fundamentalist. It would be desirable, of course, if all five characteristics were verified in each instance. But that is not always possible. Given the great variability of the cultural and historical contexts in which fundamentalism operates, it is neither possible nor desirable, to put fundamentalism in a definitional straight jacket. We have to be content, as Aristotle would advise us, with a definition that indicates the truth only "for the most part," and "roughly and in outline." The definition of fundamentalism therefore will have to remain a working definition, and any attempt to give it mathematical precision is bound to fail. In addition, with a working definition, it is quite possible to undertake serious research and arrive at valid conclusions regarding the nature and function of religious fundamentalism.

Introduction

The second virtue of this volume is its focus on the regional variants of fundamentalism, notably in South Asia. The focus on South Asia is most welcome for at least two reasons. First, it is in this region that some of the most formidable fundamentalist groups operating today had their origin. There is a symbiotic relationship between the Islamism of the Middle East and that of the Subcontinent, and it is necessary to keep a bifocal view of the matter. Secondly, it is in South Asia that we find two fundamentalisms—Islamic and Hindu—emerging as a national security issue as well. India and Pakistan, equipped as they are with nuclear weapons, have very powerful fundamentalist groups operating in them. Nuclear weapons could fall into their hands either by accident or by a coup d'etat. If that should happen, one can only imagine what the scale of violence unleashed by religious fundamentalism would be.

The focus on South Asia also helps to bring some balance in our understanding of the dangers that religious fundamentalism poses worldwide. After September 11, attention was riveted on the dangers that it posed, and still poses, to the United States, and to a lesser extent to Western Europe. The fact remains, however, the dangers facing South Asia are equally grave. Perhaps they are graver still for the reason that the region is nuclearized.

The chapters by Saha and Tummala give a panoramic view of the danger that *Hindutva* poses for the region. *Hindutva* feeds on Islamophobia, and to a lesser extent on Christianophobia. Its long-term goal is the Hinduization of the whole of India. Its short-term goal is the intimidation of the minorities, especially Muslims and Christians—their persons, properties, institutions—and places of worship are under constant threat from Hindu fundamentalists. There is a division of labor between the Bharatiya Janata Party (BJP), the Rashtriya Swayam Sevak Sangh (RSS), and the Vishwa Hindu Parishad (VHP). The first of these determines state policies, while the other two vitiate the quality of life in civil society.

Lest we get a distorted view by focusing solely on *Hindutva*, it is necessary to keep our eyes open on the history of the evolution of religious fundamentalism in the Subcontinent. South Asia spawned two fundamentalisms: Hindu and Islamic. Each was driven by the fear of the other. Islamic fundamentalism was driven partly by a revived consciousness of the imperial mission of Islam in India, and partly by Hinduphobia. The mission of Islam in the Subcontinent was thought to be the progressive Islamization of the region. It started in Sind in the eighth century, and continued through the Mughul rule. Hindus are seen as standing in the way of this program. There is in the eyes of the Islamists a life and death struggle involved here. One has only to read the works of A. A. Mawdudi to realize how seriously the Islamists take their mission. The creation of Pakistan (and Bangladesh) was only the beginning. Islamization of Kashmir is the next step. That is why the Hindu fundamentalists tend to see Islam much the same way that Muslims tend to see the West—as an imperial, expansionist force. They believe that they have been the victims of the expansion of Islam eastward.

There is therefore a "fearful symmetry" between Hinduphobia and Islamophobia. The roles that V. D. Savarkar (1883–1966) and A. A. Mawdudi (1903–1979) have played in the evolution of the two fundamentalisms are comparable. Both were born in the same region of India—Maharashtra: the one in Bhagur, near Nasik and the other in Aurangabad. They both wrote the basic texts of their respective fundamentalism. Savarkar's *Hindutva: Who is a Hindu?* (1923) and, Mawdudi's first major work, *Jihad* (1927), appeared in the same decade. It was Hinduphobia that turned Mawdudi from being a secular nationalist into an Islamic fundamentalist. Similarly, it was Islamophobia that turned Savarkar from being a friend of Indian Muslims into their implacable enemy. Jamaat-i Islami is the counterpart of the RSS: the Islamization of society is the goal of the first, and the Hinduization of society, that of the second. Their approach to modernity is also comparable. While they welcome its science and technology, they both reject its humanism, especially the fundamental rights of the individual. The use of violence in civil society is part of their program, and the capture and retention of state power their declared means. They both persecute their fellow citizens simply because of their religion. In addition, they both contribute to the destabilization of the entire region. In no other part of the world do we find a more dangerous display of the "fearful symmetry" of two contemporary religious fundamentalisms than in South Asia.

A third merit of this volume is that it sheds useful light on the darkness that religious fundamentalism is spreading in the field of secondary education. Yvette Claire Rosser's research on the Islamization of the Social Studies textbooks in Pakistan is a case in point. Her treatment of the subject is detailed and extensive. What we see here is a deliberate and sustained attempt to distort historical data known to be true by those distorting it. This calculated assault on truth is mounted not by ignorant mullahs, but by an educated elite trained in pedigreed universities.

The implication of this educational policy seems to be that religious fundamentalism can flourish only if it is fed by a distorted view of history. It cannot survive if truth and critical understanding of the past are allowed to inform young minds. The power of truth to liberate them from prejudice and hatred is denied to them. The possibility of seeing the world as a pluralist system of complementing civilizations hardly exists. Instead the educational system appears to endorse the thesis of the clash of civilizations: the Hindu, for a Pakistan Muslim, must remain his or her permanent enemy.

According to the fundamentalists, the coexistence of Islam and Hinduism on the Subcontinent for over a millennium has not brought the two cultures closer together. If anything, it has only contributed to their mutual degradation. Indeed, one of Mawdudi's major goals has been to purge Indian Islam of any "impurities" that it has contracted from Hinduism. There could be no dialogue between fundamentalist Islam and Hinduism. The treatment of Akbar the Great follows the Mawdudi line: he is either to be ignored or treated as a traitor to Islam.

The impact of the teaching of a deliberately distorted form of history on unsuspecting young minds can easily be imagined. Apart from contributing to their stunted intellectual growth, it lays the groundwork for the intensification of political tension in the subcontinent. The possibility of any rapprochement between Hindus and Muslims is being put off for the foreseeable future.

Interference with the Social Studies curriculum is not confined to Pakistani Islamists alone. The denizens of *Hindutva* are not far behind those of Jamaat-e-Islami and Jamiat-e-Ulema-Islam of Pakistan. Since the BJP came to power there has been a conscious effort to rewrite Indian history. Accordingly, Indian culture is presented as if it was a homogeneous entity. Buddhism is presented as a deviant form of Hinduism, to be rejected on nationalist grounds. As for Islam, its positive contributions in the fields of language, literature, philosophy, architecture, music, and popular culture, are either to be ignored or put in a negative light. The *Hindutva* forces are also busy undervaluing the contributions of Mahatma Gandhi and Jawaharlal Nehru. Gandhi is accused of being an appeaser of Muslims and Nehru as being hostile to Hindu fundamentalism. There appears to be a parallel between the physical assassination of Gandhi by Hindu fundamentalists and their present attempt at killing his moral and intellectual legacy.

In concluding this Introduction, it is important to keep in mind that any serious discussion of religious fundamentalism remains incomplete if it does not include a discussion, however brief, of dogmatic secularism. For, as everyone knows, religious fundamentalism arose in response to dogmatic secularism. By dogmatic secularism I mean the view that dismisses religion as either an "illusion" or as "the opium of the masses," or as the residue of past superstitions or as just the personal preference of the unenlightened. I distinguish dogmatic secularism from constitutional secularism. The latter is a practical mechanism of guaranteeing the religious neutrality of the State, with no disrespect meant toward religion.

The roots of dogmatic secularism reach back at least to the Enlightenment. The latter made a mockery of religion. Marxism, Maoism, Freudianism, and certain branches of Liberalism have built on the Enlightenment legacy, and have written their own history of dogmatic secularism. Be that as it may, there is little doubt that dogmatic secularism had misjudged, and continues to misjudge, the nature and power of the human yearning for a transcending spiritual understanding of the meaning of human existence.

Religious fundamentalism has tapped on this profound inner yearning. The tragedy is that one branch of it (the violent branch), has hijacked this yearning for its own sinister ends. It has made violence and terror, hatred and persecution, its means of operation. The other branch of religious fundamentalism (the non-violent one), which seeks the peaceful reform of religion hardly gets the attention that it deserves.

As things stand now, the majority of humankind feels the need to avoid both dogmatic secularism and violent religious fundamentalism. A middle ground between these extremes has to be found. Fortunately, it is not difficult to find guides who can point to that middle ground. The name of Mahatma Gandhi naturally comes to mind.

Gandhi has demonstrated that the alternative to dogmatic secularism is nonviolent spirituality, not violent religious fundamentalism. Some, including a few social scientists, have argued that democracy and a market economy will rid the world of the evils of religious fundamentalism. These are secular solutions, and Gandhi would endorse them conditionally. The condition is that these secular remedies have to be strengthened by the remedies that nonviolent spirituality alone can supply, viz., adherence to truth, love of the neighbor, peaceful but effective resistance to injustice in all its forms, whether racial, economic, or political. Violent religious fundamentalism is a spiritual malaise requiring, ultimately, a spiritual remedy.

Part I

Approaches to Fundamentalisms

Chapter 1

Religious Fundamentalism and Its "Other": Snapshot View from the Global Information Order

Dipankar Sinha

> Those who shout that Laden is a terrorist and Bush a vegetarian, and those who argue that Bush is a terrorist and Laden a vegetarian, drink water from the same riverbank.
>
> A contemporary Bengali song

The diabolic event of September 11, 2001—the day in which one of the worst tragedies of mankind occurred—has unleashed innumerable manifestations and consequences, perhaps too many to take into cognition at the individual level. However, the scholarly analyses of "9/11," except in rare cases,[1] seldom directly address the Global Information Order (hereafter, GIO) which is a constitutive element of the contemporary world order. The GIO[2] is assumed to exist somewhere in the background. This chapter seeks to explore the complex linkage of religious fundamentalism[3] and its "other," which we would refer to as the *other fundamentalism*, within the interactive dynamics of the GIO. The linkage, as the subsequent discussion would reveal, involves dialectics, dilemmas, and directions of the two kinds of fundamentalism, with the GIO as a *shared space*.

Fundamentalism(s) and Otherness

Before we discuss the GIO in more specific terms let us make a conceptual clarification of the two kinds of fundamentalism being referred to here. Fundamentalism has generally been defined as "belief in the original form of a religion or theory, without accepting any later ideas."[4] Fundamentalism concerns affirmation of views, ideas, and perspectives as "holistic," "absolute," and "infallible," and by the same token it declares and rejects alternative views, ideas, and perspectives as "illegitimate." The trouble with the definitions of fundamentalism is that it has almost exclusive association with religion and theology. Interestingly, the much acclaimed *The Fundamentalism Project*, based on a concerted and systematic effort at interpreting fundamentalism in social scientific terms, explains[5] it overwhelmingly in terms of religion, religiosity, and religious identity. We would argue that religious fundamentalism, so to say, has been in the limelight but there are other kinds of fundamentalism as well.

Epistemologically, the *other fundamentalism* celebrates and promotes "the apotheosis of mechanics as the highest triumph of human reason."[6] Having its roots in the Enlightenment Project, which celebrates the domination of the object world through application of human reason and scientific method, it not only interprets and announces the triumph of technocratic rationality as ubiquitous and omnipotent but it also incorporates it as a *worldview*. Technocratic rationality is thus a sort of "technology" ordained to transform "being" in the world and at the same time it is a cultural imagination.[7] Because the "West"[8] is the major innovator of science and technology, and the undisputed *epicenter* of "mechanics as the highest triumph of human reason," the *other fundamentalism* would view, define, and explain the dynamics of the world in overwhelmingly *Westcentric* terms—in the typical *West versus the Rest* fashion. Thus, Westcentrism is a core component of the rigid epistemology of the *other fundamentalism*, privileging certain specific configurations of power, knowledge, subjectivity, and language—in a specific kind of tenor—as the "only possible reality." Its major difference with religious fundamentalism lies in its *secularization criterion* in which religion is to make a retreat from the public realm. However, in its single-track promotion of knowledge and values in Westcentric terms and referents, the *other fundamentalism* would seek to establish a closed, homogenous and manipulability world order in which any alternative representation is devalued and discarded—a "political" task that remarkably coincides with that of religious fundamentalism. Thus, U.S. President Bush's invitation-cum-warning in the aftermath of September 11—that "all nations in all regions of the world must now make a decision; either you are with us or you are with the terrorists"—and Laden's call to Muslims to Shas' combat the "enemies of Islam" might have more points of convergence than it apparently reveals. The convergence, most evident in "us" and "them" categories, is bound to be dangerous in a world "where dissent is increasingly marginalised if not effaced and the peripheries ignored."[9]

Let us discuss how and why the GIO becomes a *shared space* for two kinds of fundamentalism. The dialectics of the two kinds of fundamentalism, which would engage the ensuing discussion, are most evident in the West-versus-Pan Islam variety.[10] Before we directly address it let us refer back to the concept of the Other(ness). The concept involves perspectives and relationships that are so far, yet so close. As Silverstone[11] puts it:

> It refers to the recognition that there is something out there that is not me, not of my making, nor under my control; distinct, different, beyond reach, yet occupying the same space, the same ... landscape. The Other includes others: people I know or have never heard of; my friends as well as my enemies. It includes my neighbours as well as those I have only seen in the photographs and on screens. It includes those ... (i)n my society and in yours. However, because I and the Other share a world, because I will be your Other as much as you are mine, even if I know you not, then I have a relationship to you. The relationship is a challenge. Through it I am forced to recognize that I am not alone, that I have, in one way or another, to take the Other into account.

To add, in having proposed *human salvation* through religion and technocentrism-Westcentrism, respectively, religious fundamentalism and its "other" fit the above description perfectly.

GIO Unveiled

The GIO, which holds the key to the current essay, is to be distinguished from the preceding orders, which go by the name of the International Information Order (IIO) or the World Information and Communication Order (WICO). The IIO and the WICO, at the forefront of the developing countries' struggle for restructuring the then prevalent information order, had the states/nations as fundamental units of politics. These proposed orders were to be constructed at the *world* (composed of states) and *international* (comprising of nations) levels. The GIO, on the contrary, has acquired a *global* character through the *transnational/translocal* route which by itself undermines the primacy traditionally accorded to the nations. It has often been claimed that the most important attribute of the GIO is the *compression of time and space*, which in turn has given birth to ideas like "the death of distance" and "the end of geography." While we do not subscribe to the overstretched arguments of the *compression thesis* as such, we would like to emphasize that it does imply that considerable degree of transformation are taking place now. The point assumes particular importance in view of organizations like al-Qaeda being transnational, extraterriritorial force. To add, the transformation we are referring to has been made possible by astonishing progress in the information and communication technology (ICT)—the basic infrastructure of the GIO.

There is, however, an interesting paradox associated with the GIO. On the one hand, because there is a correlation between a specific kind of communication order and the associated political economic order, the GIO theoretically requires an overhauling of existing regulatory regimes and the system of governance. On the other hand, beyond its zone of formal and explicit requirements it also gives rise to several channels of informal and latent linkages and networks, which very often escape our attention. Such linkages and networks, which largely rest on but are not limited to the cyberspace, in many cases acquire subversive character. The subversive activities directly and indirectly concern the people, groups, and communities who/which are marginalized.[12] They have little, if any, presence in the immediate cognitive map of the forces—the dominant states, the transnational institutions, and organizations—at least so far as running the "show" in the contemporary world order is concerned.

This brings us to yet another distinctive feature of the GIO. What makes it conceptually and functionally unique is that in the cases of the IIO and the WICO the dynamics of the struggle, as already indicated, had the states/nations as fundamental units. The struggle initially concerned the demand by the Third World for construction of a "just, equitable and democratic" information order which was supposed to accord equal status to the developed and the developing countries; later under severe resistance and string-pulling by the developed Western states it was converted into a demand for integration to the existing information order.[13] A detailed discussion of the politics of the New International Information Order (NIIO) or the New World Information and Communication Order (NWICO) is beyond the purview of the current essay. However, what is to be emphasized here is that in the cases of both the NIIO and the NWICO manipulations and subversion of the existing order were not exactly on the agenda. The whole thrust was on ensuring a very structured and formalistic "alternative" order, with little, if any, space left for latent, informal linkages. More specifically, in terms of conceptualization of *information* and *communication*, the former was defined more as "hard data" and the latter defined overwhelmingly in mechanistic terms—as "exchange of information." To reiterate, the parameters of the information order visualized in both the cases were utterly state—and/or nationcentric, with a vital issue like *cultural relativism* being referred to, but only within the limits of the set parameters. Interestingly, the state-nation-centric parameters remained sacrosanct to both the parties—the developing states advocating reconstruction of the existing information order and the developed states seeking status quo.

The GIO, both in its structure and process, is more reflexive in character with some space for "unintended consequences." The messages of the GIO are, to a considerable extent, sprouted through such unintended consequences. In many cases the visibility of the messages are articulated without being visible, and the audibility of the messages are articulated without being audible. In cases of "closure"—to be discussed in the following sections—on the part of the recipients, the messages are visible and audible. In being so, the GIO, in our view, is a *late-ish modern*[14] phenomenon. Despite the efforts to have formal control over it by the powers (in a major way by the powerful states and media conglomerates)—mainly through the twin mechanisms of commercialization and corporatism—its "more or less out-of-control bytes of information"[15] continue to defy the hegemony of any master narrative.

At the base of such reflexivity lies a *transforming* political economy—what has been termed as[16] "the end of organized capitalism" or more directly as "disorganized capitalism" and the consequent rise of information capital. Information capital, as David Harvey would note,[17] is much more flexible, mobile, diffuse, especially in comparison to the *sticky* industrial capital. The shift has as much to do with the rise of what Harvey, one step ahead of our designation of the contemporary process as late-ish modern, calls *postmodernization*[18]—flexible modes of production and exchange characteristic of the post-Fordist economic organization—as with the rise of an order in which the supra nation-state, transnational forces, even in the form of motley individuals and groups, are aggressively making their presence felt at the cost of the power of the nation-states. Again, one can harbor legitimate doubts about the extent to which the world through spatial and temporal compression is turning into the so-called global village but there is little doubt about the vastly increased mosaic of shifting and redefined identity, and economies of signs and space[19] in the emerging order.

As far as the GIO is concerned, the omnipresent flow of information in it leads to incessant flow of power but there is a catch. It is a moot (Foucaultian) point whether the quantum and flow of power, despite/because of the onslaught of global capital, has become less coercive and repressive but the point is that it has provided, in a comparative sense, greater scope to the assertion of identity and agency to the hitherto underprivileged and marginalized. The GIO has become a vehicle for political subversion of the contemporary world order of which it is, as has been mentioned earlier, a constitutive part. That the informatized world would have a directly proportional relationship with subversion might have disappointed publicists of the Information Society, such as Daniel Bell[20] and Stonier.[21] Both Bell and Stonier, being guided by unfettering technocentric urge, argued that the expansion of the computerized information systems and their merger with ICT would have the power to eradicate all problems. The fundamental point they missed was that whatever might be its material benefits; it would still be too little to do away with the exclusionary practices of the iniquitous world order. Thus we see today the emergence of "marginalized" *extraterritorial* forces—"global" in their thoughts, acts, activities, and objectives—which find in the GIO a useful infrastructure to indulge in subversive activities.

Such subversive acts have been traced[22] to a *new logic*, which discourages the earlier "head-on-collision" strategy with the existing information order, and calls for utilizing the order itself for promotion and dissemination of opposing ideas. In some cases, as in the case of the hacking subversive acts could be as "benign" as defacing the opponent's websites by their own messages, graffiti, and slogans, or crashing the computer networks through dissemination of virus or even effecting an e-mail jam, the later being a potent weapon for "ethical hackers" who propagate *electronic civil disobedience*. In some other cases, as in the case of the activists of militant Islam, it seemed to have acquired more intense, sweeping, and multifaceted character. There are reasons to believe that those who indulged in the horrific act on September 11 were aware of the "global mileage" that their act would get through the electronic media. In this context, one can also refer to the frequent use of e-mail by the captors of Daniel Pearl, a journalist of the *Wall Street Journal*, who was eventually murdered by the extremists in Pakistan. In a way, the GIO is more of a disorder, with contestations and ruptures intervening in the continuities that supposedly mark the rational-purposive idea of an order.

Thus, whether one likes it or not the GIO is a *shared space*. On the one hand, one just has to type and click www.alneda.com to find oneself instantly face-to-face with various pro-al Qaeda links celebrating the cause of radical Islam. On the other hand, the same click to other links would bring us face-to-face with sites extolling the virtues of the "liberal secular" West and making scathing critique of the "religio-fascists" and theocracy. And it so happens that the GIO has come to acquire a *conflictual* character—most evident but not limited to the two kinds of fundamentalism being discussed here. The GIO is being used to disseminate oppositional agendas by the fundamentalist proponents, even if there is a world of difference in terms of representations. The adherents of the *other fundamentalism* would have obvious advantage over the religious fundamentalists because the former has greater control—technological, political, and economic—over the GIO. However, that does not guarantee uninterrupted success to them. Louw's observation[23] made in the contemporary context of struggle over power and meaning is quite appropriate here:

> Power is not automatic, it is the outcome of struggle. However, such struggles are not fought on level playing fields because certain players are advantaged (or disadvantaged) by having more (or less) access to the sources of power at the start of the play. Pre-existent access to power is necessarily an advantage in the next round of the struggle over power. This means existent power elites are advantaged, *but not in a way that absolutely predetermines their success in the next round of battle.* [emphasis added]

The emphasized parts of the excerpt indicate that the GIO's status as a *shared space* can be qualitatively enhanced, leading to a more equitable, democratic, and harmonious world order, if it is freed from the clutches of fundamentalist urges.

Religious Fundamentalism of "Modern" Kind

September 11 was a cataclysmic event by any standard, but it was still a symptom, and not the cause of a deeper process at work—the closer *bond* between religious fundamentalism and modernity. As is sometimes said, the religious fundamentalists are "antimodern but not antimodernist." This is not to argue that the bond between religious fundamentalism/militancy and modernity is a development peculiar to the contemporary times. The trajectory of modernity is not straightforward; nor is it something fixed and unalterable. But the fact remains that over the centuries—say, since the days of Renaissance from when modernity has arguably taken its roots—there has been the gradual emergence of certain ideas, principles, criteria, and images which has created a sort of *crust of modernity*. As a social commentator remarks,[24] it is difficult to undermine the importance of the crust of modernity because otherwise we would have to argue that there is nothing outside modernity and there is little distinction between modernity and nonmodernity. However, the obverse of such crust also remains a distinct possibility.

Scholars such as Eisenstadt[25] have revealed that religious fundamentalist movements can combine the "traditional" and the "modernist" elements and the coexistence of the two can facilitate the fulfillment of the objectives of the religious movements. Flood,[26] in discussing religion in "late modernity," refers to tradition and community being shattered by the process of "detraditionalization" and a hidden community of "authentic individuals" developed alongside the reconstruction of tradition or "retraditionalization." His most significant observation in our context is that binding narratives and behaviors are important as ever in the contemporary transformations of religion through cyberspace. Lawrence[27] has more specifically stressed on the fundamentalists' aptitude for taking advantage of the technological advances in furthering their own cause. In the contemporary world order the bond has intensified to a greater degree and has made itself available for display. In the context of September 11 it seems that it was left to the GIO to globally publicize the reversal of the "set" perception, widely harbored in the *mainstream* arena, about the religious fundamentalists as personalities who, being guided by the cosmic vision, are strictly confined to the divine *diktats* of the sacred Book/Text/Scriptures, and are necessarily out of sync with the *modern* times.

The stereotyping has been even more possible because this "spiritual-utilitarian" aspect of religious fundamentalism, which forges its bond with "secular" modernity, is not apparent in the discourse of militant Islam. For instance, the text of *Fatwa* urging *Jihad* (*Holy War* or *Holy Struggle* as per diverse interpretations) against the Americans, signed among others by Osama on February 23, 1998, begins with this statement: "... *in compliance with God's order, we issue the following fatwa*. . . ." The following revocation to God is also a familiar part of any declaration of *Jihad*, including the one being referred to here:

> Praise be to God, who revealed the Book, controls the clouds, defeats factionalism and says in His Book ". . . fight and slay the pagans whom ye find them, seize them, beleaguer them."

Even the "severe punishment" supposedly meted out to the Americans on 9/11 is also interpreted as the "act of God Almighty" by various brands of Islamic militants.

Then again, beneath this apparent "act of God" lies the *temporal duty* of the ordinary mortals—the dedicated faithful "soldiers" of Islam—who are to execute the assignments. And when the temporal duty concerns creation, organization, and sustenance of the world's most dreaded "terror network" and its nodes—spanning as far off "centers" as Afghanistan, Bosnia, Egypt, Chechnya, Tajikistan, Palestine, Somalia, Yemen, Pakistan, Algeria, Kosovo, Kashmir, and "hideouts" in the Western states—it cannot but manipulate the most advanced "worldly resources" like aeronautics, information technology, and nuclear, biological, and chemical weapons to achieve its means. The same "resources" are being utilized for *publicizing* religion and thereby resisting the "modern" idea that religion should only concern the private self. As Pantic[28] notes, "(b)eing educated and intelligent, Osama bin Ladin (sic) and his 'folks' have studied the cultural and political effects of networked society in the context of their fundamentalist views." This of course can bring in charges of "hypocrisy"[29] against the fundamentalists who fight the "holy wars" using the weapons of mass destruction developed by the "infidels," thus adding strength to the "culture of violence" that is often viewed as part and parcel of modernity.

This also gives rise to a moot point: whether the twenty-first-century brand of fundamentalism/militancy, in comparison to its traditional counterpart, compromises its ideological fervor. It is not an appropriate place to go deeper into the debate but at the same time one has to remember that from the vantage point of religious fundamentalists, engaging with some aspects of modernity may not necessarily imply surrender or compromise; it could well be regarded as a "tactical" move, playing backfoot, so to say. This is in order to push forward the Holy Agenda, which would also lead to the downfall of modernity. Even with the "paranoid," "fanatic" band of Osama followers, who would rather sacrifice their life rather than making compromises, this seems to be the case. The Taliban chief Mullah Omar's use of "walkie talkie" to instruct followers to "embrace death as true Muslims" in the Holy War against America symbolizes "religious use" of modern technology. Such use of modern technology, with the GIO as the *backbone*, would, and has already, given rise to smarter crimes. It can, as a former director of the Central Intelligence Agency (CIA), John Deutch[30] predicted, lead to "electronic Pearl Harbor." September 11 was, from the same vantage point of modern technology, witness to what can be described as an *aerial Pearl Harbor*. Analyst Navid Kermani would even find traces of science fiction in the events of September 11 in which "mythical images and configurations are projected into futuristic scenario."[31]

The *tactical flirting* with modernity has its limitations as well. The religious militants—of whatever affiliations—should not be too euphoric about taking the modern West often for a ride just because they could do it on September 11. The fact remains that the artifacts and images of the West-projected modernity, for better or worse, continue to appeal to a large number of people in the societies from which these fundamentalist forces take root. It is true in the case of Egypt as it is true in Iran. One can have in one's "holy agenda" the resistance to the Westcentric terms of modernity but if such resistance perpetuates the pitiable condition of the people who continue to suffer from poverty, social violence, political repression, and economic deprivation in the name of "religious protection from the evils of modernity" the problem would be compounded in multiple terms to create irrepressible attraction for the "other."

Clash of Ignorance

What happened on September 11 is at the same time a clash of worldviews—most often between a *location* (the West) and religion (any religion other than Christianity, most frequently Islam). As far as the most intense flashpoint is concerned, the clash is between the West as the "epitome of modernity," and Islam as the "obscurantist," "traditional" *other*; it is between the West as the "Satan" and militant Islamism as the "godly path." By the same token it is a "clash of ignorance," with the onus on both sides propagating and celebrating such ignorance. To the radical/militant adherents of Islam (or for that matter to those of Hinduism) the West is a "monolith" of permissiveness, a sponsor of discrimination and violence, and henceforth morally corrupt and bankrupt. It is this sweeping and facile generalization, which lead to the rationalization—in the name of giving a lethal blow to what they perceive wrongly as the amorphous monolithic West—of the killing of innocent people on September 11. It is the same ignorance which removes from their sight and consciousness the happening that in the aftermath of the tragedy of September 11, a vast sea of humanity of the West and the "rest" became one—even Americans, so to say—to share grief and concern against despicable violence. Interestingly, the coming together of the West and the "rest" at that moment of crisis was precipitated by a sense of empathy and repulsion against violence.

There is, however, the other side of the proverbial coin of fundamentalism. In explaining how the West perceives its "other" and why it should take a bit more responsibility for the "clash," Ansari[32] writes:

> Of course, myths and partial images taken at face value have for long affected and often distorted understanding about Islam and the so-called Muslim world when viewed from the West. Stereotyping and conflict between Islam and the largely Christian West have repeatedly fostered levels of ignorance (a resonance of Ed Said's "clash of ignorance" to be referred to later). The irony of the present situation is increased when . . . we recognize that the West itself now

. . . forms part of the world: the two, not so separate, world, whose boundaries in fact have always been blurred, now overlap more than ever before.

Said warns[33] us of the "unedifying and inadequate labels and generalizations" associated with the *West* and *Islam* which, as he adds, lead only to "pigeonholed" views and "strapped" reality. That even the supposedly enlightened academics are not free from the clutches of the strapped reality is proved by the following comment of Bruce Cumings, a well-known historian: That such bias exists even in the mind of distinguished academics is proved by a comment by Bruce Cummings: "How many Muslims exist with passable English and the modern abilities to manipulate credit accounts, get multiple driver's licenses and fake i.d.'s, learn to fly jumbo jets, etc.—people who otherwise would be professionals? *I cannot believe that they are many*."[34] The problem with this typical view is that it loses on three major counts. First, it underestimates the "give-and-take" relationship strategy associated with religious fundamentalism and modernity, thereby reinforcing the stereotypical images of the religious militants. Second, in only scratching the surface of the problem at hand it fails to comprehend a major limitation of (late) modernity—its failure to put an end to violence, which mostly occurs because of deprivation, repression, and a sense of desperation that accompanies its achievements. Third, because of the first and the second factors it fails to comprehend the breadth and depth of the challenge. In comparison Huang Ping is more realistic when he observes[35] that because "high modernity" (Ping's designation of late modernity) has not developed a mechanism that can keep human beings safe from organized violence, nor could protect people from being attacked by "armed nobodies," the "central issue is . . . to review and rethink the system itself, to see how the global flows of capital, technology, information, and above all, people, as a consequence of the nation-state system paradoxically challenging the state itself."

Further, when viewed from the vantage point of the GIO the *ignorance* becomes a legacy of a severely blinkered technicist-instrumentalist vision born out of the *other fundamentalism*. The *other fundamentalism*, in overestimating the "universal" application of its institutions, rules, and norms, fails to take into consideration the resistance and repulsion that it invites in "enemy quarters." Interestingly, even Francis Fukuyama, who gained both scholarly fame and notoriety in presenting his thesis of *The End of History*, seems to have become less sanguine of the supposedly invincible march of Westcentrism when he writes: "Mohammad Atta and several of the other hijackers were educated people who lived and studied in the West. Not only were they not seduced by it, they were sufficiently repelled by what they saw to be willing to drive planes into buildings and kill thousands of the people among whom they lived. The cultural disconnect here . . . would seem to be absolute. Is it just our cultural myopia that makes us think that Western values are potentially universal ones?"[36] Anyone who fails to recognize the point raised by Fukuyama would fail to notice how the forces of religious fundamentalism could be manipulating the very "modern" technology both ways—to disseminate their supposedly "antidiluvian" ideas and by the same stroke, to counter the "modern evil" designs. The use of video photography, fax, e-mail, cell phones, satellite phones and the Internet by Laden and his associates, the technical training of the al Qaeda members in top institutions in the West (be it a technical university in Germany or the flight-training school in the United States, the use of the virtual network for currency transactions, and manipulation of pornographic websites for dissemination of hidden messages by Osama's lieutenants are only symptomatic of what I would prefer to call the *ad hoc appropriation of modernity*, that too limited to its material artifacts, by the religious fundamentalists.

One can also move a step further to notice the appropriation of "modern" *sartorial code* by them. The photographs of militants like Atta and his associates, who would drive the planes straight into the Twin Towers and the Pentagon on September 11, show them impeccably dressed they could be in Western clothes. The photographs of the hijackers, who grew up in secular middle- and upper-class background, challenge the familiar image of the Islamic militants—reinforced to a considerable extent by the Taliban—as bearded figures wearing loose gowns. Even Osama the person is not beyond the grid of modernity. As one comment goes[37]—"The language and context of his videotaped appeals convey more of his participation in the modern world than his camouflage jacket, Kalashnikov, and Timex watch"—along with the rider "even if only to reject (it)." Thus, notwithstanding his *fatwa* and the associated discourse, Laden can be seen as a *modernist category*, rather than as an "atavistic force."[38]

Media, a major component of the GIO itself, play an interesting role here—a role which paradoxically exposes its bias and limitations. With the ownership and control of the media and its global activities firmly located and concentrated in the West (and Japan) the projection of the non-Western "other" has been consistently negative over the years. One major consequence of the media concentration has been the stereotypical projections of militants and fundamentalists in terms of images, which situate them in premodern times. Edward Said in his less-publicized book *Covering Islam*[39] had scrutinized the news sourced from the Western media, which included the published material of major newspapers of the United States. Said's intention was to show how the media, as a sort of agency of the "complicity between knowledge, interpretation and power," creates "situational" interpretations, leading in turn to the reinstatement of the *Orientalist* and *colonialist* stereotypes. Said in course analysis deals with the nature of "facts" and "knowledge" in this scenario of "unrestrained ethnocentric" bias and asymmetry—a point which we shall discuss in the next section.

To refer back to the media's role, Akbar Ahmed, a well-known scholar of Islam, takes the point further into the realm of the media when he argues that the Western media and its "bogey of Islamic fundamentalism," in reinstating the stereotypical images, strengthen, if unwittingly, the orthodox position in Islam. As he quips: "Ironically, the media encourage what they set out to deflate."[40] The crux of the matter is that despite so much concerted and continuous efforts to expose Osama the Evil, one finds, even in a relatively "moderate Islamic" country like Bangladesh, the pictures and posters of the al Qaeda chief along with those of national leaders and popular musicians. Such *refractions*—of turning a villain into a hero—that occur when the "encoded" language, images, and messages of the global media is "decoded" by the grassroots-level reality. This even more reveals the need to avoid any technicist interpretation of the lifeworld of those who live on the other side of the fence. This is also why, as one observation[41] goes, it is futile to suppress the language of *Jihad* by the language of Crusade.

That such stereotyping has other dangers as well becomes evident by the way the militants managed to avoid any suspicion during their stay in the United States and on the d-day, that is September 11, of their "operation." At the other end of the spectrum, that the Western media itself would find itself in utter shock—as borne out by numerous "investigative assignments" in print and electronic media to reveal the background of those involved in the September 11 incident—is indicative of the futility of such stereotypes and myths. A related but less-discussed question in this context also critically scrutinizes the role of the West-dominated media from the other end—to what extent has it sought to present images of a West that is less hegemonic and more receptive? Such bridge-building exercise would weaken the practice of demonizing the West, the worst result of which so far has been the killing of innocent people on September 11 in the name of teaching the West a lesson.

Facts as Fiction?

Call it the clash of perception or that of ignorance, at the root of it lies the "changed status" of data, information, communication, and the traditionally most sacrosanct of all, truth-claims and facts. Of the last two, the former, that is, truth-claims are particularly associated with religious fundamentalism, and the latter with its "other." The GIO with all its "late modern" features and inner dynamics has put all of them in the penumbral zone. The constant packaging and repackaging of facts are part and parcel of the GIO. Whether the GIO has, as a result, already established the Baudrillardian vision of *simulation*[42]—leading to the evaporation of the distinction between truth and fiction, and to the replacement of the real by simulated models and signs of the real itself—is again a moot question. However, the fact remains that it has surpassed all its preceding information orders in which data, information, communication, and facts were, at least notionally, reliable, and in many cases inviolable.

Today with the growingly evident flux and indeterminacy in the number of data, "information," and "facts" that are produced and circulated in the GIO, their reliability and credibility in imposing singular order and meaning have been questioned—leading to multiplicity of "facts" and "truths." Is the "war on terrorism" waged exclusively against the Taliban or does it have terrorism on a broader scale in mind? To what extent is the Northern Alliance less oppressive than the Taliban? How reliable is George Bush's claim that the days of al Quaeda are over? Is the enemy confined to the few countries, which were initially identified by President Bush—or is it spread across larger space? How authentic is the claim of the Afghan warlords that Osama has been seen in a village bordering Pakistan? Where is Osama—in Afghanistan, in Pakistan, in (Pakistan-occupied) Kashmir, or in Iran? For that matter, is Osama alive or dead? If he is alive, where is he? If he is dead, how did he die—was it a kidney failure or was it breathlessness? Followers of Jean Baudrillard's theory of simulation might have found the latest and quite appropriate example in "hyperreal" Osama overshadowing the "real" Osama.

The "factual problem" is more fundamental than it apparently indicates. As Arundhati Roy[43] points out, the United States is at war with an enemy "it does not know." No one has yet formally claimed responsibility for the attack on September 11. The hijackers have not left any "suicide note" explaining their exact motives in the "mission" or mentioning the names of their leaders; nor did they leave any political message or political demand. Everything associated with the events seems to be astonishingly fuzzy in this age of Information Revolution, which is supposed to inundate us with "facts." Where does it leave us? In Roy's own words, "(I)n the absence of information, politicians, political commentators and writers (like myself) will invest the act with their own politics, with their own interpretations." In this time of diverse and often conflicting kinds of "authentic" interpretations one more pertinent point raised by Roy is the blurring vision of Operation Enduring Freedom (previously designated, raising lot of consternation, as Operation Infinite Justice) as far as the much-publicized "fight against fundamentalism" is concerned? Is it part of a general fight against fundamentalism of all kinds or is it a fight against fundamentalism in a narrow sense?

One of the greatest paradoxes of the GIO, as it stands today, is that even if it rests on the most advanced technology ever created by mankind—the ICT—the answers to the questions mentioned above are either partially known or unknown or wrongly known. Any obsessive action to establish certain selective and possibly manipulated information as "facts" all the more expose themselves as part of an fundamentalist urge that rules out the possibility, amidst much hyperbole and "strategic exaggerations," of raising questions about "facts," with different nuances at different levels. That such paradox would be the fate of the GIO was evident since 1991 when the Gulf War, which to many has led to the birth of the so-called New World Order, gained the dubious distinction of being the most publicized war in human history with least information about it.

The paradox becomes all the more evident when we find that even with the ownership and control of the world's most sophisticated surveillance technology the American rulers could not prevent the hardcore militants from infiltrating their physical (flight training schools, airports, and so forth) and air space, which led to the killings of more than three thousand innocent civilians. Huge transfers of cash, people, and various material supplies escaped detection across various international borders. In a report[44] it is mentioned that even when Atta and his accomplices were pumping huge amounts of money into the American banking system, the system with the best of alarm-mechanisms did not trip. Most important, the same surveillance technology continues to provide conflicting and confusing information and data about the whereabouts of the "most wanted" personalities like Osama and Mullah Omar. Even when the sophistication of "precision bombing" has reached an all time high, the American air raids continue to kill innocent civilians in Afghanistan "by mistake" in the "war on terror."

As far as the GIO and the dissemination of "facts" through it are concerned, the tendency to impose restrictions on the websites directly or indirectly linked to the militant Islamic activists is as problematic as the temptation to impose restrictions (such as the U.S. Patriotic Act which was passed without a Congressional hearing) on the freedom of expression of citizens. First, such censorship technology is always vulnerable to counteractions by hackers. There are reports that a group of hackers, called "Hacktivismo," is developing two programs— Camera Shy and Six/Four—which would not only make it possible to hide messages inside images but also to create a virtual network that is invisible to fireballs and filtering systems.[45] It has also been found that in the face of such restrictions, the al Quaeda and like-minded militant formations are making use of various techniques, including steganography—the *virtual* technique of disseminating concealed data or information within another. Second, it invites criticism from many, including those who are steadfastly opposed to religious militancy, on the grounds that apart from being a "fundamentalist" the urge of suppressing opposing viewpoints and information is only a superficial way of tackling the grave problem at hand, which is the perceived hostility against the U.S.-led Western policies which is under severe challenge in a region like the Middle East.

In the ultimate epistemological implications, the blurred boundary between fact and fiction makes us conscious that in view of the terms of existing epistemology of "theorization" being inadequate to deal with the emerging reality, there is a need to make refinement of the former by incorporating terms of commonsensical epistemology. However, it is not a place to develop the point in full detail. To refer back to the more specific epistemological context of the GIO, the idiosyncratic nature of formation and circulation of its messages (elaborated in the section on The GIO Unveiled) and the indeterminacy of "facts" not only lend greater legitimacy to its reflexivity, it also strengthens the *relativist* or *fallibilist* position, thereby providing greater scope for dialogical interventions—a point which would form part of our concluding observations.

Conclusion

As things stand now, one finds that two contradictory forces are globalizing themselves. We simultaneously witness the globalization of terror and the globalization of consciousness of the danger of terrorism. In view of this, the GIO has much more to offer than being a "rallying point" of organization of hatred by narcissist forces of opposing kinds. This is especially so because in being a kind of "rallying point" of contestation of such forces the GIO continues to perpetuate and aggravate the *distance* between the two modes being discussed here. On the other hand, the creation of the GIO as a shared space with *emancipatory* potential, conducive to mutual understanding and harmony to a great extent, depends on greater synergy among the forces with saner, tolerant voices and greater catholicism, which by themselves can oppose and weaken any fundamentalist urge and trend. These forces which are diverse and scattered all over the world, are making their presence felt in various ways, including physical demonstrations, silent processions, stage plays, debates, and not the least through dialogues. In a world—marked by the global-local dialectics and dynamics and still far removed from being a global village—dialogue is to play a central role.

If violence begets violence, dialogue begets dialogue. Dialogue, it is said, "rejects the tyranny of a single system or dogma; it welcomes new ideas and guarantees them equality . . . it refuses to censor 'dangerous' ideas; it cherishes and protects its capacity to learn and to grow."[46] In the specific context of the GIO, Flood reinforces the point in Bakhtinian fashion when he asserts[47] that dialogue "gives the situated observer access to universalization through cyberspace as well as being the basis of intersubjective engagement with people and texts." Thus, dialogue is the way to solving the problem of "unedifying and inadequate labels and generalizations," and the consequent *clash of ignorance*. Pantic[48] rightly refers to the "impossibility of the impossibility of the global dialogue."

The saner voices in the West, including the United States are resisting negative stereotypical view that "all Muslims are terrorists." On the other hand, a section of the Muslims are indulging in self-introspection and critical assessment relating to intolerance toward non-Muslims—the so-called infidels—not only in the Western countries, such as the United States[49] but even in Islamic countries.[50] The highway of the GIO provides a great opportunity to multiply such efforts at this critical juncture. The GIO with all its potential has come to stay, and it is better to utilize it to the greatest possible extent for constructing a more humane and tolerant world in which *straight jacketed* categories, such as "Western," "American," "*kafir*," "Muslim," "Hindu," and so forth would not automatically invite suspicion and hostile reactions. The enhanced cultural understandings that can lead to the world, as a better place is, however, contingent upon a momentous step. It is based on the understanding that there cannot be a sole "center" as far as running the world—politically, economically, culturally, or in terms of religious *diktats*—is concerned. The ordinary people are after all in desperate need of a GIO, attuned to a humane world order in which neither Laden's *Jihad* nor mindless celebration of 9/11 nor Bush's proclamation of Crusade nor Barlusconi's categorization of "superior" and "inferior" civilizations would find resonance.

Acknowledgment

The author wishes to thank Sourindranath Bhattacharya and Anjan Ghosh for their suggestions and comments. Thanks in no small measure to Santosh Saha for his encouragement to this rather unconventional theme. My thanks to Saswati Bose for her assistance in material collection and typing. Usual disclaimers apply.

Notes

1. M. Blakemore and R. Longhorn, "Communicating Information about the World Trade Centre Disaster," www.firstmonday.dk/issues6-12/blakemore/index.html, September 9, 2002.

2. To clarify a basic concept of the chapter at the very outset, the GIO is an order of a different kind—with less tangible boundary and less public visibility than a conventional order with visible center, vertical hierarchy, and formally and informally constituted contours and components. In terms of its constitutive elements, the GIO has been, and is still being, constructed by the unending "flow" of people, money, and messages (including data, information, ideas, images, perspectives, opinions, and knowledge), which in giving rise to complex interlocking of networks, are to have some degree of publicness and diffusion beyond the "local" in their aspiration to be globalized. The GIO has a structural base that owes a great deal, but is not limited to, the New Technology and New Media. However, it goes beyond its structural dimensions to be associated with a symbolic base, which works at the level of cognitions, and is itself linked to its structural base. The symbolic base is important because the functioning of the GIO, to be explicated in the subsequent discussion, in effect combines the "symbolic construction of reality" with the "reality of symbolic construction."

3. Even if in this chapter the term "religious fundamentalism" is being linked to fanaticism, militancy, terror, and violence in a specific context we remain aware that believing in fundamentals of religion does not necessarily make one fanatic or a subscriber to terrorism.

4. *Collins Cobuild English Dictionary for Advanced Learners* (Glasgow: HarperCollins, 2001), 639.

5. G. Almond, E. Sivan, and R. S. Appleby, "Fundamentalism: Genus and Species," in *Fundamentalisms Comprehended*, M. E. Marty and R. S. Appleby, eds., vol. 5 (Chicago: University of Chicago Press, 1995), 399–424.

6. N. Georgescu-Roegan, *The Entropy Law and the Economic Process* (Cambridge: Harvard University Press, 1971), 2.

7. This point comes closer to Heidegger's key concept *techne* as a technology that makes sense of the self and the world. M. Heidegger, "The Question concerning Technology," in *The Question Concerning Technology and Other Essays* (New York: Harper, 1977).

8. The West as being used here has its historical and geographical referents, with special reference to—North America and Western Europe. But more important in our context is the point that the "West" is also a mental construct, an abstract location that conjures up certain images, feelings, and perceptions among people of both sides—the West and the "rest"—which might not necessarily coincide with those of the West in the geographical sense.

9. A. Ghosh, *A World of Difference* (Calcutta: Centre for Studies in Social Sciences, 2002), unpublished paper, 2.

10. Throughout the chapter there are a greater number of references to the West's collision with Pan-Islamic fundamentalism. It is mainly due to the more frequent, more publicized, high-profile, and more widespread incidents of clash between the two. However, the point need not be overemphasized to imply that in doing so we are undermining the West's clash with other varieties. Nor does it imply that fanaticism or militancy is found only in Islam.

11. R. Silverstone, *Why Study the Media* (London: Sage, 2000), 134.

12. C. Mele, "Cyberspace and Disadvantaged Communities: The Internet as a Tool for Collective Action," in *Communities in Cyberspace*, M. A. Smith and P. Kollock, eds. (London: Routledge, 1999), 290–310.

13. D. Sinha, *Communicating Development in the New World Order: A Critical Analysis* (New Delhi: Kanishka, 1999).

14. We prefer the term and distinguish it from "postmodern" because as we view it, the GIO, despite its reflexive attributes, is not *totally free* from the *master narratives* of various kinds. We use the affix *late-ish*, rather than *late*, to avoid the host of conceptual and theoretical associations of the term *late modern*.

15. S. Lash, *Critique of Information* (London: Sage, 2002), 2.

16. S. Lash and J. Urry, *The End of Organized Capitalism* (Cambridge, Mass.: Polity Press, 1987); C. Offe, *Disorganized Capitalism: Contemporary Transformations of Work and Politics* (Cambridge, Mass.: Polity Press, 1985).

17. D. Harvey, "From Fordism to Flexible Accumulation," in *Readings in Contemporary Political Sociology*, K. Nash, ed. (Malden, Mass.: Blackwell, 2000).

18. D. Harvey, *The Condition of Postmodernity* (Oxford: Basil Blackwell, 1989).

19. S. Lash and J. Urry, *Economies of Signs and Space* (London: Sage, 1994).

20. D. Bell, "The Social Framework of Information Society," in *The Microelectronics Revolution*, T. Forrester, ed. (Oxford: Basil Blackwell, 1980), 500–49.

21. T. Stonier, *The Wealth of Information: A Profile of the Post-Industrial Economy* (London: Thames Methuen, 1983).

22. D. Sinha, "On Reworking the Global Information Order in the 21st Century—Past Lessons, Future Strategy," *Indian Journal of Political Science* 62, no. 3 (2001): 389–403.

23. E. P. Louw, *The Media and Cultural Production* (London: Sage, 2001), 9.

24. S. Bhattacharya, *Paddhatir Panchali*, The Parable of Methodology, tr. (Calcutta: Dey's Publishing, 2002), 139.

25. S. N. Eisenstadt, "Fundamentalism, Phenomenology and Comparative Dimensions" in *Fundamentalisms Comprehended*, M. E. Marty and R. S. Appleby, eds., vol. 3 (Chicago: University of Chicago Press, 1995), 259–76.

26. G. Flood, *Beyond Phenomenology: Rethinking the Study of Religion* (London and New York: Castell 1999), 51.

27. B. Lawrence, *Defenders of God: The Fundamentalist Revolt against the Modern Age* (San Francisco: Harper & Row, 1989).

28. D. Pantic, "Internet the Globalizer, and the Impossibility of the Impossibility of the Global Dialogue," www.firstmonday.dk/issues/issue7-1/pantic/index.html, 9 September 2002.

29. S. Agnivesh and V. Thampu, "Islam and Modernity: The Contradiction of Holy Wars," *The Statesman*, Calcutta, 6–7 December 2001.

30. Quoted in W. Laqueur, *The New Terrorism* (New York: Oxford University Press, 1999), 75.

31. N. Kermani, "Roots of Terror: Suicide, Matyrdom, Self-redemption and Islam," www.opendemocracy.net/forum/document_details.asp?catD=110&DocIDF=1106, 23 February 2002.

32. S. Ansari, "Islam," in *Understanding Contemporary Society*, G. Browning, A. Halcli and F. Webster, eds. (London: Sage, 2000), 376.

33. E. Said, "The Clash of Ignorance," www.zmag.org/saidclash.htm, 16 May, 2002.

34. B. Cumings, "Some Thoughts Subsequent to September 11" www.ssrc.org/sept11/essays/cumings_text_only.htm, 14 July 2002.

35. H. Ping, "September 11: A Challenge to Whom?" www.ssrc.org/september11/essays/huang_text_only.htm, 14 July 2002.

36. F. Fukuyama, "Their Target: The Modern World," *Newsweek* (December–January 2001–2002): 60.

37. D. F. Eickelman, "Bin Laden, The Arab 'Street,' and the Middle East's Democratic Deficit," *Current History* (January 2002): 36–37.

38. I owe this point to Professor Sourindranath Bhattacharya.

39. E. Said, *Covering Islam* (London: Routledge & Kegan Paul, 1981/1997).

40. A. S. Ahmed, *Islam Today: A Short Introduction to the Muslim World* (London: I. B. Tauris Publishers, 1998), 224.

41. F. Mazhar, *Crusade, Jihad O Sreni Sangram*, Crusade, Jihad and Class Struggle, Chintaa (in Bengali), September 9–13 (2001), 3.

42. J. Baudrillard, *Simulations* (New York: Semiotext(e), 1983).

43. A. Roy, "The Algebra of Infinite Justice," *Guardian*, London, 29 September 2001.

44. www.nytimes.com/2002/07/17/national/17TERR.html?todaysheadlines, 17 July 2002.

45. www.bbc.co.uk/hi/english/sci/tech/newsid2129000/2129390.stm, 2 September 2002.

46. R. Grudin, quoted in *An Introduction to Social Construction*, K. J. Gergen, ed., (London: Sage, 1999), 142.

47. Flood, *Beyond Phenomenology*, 150.

48. Pantic, "Internet the Globalizer."

49. K. Leonard, "American Muslims before and after September 11, 2001," *Economic and Political Weekly* (June 15, 2002), 2293–302.

50. www.nytimes.com/2002/07/12/international/americas/12PERU.html?today-sheadlines, 8 July 2002.

Chapter 2

Some Priority Variables in the Study of Comparative Religious Politics

Ted G. Jelen

Since the inception of political science as an autonomous discipline, political scientists have been both intrigued and repelled by the possibility of a genuinely comparative science of politics. While some analysts have been impressed with the promise of genuinely cross-national laws of political behavior,[1] others have suggested that the quest for this level of generality is misguided, and can lead to the omission of the most important aspects of social explanation.[2] In this second camp, it is often argued that the diversity and complexity of political phenomena, in particular national and subnational settings, renders the development of serious cross-national generalizations either futile or trivial. Moreover, the search for comparability in political practices and institutions may require some strong assumptions about human rationality, which might well be ethnocentric and culture-bound.[3] In other words, proponents of the "area studies" approach to comparative politics have suggested that the search for genuinely cross-national generalizations about political behavior involves assuming away the most interesting aspects of the study of politics. The generalizability offered by cross-national comparativists appears to many to compromise our ability to understand political phenomena in unique national and regional settings.

The dilemma is quite real, and of obvious importance from at least two perspectives. From a scholarly standpoint, the comparativist-regionalist controversy raises the analytic question of what features of human behavior are genuinely fundamental, and which are "merely" artifacts of particular circumstances. Normatively, the controversy over the appropriate method for studying comparative politics squarely poses the question of whether defending some conception of fundamental human rights is or is not compatible with respect for cultural diversity. From the standpoint of application, the issue of the most "correct" level of analysis for the study of comparative politics speaks directly to the question of whether, and to what extent, institutions, practices, and policies can be exported from one national or regional setting to another. For instance, the answer to such questions may impact directly the extent to which a nation such as the United States can borrow practices from other nations, as well as the appropriateness of holding other nations to a standard of "democracy" or respect for human rights.

My purpose in this chapter is to offer some observations concerning the study of religion in comparative politics, and to suggest some potentially fruitful avenues of future research. Religion appears to be a promising area for bridging the gap between the "comparativist" and "area studies" approaches to comparative politics. Depending on one's definition of religion, religion may seem a plausible candidate for a cultural universal. Conversely, religious belief and practice display the diversity, subjectivity, and variation, which characterize the human experience.

In the social sciences, the systematic study of religion has had something of a checkered past. While an appreciation of the social and political role of the sacred has generally been conceded to be essential in understanding the role of premodern or "less developed" political systems, the political role of religion was widely regarded as diminishing, and soon to be inconsequential.[4] Secularization was thought to be an inevitable by-product of modernity, and, as industrial and postindustrial societies became more "rational" and "scientific," religious belief would cease to have public relevance, and, to the extent that such values existed at all, be relegated to a private sphere of activity.[5] In the modern West, technological advances in communications, transportation, and even human genetics have seemed to some to eliminate the need for God as a first cause or as an intercessor. Indeed, it might be argued that the serpent's charge to Eve in the Garden of Eden—"Ye shall be as Gods"—constitutes a successful prediction.[6]

However, recent history has caused social scientists in a variety of disciplines to focus their attention on the political consequences of religion. The rise of the Christian Right in the United States, the political assertiveness of Islamic movements in a number of different countries, and the fall of Communism in the Eastern bloc have all, in quite distinct ways, reminded observers of the continuing relevance of religious belief in national and international politics. This trend has perhaps culminated in the recent writings of Samuel Huntington. In his seminal work, *The Clash of Civilizations,* Huntington has argued that "civilizations" are the fundamental units of analysis in comparative politics and international relations, and that, in the final analysis, civilizations are defined by religious beliefs and values.[7] Religion is a frequent focus of national identity, as well as the source of much of the "stuff" of day-to-day political discourse in a variety of cultures. Even in ostensibly "modern" settings such as the United States and Western Europe, religious values are frequently contested in the public sphere.[8] Far from fading into the historical background, religion is becoming a very important variable in the study of political institutions and behavior.

A particular advantage of religion as a variable in the study of comparative politics is that religion is often itself a cross-national phenomenon. While some religious traditions are largely confined to particular cultures or regions, such as Hinduism in the South Asian Subcontinent or Shinto in Japan, other traditions have a more global, universal identity and self-image. The most obvious example here is that of Roman Catholicism. Indeed, the very term "Catholic" means "universal," and the Church has had a strong historical evangelizing mission. Similarly, the recent history of Latin America is the most contemporary manifestation of a missionary tradition in Protestantism that was inherent in its very beginnings. Indeed, Western colonialism was to a considerable extent justified as an evangelizing mission, which spread into the Far East, Africa, the Caribbean, and Latin America. The recent prominence of Pentecostal movements in Latin American demonstrates that the export of certain forms of evangelical Protestantism continues to be a large-scale, ongoing enterprise with profound political consequences.[9] The success of such evangelism suggests that the message of doctrinally conservative Protestantism travels rather well, and may resonate with people in a variety of cultures.

The scope of international Islam extends from the Iberian Peninsula and Morocco to Indonesia, and Islam is an important political force in Africa and most of Asia (including Western China). Indeed, it might well be argued that the rise of politically assertive Islamic movements constitutes the most important international political trend of the late twentieth century. While Islamic politics is popularly regarded as a central aspect of politics in the Middle East, Islam as a political force extends from the Far East to the parliamentary systems of Western Europe.

Perhaps less publicly, but possibly as importantly, there is an important missionary tradition in Buddhism, which has caused Buddhism to be a consequential political force in a number of diverse political settings in Asia. To illustrate, Frances Fitzgerald has shown that Vietnamese Buddhism was an important source of resistance to Western forces in Southeast Asia during the Vietnam War.[10] This is a clear example of how certain sacred traditions (Buddhism, and perhaps Confucianism) possess the conceptual and theological resources to achieve an authentic syncretism.[11]

What this suggests, of course, is that certain religious traditions may provide sources of cross-national identity and identification, which may well facilitate the task of comparative political analysis. The fact that advocates of liberation theology in Latin America and former members of the anticommunist resistance in Poland profess the adherence to the same Catholic tradition (albeit with markedly different political manifestations) may make the politics of Brazil (for example) and Poland more easily comparable. Similarly, the wide scope of Islam may make it possible to compare the political consequences of Islam in a variety of national and regional settings. Is political Islam a qualitatively different phenomenon in settings in which Muslims are a clear majority (such as Iran or Tunisia) than in areas in which Islam constitutes a serious contender for national hegemony (Egypt, Lebanon, Algeria), or in settings in which Muslims are a consequential political minority (India, Western Europe)?

Moreover, it may also be possible to compare religious politics *across* different political environments. While I tend to agree with MacIntyre, who suggests that cross-national similarities should be discovered, rather than assumed, the idea that different religious/political movements may exhibit doctrinal or structural similarities which enhance our ability to compare across political cultures appears to have a great deal of intellectual potential.[12] Indeed, the studies in this volume are focused on one such concept: that of "fundamentalism," to which attention is now turned.

"Fundamentalism" as a Cross-National Concept

While religion in its various forms is clearly a theoretical priority for the study of comparative politics, it is less clear whether "fundamentalism" can serve a similar intellectual function. Technically speaking, of course, the term "fundamentalist" is properly applied only to a movement in conservative American Protestants, which began in the early twentieth century. As Nancy Ammerman has shown, the strains of "modernity" (itself a complex, multifaceted concept) led to an attempt to return to the "fundamentals" of the faith.[13] The question remains as to whether characteristics of this movement can usefully be applied to such diverse phenomena as Opus Dei,[14] the LeFebre movement in France,[15] the Khomeini-inspired Islamic republic in Iran, Rashtriya Swayamsevak Sangh (RSS) in India,[16] and the strategies of small, militant religious parties (such as MAFDAL and Shas) in the Israeli Knesset.[17]

Of course, this question has been addressed in some detail in the five volumes of the *Fundamentalism Project* edited by Martin E. Marty and R. Scott Appleby.[18] It should be noted that many of the contributors to this ambitious collection have reservations about the applicability of the concept to their countries or areas. Nevertheless, the claim is often advanced that there does exist some sort of Wittgensteinian "family resemblance" between politically assertive, doctrinally conservative political movements around the world.[19] Obviously, such a claim is controversial for scholars and believers alike. A Jerry Falwell may well bristle at being placed in the same category with Ayatollah Khomeini. Nevertheless, there may exist similarities between such movements that enhance our understanding of the public role of religion.

First and most importantly, fundamentalist movements are often political in nature, and often seek to restore a perceived historical consensus on religious and moral matters.[20] The public assertion of orthodox religious beliefs does not seem to become important until such beliefs and values are contested in the public sphere. While contemporary "fundamentalists" may seek to restore a context in which religious values are the objects of social consensus (the "canopy" model discussed below), such movements typically result from interaction between a particular religious tradition, and opposition from modern (secular) forces, or from other religious traditions. Thus, the quest to restore an allegedly historical consensus seems problematic. As I will suggest below, once citizens have been banished from a (perhaps mythical) premodern Eden, they cannot return to a previous state of innocence. It is difficult, if not impossible, for religion to recover credibility lost to the forces of science or doctrinal diversity.

Secondly, fundamentalist movements are orthodox.[21] That is, fundamentalist movements differ from other political movements (including religious ones) in that the former have a primary concern with religious *doctrine*, and with the application of such doctrine to secular life. Again, as will be argued below, the importance of doctrine does vary across religious traditions, and indeed, across different denominations or movements within the same tradition. "Fundamentalism" requires a set of "fundamentals" which can serve as the basis of political mobilization. Thus, the scope of the concept might be limited, and the notion of "fundamentalism" might properly be applied only to those religious traditions in which a set of doctrinal materials (such as Scriptures) can be regarded as somehow authoritative. It is not entirely clear, for example, how a religious tradition as decentralized as Hinduism can provide the Scriptural basis on which a religiously motivated political movement may depend, or whether the concept of fundamentalism can legitimately be applied to such creeds.

As R. Scott Appleby has suggested, the existence of a cross-national concept such as fundamentalism is perhaps more appropriately regarded as a "working hypothesis" than as an essential construct.[22] Again, taking to heart McIntyre's admonition that cross-national similarities are to be discovered rather than assumed, it is possible to use the notion of fundamentalism as a starting point for genuinely comparative inquiry.

Some Priority Variables in the Study of Political Religion

The continuing quest for "something like" fundamentalism as a cross-national concept with which we can compare the political roles of religion across cultural and political settings serves to remind us of a simple point: Religion is becoming an important variable in the comparative analysis of political systems, and future studies of politics in diverse environments are unlikely to neglect the central role played by religion. In this spirit, the balance of this essay is devoted to some general concepts or variables that seem to be promising avenues of future research in the study of religion and politics.

The Nature of Religious Markets

Among the more plausible variables for conducting cross-national inquiry into the nature(s) of political religion is the religious composition of a particular polity, or, in the vernacular of recent trends in the sociology of religion, the nature of religious "markets." That is, the number and relative strength of religious competitors seems likely to affect the political activities in which religious activists may or may not engage, as well as the likelihood of success or failure of such efforts.

Perhaps the simplest model of religious politics is that of the "sacred canopy."[23] In the "canopy" model, religion is the object of general, system-level, consensus, and thus provides a backdrop within which normal "politics" can be conducted. In such a consensual society, religion provides a shared set of norms, beliefs, and values, which impose limits on the attitudes, and behavior of citizens. For example, Alexis de Tocqueville, describing the United States in the early nineteenth century, wrote:

> The sects that exist in the United States are innumerable. They all differ in respect to the worship, which is due the Creator; but they all agree in respect to the duties, which are due from man to man. . . . Moreover, all the sects of the United States are comprised within the great unity of Christianity, and *Christian morality is everywhere the same.* . . . Christianity, therefore, reigns without obstacle, by universal consent; the consequence is . . . that every principle of the moral world is fixed and determinate, although the political world is abandoned to the debates and experiments
> of men.[24]

More contemporary analysts of political religion in the United States have also suggested that a consensus on the essentials of a "Judeo-Christian tradition" provide a foundation on which American social life depends.[25] Such arguments are often made in defense of an "accommodationist" position on issues of church and state, in which neutral government assistance to religion is considered constitutionally permissible.[26] For example, in contemporary politics in the United States, accommodationists would argue that such practices as organized prayer in public schools, or the posting of religious symbols such as the Ten Commandments, are not only constitutionally permissible, but are important carriers of a (presumably) shared religious and moral framework.

Indeed, many of the movements regarded by Marty and Appleby as fundamentalist seek to restore precisely the sort of consensus observed by de Tocqueville in the United States. Phenomena as diverse as the Islamic revolution in Iran, RSS in India, the Christian Right in the United States, and the Lefebvre movement in French Catholicism have in common the desire to regain a religious "unity" which has arguably been a recent casualty of interaction with the modern world. It is, of course, arguable that such a consensus never existed in any of these settings. However, the notion that there was once general agreement on the foundational principles of religion and morality is a powerful symbolic, rhetorical resource in political competition. In a variety of settings (including especially the Hebrew Scriptures) the prophetic voice is self-consciously reactionary, as it involves exhortations to return to a previous state of personal or collective grace.

Regardless of the historical accuracy of such claims, it seems unlikely that the canopy model of religious politics is a plausible empirical description of any contemporary national society. Religious consensus among any large group of people is threatened—perhaps fatally—by two general forces. Externally, particular sacred canopies are forced to compete with a variety of phenomena associated with globalism and modernity. Indeed, the thrust of the *Fundamentalism Project* entails the assumption that the most important religio-political conflicts in the contemporary world involve the confrontation between traditional religion and modernity. It seems unlikely that any but the most unimaginably remote cultures would be untouched by the forces of technology, religious and ethnic pluralism, and the assault on faith by "scientific rationalism." As Garry Wills has asserted, once it becomes necessary to *argue* that traditional religious beliefs are an essential part of a given culture, that proposition is no longer correct, and, indeed, becomes self-defeating.[27] Traditional religious beliefs may coexist with, compete with, or combine with elements of the modern world, but may not be able to subjugate the forces of modernity without incurring enormous (and perhaps prohibitive) social costs. Having eaten from the Tree of Knowledge, contemporary humanity is perhaps irrevocably linked with the phenomenon of secularism. That is, as an increasing proportion of daily life is explained or justified by scientific or multicultural warrants, it is difficult to imagine that such secularized human activities can become resacralized. Since religion has virtually everywhere encountered competitors from nonsacred sources, religion may not be in a position to dictate the terms of discourse.[28]

Societies in which a single religious tradition is dominant are also beset by internal threat to the hegemony of traditional religious beliefs. The recent work of Finke and Stark suggests that it may be intellectually useful to compare aspects of religious organizations to firms in an economy.[29] In settings in which religious bodies must compete for adherents, religious leaders must attempt to satisfy the needs of the laity, and to address the immediate concerns of current and potential members. Pluralistic religion, by this account, is populist religion, and tends to be doctrinally simple, and relatively strict in the behavioral demands made on members.[30] By contrast, if a religious body has a monopoly within a given jurisdiction (either de jure, by legal establishment, or de facto, by geographical or historical circumstance), it can become "lazy," and unresponsive to the needs of the laity. One obvious symptom of a "lazy" monopoly is the "professionalization" of clergy, in which the educational requirements for ordination are increased, and the discourse of religious leaders becomes increasingly remote from that of the mass public that constitute potential religious consumers. One likely outcome of religious monopolies is that the aggregate level of religious membership and practice is likely to decline.

It is important to note that the "supply-side" thesis on which the foregoing analysis is based has not been tested extensively in non-Christian contexts. Nevertheless, if this argument is substantially correct, it contains the clear implication that monopoly religions (which would be at least potential candidates for sources of "sacred canopies") empower the forces of modernity that weaken the hegemony of traditional religions. That is, it seems likely that there exist many "nominal" Muslims in Iran, Catholics in Italy, or Jews in Israel, whose religious commitments are relatively casual. Such religiously marginal citizens may well be susceptible to the appeal of the consumerist aspects of global capitalism, or other cultural aspects of modernity. While it is certainly not the case that religious belief is *necessarily* incompatible with consumerism, a lack of firmly held religious convictions might deny casual believers a means of resisting the temptations posed by modern ways of thinking and living. Alternatively, the existence of a large pool of religiously uncommitted citizens may create a potential market for religious competitors (such as evangelical Protestants in formerly Catholic nations of Latin America). Monopolistic religions may thus inadvertently create the secular space in which both modernist and religious competitors may challenge their hegemony.

Conversely, the supply-side perspective suggests that religiously competitive environments are likely to occasion higher levels of religious observance and commitment. Empirically, it appears that the aggregate level of religious membership, identification, and practice is higher where multiple versions of Christianity exist. Such competition may take place between adherents of the same religious tradition (such as different religious orders within Roman Catholicism),[31] among different denominations within a broader movement (such as the balkanization of Protestant evangelicalism in the United States), or between profoundly different religious traditions. It is not clear whether this generalization is attributable primarily to the behavior of religious leaders, to the increased salience of religious membership as a source of subnational identity at the level of the laity, or both. Nevertheless, religious competition does appear to occasion relatively high levels of religiosity.

Of course, religious competitors cannot plausibly serve as "sacred canopies," or as sources of social or political consensus. In settings in which there exist multiple religious traditions with comparable levels of mass support, the possible options would seem to range from the melding of combinations of religious beliefs and practices (syncretism) or religious conflict. The possible sources of syncretism or conflict are discussed in the next section.

It seems possible to hazard some hypotheses about the sources and consequences of various forms of religious competition. Certainly, it seems possible that the confrontation between traditional religion and modernity can result in intense and violent conflict, as was the case in revolutionary Iran. However, tension between one dominant religious tradition and secular modernity would also seem to leave open the possibility of compartmentalization.[32] That is, a rough accommodation between the sacred and the secular, in which citizens and authorities alike attempt to "render unto Caesar that which is Caesar's, and render unto God that which is God's." Such accommodation is clearly easier in instances in which the creed in question has a strong individualistic component, and permits a principled distinction between "belief" and "action." This can be seen most clearly in the history of Roman Catholicism, in which (most visibly) both Vatican I and II can be plausibly understood as efforts to accommodate the process of modernization through a process of compartmentalization.[33]

Conversely, the existence of explicitly *religious* competitors to a religion seeking societal hegemony seems likely to require an explicit accommodation, or to result in sustained conflict. Here, the case of India is instructive. Despite a commitment on the part of India's independence movement to secularism in the political realm, and despite a public commitment to the value of ecumenism on the part of two generations of the country's political leaders, religion in India remains a potent source of political division, and, indeed, of political violence. The apparent weakening of the hegemony of the Congress Party has occasioned conflicts between Hindu fundamentalists and secularists, as well as discord between Muslims and Hindus, and between Hindus and Sikhs. As religiously based demands for self-determination become more prominent, simple "neutrality" becomes difficult even to describe, and correspondingly difficult to attain.[34]

Thus, it seems apparent that future research into the nature of politicized religion in the area of comparative politics might well devote some attention to the nature and composition of religious markets. While the sacred canopy model of religious politics is no longer a plausible alternative for any society, the forms which religious accommodation or religious competition might take seem likely to vary according to the number and relative strength of religious and secular rivals for cultural influence.

The Nature of Religious Authority

Thus far, this discussion has focused primarily on the *form* that religion might take in a particular cultural or political setting. Relatively little attention has been devoted to the *content* of politicized religion. It would seem highly implausible to suppose that there are not important differences between creeds, and that these differences would not be politically consequential.

In this regard, a brief comparison of religious politics in India and Japan might well be useful. The religiously based conflicts between Hindus, Muslims, and Sikhs on the Indian subcontinent are well known to virtually all analysts of comparative politics. By contrast, the traditions of Shinto and Buddhism coexist peacefully in Japan, and, indeed, are often merged and combined within the same household. Many Japanese move with no apparent effort between Shinto and Buddhist forms of religious observance, or meld the two traditions in a form of idiosyncratic syncretism.

Why is the option of syncretism a live possibility in Japan, and apparently impossible in India? Two hypotheses suggest themselves as candidates for further investigation. First, it may be that syncretism is not a realistic possibility among religious traditions when one or more of the faiths in question are monotheistic. The admonition of the First Commandment to ". . . have no other gods before me"—a feature common to Judaism, Christianity, and Islam—may well inhibit the ability of citizens of religiously pluralistic societies to synthesize elements of two or more alternative belief systems. Thus, the presence of Islam (a faith of uncompromising monotheism) as a serious competitor in India, Pakistan, and Bangladesh may render reconciliation between Muslim, Hindu, and Sikh a practical impossibility. By contrast, the lack of single deities with human characteristics in the Shinto and Buddhist traditions may strip these faith traditions of any compelling requirement of exclusivity. In particular, Buddhism makes few demands of *religious* exclusivity,[35] allowing elements of Buddhism to combine with Hinduism on the Indian subcontinent, Confucianism in China and Vietnam, and Shinto in Japan.

Second, the development of religious syncretism may be inhibited by the existence of authoritative, written scripture. Along with constituting a strong succession of monotheistic traditions, Jews, Christians, and Muslims are "people of the book," who regard sets of partially overlapping texts as divinely inspired in some fashion, and therefore as authoritative. If one compares fundamentalist movements in Islam and Judaism with the original North American Christian variety, these movements appear to have in common a set of fundamentals to which believers can be called to return. The use of a religious tradition as a political resource is enhanced to the extent that the sacred basis is easily and publicly available to be shared.

An emphasis on scripture as an element in politically assertive religious tradition may shed some additional light on religious politics in India. Daniel Gold has suggested that a faith tradition as eclectic and decentralized as Hinduism may not provide much in the way of material for the development of religiously based *political* movement.[36] To use Hinduism as the basis for political mobilization, Hindu elites were required to (re)affirm the centrality of ancient Vedic texts, which could provide a missing "core" of the Hindu tradition. Subsequently organizations such as RSS provided instances of an arguably fundamentalist movement that is not (by most descriptions) monotheistic. Similarly, T. N. Madan has shown that a reaffirmation of the authority of the *Granth Sahib* constituted an integral component of Sikh nationalism.[37]

In other words, for religion to serve as the core of a political movement, the religious tradition in question must be regarded as somehow authoritative. Both the content and sources of religious doctrine may require a certain rigidity and inflexibility if doctrine is to exact political costs on the part of believers.

The Nature of Political Authority

Finally, it remains to consider the role of political authority in empowering or inhibiting religiously based political movements. Political legitimacy has a variety of sources in different cultural settings, and all contain different configurations of resources that can enhance or inhibit the political assertion of religious values. While government (as distinguished from other forms of authority) has often been characterized as involving the possibility of legal physical violence, most stable regimes offer some sort of non-Hobbesian rationale for their existence and their authority.[38] Some regimes may rely on shared historical memories, or shared ethnicity, or a presumably shared commitment to a set of political institutions. Even when the basis for claims of political legitimacy is not explicitly religious, it seems plausible to assert that the nature of such justifications will have substantial implications for the practice of religious politics.

In this regard, it may be instructive to begin with the radically "rights-based" political culture of the United States. Politics in the United States is often thought to have as its purpose the protection of individual rights, which exist conceptually and temporally prior to government or civil society. That is, "rights" (including the right to the free exercise of religion) are essentially nonnegotiable prerogatives of individuals, in which government policy-making itself may be regarded as illegitimate.[39] The United States Declaration of Independence states explicitly that rights are God-given, and that any limitations on such rights imposed by government are only legitimate if created by the "consent of the governed."

"Rights talk" of this sort can and does provide a rationale for religiously based activity. In contemporary American politics, church-state relations are often described in the language of the schoolyard: "They (government) started it." That is, Protestant fundamentalism in the United States is often regarded as a defensive reaction to government interference with religious free exercise. Thus, policy preferences as diverse as opposition to gender equality and gay rights, support for the teaching of creationism in public schools, and support for the regulation of "indecent" communications on the Internet are all subsumed under a general "right" to religious liberty.[40]

However, the very notion of "rights" which apparently empowers religiously motivated political mobilization also imposes certain limits on the effects of such activity. In the United States, the Establishment Clause of the First Amendment to the United States Constitution has been read to proscribe the imposition of any set of religious beliefs on citizens. Even in the absence of such an explicit constitutional prohibition, the clash of individual rights seems to ensure that there will always exist reliable opposition to the demands of religious conservatives. Unless it can be argued that a right to religious liberty in some sense "trumps" rights to privacy, equal protection, free expression, etc., the culture of individualism which prevails in the U.S. and, to a lesser extent, elsewhere in the West can easily be used to resist certain policy demands justified in the name of religious freedom. Feminism, gay rights, free communication, etc., are also generally justified under the rubric of "rights talk." Thus, a culture in which individual rights are valued provides both resources and limitations to the political mobilization of religion.

At the other extreme, a political system may derive its legitimacy directly from identification with a religious tradition. The most obvious examples of this phenomenon are the recently created Islamic republics in settings such as Afghanistan and Iran. In this context, it is perhaps useful to distinguish between the political functions of nation building and governing. In some ways, this distinction corresponds with the theological distinction between prophetic and priestly functions of religion.[41] That is, religion may serve one function in the creation of a particular regime, only to occupy an entirely different political role once the regime has been established and routinized.

It may be instructive to compare the role of Catholicism in recent Polish history with that of Islam in Iran during and after the revolution of 1979. In both instances, a religious body and a religious leader (John Paul II in Poland, Khomeini in Iran) provided a tangible symbol of opposition to a discredited regime. In addition, in both cases, the religious basis of regime opposition provided a sense of indigenous opposition to a political order that was widely perceived as having been imposed by a hostile foreign power. Indeed, it seems likely that both revolutions would have been substantially more difficult in the absence of an articulated religious ideology and organization to provide a focus for mass grievances against a domestic regime supported by an external power.

However, the political role of such "prophetic" religions has been considerably more problematic after the new regime is in place. In Poland, the Catholic Church was the dominant political actor in the immediate post-Communist era; a status attributable both to its high level of public legitimacy, and to the atrophy of other structures of civil society during the Communist period.[42] The fact that the Catholic Church was perhaps the only fully functioning institution of Polish civil society in the immediate aftermath of the fall of the Communist regime may have enabled the Church, among other things, to support passage of the most restrictive abortion law in Europe. However, while the Church may have been a dominant institution during the resistance phase of the Communist era, and in the immediate aftermath of the post-Communist era, it has not fared as well during the years that followed the revolution. Over time, other sources of social capital have developed, and other organized interest groups have formed and mobilized segments of public opinion in the Polish mass public. As a result, the Catholic Church is now but one player among many in Polish politics, and no longer enjoys the close identification with Polish national identity it had during the Communist period. Perhaps in response to the newly articulated pluralism of Polish civil society, the Sejm and Senate have substantially liberalized the earlier abortion legislation, and many Catholics have come to oppose an active political role for the Church in the post-Cold War era.[43]

Similarly, the strident, fundamentalist Islam of the Ayatollah Khomeini has proven a much more effective ideology of opposition than of governance. While the clerical rule of Shi'ite Muslims was able to undermine and ultimately overthrow an apparently strong, secular regime under the Shah, post-revolutionary Iran has been beset by the polarization of society. Since the passing of Khomeini, the leaders of most political factions in Iran have invoked religious values to warrant their political judgments and positions. Recent political struggles between "traditionalists" and "fundamentalists" in Iran suggest that the routinization of Khomeini's charismatic leadership will contain an uncertain mixture of sacred and secular elements, as well as diverse understandings of the meaning of authentic Islam.[44] At this writing, President Mohammed Khatami of Iran is engaged in the delicate task of "moderating" some of the more strident elements of political Islam in that nation without undermining the legitimacy of the Islamic revolution and the unity of the nation.[45]

Examples like this could be multiplied for pages. One might allude to the role of Quaid-i-Azam Mohammed Ali Jinnah in the creation of Pakistan, David Ben-Gurion's central role in the creation of Israel, Mohandas Gandhi's importance in achieving Indian independence, and perhaps to the theological basis of the Civil Rights movement in the United States. In the case of the latter, clergy clearly led the way, with such leaders as the Rev. Martin Luther King, Rev. Andrew Young, Rev. Ralph Abernathy, and Rev. Jesse Jackson assuming prominent public roles in the struggle for social and political equality for AfricanAmericans. The general point is that contemporary religion appears to be an extremely valuable resource in its prophetic role as social critic, or as source of regime opposition. However, the use of religion as a source of political stability and legitimacy appears more problematic. Charismatic religious leaders who were able to use religious values successfully to create new regimes found such values much less useful when applied to the more mundane task of governing.

Perhaps paradoxically, the decline in the direct political power wielded by the Polish Catholic Church, and by Shi'ite Islam in Iran, may serve to stabilize the long-term political influence of religion in these nations. Religion can easily lose its theological and political legitimacy if it is too closely identified with a discredited regime. The close identification of the Catholic Church with antidemocratic regimes in the Iberian Peninsula has served to render Spanish and Portuguese Catholicism politically impotent in recent years, and the association between the Church and authoritarian regimes in Latin America has created an opening for the rise of Evangelicalism in the Southern half of the Western hemisphere.[46] In the United States, the independent influence of the leadership of the Christian Right has been seriously compromised by the close identification of the movement with the Republican Party. In particular, Moral Majority had a very difficult time maintaining a sense of historical moral crisis among its potential members after eight years of an ostensibly friendly Reagan administration,[47] and, at this writing, has an uncertain friend in the administration of George W. Bush. Despite receiving overwhelming support from religious conservatives,[48] the early days of "Bush II" have been marked by a strong focus on economic matters, and much more limited attention to the moral priorities of moral organizations.

Thus, the infusion of sacred values into the "secular" realm of politics carries both risks and opportunities for those who would demand a more assertive public presence for traditional or orthodox religious beliefs. In a variety of settings, religion appears to be a powerful critic of prevailing secular norms, and a source of opposition and reform to a number of different regimes. Nevertheless, the sacred, prophetic character of religion can easily be compromised by close identification with secular authorities. Political religion, if it is to be politically influential *and* theologically authentic, apparently should maintain a certain distance from secular politics to retain its transcendent character. Religious leaders can serve as sources of political criticism and opposition during periods of extraordinary political upheaval, as well as providing a "priestly" source of legitimacy during the longer periods of what might be termed "normal politics." The evidence to date suggests that religion in many of its varied forms might better serve as a resource for the former purpose.

Conclusion

In this chapter, I have attempted to offer a modest research agenda for the future study of comparative religion and politics. The approach taken here involves a mix of empirical induction and theoretical deduction, with a strong emphasis on the former. Given the diversity of global religions, and the radically different contexts in which religious creeds assume political importance (or fail to do so), the attempt to build cross-national generalizations by comparing small numbers of countries or regions at low levels of abstraction seems a promising, albeit intellectually conservative, strategy.

I have tried to suggest ways in which one might steer a middle course between the Procrustean bed of "rigorous" comparative inquiry, and the intellectual balkanization that may result from ethnomethodological area studies. Indeed, as noted at the outset of this chapter, religion seems a likely source of middle-range generalizations, due to the widespread extent of religious belief in general, and to the transnational nature of several specific religious traditions.

As this chapter shows, my own area of expertise lies in the political role of Christianity in the West, and in the United States in particular. Thus, the theoretical sketches presented here are admittedly anachronistic, in that they appear to take Western, Christian patterns of religious politics as normative. This starting point, of course, is not unique, and, indeed, attempts to apply the concept of fundamentalism to non-Western settings share the same ethnocentric bias. However, I hope to have directed the attention of scholars toward three "priority" variables in the study of political religion: The structure of religious markets, the content and methodology involved in the development of particular faith traditions, and the nature of political legitimacy in the regime(s) in which religious activists seek to operate. I am hopeful that the modest hypotheses offered in the foregoing pages will provide a reasonable set of categories within which religious politics in diverse national settings can be compared and contrasted.

Notes

1. See, for example, Phillip E. Converse, "Of Time and Partisan Stability," *Comparative Political Studies* 2 (1969): 139–71.

2. Alasdair MacIntyre, "Is a Science of Comparative Politics Possible?" in *The Philosophy of Social Explanation*, Alan Ryan, ed. (New York: Oxford University Press, 1973), 171–88.

3. See Martin Hollis, "Reason and Ritual," in *Philosophy of Social Explanation*; Robert H. Bates, "Area Studies and the Disciplines: A Useful Controversy," *PS: Political Science and Politics* 30 (1997): 166–69; Chalmers Johnson, "Perception vs. Observation: The Contribution of Rational Choice Theory and Area Studies to Contemporary Political Science," *PS: Political Science and Politics* 30 (1997): 170–74; and Jan S. Lustick, "The Disciplines of Political Science and Studying the Culture of Rational Choice as a Case in Point," *PS: Political Science and Politics* 30 (1997): 175–79.

4. See, for example, the discussion in Kenneth D. Wald, *Religion and Politics in the United States*, 3rd ed. (Washington, D.C.: CQ Press, 1997).

5. See especially Jose Casanova, *Public Religions in the Modern World* (Chicago: University of Chicago Press, 1994).

6. Genesis 3:5.

7. Samuel S. Huntington, *The Clash of Civilizations and the Remaking of the World Order* (New York: Simon & Schuster, 1996).

8. See especially Stephen V. Monsma and J. Christopher Soper, *The Challenge of Pluralism: Church-State Relations in Five Democracies* (Lanham, Md.: Rowman & Littlefield).

9. See Anthony James Gill, *Rendering Unto Caesar: The Catholic Church and the State in Latin America* (Chicago: University of Chicago Press, 1998); and Anne Motely Hallum, *Beyond Missionaries: Toward an Understanding of the Protestant Movement in Central America* (Lanham, Md.: Rowman & Littlefield, 1996).

10. Frances Fitzgerald, *Fire in the Lake: The Vietnamese and the Americans in Vietnam* (New York: Vintage Books, paperback reissue, 1989).

11. It is not clear whether Confucianism would qualify as a genuine "religion." While this is ultimately a matter of definition, Confucianism clearly contains aspects of the sacred.

12. MacIntyre, "Is a Science of Comparative Politics Possible?"

13. Nancy T. Ammerman, "North American Protestant Fundamentalism," in *Fundamentalisms Observed*, M. E. Marty and R. S. Appleby, eds. (Chicago: University of Chicago Press, 1991), 1–66.

14. Opus Dei (a phrase which means "God's Work") is a conservative Catholic organization, founded in Spain in 1928. The organization is committed to the "evangelization" of all segments of public life, and is opposed to the designation of any sphere of human activity as "secular." Opus Dei was a highly visible source of support for the Franco regime in Spain during the middle of the twentieth century.

15. Marcel Lefebvre, a French Archbishop, founded the Sacerdotal Society of Saint Pius X in 1970. The Society has consistently rejected the innovations of the Second Vatican Council, especially the abandonment of the Latin Mass. In defiance of the Vatican, Lefebvre continued to ordain priests and consecrate bishops until his death in 1991.

16. RSS is a militant Hindu movement in India, which has traditionally rejected the secular, ecumenical nature of the modern Indian regime. Historically, RSS has frequently been accused of employing violence to attain its political ends.

17. MAFDAL (often termed the National Religious Party) promotes Orthodox Jewish

values in Israeli politics, but ultimately recognizes the authority of the secular government. Shas is somewhat more separationists, and regards religious law, derived from the *Torah*, to supersede the mandates of Israel's secular regime.

18. Martin E. Marty and R. Scott Appleby, *Fundamentalisms Observed: Fundamentalisms and Society* (Chicago: University of Chicago Press, 1993); Martin E. Marty and R. Scott Appleby, *Fundamentalisms and the State* (Chicago: University of Chicago, 1993); Martin E. Marty and R. Scott Appleby, *Accounting for Fundamentalisms* (Chicago: University of Chicago Press, 1994); and Martin E. Marty and R. Scott Appleby, *Fundamentalisms Comprehended* (Chicago: University of Chicago Press, 1995).

19. In his *Philosophical Investigations*, the philosopher Ludwig Wittgenstein suggested that objects which fall under the rubric of a single concept could share portions of a set of characteristics, even though no single characteristic is shared by all members of the class.

20. This point has been made quite frequently since the advent of the fundamentalist movement in the United States in the early twentieth century. For a recent formulation of this argument, see Martin E. Marty and R. Scott Appleby, "The Fundamentalism Project: A User's Guide," in *Fundamentalisms Observed*, Marty, vol. 3, vii–xv.

21. See Marty, "Fundamentalism Project." See also Ted G. Jelen, *The Political World of the Clergy* (Westport, Conn.: Praeger, 1993).

22. See R. Scott Appleby, "Observations on *Fundamentalisms Observed:* A Response," *Review of Religious Research* 35 (September 1993): 71–75.

23. Peter Berger, *The Sacred Canopy: Elements of a Sociological Theory of Religion* (Garden City, N.Y.: Anchor, 1969).

24. Alexis de Tocqueville, *Democracy in America* 1 (New York: A. A. Knopf, 1945), 314–15 (emphasis added).

25. See A. James Reichley, *Religion in American Public Life* (Washington, D.C.: Brookings, 1985); and Richard John Neuhaus, *The Naked Public Square: Religion and Democracy in America* (Grand Rapids, Mich.: Eerdmans, 1984).

26. For an elaboration, see Ted G. Jelen, *To Serve God and Mammon: Church-State Relations in American Politics* (Boulder, Colo.: Westview Press, 2000).

27. Garry Wills, *Under God* (New York: Simon & Schuster, 1990).

28. For example, in the United States, both opponents of the theory of evolution and opponents of legalized abortion have been compelled to couch their arguments in scientific, rather than religious, terms. Thus, "scientific creationism" has become a means by which creationists can advance their claims using the methods of science. Similarly, antiabortion rhetoric in the United States has increasingly emphasized the biologically "human" characteristics of the fetus, rather than invoking religious justifications. See Mary C. Segers and Ted G. Jelen, *A Wall of Separation? Debating the Public Role of Religion* (Lanham, Md.: Rowman & Littlefield, 1999).

29. Roger Finke and Rodney Stark, *The Churching of America, 1776–1990* (New Brunswick, N.J.: Rutgers University Press, 1992).

30. Laurence R. Iannaccone, "The Consequences of Religious Market Structure," *Rationality and Society* 3 (1991): 156–77.

31. Roger Finke and Patricia Wittberg, "Organizational Revival from Within: Explaining Revivalism and Reform in the Roman Catholic Church," *Journal for the Scientific Study of Religion* 39 (2000): 154–70.

32. See especially Casanova, *Public Religions in the Modern World.*

33. Gene Burns, *The Frontiers of Catholicism: The Politics of Ideology in a Liberal*

World (Berkeley: University of California Press, 1992).

34. For example, if government benefits (such as seats in a legislature) are allotted according to numerical quotas representing the religious distribution of the population, it is not clear whether such a policy is neutral, if it advantages minority religions (by insulating them from political competition), or if it advantages the majority religion (by ensuring that a religious majority is also a political majority).

35. Of course, contemporary Buddhism has served as a partial rationale for demand for Tibetan independence, and the Dalai Lama has become an internationally prominent spokesperson for this cause.

36. Daniel Gold, "Organized Hinduisms: From Vedic Truth to Hindu Nation," in *Fundamentalisms Observed*, Marty, ed., 531–93.

37. T. N. Madan, "The Double-Edged Sword: Fundamentalism and the Sikh Religious Tradition," in *Fundamentalisms Observed*, Marty, 594–627.

38. In his classic work, *Leviathan*, sixteenth-century British philosopher Thomas Hobbes argued that the sole purpose of government was the preservation of the physical safety of its subjects, and, in exchange for such safety, citizens owed government unconditional allegiance. While some readers may find such an argument compelling, the point being made here is that most contemporary governments offer other, perhaps less cynical rationales for their legitimacy.

39. See especially Mary Ann Glendon, *Rights Talk* (New York: The Free Press, 1991).

40. See especially Stephen L. Carter, *The Culture of Disbelief: How American Law and Politics Trivialize Religious Devotion* (New York: Basic Books, 1993); and Ralph Reed, *Politically Incorrect: The Emerging Faith Factor in American Politics* (Dallas: Word, 1994).

41. David C. Leege, "Religion and Politics in Theoretical Perspective," in *Rediscovering the Religious Factor in American Politics*, David C. Leege and Lyman A. Kellstedt, eds. (Armonk, N.Y.: M. E. Sharpe, 1993), 3–25.

42. See Timothy A. Byrnes, "The Challenge of Pluralism: The Catholic Church in Democratic Poland," in *Religion and Politics in Comparative Perspective: The One and the Many*, Ted G. Jelen and Clyde Wilcox, eds. (New York: Cambridge University Press, forthcoming).

43. See Ted G. Jelen and Clyde Wilcox, "Context and Conscience: The Catholic Church as an Agent of Political Socialization in Western Europe," *Journal for the Scientific Study of Religion* 37 (1998): 28–40; and Michele Dillon, "Cultural Differences in the Abortion Discourse of the Catholic Church: Evidence from Four Countries," *Sociology of Religion* 47 (1996): 25–36.

44. Wael B. Hallaq, *Islamic Legal Theories* (New York: Cambridge University Press, 1997).

45. See Mehran Tamadonfar, "Islam, Law, and Political Control in Contemporary Iran," *Journal for the Scientific Study of Religion* 40 (2000): 205–20. See also Sussan Siavoshi, "Between Heaven and Earth: The Dilemma of the Islamic Republic of Iran," in *Religion and Politics*, Jelen.

46. See Gill, *Rendering Unto Caesar*; and Hallum, *Beyond Missionaries*.

47. Clyde Wilcox, *God's Warriors: The Christian Right in Twentieth Century America* (Baltimore: Johns Hopkins University Press, 1992). Perhaps eight years of the Clinton administration will revive a sense of moral crisis for the Christian Right in the United States.

48. See, for example, Thomas B. Edsall, "The Shifting Sands of America's Political

Parties," *Washington Post Weekly Edition,* 9–15 April 2001: 11.

Chapter 3

Fundamentalist Ideology, Institutions, and the State: A Formal Analysis

Graeme Lang and Vivienne Wee

What Is Fundamentalism?

In this study, we propose a conceptualization of fundamentalism, contrasting it with the symmetrically opposite concept of pluralism to facilitate comparative analysis of religious and political fundamentalisms. Then we explore some institutional implications of fundamentalist and pluralist systems, treating fundamentalism as a variable rather than a category. Next, we turn to the concept of weak fundamentalism, and explore how such weak fundamentalisms are incorporated into national ideologies. Finally, we briefly review some developments within Southeast Asia, specifically in Singapore and Indonesia, to illustrate this kind of analysis.

The concept of fundamentalism was developed by some to describe certain movements within Protestant Christianity in the twentieth century, but has been partially generalized in recent decades to refer to a variety of religious movements with some similar characteristics. However, fundamentalism has been under-theorized in sociology, even for the analysis of religious groups, and the process of abstracting a more general definition is ongoing, and still incomplete.[1]

Some analysts provide complex definitions of fundamentalism, which combine the causes, features, and political programs of "fundamentalist" religious movements. Thus, Martin Marty and Scott Appleby define fundamentalism as a type of movement generated as a reaction to threats to the identity of the group (from aspects of modernity), which meets those threats through a selective retrieval and innovative reworking of doctrines from the past, and which leads to a political program for the transformation of society in the future.[2] They also note that a number of fundamentalist religious movements focus their energies on the family, advocating a return to more patriarchal family systems and more traditional, family-centered roles for women.

Our approach is different. We will not include in the definition of fundamentalism the *programs* of movements, since much of the content of those programs is associated with particular historical conditions or struggles, and may vary greatly between movements, which are otherwise similar. For example, defining fundamentalism by reference to a patriarchal agenda for the family is problematic even within groups, which seem to be well known for such an agenda. Marty and Appleby acknowledge that within what appear to be fundamentalist religious movements, women may succeed in using the fundamentalist canon to "domesticate" and control men.[3] Further, if we define fundamentalism by reference to "patriarchalism" and the domestication of women, we automatically exclude, by definition, the fundamentalisms of female-oriented religions such as the Shakers.[4] If such features as patriarchal revival are included in the *definition* of fundamentalism, then the concept carries too many constraining ties to particular agendas which are not, in themselves, intrinsically fundamentalist.

For the same reason, we do not wish to define fundamentalism through reference to the *causes* of fundamentalist belief systems. Those causes may be quite diverse among the historical environments in which fundamentalist movements have arisen. In any case, the causes require further research and analysis. What are the common causes of American Protestant fundamentalism and Middle Eastern Islamic fundamentalism? Perhaps it is not very useful to try to find common causes. What are important are the characteristics of belief systems, and the consequences of those characteristics. Explaining why people in different parts of the world adopt such systems is a much more complicated problem.

We also wish to avoid blurring the analytical clarity of the concept through inclusion of features of religious movements which can more properly be located within definitions of other kinds of religious and political phenomena such as "sectarianism," "millenarianism," "cultural revivalism," "ethnonationalism," "antimodernism," and so on. Militancy and a disposition to use violence are also far too variable to be included, and derive from the reactions of some groups to particular historical conditions.

We share with S. N. Eisenstadt the goal of producing a more abstract definition of fundamentalism which can be used, analytically, to compare movements which are quite dissimilar in terms of their particular beliefs and programs.[5] Eisenstadt discusses characteristics of what he calls "modern Jacobin movements," which share the goals of radical mobilization and transformation of society using some unchallengeable utopian model. He illustrates with both religious and political cases of this kind of "Jacobinism." Eisenstadt's conceptualization, however, still includes some features of particular types of movements. For example, he builds the ideas of "antimodernism" and "anti-enlightenment ideology" into his definition of fundamentalism. At the same time, he contrasts what he calls "pristine" fundamentalisms, which have some universalistic ideas and a transformative agenda, with movements, which are "particularistic and primordial," meaning that they do not include any universalistic ideas and do not promote a reconstruction of society, and hence are not truly fundamentalist. Here, we will attempt some further abstraction to free the concept of fundamentalism from such characteristics, which are in fact variable rather than analytically inescapable. In this paper, we propose a formal definition of fundamentalism based on observed properties of belief systems. With a formal abstract definition, we can also avoid the problem of trying to match such a label with the self-identification of persons affiliated with movements, which we label fundamentalist on definitional grounds. Their own emic categories are irrelevant, except where they also use such "formal" criteria to discuss and classify themselves and others. We are aware that this approach may produce partial characterizations of religious movements (as fundamentalist, by definition), which do not capture the complexity, and richness of those movements as seen from the "inside," by believers.[6] However, we are proposing to analyze only the "fundamentalist" features of those movements, and not to attempt ethnographies, which include their reactions to particular struggles and social conditions.

We also believe that with a formal definition, devoid of specific content for the beliefs, the concept can be further generalized to accommodate nonreligious forms of ideological fundamentalism, which will allow comparisons (otherwise conceptually difficult) between a variety of ideologically dogmatic groups which share properties that have important sociological consequences. For example, in China, a secular ideological fundamentalism shaped the lives of several hundred million people for a generation. We refer, of course, to Maoism before and during the "Cultural Revolution."

The Maoist state during that period, between 1966 and the mid-1970s, produced intellectual and social phenomena, which followed directly from an essentially fundamentalist vision. Like some religious fundamentalist movements, Maoism attempted to replace an earlier, more complex and subtle system with a much simpler and more forceful vision of the world and of appropriate behavior within the world, and to base that vision on writings, which were treated as virtually sacred.

Confucianism and various commentaries and adaptations of Confucian writings formed a kind of "fundamental" corpus of philosophy, morality, and statecraft in China for much of the past two thousand years. The dominance of this corpus was maintained by the state through the examination system, in which candidates had to memorize selections from the canon and the commentaries in order to be successful in the exams and gain entrance to the imperial bureaucracy. Rival systems were carefully watched, and periodically suppressed. The Confucian corpus, suitably interpreted, served the interests of the state by contributing to social harmony and to acceptance of authoritarian and hierarchical relationships.[7]

This corpus was officially replaced, after 1949, by Marxism-Leninism, as it was called, supplemented by the writings of Mao Zedong. However, the Marxist-Leninist corpus was equally complex and interpretable, and allowed a variety of "Marxisms" to coexist and contend. The Maoist Cultural Revolution attempted to replace this complex and interpretable canon by a much simpler set of writings, by Mao Zedong. The new Maoist canon had a higher status on the scale of revealed truth, and could be questioned only at the risk of severe punishment, if not death. The status of the "little red book" of Mao's writings was similar to that of religious scripture. It was as obligatory and unchallengeable during most of the Cultural Revolution period as the most zealously defended religious scriptures in other fanatical environments.

We see similar possibilities in any religious fundamentalism if its exponents capture a state and gain control over the institutions of communication, socialization, and control. Hence, we wish to propose a conception of fundamentalism, which will facilitate such comparative analysis. Here, we start with an abstract and formal account of the general properties of a belief system, which can be used to identify fundamentalism, independently of the content of the beliefs. We contrast these properties with those of a contrary system, which can be termed "pluralism." We also wish to establish these concepts as ends of a scale, not as a pair of either/or categories. Hence, we can discuss "weak" versions of both types, as well as movement along the scale in either direction because of changing conditions or historical struggles. The properties of these systems also have institutional implications, and hence, we can proceed from formal analysis of belief systems to their institutional consequences, illuminating some of the social processes and struggles which are occurring in contemporary societies through this kind of analysis.

In essence, fundamentalism has the following features. First, belief that a definitive set of principles exists which is both necessary and sufficient for the overall guidance of human behavior, and that these principles can be summarized within a small set of explicit statements. Second, belief that these principles derive from impeccable origins capable of delivering universal truth, and hence that they cannot be questioned or changed (i.e., they are "sacred"). Third, belief that these principles are available in a specific "Collection" of material compiled or received from those impeccable sources, and which therefore has sacred status. (This definition can be applied to both religious and political fundamentalisms.)

There are several social positions which follow (for many believers) from these features of fundamentalist thinking: (1) The basic principles and their applications (i.e., the Collection of unchallengeable principles, and nearly unchallengeable interpretations) provide a basis for universal socialization (e.g., parenting, education), at least within the community of believers; (2) ideological institutions and communication systems within the community or in society, including the mass media, should promote and be guided by these principles; (3) the Collection should be officially endorsed. Of course, where fundamentalist groups are in the minority, and capture of the institutions of the state seems unlikely, the institutional consequences of fundamentalism may be applied only within their own community.[8]

Complexity and Veracity of the Collection

It must be noted that the complexity of the Collection is a major factor in producing difficulties for the fundamentalist agenda. The fundamentalist impulse is to produce simple answers to questions through resort to the Collection. Most fundamentalist systems of thought also attempt to provide a simple summary of the principles.[9] The constraints on this summary derive from the fact that it must be taught and remembered by large numbers of people, and hence must be simple—or simplified—to accommodate the limits of ordinary or average human cognition.

However, nearly all Collections are far more complex than a simple set of principles, and cannot be easily summarized by any obvious exercise of logic or exegesis. Intellectual work is invariably required to extract basic principles. This means that a different selector or exegete, working independently, could produce a different set of basic principles, and a different summary of those principles. This invariably leads to emergence of rival interpretations of a Collection if there are no constraints on the production of interpretations and summaries.

Some Collections are supplemented by additional compilations of near-canonical material which comprise a second layer of authoritative interpretation or application.[10] This additional layer of material further complicates the problem of selecting and summarizing principles. Where the truth of statements in the Collections and in summaries of principles from the Collections cannot be verified by some means which compels belief even among unbelievers (e.g., by demonstration of the truth of statements through an epistemology shared with unbelievers) then there is no way to compel belief without socialization or coercion.

Hence, where Collections are complex (and they are almost invariably so), and where the truth of the Collection and of the principles are largely unverifiable by independent means, a fundamentalist agenda must be combined with some way of repressing rival interpretations, if the fundamentalist agenda from a particular interpretation of the Collection has any chance of being successfully expanded into the rest of the society. The obstacles to implementation of the fundamentalist vision derive not only from the questions and challenges of pluralists, but also from rival interpretations by other believers, and other fundamentalists. This leads to important institutional consequences, as will be outlined below.

Thus, given the exalted status of the Collection for believers—as universal truth—there are further implications in regard to rival collections of principles, or any attempts to discredit the Collection. Opposition to these principles and to the enshrined (formally endorsed and unquestionable) status of the Collection should be prevented or repressed.

The appeal of fundamentalism derives from the sense of certainty and assurance, the simple system of guidance, and the possession of compelling answers to all questions. Analysis of fundamentalism would benefit from research on some cognitive dispositions, which have been extensively studied by social psychologists, such as dogmatism and authoritarianism. An application of findings from those earlier studies to the analysis of fundamentalism and its consequences is a topic for later work. We note, however, that these cognitive features of fundamentalism are reinforced through the sense of community developed through socialization into a shared life-world, and through the self-confidence, which comes from social validation of the possession of truth. These processes include rituals and group activities designed to maintain conviction through the usual social methods of reinforcement and commitment.[11]

It is easy to maintain this kind of communal organization within a local community, which is able to control the institutions of socialization, education, and communication. It is difficult to maintain at much larger scales, although both political and theological fundamentalisms have been partially institutionalized across very large scales for a number of years in some societies prior to the evolution of more pluralist forms of organization and socialization (e.g., Maoist China, the Islamic Republic of Iran).

Pluralism: Definition and Social-institutional Consequences

The contrary mode of thought, which can be called pluralism,[12] has the following features. First, there are multiple realms of thought and action which can function according to their own principles, which are best developed by those most closely involved in those realms and hence most knowledgeable. Links among realms of thought and action are best developed voluntarily, for pragmatic reasons. Second, knowledge and principles are pragmatic, and based on what works or is functional within particular realms. Overarching principles are also pragmatic, and designed to facilitate the peaceful functioning and interaction of social and intellectual realms of thought and action. Because of interacting with fundamentalists, adherents of pluralism may add further derivations of pluralism as a response to fundamentalist claims. Third, no principles are beyond debate, while principles, which have been adopted, may need to be interpreted, discussed, revised, negotiated, or questioned, or new principles invented, on the basis of evolving situations and in view of different settings, perspectives, and experiences. Fourth, no single set of sacred principles, contained in a definitive Collection, or in any simple set of explicit statements, can serve as an unchanging and complete guide for human behavior. Fifth, there is no single and invariant Collection, which provides unchanging and unchallengeable guidelines for all human life.

This contrary mode of thought also has some social implications: (1) Education should be pluralist and pragmatic, and controlled by specialists in the various subrealms of thought and action, not by any overarching ideological authority. No sacred Collection should be imposed through universal socialization. (2) Ideological institutions and communication systems in society, including the mass media, should be open to the variety of interpretations and discussions of whatever principles are advocated within a society on the basis of different situations or experiences. (3) No official endorsement should be made of any Collection of principles (except the principles of pluralism that is, of allowing discussion, debate, and questioning of principles). (4) Questioning or challenging principles or the status of any Collection should not be prevented or repressed.

The principles of pluralism eventually may be seen as invariant and unquestionable, at some high level of abstraction, even if a detailed program for governance and behavior cannot be derived deductively from them. Pluralism and its associated values, modes of social organization, and governance can be enshrined in a Collection (such as a constitution), which achieves nearly the status of fundamentalist Collections. However, to the extent that such Collections are also subject to revision, interpretation, criticism, and debate, they are not ultimately above the pluralist principles, which they enshrine.

Fundamentalism, Pluralism, and Institutions

Societies can be analyzed in terms of the extent to which the institutional complex of the society promotes fundamentalism or pluralism, as well as in terms of historical trends in either direction. The political agendas of fundamentalists and pluralists include close attention to these issues, along with activity intended to promote or inhibit such trends. Where there are both fundamentalists and pluralists within a society, struggles over institutional issues are inevitable, not only between fundamentalists and pluralists, but among fundamentalists. Many societies in the contemporary world are characterized by such struggles, and the outcomes are important for both fundamentalists and pluralists. We will outline typical features of fundamentalist and pluralist institutional complexes. Then we will elaborate with some examples of such issues and struggles from societies in Southeast Asia.

Fundamentalist Institutional Complexes

An ideal-type of a society organized around a fundamentalist belief system includes the following features. First, the educational system teaches the Collection and its interpretations as the primary and unchallengeable source of truth. At the extreme, only memorization and recitation is allowed, along with skillful application of the memorized canon to particular situations. The educational system is under the control or supervision of ideological authorities dedicated to the protection and promotion of a particular fundamentalist interpretation of the Collection. Second, the legal system is explicitly grounded in the Collection, and passages from the Collection, as selected and interpreted by the ideological institutions, are by definition authoritative and decisive. Third, the institutions devoted to teaching and promoting the Collection and its truths include oversight of the legal system and of the educational system. Fourth, mass media are regulated or controlled by institutions devoted to teaching and promoting the Collection.

As a result of the necessity of preventing rival fundamentalist interpretations of the Collection, as well as pluralist challenges to the dominance of the Collection and its fundamentalist interpreters, it is also necessary for a fundamentalist society to employ institutionalized systems of repression, which may include censors, monitoring and policing of intellectual and cultural life by ideological agencies, and so on. Otherwise, the fundamentalist agenda cannot be sustained on a society-wide basis, and may eventually be succeeded by more pluralist governance (which is inevitable without repression in any diverse society).

The necessity of authoritative regulation and repression, on the basis of an arbitrary formulation of the principles of the ideology (arbitrary because it is only one of many possible formulations, none of which can be proven) requires a hierarchical, top-down system of control, which is not open to challenge from below. This may be charismatic (i.e., obedience is to an exceptional person at the top) or bureaucratized (i.e., obedience is enforced through systems of socialization and social control). In any case, this system must be implemented within ideological institutions, and in the relations between higher-level (political and ideological) institutions and all of the other agencies and activities which they must monitor and control. Within a small community, much of this can be done informally. Within a much larger-scale society, the informal systems must be controlled by the higher-level formal institutions devoted to protecting the supremacy of that particular formulation of principles and of the Collection from which it is derived.

There are important social-psychological consequences of this complex of institutions and processes. The educational institutions do not allow a real contest of ideas, and hence, those who are socialized are not exposed to argument and diversity. Their thinking is thus simpler than in a diverse and argumentative milieu. As "naive" fundamentalists, they are likely to be puzzled rather than hostile, when they encounter others who do not share their beliefs. However, they are left, paradoxically, less able to defend their beliefs than those who inhabit a more disputatious milieu while still being reinforced for orthodoxy. The final defense for naive fundamentalists, when arguments are lacking but it is not possible to suppress the questions, is intellectual or even physical retreat from difficult questions put by unbelievers.

Where contacts with unsympathetic and argumentative unbelievers are unavoidable, however, the community of the orthodox will often develop and provide a set of counterarguments, adamantly promulgated and defended. Where fundamentalist groups cannot avoid interaction with argumentative unbelievers and are large enough to sustain specialized production of such counterarguments, some persons will specialize in production of such material.

Adherence to orthodoxy is reinforced through formal and informal rewards. The most ardently orthodox believers are rewarded the most, pulling the psychology of the whole community toward more ardent and more orthodox belief. There will be pressure to reduce interaction with outsiders who do not share the worldview. If such interactions are minimized, there is less risk that believers will be drawn into unorthodox thinking as a result of the necessity of understanding the unbelievers in order to interact with them. If the community is large enough, it will support specialists in this role of dealing with outsiders.

Pluralist Institutional Complexes

An ideal-type of a society organized around a pluralist belief system includes the following features: (1) The educational system is pragmatic and focused on a diverse range of skills, abilities, interests, and realms of inquiry, with no attempt to unify them or provide oversight on the basis of some unquestionable principles enshrined in a Collection. Indeed, to protect these forms of education and realms of inquiry (on the basis of their pragmatic value and on the basis of explicit adherence to pluralist principles), educators will resist any such attempts. The educational system is supervised primarily by educators with pragmatic and pluralist agendas. (2) The legal system, however invariant in the short term, is based on principles and applications, which can be contested, interpreted, and revised, through some longer-term institutional mechanisms for formulating and revising principles. (3) Institutions devoted to teaching and promoting some Collection which has the status of fundamental and unchallengeable truth do not have effective control over any other institutions within the society. In that sense, they are institutionally isolated. (4) Mass media are not regulated or controlled by ideological institutions on the basis of advocacy or lack of advocacy of principles, but only on the basis of a pragmatic legal system subject to review and revision for pragmatic reasons.

Movements on the Fundamentalism/Pluralism Dimension

The characteristics of what we have called "fundamentalism" and "pluralism" can be conceived as a continuum rather than a dichotomy. Some historical societies and groups have evolved from more fundamentalist to more pluralist modes of thinking, and from fundamentalist to pluralist forms of social organization and governance. This has occurred after experience with the failure of fundamentalist ideologies and modes of governance to deal with complex realities, or with the consequences of repression resulting from fundamentalist governance, or as a result of the destructive consequences of trying to impose principles from a Collection on an ideologically diverse population, or as a result of the weakening or delegitimization of a fundamentalist state through military defeat or economic collapse.

Structural changes can also favor the evolution of pluralist principles and institutions. For example, immigration can lead to the growth of ethnic and religious diversity within a society, which can lead (after the inevitable struggles) to negotiation of a more pluralist framework for the society. Increasing differentiation within society through urbanization, the growth and diversification of a tertiary scientific, technical, and professional sector, and the resulting expansion and diversification of higher education can also lead to more pluralist accommodations to the resulting diversity of ideas, institutions, and modes of career socialization.

We do not mean to suggest that persons who have received tertiary education in such societies cannot also be fundamentalists. A narrow education in a technical or scientific specialization is quite consistent with a totalistic and intolerant worldview grounded in a fundamentalist interpretation of a political or religious canon. We are only saying that the growth and differentiation of a multitude of diverse technical, scientific, and professional sectors, and the resulting diversity in contents and forms of education, inevitably produces a population with diverse perspectives and life-experiences, including generalists who must theorize and manage the relations and coordinations among these sectors. This diversity in turn generates pluralist metadiscourses, which undermine attempts to reduce truth to any particular simple set of instructions about how to live.

Evolution from more fundamentalist toward more pluralist forms of thinking and organization has also occurred as a result of experience with the competitive advantages of a more pluralist and authority-challenging system of discussions and debates for the production of useful knowledge. For example, the institutionalized methods of producing, disseminating, and critically evaluating knowledge which we call modern science" developed out of the competitive multistate system in Europe over the past four hundred years, and that competitive system was one of the key factors in the development of modern science.[13] The growth and institutionalization of these more critical methods of inquiry naturally led to conflicts with older and more fundamentalist institutions and ideologies, but the clear or anticipated benefits of a less fundamentalist approach to knowledge within that competitive multistate system made it ultimately impossible for religious or political institutions to enforce a fundamentalist hegemony over knowledge and education. The evolution of secular pluralist educational institutions in Europe, since the thirteenth century, from what had originally been much more fundamentalist institutions, is one of the most remarkable of the transformations from fundamentalist to more pluralist institutions and discourses.

But we also do not want to suggest that scientific visions can never be incorporated into political programs, which take a fundamentalist turn. Indeed, the success of science as an enterprise has led some enthusiastic utopians to imagine that they could use scientific planning to reengineer society and nature on a large scale, using general models. When applied on such a scale, however, these models are invariably too simple to work well in the real world. Before their flaws are exposed, their enthusiastic exponents can do enormous damage if these programs are implemented in authoritarian systems. James Scott has called such programs of forced change "authoritarian high modernism."[14] Their historical failures are a result of the fact that such models are always too simple to accommodate the complexity of local conditions, and thus they lead to sterility, inefficiency, and in some cases, to society-wide catastrophe (as in the Maoist "Great Leap Forward"). These failures are not the fault of science. Instead, they are the product of the fatal combination of authoritarian systems and leaders who misunderstand the problems of applying science to the real world. More commonly, an increasingly science-oriented society is also an increasingly open and intellectually pluralistic society, since the culture of science is critical, skeptical, egalitarian, and tolerant of experiment.

Some historical societies, however, have evolved or been transformed from pluralist to fundamentalist forms of social organization and governance. This has occurred as a result of the capture of the state by ideologically fundamentalist groups, sometimes after the institutions of the pluralist society (particularly, the state) have been weakened or discredited by social conflict, military defeat, economic collapse, or other turmoil.[15] In such societies, large numbers of people seek the kinds of simple solutions typically promised by political or religious fundamentalists, at the same time that the governing institutions of the society are least able to resist being captured by zealous fundamentalist minorities.

It should be noted that pluralism also facilitates the activities of ideological minorities—including fundamentalist groups—by allowing competition for resources and adherents, rewarding the most energetic groups with growth and greater influence, and thus stimulating greater zeal among the organizers and beneficiaries of such groups.[16] Thus, a pluralist society is bound to contain more tensions and struggles between fundamentalist and pluralist principles than a fundamentalist society. A growth in pluralism may, paradoxically, lead to a rise in the strength of fundamentalist minorities and their influence within the political system. In the presence of strong antagonisms between groups inhabited by fundamentalist minorities, and without institutionalized ways of mediating and resolving those antagonisms, growth in pluralism may lead to increasing conflict between those groups as the most intolerant members of each group take the lead in pursuing their totalistic agendas at the expense of their rivals and of other groups who reject their visions.

In short, the balance of fundamentalist and pluralist forces and trends within a society is likely to be complex and dynamic. Internal and external factors can provide opportunities for the agents of these forces to gain advantages. In turn, these shifts may precipitate aggressive and innovative reactions to such changes. These tensions and interactions can be observed in many contemporary societies.

The stakes are high. The capture of institutions by fundamentalists has huge consequences for pluralists and even more so for other fundamentalists, since it may represent the beginning of the end of their freedom to pursue and propagate their own versions of truth. The capture of those institutions by pluralists, by contrast, will seem to fundamentalists to represent a threat to the Truth, and to lead down the slippery slope to social and moral chaos (unless of course the pluralists are capturing these institutions from *other* fundamentalists, in which case the formerly excluded groups will applaud, and then begin to exploit the new opportunities to find niches within newly pluralist institutions).

One of the complicating factors in this struggle is the widely recognized need of a society for some basic principles, which can serve as the common framework for order and collective morality. We could call this framework the prime principles. They may or may not be enshrined in a constitution, but they are likely to be propagated on public ceremonial occasions as the alleged common identity and morality of the community. They may also comprise a kind of "preface" to education, recited or acknowledged regularly to frame the processes of learning for other more specific matters. These principles or themes may also be attached to the ethnic and cultural identity of a people, and hence to be beyond challenge, at least for people who acknowledge that identity.

Where do these prime principles come from? There are no societies in the contemporary world where the prime principles are simply the minimal code of law needed to provide peaceful conditions for collective life. Almost every society grounds its prime principles at least in part in an earlier religious code, often canonized in a sacred Collection. Thus, there is a fundamentalist "Trojan horse" within the most basic principles of every society's institutional and ideological framework.

When a society originated in a culturally homogeneous population with a compact ideological vision, these principles are grounded in that vision, and may continue to provide a reference point for fundamentalists long after the society has incorporated a much more diverse range of ideologies through immigration and structural differentiation.[17]

At the same time, the prime principles of a modern state also must provide a framework for collective life. Where collective life is diverse, complex, full of historic accommodations among groups with different cultures or subcultures, and has produced abstract codes for regulating economic exchanges and other public activities, there will also be a universalistic and abstract component to the prime principles, based on whatever abstract principles seem to summarize these codes and accommodations up to the time when the prime principles were formulated. Hence, we can analyze the extent to which a society's prime principles are particularistic (requiring adherence to specific beliefs and behavior) or abstract (providing a common framework of general principles but allowing pluralistic diversity within that framework). This balance between particularism and abstraction is extremely important for all subsequent interactions between fundamentalists and pluralists.

We could sketch the conditions under which a society's prime principles and its institutional framework are likely to be more or less fundamentalist or pluralist, and more or less particularistic or abstract. These conditions would also largely determine whether a fundamentalist revolution within a society can be sustained over the longer term, or whether the society will inevitably drift back again toward pluralism, or whether it will continue to be riven by conflict among fundamentalists, and between fundamentalists and pluralists. We do not have space in this chapter to carry out this analysis here, but we suggest that it would be useful for understanding the changes and trends in many countries in the contemporary world.

However, we do wish to pursue this line of analysis into one of the kinds of phenomena which can be observed and described, and which is far more common than the capture of a state by fundamentalists: the institutionalization of a weak form of fundamentalism among the prime principles of a society, usually as a result of social pressure from fundamentalists. A partial institutionalization of fundamentalism is never completely satisfactory to fundamentalists, and thus we can expect, and typically find, a continuing contest between fundamentalists and pluralists about whether to expand, hold, or reduce the scope and coerciveness of these principles throughout the society. Examples of this phenomenon can be studied in a number of societies, and such analysis is facilitated by our use of fundamentalism as a scale rather than simply as a category.

Weak Fundamentalism

A state may institutionalize a weak version of fundamentalism within a common framework, which also includes some pluralistic characteristics, and in regard to further modifications to that framework, the society may be moving in either direction. We suggested that premodern China had institutionalized a weakly fundamentalist vision through state support for the Confucian writings and commentaries (through the examination system), combined with some suppression of rival systems. This weak fundamentalism made only mild claims about the inerrancy of the corpus, and there was no formal organization of approved interpreters who could enforce orthodoxy throughout the educational system.[18] The magistrates watched carefully for heterodox philosophies, which might challenge the authority of the regime, and the imperial examination system mainly required a massive effort to memorize the corpus. Revolutionaries in twentieth-century China rightly saw this system as a barrier to the implementation of their own plans, whether those plans were pluralist (as among some reformers) or fundamentalist (as among some of the religious and political revolutionaries).

In other parts of East and Southeast Asia, other kinds of "weak fundamentalism" have been implemented through partially abstract and pluralist sets of prime principles, with varying degrees of success or failure and with continuing pressure from both fundamentalists and pluralists to move in opposite directions. We can observe these experiments and trends, for example, in Singapore, Indonesia, and Malaysia, and the struggles are ongoing.

These weak fundamentalisms, when implemented by the state, can be considered a form of statecraft, since the intention is to provide an ideological framework for managing interaction by forging a compromise between different sets of principles held by subgroups within the society. This is achieved by extracting principles, which those groups are supposed to share in common. Because of the ideological diversity of these societies, however, this extracted set of principles is necessarily far simpler than the elaborate sets of principles and legitimations which Peter Berger calls the "sacred canopy."[19] An elaborate code drawn from a particular religion is only possible in societies where belief is far more homogeneous than in most of Southeast Asia. We will illustrate with a brief review of developments in Singapore and Indonesia, with some reference to the equally fascinating ongoing developments in Malaysia.

Singapore

In Singapore, an authoritarian regime has ruled this multiethnic but Chinese-dominated city-state since the 1960s. The society is comprised of about 77 percent ethnic Chinese, about 14 percent Muslim Malays, about 8 percent persons of South Asian descent, and some others. The program of the ruling People's Action Party (PAP) had been formulated in the 1950s with some social-democratic features, but quickly evolved after the PAP gained power into an ideology of meritocracy, one-party rule (on the basis of the PAP's meritocratic expertise), capitalist economic growth, interethnic harmony, and whatever repressive measures were required to assure that none of these basic principles were challenged by any social or political groups within Singapore society. During the 1980s, the secular regime attempted to bolster this set of ideas, and ensure its own continuing ideological hegemony in an increasingly prosperous and Westernized society, by promoting a kind of weak fundamentalism. Part of the reason for this development was that the regime was determined to counter criticism of Singapore's authoritarian system by Western critics on the basis of supposedly universal human rights, including much more freedom of expression than the city-state was prepared to tolerate. Internally, the goal was to help unite the city-state's population around a common set of principles which could be enforced through more specific policies and measures in courts, schools, and the media, and which could help to promote continuing "social stability."

Initially, it was proposed that this could be done in part through moral education, with a complementary and compulsory religious education curriculum called "Religious Knowledge" (RK). Students would be allowed to choose from among Catholic, Protestant, Buddhist, Confucian, Hindu, Islamic, and Sikh classes as part of their RK program. However, the courses were also expected to support a more general set of values considered essential for Singapore's stability and prosperity.[20]

Some of these principles were intended to support Singapore's capitalist economic system, and some were intended to help preserve stability by minimizing ethnic particularism and the possibility for ethnoreligious conflict. Some principles were also intended as a bulwark against "decadent" Western values, which were alleged to be drawing young people in Western societies into hedonistic individualism and loss of respect for moral values and for their elders, and influencing the increasingly affluent young people of Singapore in similar directions. During this period, the phrase "moral ballast" was frequently used in speeches by government figures to indicate what they hope to achieve with the RK program—to anchor the values of youth in religious traditions emphasizing good behavior and social responsibility, rather than allowing the youth to drift with the tides of materialism and individualism washing over the city-state from the West. In any case, it was intended that the teaching of all of the religions in the RK program would include support for morality and for communitarian principles of social responsibility.

However, there was some conflict between the ideals of a pluralist (albeit unchallengeably capitalist) and universalistic framework, on the one hand, and education in more particularistic religious knowledge within the RK curriculum. Thus, "tolerance of other creeds" was supposed to supercede any teachings within particular religions, which could be interpreted to support intolerance of other creeds. However, monotheistic faiths such as Christianity and Islam can be interpreted, and are interpreted by many believers, as intolerant toward other faiths. In effect, this general set of universalistic values was designed as a higher-order secular ideology within which the particularistic RK classes were expected to promote social morality. It seems that the regime did not at first see the potential conflicts between promoting particularistic and potentially intolerant religious socialization while at the same time promoting higher-order pluralist and universalistic principles. However, the government noticed that Christian evangelical groups were in fact often dismissive or intolerant toward other faiths, and the same attitudes could be found among some people in the Muslim community, toward non-Muslims.

In addition, some Christian groups and thinkers advocated a "social justice" orientation, which could bring them into conflict with the state over welfare, human rights, and the unfettered operation of the capitalist system. "Leftist Christianity" was a potential threat to the dominance of the ruling party (the People's Action Party) in regard to its positions on political discourse and social policy.

An equally serious problem for the RK curriculum, from the "demand side," was that it also did not provide any benefits within the opportunity-structure of Singapore's economy. Indeed, the students in Singapore's technocratic and meritocratic system of education are primarily oriented toward acquiring the secular professional and technical credentials to get good jobs. The economic system in Singapore rewards such knowledge and credentials, and does not reward mastery of RK.

The regime evidently hoped that the Chinese majority among the students would choose Confucianism as their RK option, and thus help to enshrine Confucianism—the most secular of the RK components—as part of the national ideology, at least for the 77 percent of the Singaporean population who are Chinese. The government went so far as to send Confucian scholars to the National University of Singapore to instruct the lecturers in how to appropriately teach and promote Confucian values and attitudes among their students. However, Chinese students in the secondary schools proved to be uninterested in the Confucian curriculum, mainly because they wanted good marks for university entrance and career advancement, and Buddhism was seen to be an easier subject than Confucianism, and hence an easier way to get good marks.[21] Further, while about 64 percent of the Singaporean Chinese identify themselves as Buddhist or Taoist in government surveys, none claim to be "Confucianists" since Confucianism (at least in Singapore) is considered to be a philosophy rather than an everyday religious practice.

Eventually, in the face of student disinterest in Confucianism, the experiment in compulsory RK was abandoned. While the religious leaders with whom the government consulted in Singapore almost universally wished to retain compulsory religious education in Singapore's curriculum, the regime had decided to take another route to national ideological socialization, and RK was converted into an optional subject, to be taken, if at all, outside of school hours. It is possible that the regime was also worried by the tendency of Christianity and Islam to generate social-justice movements, which challenge the government

Instead, the regime adopted a secular set of principles, which was announced as the new "national ideology." The most basic principles of the ideology, as summarized by Joseph Tamney, were: "nation before community and society above self; family as the basic unit of society; community support and respect for the individual; consensus and not conflict; and racial and religious harmony."[22] These principles were intended to enshrine an "Asian" set of values conducive to prosperity, social stability, and social responsibility. The regime believed that such a set of principles is necessary for Singapore's multiracial, multireligious society to remain politically stable and socially harmonious (i.e., free of conflict and "communal disturbances"), which in turn are essential for its continuing economic development.

Singapore is an authoritarian state which tried during the 1980s to implement a weak fundamentalism, partly religious and partly secular, to preserve what were claimed to be the Asian values and social harmony of the society, and to ensure suitably communitarian values (as well as to provide local means of countering Western criticism of Singapore's authoritarian political system). However, there are structural conditions, which make it difficult to implement such a solution, particularly, the variety of ethnic groups, which comprise Singapore's population. The major ethnic divisions between Malays, South Asians, and ethnic Chinese are further complicated by religious divisions within each of these groups. For example, Singaporeans of South Asian origin include Theravada Buddhists from Sri Lanka, Hindus and Christians from India, and South Asian Muslims from India, Pakistan, and Bangladesh, while the Singaporean-Chinese population includes Christians, Buddhists, people who practice Chinese "popular religion" or follow various Chinese sectarian religions, and a few Chinese Muslims. These diverse groups do not share any common religious or philosophical heritage, which could be used as a foundation for state ideology.

The technocratic capitalist system in Singapore has also led to an inevitable emphasis on technical and professional knowledge rather than fundamentalist-cultural knowledge. While it is perfectly possible for members of technical and scientific professions to be religious fundamentalists (and indeed, many such persons in Singapore hold such beliefs) the overall character of the educational system and the principle of meritocracy are necessarily pluralist and pragmatic. The focus on high-technology economic development as the key to Singapore's success is strenuously advocated by the state, and ensures that this goal always supercedes cultural knowledge in the Singaporean educational system. The supreme value of technical and professional expertise is further reinforced by the regime's claim that Singapore is a meritocracy (not least, in the methods of recruitment for positions in government and in the principal sectors of the Singaporean economy). Hence, the technocratic-capitalist system provides much of the content for the state ideology, crowding out particularistic elements.

In short, these characteristics of Singapore society have produced a society too differentiated in educational levels, lifestyles, and religious interests, and too committed to secular values related to pragmatic expertise, to support a single unifying ideology which has particularistic components.[23] The Singaporean regime has therefore settled on a more abstract version of the "national ideology," abandoning its earlier attempt to include religious values within the prime principles of the state.

Indeed, religious fundamentalists among all the religions within Singaporean society are still closely watched, and are actively prevented from taking their fundamentalist institutional agenda into the realm of political discourse. This determination even extends to the continuing enforcement (up to the date of writing, in early 2003) of a ban on Muslim Malay schoolgirls wearing the headscarf at public schools.

If Singapore were to become more pluralist in terms of political democracy and political discourse, the visibility and influence of fundamentalist groups would probably increase, and it is possible that divisions amongst Singapore's ethnoreligious groups would become sharper, particularly if these groups begin to serve as advocates for their ethnic constituencies in debates over ethnic stratification within Singaporean society. This is certainly the regime's argument for maintaining tight control over such discourse, while institutionalizing a pluralist-universalist set of prime principles as Singapore's national ideology.

Indonesia

During the same period when Singapore was attempting to institutionalize a national ideology, which included both particularistic religious education and secular universalistic principles of association and tolerance, its giant neighbor to the south, Indonesia, was also engaged in debates about the official national ideology, known as "*pancasila*." Announced in 1945 by Sukarno, the president of the newly independent nation of Indonesia, *pancasila* (literally, the "five principles") can be summarized as follows: (1) belief in god; (2) a just and civilized humanitarianism; (3) national unity; (4) Indonesian democracy through consultation and consensus; and (5) social justice.[24] These principles were included in the Indonesian constitution, and contain both religious and secular ideas. They have been taught throughout the school system in Indonesia for the past fifty years. Unlike Singapore, Indonesia did not eventually abandon or exclude the religious component of this ideology, that is, the inclusion of "belief in god" within the prime principles of the nation. In addition, unlike Singapore, Indonesia successfully strengthened the institutionalization of this national ideology during the 1980s.

The principles are weakly religious, since they include "belief in god" but nothing more specific. The weakness of the religious principle is deliberate. In effect, *pancasila* institutionalizes tolerance among religions, since any theistic religion which advocates benevolence and national unity can claim adherence to the national ideology. However, this ideology is not entirely pluralist, since it does specify belief in god. Many of the Muslims who wished to convert Indonesia into an Islamic state (for example, by implementing *sharia* law) were dissatisfied by the absence of any reference to Islam, but at the same time the secularists were required to adapt to a constitution which now requires all individuals and organizations to endorse religious belief as a basic requirement of citizenship.

Why did Indonesia adopt this mixed charter for the nation? In what ways were these principles used and institutionalized in public life? What pressures are currently pushing Indonesia toward a stronger or weaker fundamentalism in its national ideology and national institutions? We wish to make some brief comments on this national ideology, and on the pressures in Indonesia which could produce further movement along the fundamentalism/pluralism continuum.

First, why did Indonesia adopt this kind of weakly religious set of prime principles? Indonesia is a predominantly Muslim country, but the Islam of a large proportion of the population is too mixed up with other local religious beliefs and practices to allow a purist version of Islam to be enforced nationwide. Indonesia was, before the creation of the modern state, an archipelago of diverse populations, which had never been subjected to ideological homogenization by a centralized regime. Comprising several hundred different ethnic groups, these diverse populations were spread among what Robert Hefner has characterized as "a multi-centered system of mercantile city-states, inland agrarian kingdoms, and tribal hinterlands."[25] While more than 80 percent of this population are Muslims,[26] there are also Christians (about 7 percent of the population), Buddhists, Balinese Hindus, and followers of various local folk-religions. Muslims in many regions of the archipelago had interacted with Buddhists and Christians for generations, and evolved models for civil relations, which constituted a kind of on-the-ground cultural pluralism.

Moreover, since the Muslims had no central authority to enforce any particular version of Islam, and since the Collection (the Quran and *hadith*) admits a variety of interpretations, as do all Collections, there were inevitably a wide range of views among these diverse populations about the interpretation of the Collection, and about how Islam can be applied to daily life. There were also many Muslim intellectuals who believed that it was undesirable to try to enforce an Islamic orthodoxy, and that a flourishing but tolerant and multivocal Muslim civil society offered the best model for progressive development of Indonesian society.

Equally important was the fact that the army, which led the fight for independence and played a key role in government and the economy after independence, was led mainly by secular nationalists who rejected any dogmatic religion as the basis for nation-building. The secular nationalists also knew that they needed to accommodate other religious groups besides Muslims. To unite this vast and diverse population, it was impossible to enforce a cultural orthodoxy, and essential to find some common but necessarily vague ideological ground upon which to build national institutions and national identity.

In order to find common ground between the opposing views of the various groups of moderate Muslims, Islamists, secular nationalists, and non-Muslim Indonesians, Sukarno proposed to adopt a religious idea compatible with nearly all of the religions of Indonesia. *Pancasila* was intended to provide a nonsectarian framework for the nation, which would not exclude or alienate secular nationalists and believers in other faiths, while also institutionalizing some acceptable common values and beliefs beyond the principles of mere pluralistic tolerance. Thus, belief in god was considered acceptable to all social groups and religions (despite excluding atheists).

Some Indonesian Muslim organizations, however, have been trying to increase their influence over the state from the beginning, in order to implement a more fundamentalist vision for the country, and because some of them had led or participated in anticolonial struggles and felt entitled to make demands in regard to the character of the new regime.[27] Indeed, the first drafts of the constitution, responding to pressure from Muslim leaders, had actually added to the first principle (belief in god) a reference to the requirement that Muslims must implement *sharia* (Islamic law), and that the president of the new republic must always be a Muslim. These stipulations were dropped from the final draft, leading many Muslim fundamentalists to conclude that they had been betrayed.[28] Nevertheless, the secular nationalists had prevailed, using the argument that only with such a nonspecific national ideology could they succeed in uniting a religiously and ethnically disparate collection of populations under one national regime.

Sukarno had many other ideas and programs related to ideologies with which he sympathized, including communism, and *pancasila* was a strategic ideological compromise rather than a simple summary of his own beliefs. He tried to engage in further ideological innovation, as for instance in 1959 when he proposed the principle of *"nasakom,"* which was an attempt to combine the basic principles of nationalism, communism, and religion, and was said to be the real meaning of *pancasila*. Sukarno's links with and support from the Communist Party of Indonesia (PKI) were part of this unlikely ideological fusion. In any case this innovation was much less successful than the adoption of *pancasila* within the constitution.

After Suharto replaced Sukarno as president in 1966, following a coup attempt by some alleged PKI supporters and a bloody purge of the PKI and anyone suspected of communist sympathies, Suharto discarded much of Sukarno's eclectic accumulation of ideological themes (eliminating "communism" completely from the mixture), and focused much more narrowly on *pancasila* as the ideological foundation of the state. Beginning in 1978, all civil servants and all school children were required to engage in regular study sessions devoted to the principles of *pancasila*. In 1985, the Suharto government went further, and passed a law specifying that all organizations in the country must formally adopt *pancasila* by incorporating it into their charter or bylaws. Any organization, which refused to do, so would be banned. This extraordinary measure provoked fierce debate, but was eventually implemented. *Pancasila* thus constituted a kind of weak fundamentalism which was adopted within all of the major institutions in Indonesian society, not only in the educational system but within all other organizations as well.

After the fall of Suharto during the economic crisis and its repercussions in the late 1990s, the country's political system became more open and democratic. The Golkar Party which ruled Indonesia under Suharto since the 1960s lost power to a new coalition, after several vigorously contested elections, and the press and mass media were much less controlled by the regime, while political parties became far more aggressive than they dared to be during Suharto's authoritarian regime. As we would predict, this increase in openness led to a resurgence of pressure from advocates of strong fundamentalism to tilt the nation toward a much closer integration of Islam into the laws, education, and governance of the society.

However, the structural changes within Indonesian society have also facilitated the growth of a diverse range of Muslim organizations and increasing intellectual space for Muslim intellectuals, who now contend with the fundamentalists for political influence. There is no better example than the former president, Abdurrahman Wahid, who for many years headed one of the principal Islamic organizations in Indonesia before his entry into national politics. Wahid's strong commitment to pluralism, tolerance, and what Robert Hefner has called "civil Islam" contrasts sharply with the aims and mentality of the proponents of what Hefner calls "statist Islam," that is, the determination to graft Islam into the institutions and national ideology of the state.

In the world's largest Muslim country, there is an ongoing contest over whether the national ideology will retain its current combination of a weak religious prime principle (belief in god) and several strong pluralist-secular principles (i.e. the other four principles in the current version of *pancasila*), or whether instead the fundamentalists will succeed in capturing key organs of the state. If they manage to do so, they would undoubtedly begin to bend those institutions to the implementation of a strong fundamentalism within education, law, and the regulation of the mass media.

Similar pressures are at work in Malaysia, where the society is also structurally diverse because of large differences between regions in the degree of urbanization and educational levels. Further complicating Malaysia's ideological landscape is the fact that while about 61 percent of Malaysians are ethnic Malay Muslims, about 34 percent of the country's population are ethnic Chinese and Indians, almost none of whom are Muslims. Thus, like Singapore, Malaysia must try to find pluralist accommodations with its large non-Muslim populations, which greatly reduces the prospect of implementing a particularistic national ideology.

Complicating this dynamic struggle is the fact that Indonesia and Malaysia are both federal systems (unlike Singapore), with considerable variations between provinces in regard to the prevalence and strength of fundamentalist movements and parties. Both states have been led by secular and (at least in regard to religion) pluralist leaders for most of the past fifty years. However, within both federal systems, there are regions where very conservative versions of Islam, promoted by fundamentalist groups, are strongly entrenched. Within both federal systems, at least one province has implemented some features of S*haria* law (in Indonesia, Aceh; in Malaysia, Kelantan and Terengganu). Thus, both Indonesia and Malaysia contain fundamentalist subsystems within a more pluralist national polity, and there are continuing struggles between these opposing forces in both societies.

Conclusion

We have argued that a more abstract definition of fundamentalism is a useful way to facilitate comparative analysis. Our definition does not try to accommodate the historical (and variable) causes, doctrinal contents, or specific programs of such movements. Instead, we focused on the institutional and programmatic consequences of the formal characteristics of such movements—in particular, the consequences of their formulation and authoritarian promulgation of a simple set of unchallengeable principles derived from a sacred Collection. We contrasted this type of belief system with a contrary mode of belief and practice, which can be called pluralism, and suggested that fundamentalism and pluralism can usefully be conceived as ends of a scale, rather than as a simple dichotomy.

This analysis led us to a consideration of the implications of these belief systems for states and statecraft. We suggested that many contemporary states are embroiled in the issues raised by the contest between fundamentalism and pluralism, and then proceeded to consider how such issues and tensions are played out in multiethnic and multireligious states in Southeast Asia, in several of which we can observe a kind of weak fundamentalism at the level of state ideology, but with continuing pressures on this ideology from both fundamentalists and pluralists. Such struggles for the "soul" of the nation are ongoing in Singapore, Indonesia, and Malaysia.[29] The outcomes will depend in part on structural characteristics and trends with those societies. The consequences—for the future intellectual and social life of such societies—are as important to pluralists as to fundamentalists.

Notes

1. On reasons why "fundamentalism" has been undertheorized in sociology, see Martin Reisebrodt, *Pious Passion: The Emergence of Modern Fundamentalism in the United States and Iran* (Berkeley: University of California Press, 1993), 3.

2. See Martin E. Marty and R. Scott Appleby, "Introduction: A Sacred Cosmos, Scandalous Code, Defiant Society," in *Fundamentalisms and Society*, Martin E. Marty and F. Scott Appleby, eds. (Chicago: University of Chicago Press, 1993), 1–19.

3. Marty and Appleby, "Introduction," 9.

4. See William Kephart, *Extraordinary Groups: An Examination of Unconventional Lifestyles*, 3rd ed. (New York: St. Martin's Press, 1987).

5. S. N. Eisenstadt, *Fundamentalism, Sectarianism, and Revolution: The Jacobin Dimension of Modernity* (Cambridge: Cambridge University Press, 1999).

6. See Judith Nagata, "Beyond Theology: Toward an Anthropology of 'Fundamentalism,'" *American Anthropologist* 103, no. 2 (June 2001): 481–98.

7. See, for example, Wen-yuan Qian, *The Great Inertia: Scientific Stagnation in Traditional China* (London: Croom Helm, 1985).

8. For the wider social context, advocacy of pluralism may be the best strategy for minority fundamentalist groups. Some have embraced pluralism—as a legal framework for a society—because it allows them to adhere to fundamentalist principles without repression from majority groups.

9. Within both Christianity and Islam, for example, "short-lists" of basic principles or "fundamental beliefs" have been developed by some believers to indicate the "core" or essential beliefs and practices in the faith, adherence to which defines the community of the faithful. Similar summaries occur in fundamentalist political systems.

10. Examples of this additional "layer" of interpretive or near-canonical material, with a status somewhat below the official "Collection," but with considerable authoritative status for believers, have included the *hadith* (for Islam), the works of Aquinas (for Roman Catholicism over a number of centuries), the Talmud (for Judaism), and the Doctrine and Covenants (for LDS Mormonism). Some commentaries have also been accorded a nearly similar status within philosophical traditions managed by ideological institutions, such as the status (for examination purposes) of some neo-Confucian commentaries during the Ming and Qing dynasties in China. Political fundamentalisms may also include these secondary works (while also restricting or banning rival commentaries).

11. Research since World War II has investigated the correlates and appeal of dogmatism, authoritarianism, ethnocentrism, and related cognitive dispositions. Much of this research is relevant to an analysis of the appeal of fundamentalism and the social conditions most conducive to increasing appeal for such systems of thought. In regard to methods of reinforcement and commitment, there is also a large body of research on mechanisms used to socialize members and maintain commitment. This kind of analysis has been incorporated into work on a variety of ideological communities. See, for example, Rosabeth Moss Kanter, *Commitment and Community: Communes and Utopias in Sociological Perspective* (Cambridge: Harvard University Press, 1972).

12. See also Eisenstadt, *Fundamentalism, Sectarianism, and Revolution*, 68.

13. For a structuralist analysis, see Graeme Lang, "State Systems and the Origins of Modern Science: A Comparison of Europe and China," *East-West Dialogue* II (February 1, 1997): 16–31.

14. James C. Scott, *Seeing Like a State: How Certain Schemes to Improve the Human Condition have Failed* (New Haven: Yale University Press, 1998).

15. This is one of the main theses in Theda Skocpol, *States and Social Revolutions: A Comparative Analysis of France, Russia, and China* (Cambridge: Cambridge University Press, 1979). Skocpol analyzes conditions which facilitate capture of the state by revolutionary groups.

16. The "religious economy" paradigm in the sociology of religion has produced compelling theory and much evidence that conditions of religious competition can produce higher rates of religious activity and religious membership than religious monopoly.

See, for instance, Rodney Stark and Roger Finke, *Acts of Faith: Explaining the Human Side of Religion* (Berkeley: University of California Press, 2000).

17. In the United States, for example, the use of the words "under God" in the pledge of allegiance is considered essential by many fundamentalists, but anathema by many pluralists, and has recently been a subject of fierce controversy in the courts and in the media. See Adam Liptak, "Court Lets Stand the Ban on 'God' in Pledge," *New York Times*, March 1, 2003 (online edition).

18. See also Eisenstadt, *Fundamentalism, Sectarianism, and Revolution*, 16–18.

19. Peter Berger, *The Sacred Canopy: Elements of a Sociological Theory of Religion* (New York: Doubleday and Co., 1967).

20. This account of Singapore's policies is derived from the analysis by Joseph Tamney, *The Struggle for Singapore's Soul: Western Modernization and Asian Culture* (New York: Walter de Gruyter, 1996), 19–50.

21. Tamney, *Struggle for Singapore's Soul*, 38.

22. Tamney, *Struggle for Singapore's Soul*, 19.

23. Beng-huat Chua, *Communitarian Ideology and Democracy in Singapore* (London: Routledge, 1995), 200.

24. These are the translations of these principles in Douglas E. Ramage, *Politics in Indonesia: Democracy, Islam and the Ideology of Tolerance* (London: Routledge), 1. Our account of the national ideology in Indonesia relies heavily on Ramage's excellent analysis.

25. Robert Hefner, "Public Islam and the Problem of Democratization," *Sociology of Religion* 62, no. 4 (2001): 500.

26. The proportion of Indonesia's 200+ million people who self-identify as Muslims is about 88 percent Hefner, "Public Islam," 492.

27. Vivienne Wee, "Sacred Worlds and Secular States: The Islamist Governance of Gender and Everyday Life in Southeast Asia," presented at the conference on "Islam in Southeast Asia and China: Regional Faithlines and Faultlines in the Global *Ummah*," November 28–December 1, 2002, City University of Hong Kong.

28. Ramage, *Politics in Indonesia*, 14–15.

29. On Singapore, see Tamney, *Struggle For Singapore's Soul* (see fn. 20). On Indonesia, see Ramage (fn. 24). On Malaysia, see Raymond L. M. Lee and Susan Ackerman, *Sacred Tensions: Modernity and Religious Transformation in Malaysia* (Columbia, S.C.: University of South Carolina Press, 1997).

Chapter 4

Religion between Universal and Particular: Eastern Europe after 1989

Alexander Agadjanian

This chapter primarily focuses on postcommunist nations of Eastern Orthodox cultural area (with a special case study from Russia and with additional material from Greece and Poland), to explore the variety of religious responses to the global culture of the late modernity. It proposes several ideal-typical models of such responses. It holds that most religions of the area abandoned the universalistic discourse and assumed strongly particularistic links with ethnic, national, and cultural identities. However, for a religion, this explicit particularism is, paradoxically, the most efficient way of de facto self-inclusion into a field allotted to it within the new global taxonomy.

Religion vs. Global Culture: To Resist or to Accept?

This chapter will attempt to summarize some recent religious developments in Eastern Europe[1] with one specific perspective in mind: to investigate the ways religions of this area in the post–Cold War era have responded to the advance of "global culture."

Responding to global culture—or to whatever we can call a trend thereto or an expression thereof—means to revisit a religion's eternal claim to represent the *universal* while being constantly bound to a *particular* entity: community, ethnos, polity, or tradition. Universal and particular have been always dialectically linked in the history of religions. They might simply ignore this distinction as a problem, as in isolated tribal communities whose particular gods were the only conceivable source of universal order; they might have tried to cultivate a certain universal divine space that would overcome particular regional preferences while at the same time tolerating them, as in classical ancient *oecumene*; they might have posited a hierarchy of access to the ultimate universal truth, with a particular community being clearly marked as having an exclusive mission to be God's people, as in the Judaic theology of covenants; they might have established an imperial expanse combined with exclusive dualistic regime of messianic warfare with infidels, as in classical Islam or medieval Christianity; or to postulate a more inclusive universalism recognizing particularities as only accidental, outer forms of an essential inner unity, as in modern colonial Christianity.

The contemporary situation seems to create, however, a new intricate complexity. In a *Problemstellung* article R. Robertson and J. Chirico were the first to explore the religious resurgence against a backdrop of a new condition of globality. They indicated the tendency toward a "relativization of personal identity" and "a near-global conception of selfhood," as an expression of the broad globalization process. An outcome of, or a response to, this tendency, "[t]he resurgence of fundamentalistic promotion of particularistic ideologies and doctrines (local, ethnic national, civilizational and regional)," may be seen as a backlash, a reestablishment of clear contours of identity. This outcome, as Robertson and Chirico emphasized, "does not by any means constitute counter-evidence [against globalization], for . . . the recent world-wide assertion of particularistic ideas is heavily contextualized by the phenomenon of increasing *globality*."[2] In what way, then, may religion be thought of in this new global context? In another article W. Garrett and R. Robertson posit four possible answers:

1) The global order is predicated on normative rubrics . . . without a vital connection to any religious tradition; it would mean to assert that there is no place for religions in this radically secular global order.
2) On the contrary, religions may be thought of as "contribut[ing] significantly to the development of patterns of universal order."
3) As an intermediary position, the essentially secular universal order would, nonetheless, "afford niches wherein religious groups or sentiments may find some degree of security."[3]
4) As the fourth possibility (which means, in fact, to conceive of religion in an "entirely different mode"), religion may become a "*genre* of expression, communication, and legitimation [of collective identities and individual needs] rather than simply an institutional enclave alongside political, economic, and familial entities, as was [religion's common image] during the modern era.[4]

While providing these four patterns of possible development, W. Garrett and R. Robertson judiciously abstain from viewing them as excluding each other; in fact, as the totality of further studies show, each of these four patterns is partly, if not exclusively, valid.

Further in the same article, W. Garrett and R. Robertson treat the issue of universalism and particularism. Deriving from the general notion of the dialectical relationship between the two concepts, they articulate an important idea: the assertion of particular cultural enclaves, of particular identities (national, ethnic, linguistic, religious, or, indeed, those that intermix all the previous), is a necessary means of their self-preservation "in face of their global participation."[5] In other words, a human community (as, indeed, an individual, too) must protect its particular self, in order to participate in the global culture as *a* self. In my opinion, this law is valid for all four tentative prospects described above: to inscribe one*self* into the universal is only conceivable through *self*-determination.

P. Beyer makes the same point: all religious responses to the global *universum* are driven by an objective need not to reject it, but to become a part of it. In the Iranian revolution, he assumes, "the central thrust was [only] to make Islam and Muslims more determinative in the world system, not to reverse globalization;" in this way all religions, therefore, were instrumental in the elaboration and development of the global culture.[6] As P. Beyer proceeds, he refers to modern movements (such as *Boxer* rebellion, *Arya Samaj*, and others—a list that might include, indeed, the more recent ones), which constituted themselves as "religions" or "traditions" and thus inscribed themselves into the new cultural order.[7] For Robertson, "globalization itself produces variety–more accurately, it encourages heterogeneity-within-homogeneity. . . ."[8] At the same time, can we expand, the global culture, or, more specifically, a *new universal taxonomy* is being spelled by the self-asserting narratives of particular identities, by their very effort to inscribe themselves into the global whole.

P. Beyer speaks of two major religious responses to global culture: the fundamentalist negative rejection and the inclusive positive acceptance. A striking paradox that he points out is that the first, *negative* reaction may be considered as more instrumental in the creation of this new universal taxonomy than the second, *positive* one. Why? Because in the second case a religious tradition "is reoriented toward the global whole and away from the particular culture with which this tradition identified itself in the past;" instead of its past content, this religion "takes up the values of the emerging global culture."[9] After such a transformation, religion is dissolved in the global culture and loses the ability to convey "specifically religious information . . . that people could not get from nonreligious sources."[10] Not only is such religion deprived from its particular cultural identity, it even loses its specifically *religious* content. This unidentified *self* contributes nothing to the universal.

On the contrary, a religion that is resistant, well articulated, and clearly conscious of its particularity, assumes a certain locus in the new universal taxonomy. The more expressively particular is the *self* of a religion (religious movement, community, or group), the stronger is its specifically religious symbolic and social capital. Therefore, the particularistic expression and the resistance against the universal may be inferred as a typical religious strategy and, paradoxically, a more assured way to be inscribed into the new universal taxonomy. Let us pause upon this preliminary hypothesis and move on to its further elaboration, while directly tying it to the East European data.

Eastern European Religions: Choosing Particularistic Strategies in Negotiating a New Field

Religion has been omnipresent in former communist countries since the late 1980s in a number of ways, in full conformity with a general trend of public religion's resurgence.[11] After the collapse of communist ideologies and liberalization, religions quickly moved to the center of public discourse. Religious leaders and organizations suddenly became prominent players in political games. Religions provided a set of references both for dismantling of communist regimes and for a swift ethnonational mobilization, leading to ethnic clashes but sometimes creating islands of social stability in the critical and chaotic times of transition.[12] Postimperial wars in former Yugoslavia and the Soviet Union were at least partly orchestrated and sometimes motivated religiously. The introduction of religious pluralism was followed by direct interdenominational tensions and clashes both over property and souls along traditional and new lines.[13]

These evidences of religious presence seem to be a rather motley bunch of ill-assorted phenomena. Let us try to introduce some qualifications that would help us to comprehend it in a more methodical way. The first statement to be made is that in spite of a significant growth of religious presence or religious prominence, in no case were religions able to claim any determinate, let alone exclusive, role in defining the nation-building or cultural climate. Although religious references, in most cases, have directly entered into the discourse of national identity and political practice, the religious legislation reflected this discourse only in a muffled way and handled religion in a clearly secular manner.[14] Overall, after fifteen years of change, religions seem to be included as an institutional and discursive *field* in the diverse, complex, and predominantly secular texture of new societies. Therefore, religions faced the need to reshape themselves in such a way as to be able to operate within this newly defined field.

For a religion, this "being-in-the-field" means to engage in two types of negotiation. First, it is the negotiation with other societal fields in the new open space—in fact, transnational, global space. The issue at stake here is the *relevance* of religion to the secular and global world, and it requires each religious tradition to elaborate a new set of ideas and mechanisms that would define the measure and the model of its relations with political power, legislation, civil society, economy, new mass cultural idioms, and the condition of globality. For Eastern Orthodox Churches it was a task of dramatic opening, of profound (and painful) restructuring, of acquiring and interpreting of a new language of modernity, of which they were cut off for decades of isolation and repressions.

The second type of negotiation, which partly originated from the same fact of a new global openness, is the negotiation *within* the religious field, or the competition *for* this field, with other religious forms of an unprecedented variety. The main issue here is that of *domination*. "Religious pluralism" that the Eastern Orthodox Churches faced in the 1990s is a new context, even in comparison to the religious diversity that they might have experienced in old imperial settings of the early twentieth century. The negotiation and conflicts that have arisen within the religious field of this area belong to four major cleavages: Orthodox versus Roman Catholics and Uniates, or Greek Catholics (all along the line of the old Latin-Greek divide); Orthodox versus Western and local Protestants; Orthodox versus Muslims; Orthodox versus New Religious Movements.[15]

The process of self-reshaping along these two lines exacerbated the fundamental internal tension, or problem, within each Eastern Orthodox tradition: the problem of identity. On the one hand, the new situation of openness prompted an overture and change. On the other hand, any change is always accompanied by a clear redefinition of the *self* of a tradition. While opening it*self*, a tradition simultaneously has to clearly define the limits of this opening, and thus the limits of the *self*. While inscribing itself in a new order of things, the borders of *self* should be clearly circumscribed. A religious tradition, being exposed to the challenge of openness, reacts by folding up, or compressing. We can call this process *the dialectic of overture and compression*, in which a tradition tests a precarious balance of reform and identity-protection. Correspondingly, overture implies a universalist discourse, while the compression, a particularistic discourse.

In practical terms, this innate tension, revealed through negotiating of both relevance and domination (as described above), often leads to ideological and/or institutional divisions within each religious tradition. Some churches were on the brink of complete schism but it did not occur in most cases;[16] it is certain, however, that everywhere the strain along these lines was and remains very tight. The famous Serbian bishop, Nicolaj Velemirović (1880–1956, canonized posthumously), reflected this strain in his theology: his initially opening project of going beyond Christian East-West rupture was finally replaced by a staunchly protective and particularistic emphasis on St. Sava's legacy implying two key patterns: Orthodox monasticism and Serbian ethnic identity. Justin Popović (1894–1979), Velemirović's younger contemporary (and also a saint of the Serbian Church), carried this trend of compression to a radical intolerance toward "heretical" Western Churches and the West in general.[17] In Greece, trends of renewal and ecumenism anchored in such periodicals as *Sunaxe* and *Kath Hodon* and such institutions as Society for Ecumenical Studies in Thessalonica, are counterweighed by the lingering monastic fundamentalism (centered at Mt. Athos), diffused Old Calendarist movement, and widespread anti-Latinism and anti-Westernism.[18] In the Catholic Poland similar tensions occurred after the same pattern, with two clearly discernible religious currents formed in the middle of the twentieth century, liberal and populist;[19] within the clergy, this division put forward people like the late Joseph Tischner or Archbishop Joseph Zycinski of Lublin, as compared to a much more conservative mainstream clergy and the Lublin Catholic University in general.

The internal tension has been also reflected in an alteration of various phases of postcommunist religious developments. In the last years of communist regimes, the religious language was largely interwoven into the anti-communist liberal discourse; in this mixture, religious symbolic capital enhanced the liberal political agenda, whereas the religious vocabulary developed strong universalist connotations: religion was believed to be the utmost expression of "universal values," repressed, repudiated, and distorted by particularistic, class-bound, and partisan communist ideology. Catholic or Orthodox traditions were referred to as repositories of universalism. This was a common motif of the *glasnost* discourse in the late Soviet Union. Polish Catholicism was the most effective religious force contributing to anticommunist mobilization, partly because, in contrast to the Orthodox Churches in the region, it had an international scope and largely intact symbolic resources;[20] another telling example from Poland would be the evolution of a popular Catholic "Oases" movement from being a germ of the civil society under the communist regime to becoming a grouping with a conservative "integralist" agenda in the 1990s.[21]

This religious universalism was, however, a part of a predominantly lay, not clerical, discourse. Nevertheless, the degree of the Churches's direct social and political involvement soared. Immediately, this involvement became highly controversial both within and outside the Churches. Rather quickly, the process of overture has been replaced, or overweighed, by the opposite trend of compression, and the particularistic discourse has become clearly dominant among the clergy. The mainline religious institutions were becoming more and more conservative in most cases, with modernist and antimodernist extremes occupying marginal niches, the latter being much more visible and articulate than the former. The same Catholic Church in Poland, after playing a crucial role on the initial stage of "transition," moved significantly to the pole of particularism, assuming the highest degree of nationalism that the global structure of the Roman Church can allow to a national ecclesiastical body; this nationalism is expressed by some organizations with a strong Catholic identity, such as Fellowship of Christian Nationalists (who were once a part of *Solidarnosć*), *Liga Polskich Rodzin* (Polish Family League) party, *Radio Maryja*, and peasant *Samooborona* party. On most issues the Church lost the dynamism of overture and entrenched herself on definitely conservative stands.[22]

The central issue where the compression phase became the most visible is that of religious pluralism, the issue where the dominant religions felt most vulnerable; the theme of identity and the theme of domination over the newly outlined "religious field" are tightly intermixed in this issue. To insure their continuous control over the field, the dominant Churches developed a discourse of the *spatial* and *temporal* privileges. In terms of *space*, they claimed their responsibility over certain territories by right of canonical law or custom (such as "canonical territory," ascribed to each Orthodox Church according to norms of ecclesiastical autocephaly). In terms of *time*, the Churches put forward the notion of "traditional religion" as opposed to all the rest, a new cultural dichotomy construct legitimizing a special historical link to a nation or ethnicity.[23]

Ethnic and/or national particularism that religions tend to express is definitely the major phenomenon. Now, in almost all Eastern Orthodox countries the denominational line concurs with ethnic boundaries, and the level of religious "compression" positively correlates with the level of ethnonationalism: groups such as some brotherhoods in Russia, are both most fundamentalist (and anti-ecumenical) and nationalistic.[24] Russian Orthodoxy's ostensibly *transnational* discourse of a "canonical territory" roughly corresponding to the former imperial space is clearly particularistic—first, because of its obvious denominational sensibility, and second, because this discourse is by no means *transethnic*, for their main addressees are ethnic Russians everywhere. Even in those cases when, such as in Ukraine or Belarus, the Moscow Patriarchate speaks of a transnational "spiritual unity," the ethnocentric (Slav, or Eastern Slav) implication is inherent.[25]

Ukraine represents an interesting and convoluted example. The main religious developments there are very much defined by the vicissitudes of the quest for ethnonational identity: as *ukrainstvo* (Ukraineness), an ethnocultural entity, should get free from Russian imperial legacy, so must a new ecclesiastical entity be created to match the new national project. An immediate result was the split of the Church: one part being dependent upon Moscow patriarchate and another one independent (and further divided, however).[26] The idea of an independent "national Church," which is a clear opposition to Moscow's "transnational" claim (and which is rather eager to go under jurisdiction of the ecumenical patriarchate of Constantinople—the last symbol of Orthodox universality),[27] was an ongoing national debate from the very declaration of Ukraine's independence.[28] The symbolic allure of *the* (yet virtual) national Church is so strong that the third player of the Ukrainian religious field, Greek Catholics (the Uniates), who claim to represent the primordial true *Ukraineness*, consider to overpass the age-old denominational rivalries and to join the independent (not pro-Moscow) Orthodox for this national religious project.[29]

The situation in Ukraine is indeed quite unique because the ethnic identity is split between two forms of religious expression, Greek Catholic and Orthodox, and the creation of *the* national religion (if at all imaginable) is an ongoing process of interdenominational interaction. In most other countries of the area the identity link with Orthodoxy is clear. *Srpstvo* (Serbdom), a term analogous to *ukrainstvo,* is an unequivocal alloy of ethnicity and religion. This phenomenon is quite common for the area.

This link of religion and ethnicity/nationality has strong roots in the history of Eastern Orthodoxy: one factor is ecclesiastical *autocephaly* (autonomy) that was always a formative principle, making the Churches directly dependent on local secular forces; another reason (applied to the peoples subject to long Turk domination) was the *millet* system in the Ottoman Empire, which managed ethnic minorities as religions communities; consequently, the rise of ethnic consciousness in the nineteenth century (when the *Rum* millet, administered by the patriarch of Constantinople disintegrated, was largely expressed in particularistic religious terms. To be sure, the so-called phyletism, or the ethnonational principle in church organization, was officially condemned in 1872 by a synod under the patriarch, but this principle continuously dominated modern religion history of the whole region, along with what V. Roudometoff calls "redeployment of Orthodoxy" on a national basis.[30]

The spatial and temporal borders mentioned above—the "discourse of the territory" and "the discourse of tradition"—besides expressing ethnic particularism, also mirrored increased denominational sensibilities: the barriers were erected against the established Western denominations, first of all (in Orthodox countries) Roman Catholicism, sharpening the old hostility toward the Uniates (especially in Romania);[31] and then against a sweeping growth of new religious movements and the influx of Protestant missionaries. For example, the revived missionary work is mostly aimed at "protection of our Church and our Orthodox people from a variety of foreign proselytizing activities."[32] The Christian mission, which is apparently a universalistic endeavor, is clearly reinterpreted here in a defensive, protective way. Proselytism is seen as the main form of the "war for souls," waged by foreign denominations.[33] The term proselytism is defined here broadly, meaning not just reconverting a person from one religion to another, but also converting those who belong to no religion, precisely because, according to a dominant interpretation, all people living on this particular "canonical territory" and belonging to this particular ethnos (for example, Russians) are *endemically* Orthodox, independently of their religious beliefs and practice or the absence thereof (which is largely the case in most post-communist societies).

Therefore, proselytism is seen as creating a threat not only to the dominant Church but also to the whole ethnonational community. In the same vein, "[t]he Protestant evangelization of Ukraine" is said "to destroy the sense of togetherness, of ethnic unity, and to lead to individualism;" the Protestant missionaries want to "alter the spiritual ethno-type of Ukraine."[34] In Romania, the conceptualization of "heresy," alien and detrimental for national identity, is an ongoing discourse within Orthodoxy, which is by definition equated to national tradition. The Orthodox Church rejects the notion of postcommunist "religious vacuum" or "spiritual desert," assuming (as is the case of Russia) that Romanians are *endemically* Orthodox (even those who do not practice), and thus the "sects"—a term applied mainly to Protestant groups—carry out proselytism that must be outlawed.[35] In Greece antiproselytism legislation has been in force since General Metaxas (in the late 1930s) and served the same goals.[36] These examples from

Eastern and Southeastern Europe reflect a ubiquitous antiglobalization pattern found in different parts of the non-Western world.[37]

The "war for souls" was waged to ensure the domination-in-the-field and against something that was supposed and labeled to be foreign, alien, detrimental to *this* territory and to *this* people. With a shift to particularistic conservatism, it was only logical to associate the source of this foreignness, in the final analysis, with that which represents the claim for the universal, the West. The unacceptable foreignness of this universalism is twofold: not only does it stem from another sociocultural setting, but it also is largely secular. Therefore, the whole Western ethos is thought of as bringing an ontological threat; in particular, new religious forms of Western origins are suspected to bear not just a competition *within* the religious field but the very trend to *reduce* this field.[38] In 2000, the government's plan to remove religion from identity cards in Greece ignited mass demonstrations led by Church hierarchy with a clear anti-Western agenda. This agenda pinpointed two dangers: first, de-Hellenization of Greece, and second, "marginalization of religion" in "global consumerism," quite significantly, both were closely linked.[39] Russian Orthodox antiglobalists of the late 1990s, an uncoordinated collection of variously radical groups, were speaking of the Western threat both to the Russian Church and to the Russian people.[40] Again, the Church in Poland, in spite of Catholic structural internationalism, is split on the issue of Polish integration into Europe, accepting it (in accordance with Vatican's recommendations) only under the condition of promoting a "Christian spirit" of the Union and on a principle of "homeland of homelands."[41]

Overall, in the course of last decades, the dominant religions have practically yielded the sphere of the universal, de facto recognizing that the Western liberal secular ethos acquired exclusive rights to claim the universal and to represent it. Most theological, political, and institutional efforts have been spent to create the whole concept of particular religious tradition and its various parochial linkages with territory, ethnicity, language, culture, history, power system, and worldview.

Russian Orthodox Conundrum of Overture and Compression: Preserving Uniqueness (A Case Study)

Let us observe this twisted internal strain between impulses of overture and compression in the case of the Russian Orthodoxy. Although the size of the Russian Church makes the degree of this strain unique, its experience is typical to the area, as indeed it may reveal some promptings for understanding the religious dynamic the world over.

I would like to track a discursive thread of Russian Orthodox rhetoric through an exegesis of one text, called the Foundations of the Social Concept, a programmatic official document conceived in 1994 and adopted in 2000 by the Moscow Jubilee Bishops Council.[42] This semitheological document was a new type of text for the Christian Orthodox tradition: its main goal was a direct treatment of both fundamental and topical issues of society: from the nation to the death penalty to war to bioethics to globalization.

The text clearly reflects various competing voices within the Church officialdom, as, indeed, within the Church at large; it is multivocal in many senses: in vocabulary, in concepts that are used, in references to traditional authorities, and in ideas. An analysis of the whole document goes beyond this chapter. I only wish to pinpoint one striking contradiction of this text, which I believe to be strategic.

On the one hand, it shows an obvious intention to become modern and relevant, to cut off the inherited endemic other-worldliness and cultural isolation, to build a bridge between natural and supernatural, to affirm the value of *this* world. It calls the Church "not to shun the world," to consider human activity as a cowork, a *synergy* with Creator. It fights the staunch Manichaenism and promotes a social openness and inclusive activism, a kind of Orthodox version of *aggiornamento*. The document ipso facto is a thrust to modernity.

On the other hand, with a closer approach to the text, you would find something quite different from, if not the opposite of, the previous. For example, you can see in the document extremely strong *border sensitivity,* a constant concern, sometimes an obsession with self-identity, and a permanent reification of the "us-them" dichotomies operating on several levels. The presumption that the Church is opposed to the rest of society is quite explicit; in most cases, in this opposition the Church is conceived as an institution with certain corporate interests, rather than an open and inclusive community. The Church as a Christian institution is juxtaposed to the "non-Christian state, associations, and individuals." The following quote is typical in both its tone and theological argument " . . . The internal law of the Church is free from the spiritually fallen world and even opposed to it" (IV.4). It is one of the major themes of the document to clearly define the institutional borders of the Church: "clerics, monks, and laity," whose activities are controlled by the hierarchy (i.e., Church authorities; see V.2, V.4, XV.2).

In other cases the text emphasizes the Eastern Orthodox identity in general, or even more specifically, the Russian (national) form of Eastern Orthodoxy. The structure of authoritative references found in the text clearly reveals this denominational bias: 140 out of 147 nonbiblical references are to Eastern Orthodox theologians, rulers, and ecclesiastic documents.[43] The adjectives "Christian" and "Orthodox" (*pravoslavnyi*) are used almost interchangeably in the text, though sometimes "Orthodoxy" seems to be used in contrast to a broader category of "Christianity."[44] At some places, through using archaisms or old religious vocabulary, a specifically Russian linguistic flavor comes to the foreground in text, or specifically Russian historical images and events are evoked, to attach to Orthodoxy a more national appearance.

Thus creating several implicit particularistic definitions, the document establishes a sequence of barriers that stand against the initial overture and decisively limit the degree thereof. The purpose of all these barriers is self-definition, protection of a certain identity, a certain theological, denominational, and institutional purity that is threatened by this risky process of self-inscribing in a virtual universal taxonomy. Therefore, we can call them *purity-protective taxonomic barriers*.

What stands behind this particularistic impulse is another strong paradigm of the text, a second leitmotif directly contradicting the initial world-affirming effort. The world is described as still extremely dangerous and inimical, especially the *contemporary* world (this actualization of the discourse is obvious, too). The criticism of the contemporary world is overwhelming and relentless, sometimes assuming prophetic and apocalyptic pathos. In a number of instances the document calls the world "fallen" and "degrading," refers to demographic crisis, family breakdown, ecological catastrophe, blooming "industry of vices," "spiritual void, the lack of meaning of life, the erosion of moral guidelines" (XI.6 and passim). This kind of world can never be accepted, embraced, or justified.

What is perceived as the origin of this poor condition, with such a clear emphasis on *latest days*? Basically, at the bottom line, it is the apostasy, or secularism, an anthropocentric self-aggrandizement of the godless human being: "Seduction by the achievements of civilization moves people away from the Creator and leads to a deceptive triumph of reason, which attempts to arrange the world without God" (VI.3). To describe this challenge, the document uses the term theomachism (*bogoborchestvo*) that has a long history in the Russian thought (XII.4).[45] As a matter of fact, what is rejected is, to use J. Habermas's term, the modernity-project seen as a Tower of Babel sort of challenge to God, an old anti-Enlightenment and romantic discourse going back to de Maistres, Dostoyevsky, the neo-Thomistic revival of the nineteenth century, and even to Heideggerian concern to return to "the power of being" as opposed to the rootless universalism; and it is similar indeed to what we can find in a cross-cultural, cross-denominational, antimodernist and antisecular discourse everywhere.

Opening itself to the new global order, inscribing itself therein, the tradition simultaneously resists it, because this global order is defined, according to the tradition's constituent assumptions, as "a universal de-spiritualized culture" (XVI.3). Impulses of "overture and compression" are dialectically inseparable.

This inherent ambiguity of responses becomes even more intriguing when we go further in the deconstruction of the text. One major emphasis is on the *dignity of human person*, a concept widely used in contemporary Western theology and in global secular discourse, but quite unusual in the Russian Orthodox theological context, at least in traditional scholastic vocabulary.[46] Yet another surprising emphasis is the one on *diversity*, something not quite common for the conservative traditional discourse; diversity is extolled both in biological and cultural realms.

Both concepts of dignity and diversity appear to belong to the modern discourse and thus attest again to an ongoing *aggiornamento,* an overture. In addition, it is certainly the case, because both concepts were unmistakably new for Russian Orthodoxy, although they were theologically contextualized as deriving from the tradition of Christian personalism and tolerance. However, in the very process of this contextualization the whole semantic field associated with these concepts changes dramatically. In no way does "the dignity of human person" lead to fully accepting the universality of human rights or liberties; in no way does diversity mean pluralism with the slightest degree of liberal connotations. What is at stake in both cases is preserving individual *uniqueness* in all forms and contexts, preserving uniqueness as such, uniqueness as a primary principle of being.

Uniqueness is endangered by the "contemporary world," and this is the point where the theologians directly address globalization. While they do admit some achievements of globalism, their overall pathos is to resist "the spiritual and cultural expansion fraught with total unification," the "universal culture devoid of any spirituality and based on the freedom of fallen man unrestricted by everything . . . " (XVI.3), or "the world order in which the human personality, corrupted by sin, is placed at the center of everything" (XVI.4). As the inspirer of the whole project, metropolitan Kirill, the second person in Church hierarchy, wrote in another publication, the Russian Church rejects "an aggressive globalizing monoculture that dominates and assimilates other cultural and national identities."[47]

Here is the focal point. What harbors a real danger is *unification*. What is endangered is *identity*. It may be individual identity ("uniqueness of the human person"); but it will be, more likely, the "identity of nations and other human communities" (XVI.3). The Church itself is implied here as a community, and the nation is another one. The document explicitly speaks (in chapter 2) about the *national* tradition as congruent, and actually interwoven, with a *religious* tradition. It refers to the Old and New Testament to prove, basically, that the particularity of a national Christian community (such as the Russian) does not contradict the universality of Heavenly Jerusalem. It refers to the people of Israel as the epitome of the accent idea, and yet a chosen people who clearly opposed themselves to others (*'am* to *goyim* in Hebrew, *laos* to *ethne* in Greek), a community tied together by ethnic and linguistic bonds and rooted in "a particular land, the Fatherland." It refers to Jesus Christ, who, in spite of the ultimate universalism of his message, was clearly conscious of belonging to the Jewish nation (II.1, 2).

While the document tries to negotiate a balance of universal and particularistic messages, its overall emphasis is certainly to endorse the "Orthodox people," an ethnically and religiously defined "nation," a particular traditional identity mobilized against the pressure of global secular universalism. The overture to the discourse of human dignity and diversity turns out to be submerged in the strong particularistic compression.[48]

Elaboration: Strategies of Religious Response to New Universalism

The Russian and other East European examples show how intrinsically convoluted is the religious response to globality, how intermixed and dialectically interrelated are the impulses of acceptance and resistance, fundamentalism and reform, universalism and particularism. It also proves our initial presumption that the ultimate goal of such a response is to find a place in the new global taxonomy, or "global culture." As a matter of fact, the resistance, reluctance, even repugnance toward modernity (or late modernity) that a religious mind can experience and express do not necessarily mean that modernity is not accepted as a general framework; and vice versa, adjustment, reform, "*aggiornamento*" do not necessarily mean embracing something more than just this general framework.

Moreover, typologies of responses to globality need more elaboration beyond a rough dichotomy of rejecting or embracing. We can think of at least *three* major strategies of response and *seven* ideal-typical religious dispositions:

I. *The strategy of rejection* includes two possible religious dispositions:
   (a) Reactive—when a religious group maintains a strong fundamentalist coherence and delivers a conscious aggressive response (a *guerilla* model);
   (b) Protective—when a religious group links its own tradition with a particular subject of identity (a social community, an ethnos, a nation, etc.) and chooses to protect itself from expansion (a *fortress-under-siege* model);

II. *The strategy of coexistence* includes three religious dispositions:
   (a) Isolationist—when a religious group overtly accepts the framework of globality and claims an isolated locus reserved for itself, without fighting against globality or even trying to negotiate with it (*ivory tower* model);
   (b) Consumerist—when a religious group retains a particular identity instrumentalized as exotic ethnic attraction that sells in a global cultural "market" (*curiosity shop* model);
   (c) Negotiating—when a religious group maintains a constant dialogue within the global culture, negotiating functions, rights, and privileges of a certain space it occupies (*bargain* model);

III. *The strategy of embracing* includes two religious dispositions:
   (a) Reformist—when a religious group accepts globality not only as a framework, but also deliberately chooses to adjust its own core of traditional beliefs by including some foundational values of what is believed to be the global culture (*reform* model);
   (b) Globalist, when a religious group embraces all core values of the global culture, thus eventually losing its own particular identity

and actually ceasing to represent a specifically religious message (*disbandment* model).

These are ideal-typical models that may be simultaneously manifested in a religious community, even in one party within it, even, indeed, in one and the same document: we have seen that the Russian Orthodox social doctrine contained elements of all three strategies, combining protective, negotiating, and reform dispositions, with the latter one, reform, being much less outspoken than the former two. This posture may be also considered as a median, *mutatis mutandis*, to most of Eastern Orthodox Churches, although the subgroups with all dispositions can be found in each Church. Common to all of them is a strong sense of religious identity, a clear reference to ethnonational cultures, and the perception of the "global secular culture" as a threat. Overall, these Churches have a clear particularistic penchant, and they develop practically no substantial universalistic discourse except for interfaith and ecumenical contacts. Their main ideological and theological position is to insure the endurance of unique national cultures whose spiritual ethos they believe themselves to embody.

It goes without saying that this particularistic disposition is not unique to Eastern European religious cultures. In no way can this phenomenon be seen as specifically recent or isolated. In fact, this trend to preserve uniqueness has to do with a profound and perennial tension in the history of human culture: between the "threat" of unification and the "shelter" of difference; it is true, however, that this tension became especially obvious with the advance of the great macronarratives of modernity.

On the other hand, historically, the world religions that after Karl Jaspers are sometimes called postaxial, always expressed a strong and elaborated quest for universality. This concept of a "notional, ideational oneness of the world" is certainly a part of world religions' narratives.[49] To repeat once more what I have said earlier: it seems that religions are now loosing this ability to define a universal discourse; the quest for universality is not associated with religions any more, at least in the way it seemed to be, for example, at the World's Parliament of Religions in 1893 or during the rise of ecumenism after World War II. The discursive space of the Universal seems to be firmly ceased by the new global culture based on the core values of Western secular liberalism.

However, one significant shift in this universal discourse of *late* modernity (perhaps, in the last third of the twentieth century) consists of the emphasis on cultural relativism and acceptance of difference, partly as a reaction to a sweeping standardizing effect of consumerism. This late modernity discourse apparently rejects the teleological idea of uniform progress and offers instead the idea of *universal humanity*, which celebrates the plurality of particular identities. Now, to become a part of the global project, communities are not explicitly urged to match one universal standard, but they are prompted to retain their particular traits.

In this new framework, religions are reconceptualized as a form of symbolic expression of these particular identities, of a particularistic cultural resistance to the new, apparently metacultural, universalism. Religion became a symbolic language for protecting, enhancing, and sometimes creating particular identities, in accordance with R. Robertson, when he speaks of religion as a new "genre of [particularistic] expression, communication and legitimation."[50] As R. Friedland strongly puts it: in times when cultures and capitals become *sans frontières*, "religious nationalism represents the return to text, to the fixity of signs, the renarrativization of the nation in the cosmic context." Thus, religion helps "to fabricate a discursive space in which they can breath easily."[51]

These roles for religions, as well as a certain institutional space (field), are allotted to religions within the new universal taxonomy by the new ethos of world culture. Thus it is only seemingly paradoxical that a straightforward, ostensible particularism, shown by Eastern European religions, turns out to be in fact the only tactic for them to retain a substantial symbolic power in the era of global culture. On the contrary, those eclectic and overinclusive religious movements that claim to express a universal message lose the touch of the primordial power of soil and a specifically religious quality by simply dissolving in the "global culture" (many New Age movements, Scientology, Bahai). The same can be said about recent examples of Roman Catholic and Protestant *embracing* strategies: the more they assume the mainstream values of secular liberal universalism, the more they lose the power of carrying a specific message.[52]

Not every instance of particularism and open antiglobal religious resistance is, therefore, an indication of the rejection of the global discourse as such; not every impulse of fundamentalism is, accordingly, an indicator of aggressive militancy, as in the *guerilla* model of my classification. The *guerilla* model is just an extreme expression of a broad tendency—an obvious invigoration of traditional religious particularism and, consequently, of both interreligious and secular-religious divides. In most cases this broad tendency has two constituents. One is the concern to secure a certain space in the religious field allotted by a new global taxonomy whose domination is reluctantly but realistically accepted and whose apparently pluralist agenda does create this opportunity. The second motive is more fundamental and tenacious: a profound distrust of the secular liberal universal ethos as such, an ethos that is felt to be what it really is: only apparently pluralistic but intrinsically as absolutistic as all other previous forms of universalism.

However, this last presumption requires further special study.

Notes

1. My special focus will be primarily on postcommunist Eastern Orthodox nations, with addition of the cases that do not fall into this category but share some commonality, as well as providing partly contrasting properties, such as Greece (Orthodox but never

communist) and Poland (postcommunist but Roman Catholic). My focus, however, will be Russian Orthodoxy.

2. R. Robertson and J. Chirico, "Humanity, Globalization, and Worldwide Religious Resurgence: A Theoretical Exploration," *Sociological Analysis* 46, no. 3 (1985): 233, 235, 237.

3. R. Robertson and R. Garrett, "Religion and Globalization: An Introduction," in *Religion and Global Order,* R. Robertson and W. Garrett, eds. (New York: Paragon House Publishers), xv. In the third case the authors refer to D. Martin, *A General Theory of Secularization* (New York: Harper & Row, 1978).

4. Robertson and Garrett, "Religion and Globalization," xv. This is the view that Robertson seems finally to embrace; see R. Robertson, "Globalization, Modernization, and Postmodernization: The Ambiguous Position of Religion," in *Religion and Global Order,* Robertson and Garrett, 282.

5. Robertson and Garrett, "Religion and Globalization," xix.

6. P. Beyer, *Religion and Globalization* (London: Sage, 1994), 3.

7. Beyer, *Religion and Globalization,* 54.

8. Robertson, "Globalization, Modernization," 283.

9. Beyer, *Religion and Globalization,* 10.

10. Beyer, *Religion and Globalization,* 87.

11. J. Cazanova, *Public Religions in the Modern World* (Chicago: University of Chicago Press, 1994); S. Ramet, *Whose Democracy? Nationalism, Religion, and the Doctrine of Collective Rights in the Post-1989 Eastern Europe* (Lanham, Md.: Rowman & Littlefield, 1987); S. Ramet, *Nihil Obstat: Religions, Politics and Social Change in East Central Europe and Russia* (Durham, N.C.: Duke University Press, 1998).

12. A. Agadjanian, "Revising Pandora's Gifts: Religious and National Identities in Post-Soviet Societies," *Europe-Asia Studies* 53, no. 3 (September 2001): 472–88.

13. J. Witte and M. Bourdeaux, eds., *Proselytism and Orthodoxy in Russia: The New War for Souls* (Maryknoll, New York: Orbis Books, 1999).

14. The level of constitutional disestablishment varies. "Eastern Orthodox Christianity shall be considered traditional religion in the Republic of Bulgaria" (Article 13.3). In Georgia "[t]he state recognizes the special importance of the Georgian Orthodox Church in Georgian history but simultaneously declares complete freedom of religious belief . . ." (Article 9). In Macedonia the Orthodox Church is singled out in an educational clause with "other religions" (Constitution of 1991, Article 19.3). Romanian Orthodox Church is not mentioned in Romanian constitution but the State supports religions in organizing charities and education in public school (Constitution of 1991, Article 29 and 32.7). The most clear establishment statement is found in Greek 1975 Constitution, which is adopted "[i]n the name of the Holy and Consubstantial and Indivisible Trinity" and proclaims Orthodoxy "prevailing religion" and prohibits proselytism (Part I, Section II, Article 3.1–3; Part II, Article 13.2). Poland is another case with a special constitutional mention of one, Roman Catholic, denomination (Constitution of 1997, Article 25). In all these cases freedom of (other) religions is, however, constitutionally guaranteed. Other constitutions abstain from making any special references, while some, such as the Ukrainian, does refer to "our responsibility before God" (Preamble of the 1996 Constitution), while some, such as the Russian, clearly declares secularism (Constitution of 1993, Article 13). Special religious legislation, however, may introduce substantial corrections (like in the Russian case where a special 1997 law clearly created a hierarchy within religious pluralism).

15. It is out of the question that most of these cleavages (except the last one) are by no means new, but they have been exacerbated in the last decades and especially after the disintegration of the communist system that managed to muffle them up.

16. In Bulgaria we can speak of a split between the Synod headed by Patriarch Maxim and a rival synod headed by Bishop Inokenti (Petrov); in Ukraine the Church schism in the early 1990s (in fact, institutionally, it was a schism within the Russian Church) was caused by other reasons (see below in this section); in Russia the split between Moscow patriarchate and the Russian Church abroad goes back to early 1920s.

17. Thomas Bremer's presentation at the conference on Christian Orthodoxy in contemporary Europe, Leeds, 2001; B. Groen, "Nationalism and Reconciliation: Orthodoxy in the Balkans," *Religion, State, and Society* 26, no. 2 (1998): 120–22.

18. Groen, "Nationalism and Reconciliation," 117–20.

19. See, for example, E. Pace, "The Crash of the Sacred Canopy in Polish Society: A Systems Theory Approach," in *Religion and Politics in Eastern and Central Europe. Traditions and Transitions*, W. Swatos, Jr., ed. (London: Praeger, 1994), 133–44.

20. Another factor was certainly its rigid authoritarian structure, but its effectiveness was largely due to the fact that the focus of authority was located abroad, in Vatican. See: H. Johnston, "Religious Nationalism: Six Propositions from the Eastern Europe and the Former Soviet Union," in *Religion and Politics in Comparative Perspective: Revival of Religious Fundamentalism in East and West*, B. Misztal and A. Shupe, eds. (London: Praeger, 1992), 78–79. Yet another huge factor that cannot be omitted was the Polish Pope.

21. Cf. Patric Michel's important thesis about the Catholic Church being a location of civil society in communist Poland: P. Michel, *Politics and Religion in Eastern Europe* (Cambridge, Mass.: Polity Press, 1990). On the evolution of "The Movement of Living Light," or "Oases," in Poland see, J. Mucha, "Religious Revival Movement in Changing Poland: From Opposition to Participation in the Systemic Transformations," *The Polish Sociological Review*, vol. 2, no. 2 (1993): 139–48. This last case suggests an interesting precision in the pattern I am illustrating: the pulsating rhythm of opening and closing, overture and compression, is patterned by larger trends of social change.

22. T. Szawiel, "Religion and the Church in the New Democracy," *Polish Sociological Review*, no. 4 (2000): 447–60. Although not as endemic and far-reaching as in Eastern Orthodoxy, ethnic and national particularism within Roman Catholicism has a long history, going at least to the creating of Gallicanism in fifteenth-century France; contemporary Mexican or Philippine Catholicism are unmistakably parochial.

23. The Russian legislation singles out "traditional religions" enjoying a preferential treatment; in Rumania the same discourse goes back to the 1930s, see, A. Gurau, "The Policies of Heresy in Romania: The Influence of the Orthodox Church's Nationalist Ideology on the Regulation of Proselytism" (paper presented at the Annual meeting of the Society for the Scientific Study of Religion, Houston, October 2000); in Bulgaria Orthodoxy is set apart in constitution as "traditional"; in the same vein, Greek Constitution distinguishes so-called known (gnostes) religions, also a rather old term of legal classification. N. Alivizados, "A New Role for the Greek Church?" *Journal of Modern Greek Studies* 17, no. 1 (1999): 28.

24. The most powerful brotherhood of this kind is "Radonezh Society," created on the base of *Sretensky* monastery in Moscow (see, their website at www.pravoslavie.ru); on Russian Orthodox radical groups see: A. Verkhovsky, "Orthodoxy in Russian Nationalist Radicalism" (paper presented at the National Convention of the American Association for the Advancement of Slavic Studies, Washington, D.C., November 2001).

25. Once again, this general tenor might be manifested in a relatively moderate, although quite tenacious, nationalist stance of the Moscow patriarchate hierarchy, or in an openly xenophobic, Russo- or Slavo-centric, and unequivocally imperial appeals of relatively marginal ultranationalist groups.

26. As for the beginning of 2002, major Orthodox denominations in Ukraine were: Ukrainian Orthodox Church in union with Moscow patriarchate (about 9,500 congregations); Ukrainian Orthodox Church—Kiev patriarchate (about 3,000); Ukrainian Autocephalous Orthodox Church (about 1,000). The Greek Catholic (Uniate) Church had about 3,300 congregations, densely concentrated in western Ukraine. See, V. Yelensky, "Religioznye obshchiny Ukrainy v tsyfrakh: poslednie izmenenia," *Religiia i obshchestvo*, Bulletin by *Liudina i svit* magazine and Ukraine-American Bureau of Human Rights, no. 15 (Kiev, 2002) (Statistical data are from the Ukraine State Committee of Religious Affaires). However, other surveys suggest a substantial correction of this official institutional picture, as the majority of people seem to declare their affinity with the Kiev independent Church rather than with the Moscow-led Church (See V. Yelensky, "Mezhpravoslavnyi konflikt v Ukraine (1990 gody)," *Religiia i obshchestvo*, Bulletin by *Liudina i svit* magazine and Ukraine-American Bureau of Human Rights, no. 12 [Kiev, 2001]).

27. See Groen, "Nationalism," 122–23, on the role of the patriarchate of Constantinople.

28. The independent Ukrainian religious identity actively involved the North American Ukrainian Diaspora, thus creating a symbolic and institutional alternative to Russian "transnationalism," however, as in Russian Orthodox case, this "transnationalism" is unmistakably ethnocentric.

29. See N. Boiko and K. Rousselet, "L'Ukraine entre Rome, Moscou et Constantinople" (an unpublished paper, cited with authors' permission), who believe that the "national values draw together the [independent Orthodox churches] and Greek Catholics above the denominational cleavages. . . ."

30. V. Roudometoff, *Nationalism, Globalization and Orthodoxy: The Social Origin of Ethnic Conflict in the Balkans* (London: Greenwood Press, 2001), 106, 124, 135.

31. The Uniates of Transylvania created an important (and complex) stimulus for the formation of Romanian national consciousness; Orthodox clergy regard this "hybrid faith" as "the most grievous injury done to their world by the West since the Fourth Crusade of 1204," as "a kind of artificial insemination" (as phrased by a priest) that corrupted the purity of the nation. V. Clark, *Why Angels Fall? A Portrait of Orthodox Europe from Byzantium to Kosovo* (London: Macmillan, 2000), 217.

32. From the documents of the First Congress of Orthodox missionaries of the Russian Orthodox Church, held in Belgorod, Russia, in 1996. Cited in, V. Yelensky, "Proselytism, Missionerstvo i bor'ba vokrug identichnosti ukrainskogo obshchestva," *Religiia i obshchestvo*. Bulletin by *Liudina i svit* magazine and Ukraine-American Bureau of Human Rights, no. 15 (2002).

33. See Witte and Bourdeaux, *Proselytism and Orthodoxy*.

34. See Dmitry Kanashkin, "Politichnyi sens okkultnoi pandemii v Ukraine, in "Visti z Ukrainy" (1994, no. 45), published by Kiev Patriarchy, cited in Yelensky, "Proselytism, Missionerstvo."

35. Gurau, *The Policies of Heresy*.

36. N. Alivizatos, "A New Role," 29–30.

37. One region with a particularly strong similarity is Latin America that witnessed a major rise of Protestantism and especially Pentecostalism in the latter part of the twenti-

eth century, see, S. Platero, *Globalizacion y reconversion religiosa: Un reto a la identidad Latinoamericana?* paper presented at the Conference of the International Society of Sociology of Religion, Mexico, August 2001. In Latino countries Roman Catholicism, as universal as theoretically it can be, clearly associates itself with particular Latino identities that are endangered with Protestant invasion. Again, like in "Orthodox" countries of Europe, traditional religion refashions itself as ostensibly particularistic and protective against global (Western) alien intrusion.

38. "Just remember," Victoria Clark's Serb interlocutor told her, "the Orthodox Church looses by every inch of Western progress—telephones, roads, the Internet, whatever" (Clark, *Why Angels Fall*, 59). The anti-Westernism in this area has had a long history that goes back to the nineteenth-century anti-Europeanism, expressed by the Russian Slavophile movement (that affected Balkan Slavic religious thought) and by indigenous Orthodox identity founders; it was a more complex process than just a blunt rejection, but rather a "cultural schizophrenia between xenophilia and xenophobia," an anti-Orientalist discourse that unwillingly reproduced crucial elements of European Orientalism (V. Makrides and D. Uffelmann, "Studying Eastern Orthodox Anti-Westernism: The Need for a Comparative Research Agenda," in *Orthodox Christianity and Contemporary Europe*, J. Sutton and W. van den Bercken, eds. (Leuven: Peeter Publishers, forthcoming).

39. "Resist, my dear Christians," Archbishop Christodoulas, the Church Primate, told the protesting crowd. "The forces of globalization and religious marginalization are out to get us," *New York Times*, 25 June 2000. He contended that the measure (removal of religious line) was a part of a sinister plot to de-Hellenize Greece, "Our faith is the foundation of our identity. If you abolish one, you abolish the other," *New Statesman*, August, 2000, 21.

40. Verkhovsky, *Orthodoxy*.

41. E. Halas, "Rola Kosciola rzymskokatolickiego w procesie integracji europejskiej," in *Spoleczenstwo Polskie w perspektywie czlonkostwa w unii europejskiej*, J. Muchy, ed. (Warzawa: Wydawnictwo IfiS PAN, 1999), 201–16. On the issue of "Christian values," as the central identity-defining discourse of the Polish Church, and its application to abortion controversy, see, S. Miller, "Religion and Politics in Poland: The Abortion Issue," *Canadian Slavonic Papers* vol 39, no. 1–2 (1997): 63–86, 77–79.

42. "Osnovy sotsialnoi kontseptsii Russkoi pravoslavnoi tserkvi," in *Uibileinyi archiiereisky sobor Russkoi pravoslavnoi tserkvi, 13–16 augusta 2000. Materialy* (Moscow: Publishing Council of the Moscow Patriarchate, 2001), 329–410 (Foundations of the Social Concept of the Russian Orthodox Church, in *Proceedings of Jubilee Bishops Council of the Russian Orthodox Church*). The word "concept" which is used in the official rendering of the title in English is in fact closer to what is called "social doctrine" in Roman Catholicism. The references to this document hereafter will include the number of the chapter (Roman figures) and the number of the section (Arabic figure).

43. For a detailed analysis of references, which reveal interesting clues in understanding self-consciousness of the tradition, see, A. Agadjanian, "Seeking the Balance between the Relevance and Identity: Official and Popular Formulations of the Social Teaching of Russian Orthodoxy," in *Orthodox Christianity and Contemporary Europe*, Sutton.

44. For example, speaking of the "Christian states" (IV.5), the authors mean both Western and Eastern Christendom; but the expressions "Orthodox politician" (V.3) or "Orthodox physician" (XI.2) are evoked to convey a denominationally charged meaning. "Western Christian tradition" is explicitly defined as being different from the Eastern one (e.g., VIII.3).

45. By the way, this same classical thesis was pivotal, for example, in Nicolaj Velemirović,' Serbian version of theological anti-modernism that I mentioned in the previous section.

46. The expression "dignity of the person" is mentioned twelve times throughout the document in various contexts: in connection to the private property, gender equality, and bioethics. "Uniqueness of personality" is another adjoining form used mostly in the chapter on bioethics.

47. Kirill, Metropolitan of Smolensk and Kaliningrad, "Gospel and Culture," in *Proselytism and Orthodoxy in Russia: A New War for Souls*, J. Witte and M. Bourdeau, eds. (Maryknoll, N.Y.: Orbis Books, 1999), 66.

48. On Russian media discourse about religion and nation, see A. Agadjanian, "The Public Religion in Russia and the Search for National Ideology," *Journal for the Social Scientific Study of Religion* 40, no. 3 (September 2001): 351–65.

49. J. Simpson, "Globalization and Religion: Themes and Prospects," in *Religion and Global Order*, R. Robertson and W. Garrett, eds. (New York: Paragon House Publishers, 1991), 14.

50. Simpson, "Globalization and Religion," xv.

51. R. Friedland, "When Gods Walks in History: The Institutional Politics of Religious Nationalism," *International Sociology* 14, no. 3 (September 1999): 314, 317. I cannot share the whole Friedland's paradigm. He believes religion to provide *the only* possible language on which non-Western nations can express cohesive cultural response to Western secular globalization; he idealizes to an extreme degree the religion's role as a redemptive alternative to the oppressive and ephemeral global culture, as a way "to secure morality against an increasingly post-humanist world" (Friedland, "When Gods Walks in History," 317). This inexorable dichotomy, reviving global dependency and Orientalist constructs, distorts, in my opinion, the true picture of variety of responses and of the dialectic with which religions negotiate their space within the global taxonomy. Friedland's very strong point, nevertheless, is his tangible and lucid articulation of this special power that religion extracts from associating itself with particularistic identities, thus creating a meaningful response to globality.

52. The case of Western religions has its particular profundity because of the genealogical kindred of modern Western theologies and the liberal universalistic ethos. Western religious universalism grounds itself on the claim that contemporary "secular liberal civilization" originated from the Judeo-Christian religious tradition. The embracing strategy toward global culture seems therefore more natural in the case of Western religions. Roman Catholicism has an especially strong universalistic appeal because of its metanational structure and its post-Vatican inclusiveness. However, Vatican constantly emphasizes the distance of its teaching of *catholicity* from the secular ethos; even more important is the fact that most national Catholic Churches retain, as the Polish example shows, strong particularistic tendencies diverging from metanational catholicity.

Part II

Regional Fundamentalisms

Chapter 5

Phases of Political Islam

Tamara Sonn

Many scholars try to deal with the variety in contemporary Islamic movements by distinguishing between "conservative" or "traditionalist" Islamists and those of a more "moderate," "liberal," "modernist" or "progressive" bent.[1] The determining factor in these distinctions seems to be how closely the ideas involved accord with modern Western ideals of democracy and human rights. I believe, however, that the most recent developments in the Muslim world make clear another kind of distinction, one based not on comparison with Western values but based on the various goals with which the movements involved are concerned. In this chapter, I will identify two major phases in modern/contemporary Islamic movements, each with distinct goals and discourse appropriate to them. One phase is geared toward developing a sense of unique identity and empowerment in a populace under totalitarian control, whether foreign or domestic. Its goal is to awaken social and political awareness in people accustomed to passivity due to political marginalization. Accordingly, its tone is often agonistic, drawing upon emotions associated with humiliation suffered under imperialism;

defensive when referring to those accused of being responsible for the community's current disenfranchised status; and utopian in references to Islam, the perceived solution to the community's problems. The second phase focuses more specifically on a given community's immediate economic, social, and political challenges. As such, its discourse tends to be more analytical, self-critical, and practical. This phase often follows the first phase, dominating Islamic discourse in a community that has already achieved its goal of political/economic independence, as in the case of Iran, while the first phase tends to dominate in communities still struggling toward that goal, as in the case of Palestine, although the two strains are often found intermingled. This study will also examine the case of Pakistan, in which the transition from motivational to practical Islamism has not occurred, and people's hopes for practical results are thwarted, despite the achievement of independence and implementation of Islamic law. The result is increased frustration, and fertile ground for radicalization.

Phases of Political Islam

In order to understand the last century of Islamic history, it is essential to grasp the significance of colonialism and the postcolonial condition. Virtually the entire Muslim world was colonized and this is the dominant reality in its modern history; developments in twentieth-century Islamic thought can be viewed as a series of efforts to deal with colonialism and postcolonialism. In other words, the ongoing effort is to achieve not only political but also economic independence, stability, and prosperity.

In broadest terms, there are three major stages. The first preceded World War I, and was characterized by efforts to achieve independence, which were based on the European model of secular philosophies and political parties. Egypt, Syria, and Iraq were leaders in these efforts. All developed political parties, platforms, and some form of parliamentary democracy. The results of World War I caused this approach to lose what appeal it had had, which was generally limited to the urban elites who were its vanguard. Instead of independence, more direct colonial control was imposed throughout most of the Muslim world. France, Italy, Britain, and Holland gained control of the Muslim world from Morocco to Malaysia and Indonesia.

The next effort then was based on the Soviet model. The Soviets's militant socialism had been effective in overthrowing the powerful czars of Russia. Perhaps it would work in the Muslim world, too. The Baathists of Syria and Iraq, as well as Egypt's Nasserites date from this period, as does Pakistan's socialist Pakistan People's Party. Again this effort failed, as was evidenced by the 1967 defeat of the combined Arab forces, and the 1971 civil war in Pakistan.

It was only after the failure of these two initiatives that a more indigenous, populist approach to political and cultural empowerment gained ascendancy, one that appealed to the core of Muslim identity. Based on Islamic symbols and values, this movement is usually called fundamentalism by journalists, and Islamism or political Islam by scholars, following the terminology developed by the people involved in the movement. The two earliest representatives of this movement were the Muslim Brotherhood in the Arab world and the Jamaat-i Islami in South Asia. They had originated long before the 1960s (1926 and 1941, respectively). But as populist, nonelite movements, they took much longer to spread and gain their chance to demonstrate their effectiveness than did the Western-modeled approaches of the educated elites. These two groups differ in organizational styles, but their major ideologues influenced one another and their formative ideologies were virtually identical. After the failure of the earlier "foreign" models of reform, both groups raised the call for the replacement of foreign models with Islam, claiming, "Islam is the solution."

This approach is generally revolutionary, calling for radical changes in society. Its ultimate goals are the same as those of the earlier movements: independence, peace, and prosperity. However, the means of achieving these goals have changed. Islamism calls people to recognize their unique Islamic identity. This, in contrast to pre–World War I movements that stressed an identity based on rationality and cultural sophistication vis-à-vis Europe, and tended in fact to deny major cultural differences; and in contrast to specifically Arab or Third World cultural identity, stressed in the socialist phase. Islamists believe that solutions to their problems will be found in Islam. The mass popular appeal of Islamism is to be found in its insistence that Islam alone—its teachings, norms, institutions, and coping mechanisms—are both necessary and sufficient to produce a just society.

But there are two identifiable phases of Islamist discourse. One phase stands in stark contrast to the confident optimism of its secularist predecessors. It is defensive, characterized by deep distrust of a stereotypical "West" that seems bent on undermining and even destroying the Muslim world. In this perspective, virtually all the Muslim world's problems are the fault of "the West": poverty, lack of development, alienation, and social turmoil are all laid at the feet of the foreign interlopers. Although the need for revising Islamic law to suit changing realities, and criticism of traditional religious leaders for passivity in the face of oppression are recurrent themes, few details are spelled out. Instead, in further contrast to its predecessors' tendencies toward strategic tracts, this phase of Islamist discourse tends toward utopianism, born in suffering, humiliation, frustration. Its hallmark is the claim that Islam is the solution to everything—moral, social, economic, political, physical, psychological, and even environmental problems. It is not concerned with the details of achieving power or running governments so much as it is concerned with motivating people to assert their noble Islamic identity, to get involved, to rise up against the oppressors in the name of all that is right. With its rhetorical flourishes and emotional appeals, this phase of Islamic discourse can therefore be described as concerned with consciousness rising on a mass scale (rather than simply among the educated elite).

Ayatollah Khomeini's movement was the quintessential example of this phase of Islamism, and its success in 1979 gave a tremendous boost to the popularity of political Islam throughout the Muslim world. Hopes were very high that a return to "true Islam" would restore dignity, autonomy, and solidarity among Muslim countries. Islamist groups in various countries became very bold in their agitation for return to an Islamic state, beginning with implementation of Islamic law. They stepped up their attacks on the effects and affectations of "Westernism," and proudly displayed their commitment to Islamic identity by wearing the veil or growing a beard.

However, the 1980s dragged on without another victory for political Islam. The Iran-Iraq war ended in a stalemate, devastating both secularist/socialist Iraq and Islamist Iran. Sudan had also embarked on a well-publicized Islamization program, but it remained—as it does today—enamored in a civil war.

The 1990s seemed even worse for this phase of Islamism. Algeria's Islamists were on the verge of parliamentary victory, when democracy was overturned by a military coup and the country descended into a hideous civil war. Its combatants—some claiming the Islamist mantle—drenched the country in blood. The Soviets' departure from Afghanistan had appeared at first as a victory for the Mujahidin, valorized by Islamists worldwide in their victory. However, their victory was followed by a civil war of attrition so vicious that those who could leave the capital and those who remained feared for their lives. The result was the ascendancy of the Taliban, who perhaps epitomize the utopian and exclusivist characteristics of Islamism, but do not represent political Islam's reformist tendencies. Indeed, their failure to address the need for reform alienated them from many Islamists.

By the time of the Algerian civil war and the Taliban victory in Kabul in the mid-1990s, there was mounting evidence that many Muslims were moving beyond the utopian and defensive elements of Islamist discourse to development of its more analytic or rational side. They were focusing on the more nuanced, practical, and inclusivist themes of reformist Islamism: recognition of the complexity of the challenges facing Muslim communities today, emphasis on the flexibility of Islamic law, and willingness to accept the responsibility to find solutions for their problems rather than simply to blame "the West" and its minions. Evidence of the growing popularity of this phase of Islamist discourse is clear in Iran, for example, in the landslide victory of Mohammad Khatami in the 1997 and 2001 elections, as well as those of his colleagues, often characterized as "reformist" in contrast with their opponents, the "traditionalists."

It is important to recognize that representatives of this phase of political Islam remain committed to the grand Islamist goals of independence from foreign domination, to justice, and to peace. But they no longer focus their energies on raising Islamic consciousness. They seem, in fact, to assume Islamic consciousness as they direct their efforts toward developing practical programs for achieving these goals. As a result, their discourse is characterized by concern with interpretation of legal codes to deal effectively with specific questions confronting all peoples in the modern world, such as the rights of citizens, including women and religious minorities, and international relations.

In this chapter, I will distinguish between these two phases of Islamism according to their goals: the motivational phase focused on consciousness-raising and the practical phase focused on dealing with regional-specific organizational/institutional issues. I will analyze their discourse accordingly, paying particular attention first to defensive, utopian, and emotional elements of political Islam and demonstrating that these are geared to the specific goals of this phase, and then to the more practical and rational elements, again associating them with their distinct goals. I will conclude with observations about frustration and radicalization resulting from long-term failure to achieve the goals of political Islam.

The Motivational Phase of Political Islam

It is difficult to pinpoint the actual beginning of the Islamist movement, but it is possible to identify articulation of some its key ideologies. Among those defining moments was when Jamal al-Din al-Afghani (d. 1897), one of the fathers of Islamism, identified "the West" as the nemesis of the Muslim world.[2] Other major thinkers, such as Sir Syed Ameer Ali, had tried to conform to Islamic and European heritage, attempting to show that Islam is but another step in humanity's quest for a "conception of an Universal Soul pervading, regulating, and guiding all existence."[3] Because "[t]he holy flames kindled by Zoroaster, Moses, and Jesus had been quenched in the blood of man," Prophet Muhammad was sent to remind humanity of its divine origins and destiny. Thus, Ali explained that Islamic teachings on war, for example ("purely defensive"), tolerance, the status of women and slaves, science, reason, and spirituality are all in accordance with the highest ideals of Jewish and Christian thought—implicitly identifying Jewish and Christian ("Western") thought as the standard by which Islam was to be judged. But Afghani established the framework for Islamist discourse by articulating the notion of "the West" as the enemy of the Muslim world, defectors from true religion by contrast to whom Muslims were unquestionably morally superior. "The West" was never more clearly identified than as the source of imperialism, colonialism, and the impoverished orientalist discourse through which these evils were rationalized. But in identifying the foil to Islamic group identity, Afghani provided a framework for Islamist discourse: a world bifurcated into Muslims and those who are hostile to Muslims and Islam, or at least potentially so.[4]

This theme came to dominate in the work of the founder of the Muslim Brotherhood (*Ikhwan al-Muslimin*, or *al-Ikhwan al-Muslimun*), Hasan al-Banna' (d. 1949). In a description of why he founded the Muslim Brotherhood, al-Banna' paraphrased the plaint of a group of laborers employed by the British on the Suez Canal who came to him in the early days of his organization in his village:

> We know not the practical way to reach the glory of Islam and [to serve] the welfare of Muslims. We are weary of this life of humiliation and restriction.... [W]e see that the Arabs and the Muslims have no status and no dignity. They are no more than mere hirelings belonging to the foreigners.... We are unable to perceive the road to action as you perceive it, or to know the path to the service of the fatherland [*watan*], the religion and the *ummah* [Muslim community] as you know it.... All that we desire now is to present you with all that we possess, to be acquitted by God of the responsibility, and for you to be responsible before him for us and for what we must do. If a group contracts with God sincerely that it live for his religion and die in his service, seeking only his satisfaction, then its worthiness will assure its success however small its numbers or weak its means.[5]

This description of the early Brotherhood is clearly offered as an appeal to the emotions of an oppressed people, drawing upon their experience of suffering and sense of impotence. And from the beginning, it is "the foreigners" who are to blame. Indeed, the Brotherhood taught, "The West surely seeks to humiliate us, to occupy our lands and begin destroying Islam by annulling its laws and abolishing its traditions."[6]

"The West" here seems to indicate generic European culture, but al-Banna' distinguishes between the evils of Western European culture and those of the then-Soviet bloc. By contrast to either one, Islam compares positively. The West's capitalism has its good points: intellectual advancement, material benefits, and democracy. But it is too materialistic and leads to oppression of the poor by the wealthy. Besides, its excessive individualism breeds personal and class competition, rather than cooperation. Similarly, communism has some positive concerns, including social justice, egalitarianism, solidarity, and humanitarianism. But its dominant characteristics are atheism, dictatorship, tyranny, and lack of freedom, collectively described as "Red barbarism," nothing more than a new version of czarist Russia's "slaughterhouse of religion."[7]

These Western ideologies have produced "a deadening of human sentiments and sympathies, and ... the extinction of godly endeavors and spiritual values," the Brotherhood claims.[8] Therefore, Muslims must reject them and resort to their own heritage, Islam. Islam will provide the solution to all problems:

> We believe the provisions of Islam and its teachings are all inclusive, encompassing the affairs of the people in this world and the hereafter. In addition, those who think that these teachings are concerned only with the spiritual or ritualistic aspects are mistaken in this belief because Islam is a faith and a ritual, a nation and a nationalism, a religion and a state, spirit and deed, holy text and sword.[9]

The all-inclusiveness of the Brotherhood's description of Islam is part of its appeal. It is a mass-based movement, originating in rural areas, among peasants who, as noted above, specifically pled their ignorance of solutions to their plight and their desire to be free of the responsibility to address them. Blaming their problems on "the West," rather than their own inadequacies, and simplifying the solution to "Islam," was no doubt more appealing in this context than rational strategies like those worked out in the socialists' political manifestos. In fact, this utopian view made Islam so complete that it even provided for colonialism—Islamic colonialism, which is also good because it is motivated by the desire to establish "the best system of colonization and conquest, as indicated by the Qur'an (2:193/189)."[10]

The defensive and utopian themes echo as well in the work of the second great ideologue of the Muslim Brotherhood, Sayyid Qutb (d. 1966). As in the work of his predecessors, Sayyid Qutb positions Islam as the only correct alternative to the hostile powers and failed ideologies of the West.

> There are two huge blocs: the Communist Bloc in the East and the capitalist Bloc in the West. Each disseminates deceptive propaganda throughout the world claiming that there are only two alternative views in the world, communism, and capitalism, and that other nations have no alternative but to ally themselves with one bloc or the other. There is no other way out. . . . It is clear that both the Western Bloc and the Eastern Bloc are fighting over the world, manipulating battles for their own interest at the expense of the nations and peoples who are in their orbit. . . . As for us, what is our stake in this struggle? We have recently experienced in Palestine that neither the Eastern Bloc nor the Western Bloc gives any credence to the values they advocate, or consider us ourselves as of any consequence. . . . We will receive no mercy from either bloc. We are oppressed strangers in the ranks of both. We are therefore the tail end of the caravan regardless of the road we take.[11]

Simply put, the West is the enemy of Muslims. This has been true since the beginning of Islam, according to Sayyid Qutb; it is a millenarian struggle of belief and unbelief:

> The struggle between believers and their enemies is in essence entirely a struggle of belief. The enemies are angered only because of the believers' faith, enraged only because of their belief.
>
> This was not a political, an economic, or a racial struggle. Had it been any of these, its settlement would have been easy, and the solution of its difficulties would have been simple. But essentially it was a struggle between beliefs, either unbelief or faith, either jahiliyya [the moral ignorance of pre- or non-Muslims] or the eternal and universal din [religion/way of life] of Islam.[12]

And again we find that "Islam is the solution" to all problems:

> If it becomes clear that Islam possesses or is capable of solving our basic problems, of granting us a comprehensive social justice, of restoring for us justice in

government, in economics, in opportunities and in punishment . . . then without doubt it will be more capable, than any other system we may seek to borrow or imitate, to work in our nation.[13]

Indeed, Islam is the only solution. It is the only "true religion," the only proper "course for humanity." In a chapter entitled "The Singular Path" Qutb explains why only Islam will solve humanity's problems. He lists several reasons, including that Islam is "the only path that grants man the excellence, bestows on him true freedom, and saves him from the curse of slavery"; Islam is the only way of life that is "free from the defects of human ignorance and weakness;" and it is in "complete concordance to the comprehensive system of the universe." Again these virtues are contrasted with the defects of the dominant West. Under Western tutelage, people are miserable:

[The m]an of today as a whole is the physical structure of grief, sorrow and uneasiness. He is miserable, distressed and prey to confusion. He seeks escape from life. Sometimes he takes refuge in opium, hasheesh and wine and sometimes wishes to forget his inner anxieties through the craze of rapidity and idiotic ventures. Despite all his materialistic prosperity, plentiful productivity, pleasures, luxuries and abundance in life, man is distressed. . . . It seems as if it were a hoard of demons who were chasing man and he were trying to flee and evade it, but it were always taking hold of his neck.

This fact is quite vivid when we look towards the prosperous and rich nations of the world. The plight of most nations led by the U.S.A. and the U.S.S.R. is such as a host of demons were running after them and they were trying to get rid of demons as lost as themselves.

The modern conception of human life, which the cultured man of today has in mind, seems nothing but a curse, in comparison to that of Islam.[14]

How will an Islamic "system" work? Although for Islamists, the path seems eminently "clear," as the Qur'an describes itself, Qutb's explications nevertheless retain Islamists's characteristically utopian outlook. For example, Sayyid Qutb says that in the Islamic system, only God is sovereign. Therefore, human governments are illegitimate:

This religion is a general proclamation for the liberation of "man" on "earth" from bondage to creatures. . . . The proclamation of the sole Lordship of God over the worlds means: a comprehensive revolution against the governance of humans in its various shapes, forms, systems and conditions and total rebellion against all conditions in the world where government is [controlled] by humans.[15]

Therefore, Islamic government must be based on Islamic law. Sayyid Qutb does discuss the need for flexibility in the interpretation of Islamic teaching. "The Islamic system has room for scores of models which are compatible with the natural growth of a society and the new needs of the contemporary age as long as the total Islamic idea dominates these models."[16] In addition, he believes that people with sincere intentions and proper education are capable of receiving guidance, quoting the Qur'an: "And for those who strive in Us, We surely guide them to our paths."[17] But specific details of Qur'anic legislation appropriate for contemporary circumstances are left for others to determine. The focus of Sayyid Qutb's work remains simply motivating people to do so, often by referring to the glorious past: "The ideal Islamic age of glory has granted man some principles, thoughts, value and standards of testing and examining."[18] Details of Islamic government are treated in a similar way. It must operate on the basis of consultation (*shura*), a Qur'anic principle, but specifics concerning the range, means, and relative authority of consultation is left for a later time. Among the few details of which we can be certain are that Islamic society rejects discrimination based on ethnicity or gender, and an Islamic government will reject usury, replacing it with *zakat* (the required Islamic charity), and with "cooperation and mutual solidarity."[19] Society must be transformed from its current "bestial excitement, its lunatic intoxication, its uproar and confusion." But, as in the case of Islamic legislation and government, Sayyid Qutb concentrates on convincing his readers of the need for transformation, rather than on the precise means of achieving it:

> What is required is that a believing group place their hands in the hands of God and then march forth, the promise of God to them being overriding reality for them, and the leisure of God being their first and last aim.
> Through this group God's way for the realization of His path will be applied. It will disperse the clouds of ignorance from human nature. It will give expression to the will of God that His word is supreme on earth, and the reigns of power are in the hands of His faith.[20]

Utopian visions and a defensive outlook are also found in the writings of Abu A'la Mawdudi (d. 1979), founder of the Jamaat-i Islami. The West is still the benchmark against which Islamic society is to be measured. And Mawdudi, like the Muslim Brotherhood ideologues, insists that Islam is superior to a hopelessly degenerate West. Living as he did in prepartition India and convinced that Muslims would lose their freedom and identity in a secular India, Mawdudi set about establishing his organization (1941) in order to expose the evils of the West and present Islam as the only acceptable choice for humanity.[21] Even his description of the status of women in Islamic society assumes this defensive posture vis-à-vis the West:

> The woman is still inferior in the Western eyes as she was in the past ages of ignorance. In the West a real genuine woman has yet to have respect as the queen of a home, the wife of a husband, the matron of children. The so-called respect she enjoys today is in fact for her being the he-woman or the she-man who is physiologically a woman, but mentally a man, and who pursues masculine activities in life. Obviously, this respect is for manhood, not for womanhood. Another manifestation of the female inferiority complex is that the Western woman fondly puts on the male dress whereas no man can even think of

putting on the female dress in public. To be the wife is disgraceful for hundreds of thousands of Western women, but to be the husband is not disgraceful for any man. . . . It can, therefore, be said without fear of contradiction that the West has not honoured the woman because she is the woman. This was done by Islam alone, which accorded woman the place of pride in her own natural sphere in society and civilization, and thus raised the status of womanhood in the real sense.[22]

Western life, Mawdudi recognizes, is secular. This is how he explains its debauchery, because for Mawdudi, "secular" means utterly devoid of religion, effectively atheist and therefore amoral. The antidote, of course, is Islamic law, again presented as the source of resolution of all problems: "family relationships, social and economic affairs, administration, rights and duties of citizens, judicial systems, laws of war and peace and international relations. In short it embraces all the various departments of life. . . . [It] is a complete scheme of life and an all-embracing social order where nothing is superfluous and nothing lacking."[23]

Although Mawdudi was opposed to the creation of the state of Pakistan, he later accepted it, provided its laws were Islamic. In that case, he determined, "the struggle for obtaining control over the organs of the state when motivated by the urge to establish the *din* (religion) and the Islamic *sharia* [divine law] and to enforce the Islamic injunctions, is not only permissible but is positively desirable and as such obligatory."[24] Yet Mawdudi's description of the mechanisms of policy and statecraft remain sublime ideals: divine sovereignty, Prophetic authority, human "viceregency," and rule by consultation (*shura*). He does allow that human beings may extend existing legislation to cover novel cases. He believes that God's will has been revealed in the Qur'an, the normative example of Prophet Muhammad (the Sunna), and is therefore accessible to all, not just a privileged elite. All qualified citizens have the right to participate in legislation in the Islamic state, not just those of a particular class, family, or profession. Their legislative work will be bound by the eternal principles of the *Sharia*, but within that framework they may exercise the right of interpretation (*ijtihad*). "Every Muslim who is capable and qualified to give a sound opinion of matters of Islamic law is entitled to interpret the law of God when such interpretation becomes necessary. In this sense, the Islamic polity is democratic."[25] Again, details concerning these issues are quite overshadowed by the language of motivation. Among Mawdudi's most practical specifications for the Islamic state is that non-Muslims, while guaranteed security and freedom of faith, are not to be significant participants in the government:

> That this is the standpoint of Islam is proved by the utter absence of even a single instance in the days of the Holy Prophet (peace be on him) or the Caliphs where a *Zimmi* [*dhimmi*] (non-Muslim citizen) may have been made a member of the parliament, or the Governor of a province, or the Qadi [judge], or the Director of any Government department, or the commander of the Army or a

Minister of the Government or may have been ever allowed to participate in the election of the Caliphs.[26]

Once again we see the Islamist perception of a world divided into Muslims, who may be trusted, and all others, who may not.

Ayatollah Khomeini of Iran (d. 1989) perhaps put the finest point on the major characteristics of Islamism. Like that of Muslim Brotherhood and Jamaat-i Islami ideologues, the focal point of his discourse was social justice through Islam. In addition, like them, his rhetoric was emotional, defensive, and utopian. He often began his orations with appeals to Shī'i heritage designed to arouse pathos. Michael M. J. Fischer observes that this emotional appeal, known as a *rawzeh*, ordinarily was placed at the end of a sermon. Fischer quotes an address delivered by Khomeini on the tenth of Muharram, already an emotionally charged day in the Shī'i calendar, which he began with the *rawzeh*. In this case (June 3, 1963), Khomeini was addressing crowds in the aftermath of the Shah's troops' attack on a seminary in Qum, which had resulted in the deaths of several students. He brings the audience to tears by reminding them of the deaths of women and children when the Sunni Umayyads attacked Husain, the grandson of Prophet Muhammad considered by the Shī'i to be the legitimate ruler (vis-à-vis the Umayyads, whom they considered illegitimate). He then asks:

> If the brutal regime of Iran is engaged in a war with the ulama [religious scholars], why did it tear the Qur'an apart while attacking the Faisiyeh Seminary? What did it have against the Faisiyeh Seminary? What did it have against the students of theology? What did it have against our eighteen-year-old Sayyid [Sayyid Younes Rudbari who had been killed in the March assault]? [The audience cries.] What had our eighteen-year old Sayyid done to the Shah? What had he done against the government? What had he done against the brutal regime of Iran? [The audience cries.] Therefore we must conclude that it wanted to do away with the foundation. It is against the foundation of Islam and the clergy. It does not want this foundation to exist. It does not want our youth and elders to exist.[27]

Such appeals were among Khomeini's most effective rhetorical devices. Their effect was heightened by his ability to then focus blame for the sufferings of Iranians, allowing his listeners to vent their emotional energy. Unlike pre-Islamist reformers and even some other Islamist reformers, Khomeini's criticism was not directed internally, at the religious leaders, for example, for failing to provide adequate leadership or education to the Muslim community. The blame was characteristically placed on foreigners or the regime, itself merely a tool of foreigners. For example: "All of our troubles today are caused by America and Israel. Israel itself derives from America; these deputies and ministers that have been imposed upon us derive from America—they are all agents of America, for if they were not, they would rise up in protest."[28] Elsewhere: "Are we to be trampled underfoot by the boots of America simply because we are a weak nation and have no dollars? America is worse than Britain; Britain is worse than America. The Soviet Union is worse than both of them. . . . But today it is America that we are concerned with."[29] By contrast to those "agents of the enemies of Islam," Khomeini demands that Iran's youth rise up:

> to awaken people, to expose the sinister and destructive designs of imperialism. . . . With utter devotion, exert yourselves to diffuse and propagate Islam among non-Muslims and to advance the great aims of Islam. . . . Do your utmost to expose the plans of the tyrannical regime of Iran against Islam and the Muslims. Convey to the world the voices of your tortured Muslim brothers in Iran and demonstrate solidarity with them.[30]

The emotional appeal, the external focusing of anger, and the general call to action were all extremely effective in raising consciousness. Building upon the work of his predecessors, such as 'Ali Shariati' (d. 1977), Khomeini's skillful articulation of these themes ultimately resulted in the Iranian Islamic Revolution of 1979, which became a paradigm for Islamists. Indeed, in the words of Richard Cottam, it was one of the "greatest populist explosions in human history."[31] For Muslims, as Esposito and Voll observe, it symbolized "restoration of Muslim pride and power in a world long dominated by foreign superpowers."[32] Shireen Hunter says of Khomeini that he was "the man who brought down the shah, ended a 2,500-year tradition of monarchy in Iran, turned three decades of U.S.-Iranian amity into bitter enmity, and for ten years was the uncontestable leader."[33] But while the Iranian "experience and agenda" offered a "guide to the political and ideological transformation of the worldwide Muslim community," as Esposito and Voll point out,[34] it would eventually become obvious that they were not a formula for effectively running a government.

Iran's Islamic Republic was institutionalized by 1981, in the *velayat-e faqih*, or government by the legal scholars. Based on no existing model, it incorporated the Qur'anic principle of consultative government; the *majlis-i shura* is the National Consultative Assembly and its members, as well as a president, are popularly elected. However, ultimate approval of candidates and legislation rests with the religious scholars. In addition, within twenty years after its institutionalization, it became clear that some adjustment was needed. Emotional reaction against injustice, posturing against perceived enemies, and single-minded commitment to a religio-moral alternative to the status quo had served their purpose. They had raised people's awareness of the need for change, they had heightened people's confidence in their own culture and religion, allowing sufficient solidarity to effect change. But after the revolution's success, there was a need for solving practical problems on a day-to-day basis. This was recognized by enough of the Iranian voting populace to elect Mohammad Khatami as president in 1997. Khatami seemed to be the candidate who recognized that adjustments to the status quo—not so much to the system itself, and certainly not to its Islamic basis, but to the attitudes and interpretations of those working within the system—were still necessary. This recognition is evident in his writings, where we see perhaps the best example of the practical phase of Islamism.

The Practical Phase of Political Islam

Following the demise of Ayatollah Khomeini in 1989, Hashemi Rafsanjani had become president of Iran. His was a transitional presidency, his policies focusing on recovering from the Iran-Iraq war and stabilizing the economy. There was virtually no ideological development evident during his regime. But below the surface, there was growing frustration with the isolation of the country and stagnation of the economy, and increasing discontent with the lack of personal freedoms among the populace. These sentiments surfaced in the 1997 election of Mohammad Khatami. A respected religious scholar and philosopher, Khatami developed a very sophisticated worldview focusing on the need for progress in the Muslim world. Integral to that progress is the need to establish what he calls a "new Iran." His landslide victory in the 1997 and 2001 elections demonstrates the popularity of his views.

As Khatami describes the "new Iran," it will be part of a comprehensive Islamic civil society. At a 1997 meeting of the Islamic Summit Conference, he described it as one that lives "in peace and tranquility with other peoples and nations."[35] Immediately, the shift from Islamism's defensive attitude is obvious. President Khatami believes all Muslims must understand and accept other cultures, working with them toward shared goals of social justice. His views on these subjects have been carefully articulated in a series of addresses to international audiences, as well as several articles collected in two books recently published in the United States.

Khatami begins his analysis by accepting the need for development in Islamic society. To him it is undeniable that the Muslim world is in need of what he calls "a desirable transformation in society."[36] Despite continued efforts, Islamic societies have not achieved development. Muslims are still struggling economically, socially, and politically. There is no doubt that global factors share a significant portion of the responsibility for this situation. However, it seems clear to President Khatami that there are factors in Islamic society itself that are hindering the requisite transformation in society. Thus, critical self-analysis on the part of Islamic society replaces defensiveness. Accordingly, Khatami claims that the essential element lacking in Islamic societies is freedom of thought and expression—in his words: "the freedom to think and the security to express new thinking."[37] "[T]ransformation and progress require thought," he says, "and thought only flourishes in an atmosphere of freedom. But our history has not allowed human character to grow and to be appreciated, and thus the basic human yearning for thinking and freedom has been unattended at best and negated at worst."[38]

The need for intellectual freedom and freedom of expression dominates Khatami's recent writings. Khatami is not advocating intellectual or religious anarchy, of course. He says, "For those without formal religious training, heeding the prescriptions of the clergy is necessary in practical matters." But, he continues, "[I]n the realm of thought, no thinker can blindly follow the clergy, however outstanding they are. . . ."[39] What he is advocating, therefore, is the right to achieve and express intellectual insight without fear of censorship or persecution.

The importance of freedom of thought and expression lead Khatami to an attitude toward the West that is quite unique among Islamic reformers. Rather than the sweeping condemnations of an essentialized "West," so familiar to Muslims since the time of Afghani, Khatami says that Muslims should learn from Westerners. He says that the Muslim world must learn from all of Western history: "[T]he vast experience of Westerners is before us, and if we are thoughtful, we must choose our future path on the basis of this experience."[40] He even goes so far as to say that there are positive strengths in Western society and achievements that Muslims have to incorporate into their own societies.

In an even more obvious break with the mainstream Islamist thought, Khatami says that modernity itself is at the root of the positive elements of Western development. He says, "the goal of this familiarity with the West is understanding the main tenets of modernity."[41] And what is modernity? While most Islamists, following Mawdudi, see modernity merely as a rejection of religious authority and the root of the ungodly forces of humanism, Khatami's view is far more nuance. For him modernity is essentially linked with freedom from the "autocratic and whimsical rulers" who plagued the premodern West and continue to plague the Muslim world. Portraying the lessons of European history very accurately, in fact, he claims that it takes freedom of thought and expression to cast off the shackles of these autocrats who base their legitimacy on traditional interpretations of religion.

Khatami is not uncritical of the West, of course. Although the West has permitted great intellectual freedom and, as a result, has been able to cast off tyranny, its record is deeply flawed. It has failed to concern itself with individual rectitude or virtue, he says, and this is because when the West overthrew its religiously legitimized dictatorships, Khatami thinks that the West also overthrew religion itself. This is a view Khatami shares with mainstream Islamists. The general view is that the West's development is largely dominated by "hedonism and greed."[42] Because these pursuits are ultimately unsatisfactory to the human spirit, Khatami sees Western society as now "worn out and senile."[43] In fact, he thinks Karl Marx was partly right about the West. He says Marx "was a great pathologist of the capitalist order," even if Marxism itself was "an impractical and unrealistic philosophy."[44] But what that means is that both the Muslim and the Western worlds are in crisis. He believes that the West's time in the sun is just about over, while Islam's new civilization is just beginning. However, the point is that both the essentialized "West" and "Islam" are viewed critically.

Gone with the utterly evil West is the uniformly good "Islamic system." In other words, the defensive utopianism of many popular Islamists is being replaced by critical analysis.

The dawning of this new era gives urgency to Khatami's calls for reform in Islamic society. In addition, his analysis shows that the essence of modernity for Khatami—intellectual freedom—is not new in Islamic heritage.[45] Khatami believes that at the time of Prophet Muhammad, freedom of thought and expression were respected. But, as he says, "[A] mere 40 years after the coming of Islam . . . authoritarianism of a more dangerous form [than that of pre-Islamic times] came to govern the destiny of the Islamic community, for this time authoritarianism and tyranny adopted the guise of Islamic legitimacy."[46] That is why for Khatami the Islamic revolution of 1979 signaled a reawakening of intellectual freedom in Islam. It is an example of the power of intellectual freedom. Unfortunately, however, he says the strict measures required after the revolution to keep the country from sinking into anarchy allowed some authorities to suppress freedom. However, it is particularly offensive to him that this suppression of freedom was done by some revolutionary leaders in the name of religion. According to him, "They covered their closed-minded ways under the guise of religion, when in fact their religion was nothing but a series of mental and emotional habits. . . ."[47]

In fact, Khatami says, we have to be careful about what we call tradition. The mere fact that something is old does not make it tradition. Nor does that fact that something is traditional make it good. The only "good traditions" are the immutable laws of God—what Khatami calls the "laws governing existence." He says these are "divine or natural traditions."[48] However, human beings make mistakes interpreting God's law, so no human tradition should be considered sacrosanct. It is the confusion of human interpretation with divine law that has caused the lack of intellectual freedom in Islam, says Khatami.

Continuing his rational critique of Islamic tradition, Khatami says that in order to deal with the debilitating lack of freedom in Muslim societies, the weight of falsely sanctified tradition must be lifted. In addition, Khatami boldly criticizes a number of respected Islamic intellectuals in this regard, drawing on his earlier philosophical writings. He says that respected medieval intellectuals had "implicitly legitimized . . . authoritarianism."[49] Even worse, he claims, the few who tried to resist were left with only violence to redress their grievances, resulting in factionalism.[50] The majority, on the other hand, adopted fatalism about their destiny, opting out of any kind of resistance at all. Then, because the autocrats "stifled" reflection on politics and society—"the sphere of secular affairs," the only intellectual arena left open was in speculative mysticism. This he believes was "a wrong and ill-fated response" because it negated the relevance of politics and political thought altogether."[51]

Stressing the importance of reason, Khatami specifically condemns excessive emotionalism as detrimental to Iran's progress. "In my view," he says, "reason is the common bond of all humans, a means of connecting to the world and to others, the same reason through which Plato and Aristotle communicated their views."[52] Therefore, it is on this level that the West may and indeed must be dealt with. For, as Khatami puts it, "Our vision of consolidating a system of religious governance in our future-oriented society cannot be materialized in a vacuum. We cannot implement this vision without full contact with the international community."[53] The West, in short, must be constructively engaged, through "rationality and enlightenment and through offering more powerful and compelling counter-arguments."[54] Just as the West's military might rules out military confrontation, its rationality makes "heated, flag-waving emotionalism" ineffective in dealing with the West.[55] In Khatami's words, this kind of "fanaticism . . . merely harms Islam."[56] Therefore, while many popular Islamists stress the need for martyrs, Khatami says that the greatest need right now is for what he calls "religious intellectuals." They are the ones who have to overcome emotionalism and traditionalism, the tendency to adhere blindly to precedent regardless of its appropriateness or lack thereof to current circumstances.

Reiterating the openness he showed toward learning from the lessons of the West, Khatami cautions people against unwarranted certainty that they are right. With openness and clear reason, Muslims should be able to hear and evaluate all manner of positions. To do otherwise is to run the risk of silencing a view that could prove helpful in achieving the overall goals of Islamic society. Since those goals are clearly not being met in the modern age, it seems that it is time to explore new options. Besides, societies change and with social changes come changes in religious interpretations. That is as it should be. Khatami says, "When conditions change and times change, new questions arise that in turn require new answers—and hence a new civilization."[57] Again, finding these new answers required reason and the freedom to use it. Therefore, Khatami's mission is to avoid emotionalism, to reawaken intellectual freedom in Islamic society. In addition, here again we see the self-critical approach of Khatami's work. The purpose of the freedom Khatami is advocating is to allow Muslims to create a just society. That is what he means when he talks about a transformation of society, and it is why Muslims must eradicate what Khatami calls "the effects of despotism [that] have become second nature to us." In our narrow-mindedness, he says, "[w]e are all individually dictator-like in our own ways, and this unfortunate condition is evident in all strata and spheres of society."[58] Until tyranny is wiped out on all levels of society, no progress will be made toward the goal of social justice.

In answering the question of what an Islamic Iran would look like, then, Khatami directly confronts some of the policies followed by earlier reformers, especially those who limited freedom in favor of centrally directed development. Rather than suppressing freedom in the interest of directing society to progress and development, Khatami says that people's "freedom [must have] priority over growth."[59] The detrimental effects of lack of intellectual freedom are expressed most obviously in irrational intolerance, resulting in a fragmented society incapable of benefiting from any positive results of technological developments. In sometimes barely veiled references to his predecessors, Khatami claims that those who legitimize the curtailment of freedom through tradition must recognize, he says, that "our tradition is more suitable for another civilization," one that "no longer exists. . . ." Thus, he says, people must be free to develop new ways to deal with the new civilization.[60]

In a particularly interesting comparison, Khatami says that the decline of the Muslim world resulted from the limitation of virtue to the personal level, just the opposite of the West's approach. Individuals were expected to be righteous, but the government was never held to the same standard. He says that "[s]ocial rectitude has no precedent in our history. The same Muslims who believed in [personal] rectitude committed many social injustices in the Muslim world, and individual rectitude has not been able to overturn these inequities."[61]

In order to bring personal virtue to the social and governmental level, then, Khatami says democracy is essential. That is its role, in fact. Furthermore, democracy is unquestionably indicated in Islamic source, he claims: "The legitimacy of concepts such as collective decision making, reconciliation, and the supremacy of the public interest was upheld by the behavior of [Prophet Muhammad] himself and to some extent by the caliphs who succeeded him, especially by Imam Ali."[62] Here again Khatami praises, rather than condemns the West. According to Khatami, the West is way ahead of the Muslim world in institutionalizing collective decision making.

Accordingly, Khatami's vision for Iran, and by extension for all Islamic societies, is a free and tolerant, reasonable and flexible society, based on a holistic understanding of human beings. In other words, he envisions a society that meets both the material and spiritual needs of its citizens. In his inaugural address, he described the ideal society for Iran. Iran should be a society that respects "social and individual security within the framework of the Constitution." It should have "clearly defined rights and duties for citizens and the government." Its government should "officially recognize the rights of the people and the nation within the framework of law. . . ." Such a government needs "organized political parties, social associations, and an independent free press." This is a society "where the government belongs to the people and is the servant of the people, not their master, and is consequently responsible to the people."[63]

Overall, the views expressed by Khatami are confident rather than defensive, rational, and analytic instead of emotional, and based on critical thinking in search of practical solutions rather than utopian expectations. Under his leadership, Iran has made significant steps in the areas of individual liberty and development. After his 1997 election, President Khatami's government oversaw Iran's first local elections in 730 cities and 40,000 villages. *The Washington Post* recently reported on the village of Lazoor, for example, where "the people run the show, and ideology has yielded to practicality and the common craving for a better life." The townspeople have formed their own government, and successfully initiated training sessions for identifying and implementing solutions to local problems. Community leader Ali Esfandiar is quoted as saying, "The most important impact is that people are really self-confident, and they have started to believe in themselves. We are capable of finding solutions for every problem."[64]

It is too early to predict the ultimate outcome of Khatami's political Islam. Despite his overwhelming popularity among the Iranian populace, there is still opposition to him in the government. In addition, although Lazoor is not unique, it is ahead of the curve. Still, it is an example of the effective transition from motivational to practical Islamism advocated by Khatami. It is an example of how careful analysis of specific circumstances can make the difference between a sense of empowerment and actual empowerment.

Muslim Minority Communities: The South African Example

The contrast between these two approaches to Islamic reform is evident in Muslim minority communities as well. Perhaps the most telling example can be found in a comparison of the records of Muslim communities in South Africa. South African Muslims are mainly the descendants of the slaves and indentured laborers brought in by the Dutch and the British in the seventeenth and nineteenth centuries. A small group of Muslim former slaves, commonly known as "Zanzibaris," arrived in Durban in the last quarter of the nineteenth century, and many Africans and some Europeans in South Africa have become Muslim, as well. However, the predominant ethnic groups among South African Muslims are the "Malays" and Indians.[65] Like all "people of color," Muslims of South Africa were subjected to enormous suffering under the apartheid system of racial segregation, and many joined the struggle to end the unjust system. Yet not all South African Muslims became engaged in the struggle. For many, meeting daily responsibilities was challenging enough to preclude social and political activism. For others, traditionally exclusive sectarian identities, reinforced by their current oppression, made it impossible to join in a movement—even one dedicated to their own well being—that included non-Muslims. This exclusivity was reinforced again by Islamist rhetoric, such as that of the Muslim Brotherhood and the Jamaat-i Islami, which identified the source of all evil as the religious "other."

Indeed, many Muslims who wished to work against the system were forced to work outside their religious identity. Many Muslims joined in secular movements opposed to the apartheid system, including the African National Congress, from its earliest days in the early twentieth century.[66] It was not until the 1950s and 1960s that many in the younger generation of Muslims began to look to their religion for organizational and ideological bases of resistance. Several organizations were founded expressing this generation's discontent with complacency, defensiveness, and defeatism of the many Muslims who did not join in the resistance.

Phases of Political Islam

The first organizations of this kind were formed around Cape Town. In 1961 a general "Call of Islam" movement was launched in the Cape—which set the tone for Islamic activism against injustice with the publication of its principles:

> For too long a time now have we been, together with our fellow-sufferers, subjugated; [we have] suffered humiliation of being regarded as inferior beings, [and] deprived of our basic rights to Earn, to Learn and to Worship. We therefore call upon our Muslim Brethren and all brothers in our sufferings to unite under the banner of Truth, Justice, and Equality to rid our beloved land of the forces of evil and tyranny.[67]

This call for Islamic resistance was unique in a number of ways. First, unlike earlier protests by Muslims in South Africa, the new resistance was not directed against specific rulings. It was aimed against an entire system deemed essentially unjust. Second, and more significantly, the injustice being protested was not those suffered by Muslims alone, but by all victims of oppression, regardless of religious affiliation. The premise of this "call" is that Islam is above all a struggle against injustice. The purpose of human life as revealed in the Islamic sources is to create a just society. Just as in other parts of the Muslim world, the imposition of colonial rule had shaken Muslims out of a kind of moral slumber and reminded them of the challenge posed by God at creation to be his stewards, to create and maintain a society reflecting human dignity and equality.

Islamic resistance organizations in South Africa from this time on focused on explicating the centrality of justice to Islamic values, articulating the implications of that centrality for their daily lives, and defining the entire process as essentially religious activity vis-à-vis those Muslims who denied the possibility of working religiously with the religious "other." Imam Abdullah Haron was a leading figure in this movement. He was active in several Islamic resistance organizations in the 1960s, and edited the Cape's *Muslim News*. He was particularly influential among the youth. Because of his activism, he was taken into detention by security forces in 1969. After four months of detention, the police announced that he had "accidentally" died. The public outpouring of grief and anger over his death was overwhelming. Thousands of antiapartheid strugglers from across the South African spectrum marched in his funeral, defying police orders. Imam Haron became a hero not just of Islamic activists, but also of the anti-apartheid movement overall. One of his colleagues in the resistance, Bernard Wrankmore, a Christian, undertook a hunger strike, demanding an inquiry into the death. After sixty-seven days, the government showed no signs of relenting, and Wrankmore ceased his strike. However, the solidarity of all those motivated by social justice, regardless of communal affiliation, had been demonstrated.

In the 1970s and 1980s, more Muslims were attracted to the liberation agenda. New organizations appeared. Not all of them accepted the premise of interreligious solidarity. They all accepted the centrality of social justice to Islam, and the need to work for it, even to work for justice for non-Muslims. However, some still believed that Muslims must work only with Muslims. It was in this context that the key issues involved in interreligious pluralism and solidarity were articulated by political Islamists in South Africa.

Overall, people in these movements found inspiration in their renewed understandings of Islamic teachings. Islamic "study circles" (*halaqat*) proliferated at the same time, as did university programs in Arabic and Islamic studies.[68] As in the rest of the Muslim world, encouraging believers to demonstrate their commitment to egalitarian values through social action was a central theme. The writings of Sayyid Qutb, for example, Mawdudi, and Iranian ideologue 'Ali Shari'ati, and were studied with enthusiasm. But the challenges of South African Muslims were unique, most obviously because Muslims in South Africa are a very small minority. Of a population of around 40 million people, Muslims make up less than 1.5 percent. Many had been raised with a very strong sense of religious exclusivity, which conveniently, as noted above, reinforced by apartheid. The South African Muslims, in fact, had come to identify all non-Muslims as kaffirs (*kafir*, pl. *kuffar*), which means "unbeliever" in the original Arabic, but with even more derogatory connotations in South African usage. One of the leading activists, Farid Esack, tells of being taught as a child to greet non-Muslims with "*samm alaykum*" instead of the standard Islamic greeting, *salam alaykum*. *Samm alaykum* means "poison on you," instead of the Islamic "peace on you." In this view, supported by some religious sources, Muslims should only associate with Muslims.

Thus, in the context of apartheid, not associating with non-Muslims had become an essential part of being Muslim, part of the very identity of a Muslim. Even while accepting the centrality of social justice to Islamic values, making common cause with the dreaded kaffirs seemed to be an insurmountable obstacle to many. Those Muslims who did work with non-Muslim groups were looked on by religious exclusivists as engaging in secular, not religious activity. However, the activists who worked with the religious other were not content to allow them to be excluded. To them, their activism alongside the religious other was at the core of their religious identity. Accordingly, the activists went back to traditional religious sources for support of their position. As Esack put it, rather than allowing the exclusivists' interpretation of religious sources and the terms used to identify Muslims and "others" to go unchallenged, political Islamists undertook "the rediscovery and re-appropriation of the meaning of these terms." In his words:

> It is possible to re-deploy these terms in a way, which enables one to live alongside others with integrity. Because ultimately the Qur'an . . . presents Allah as a being that is concerned with something that people *do* and with the people who *do* it, rather than with an abstract entity called faith. . . . Thus, *muslim* and all its positive connotations (including eschatological) cannot refer to

Phases of Political Islam 113

the biological accident of being born in a Muslim family. Similarly, *kafir* cannot refer to the accident of being born outside of such a family.[69]

By focusing on Islam as a set of values in action—not simply belief in the central Islamic value of justice, but the active struggle (*jihad*) to achieve justice—the obstacle of working with non-Muslims was transcended. Communal exclusiveness was superseded by the call to moral action. In Esack's analysis, the overall spirit of Qur'anic teaching is personal accountability, not group identity, personal accountability for actions, their motivations, and consequences. But actions are by nature dynamic: As Esack put it: "[E]very deed that we do or refuse to do is a step in our personal transformation." There is no single action or set of actions that encompasses an entire life; moral behavior is an ongoing enterprise, evident in every interaction and choice. It is effort, not a fait accompli. The same is true of Islam, Esack believes. It is not an identity given by birthright; it is continuous responsiveness to injustice in all its forms.

This "reappropriation" of Islamic terms in the service of the Qur'an's overall teaching of justice provided the basis of the South African activists' religious pluralism. In addition, just as the traditional sectarian divisions faded in importance, so did the distinction between religious and political activity. As the discourse on religious identity continued within the Islamic community, activists increased their involvement with peoples of various faiths—Jewish, Christian, Hindu, and African Traditional Religions—who were likewise committed. Interfaith services proliferated. Muslims like Farid Esack, Rashid Omar, and Ebrahim Moosa were invited to address Christian congregations, and people like antiapartheid activist, Alan Boesak, Gerrie Lubbe, and Martin Prozesky addressed Islamic activist meetings. In 1984, interfaith activism was institutionalized in South Africa. That was when the South African chapter of the World Conference on Religion and Peace (WCRP) was formed, under the aegis of Bishop Desmond Tutu and convened by Archbishop Trevor Huddlestone, with active participation by Muslim leaders.

Demonstrating the effectiveness of the organization—and the empowerment of Muslims through their commitment to pluralism, in 1992 WCRP members were asked to draw up a "Declaration on Religious Rights and Responsibilities" that serve as a guide for the new South African constitution, then under negotiation. The values incorporated in the document reflect the values shared by the diverse religions represented:

1. All persons are entitled:
    1.1 to freedom of conscience,
    1.2 to profess, practice, and propagate any religion or no religion,
    1.3 to change their religious allegiance;
2. Every religious community and/or member thereof shall enjoy the right:
    2.1 to establish, maintain, and manage religious institutions;
    2.2 to have their particular system of family law recognized by the state;

2.3 to criticize and challenge all social and political structures and policies in terms of the teachings of their religion.

This declaration played a major role in negotiations for South Africa's new constitution. It does not appear as such in the final draft of the constitution, which was adopted in 1996, but its ideas were incorporated into several of its sections.[70] Those Muslims who retain their exclusivist stance and reject working with "non-Muslims" maintain that Esack and his colleagues have gone beyond the pale; they are no longer working in "Islam." Yet those exclusivist Muslims continue to dream of "the Islamic solution," while the pluralist Muslims have become actually effective in the politics of South Africa. Esack himself was appointed by Nelson Mandela to the Commission on Gender Equality. Numerous other Muslims were appointed or elected to high positions in the government, including Dalla Omar, who became minister of justice.

Like that of Khatami and his supporters, the effectiveness of pluralist South African Muslims is an example of empowerment through political Islam by taking the natural step of transforming Islamist motivational rhetoric into practical programs for organizing and governing society. The milieu is still Islam, of course; the transformations are all based on careful analysis of Islamic sources. Only interpretations of appropriate ways to apply the teachings in the sources change. The transformation is similar to the one that took place in the American Civil Rights movement. The first step is achieving rights, and that often begins with recognition that one's group has been systematically denied rights. However, once rights are achieved, then it is necessary to figure out how to use those rights to achieve specific socioeconomic and political goals. The transition is from a desire for empowerment to the effective use of power—as popular jargon has it, a transition "from victim to victor."

What Happens When Goals Remain Unattained

The first phase of Islamism, as I describe it, motivates people to demand their rights as Muslims, through appeal to Islamic core values of justice and human dignity, in opposition to an essentialized "the West" which has denied their rights, and based on the conviction that an essentialized "Islamic system" is sufficient to resolve all their problems. Observers may disagree that Islam really is the solution, but Muslim communities still struggling for their rights cannot be faulted for placing their hopes in it. However, once independence is achieved, the "Islamic system" has to be worked out in practical terms. Without doing so, the acquisition of rights becomes meaningless. There are examples of Muslim states that have achieved independence but have so far failed to find ways to use that independence effectively. The phrase being used today for such cases is "failed states."[71] Olivier Roy described these failures in his book *The Failure of Political Islam* (Harvard, 1994). But the failure he described was not the failure of political Islam as such. It is actually the failure only of some political Islamists to make the transition from attitudes appropriate for consciousness-raising to those necessary for practical implementation of ideals in the competitive global village of the twenty-first century.

This is how analysts in Iran describe their own process of transition. Mahmood Sariolghalam, an Iranian political scientist, says, "It's a matter of efficiency. The religious establishment has always claimed political authority and legitimacy. However, they had their chance, and they didn't deliver. Historically, it's a very important development in Iran."[72] Mohammad Javad Larijani, described as "one of the chief theoreticians of the right wing," described the need for Iran's clerical rulers to "modernize" as a "practical urgency . . . so educated, young, devoted Muslims know how to be devoted and faithful Muslims at the beginning of the twenty-first century."[73] For failure to address the social and economic needs of a growing population in today's world results not only in the failure of the government, but it potentially alienates people from the self-proclaimed basis of its legitimacy—from Islam itself. As Taha Hashemi, owner of the conservative newspaper *Entekhab*, put it, "The wrong presentation of religion and the wrong interpretations of [Iran's] constitution have caused the youth to hate this state, and because the wrong face of Islam is being presented, secularism is on the rise. . . . It has alienated our people . . ." Summarizing the problematic elements of Islamist thought in Iran, he said, "This stream of thought, which is against scientific movements, against development, against cooperation with the West, against maintaining constructive relationships with modern society, can never reflect the right understanding of Islam and can never be in coherence with the modern world."[74]

This disaffection with Islamism in power is also evident in Pakistan, where the contrast with Iran is instructive. Islamists have been involved in the Pakistani government since its very creation. After initial opposition, Mawdudi and religious scholars in general approved the creation of the state as an Islamic state, requiring a Muslim leader, and an Islamic Objectives Resolution passed by the Constituent Assembly in 1949, included as the preamble to the first constitution (1956) as well as subsequent constitutions. The Objectives Resolution reads:

> Whereas sovereignty over the entire Universe belongs to Almighty Allah alone, and the authority to be exercised by the people of Pakistan within the limits prescribed by Him is a sacred trust . . .
> And whereas it is the will of the people of Pakistan to establish an order;
> Wherein the State shall exercise its powers and authority through the chosen representatives of the people;
> Wherein the principles of democracy, freedom, equality, tolerance, and social justice, as enunciated by Islam, shall be fully observed;
> Wherein the Muslims shall be enabled to order their lives in the individual and collective spheres in accordance with the teachings and requirements of Islam as set out in the Holy Qur'an and Sunnah . . . ;

[provisions guaranteeing the rights of minorities, "fundamental rights, including equality of status, of opportunity and before law, social, economic and political justice, and freedom of thought, expression, belief, faith, worship and association, subject to law and public morality;" independence of the judiciary, etc.]

Now, therefore, we, the people of Pakistan,
Conscious of our responsibility before Almighty Allah and men;
Cognisant of the sacrifices made by the people in the cause of Pakistan;
Faithful to the declaration made by the Founder of Pakistan, Quaid-i-Azam Mohammad Ali Jinnah, that Pakistan would be a democratic State based on Islamic principles of social justice;
Dedicated to the preservation of democracy achieved by the unremitting struggle of the people against oppression and tyranny.[75]

Pakistan's history, unfortunately, has not lived up to those expectations. Roughly half of its brief life has been spent under military government, it has been involved in an ongoing border dispute with India that has erupted into full-scale war twice, it has endured a civil war and the secession of former East Pakistan, communal and ethnic strife continue to plague many regions, and its economy is stagnant.

Efforts to address these issues have frequently involved further "Islamization," a trend that achieved its highest visibility under Zia al-Haq in the 1980s, although it actually began under Zulfikar Ali Bhutto. Zia sought legitimacy for his military rule by acceding to Islamists's demands for "returning to the Shari'ah." Prior to his regime, the newly established state of Pakistan had implemented a variety of laws, many of which were decried as secularist, but in the minds of progressive/reformist Muslims, represented reforms of traditional fiqh statutes in accordance with the demands of a modern state. For example, the medieval law limiting the legitimacy of women's testimony in court was revised in accordance with Qur'anic teaching on human equality in moral responsibility and recognition of the change in women's social status through education. Similarly, the medieval equation of *riba,* forbidden by the Qur'an, with any level of interest whatsoever, was revised. According to the new interpretation, *riba* was identified as usurious interest rates, which continued to be forbidden, while reasonable interest rates were determined to be permissible in order to allow Pakistan to participate in the global economy. However, this type of "modernist" legislation was characterized as un-Islamic by conservative Islamic elements, whose support was considered essential for the success of Zia's regime.[76] As a result, the legal reforms of the 1960s were struck down; women's legal testimony was again limited, efforts were made to forbid all charging or paying of interest, *hudud* ordinances were institutionalized, including amputation for theft, and certain other high-profile "Islamic" legislation was enacted, including government regulation of the collection and distribution of *zakat* and *'ushr,* Islamic charity taxes.

The symbolic nature of these "Islamic reforms" is evident in the discrepancy between legislation and implementation. In reality, for example, the charging and paying of interest has not been prohibited in Pakistan; only compound interest was actually prohibited. Similarly, legislation stipulates that physicians must perform amputations. But physicians consider "judicial" amputations a violation of the Hippocratic oath, so amputation sentences are not actually carried out. A recent study has even shown that while *zakat* and *'ushr* are duly collected by the government, their distribution is sporadic, at best. Yet so important is the symbolic value of "Islamic law" or "Shari'ah"—the two are equivalent terms in the language of the Islamist groups—that even Pakistan's twice-elected female prime minister, Benazir Bhutto, was unable even to influence legislation concerning women.

Perhaps most significant, Zia went one step further than Bhutto in empowering the Islamists. The Council of Islamic Ideology, established by Ayoub Khan's 1956 constitution as an advisory body, was entrusted with the task of reviewing existing laws for conformity with their view of Islam. Zia gave this task to the Federal Shariah Court, which could "examine and decide . . . whether or not any law or provision of law is repugnant to the Injunctions of Islam . . ."[77] It was staffed by traditionally trained religious scholars who maintained the no doubt sincere belief that enforcement of traditional Islamic laws and norms would result in social well-being. Rethinking or expanding those interpretations for new circumstances was considered by some to be neither necessary nor advisable, and by others to be best deferred until a more appropriate time. Accordingly, "Islamic authenticity" came to be equated with traditional Islamic legislation. Concern with that "authenticity" overshadowed the challenge of rethinking Islamic sources for legislation in new circumstances (*ijtihad*) and the requirements of good governance.

Yet each successive government had recourse to this kind of legitimation. The last decade of the twentieth century started with Act X of 1991—the "Enforcement of Shar'iah Act." This act reiterated: "Islam has been declared to be the state religion of Pakistan and it is obligatory for all Muslims to follow the Injunctions of the Holy Qur'an and the Sunnah. . . ." The Act continues: "Shariah means the Injunctions of Islam as laid down in the Holy Qur'an and Sunnah." Who is going to determine what those are? The Act explains:

> While interpreting and explaining the Shariah, the recognized principles of interpretation and explanation of the Holy Qur'an and Sunnah shall be followed and the expositions and opinions of recognized jurists of Islam belonging to prevalent Islamic schools of jurisprudence may be taken into consideration.

That is, traditional (as opposed to reform- or *ijtihad*-oriented) religious scholars shall determine Islamic legitimacy. In any case, the Act concludes: "The Shari'ah . . . shall be the supreme law of Pakistan." And, "All Muslim citizens of Pakistan shall observe Shari'ah and act accordingly. . . ." The process of achieving that goal is then described as "Islamization," so that all aspects of Pakistan's society shall be Islamized, with the goal of eliminating bribery, corruption, obscenity, vulgarity, social evils, false imputations, etc.[78]

Again, there is no mention of social, economic, or political development. The statement clearly reflects the unquestioned belief that following of traditional injunctions of Islamic law (prayer; charity; fasting; modest dress; refraining of alcohol, gambling, and mixing of sexes) will result in good governance, accountability, and economic prosperity, although those practical issues are discussed only in the most general terms.[79] Perhaps not surprisingly, the same decade ended with allegations that under the government of Nawaz Sharif, "bribery, corruption, obscenity, vulgarity, social evils, false imputations, etc." remained. Before it was overthrown by the current Chief Executive General Pervez Musharraf (October 1999), convicted of bribery and exiled, the government of Nawaz Sharif was proposing more "Islamization."

The problems that continue to challenge Pakistan are institutional, structural, multidimensional, and far too complex to analyze in the present context. The fact that they continue to plague Pakistan is not the fault of Pakistan's Islamists. What is at issue here are the hopes generated by Islamist claims that "Islamization"—construed as the enforcement of traditional Islamic laws—will resolve those problems, and the government's continued reliance on the appeal of this kind of Islamism for legitimacy. That reliance, in lieu of practical programs for good governance and economic development, has had serious repercussions for Pakistan. The impact on Pakistan's efforts to develop democracy is self-evident. To the extent that Nawaz Sharif was able to maintain popularity, like many of his predecessors, it was by appealing to the symbolic value of Islamic legitimacy. This despite lack of real democratic development. In the case of Nawaz, it was despite moves to undermine the most basic elements of democracy, such as the freedom of elected representatives to vote their consciences or the will of their constituents. Instead, under Nawaz, Amendment 14 required that they vote with the party or lose their elected seats.

History demonstrates, in fact, that democracy has not been the key to the Islamists's success in Pakistan. Their parties and those of traditional religious scholars have never been able to muster more than 3.43 percent of the vote in federal elections (1988).[80] Rather, their parties' power is characterized as "street power." They can bring pressure upon the government by bringing people into the streets for demonstrations. This pressure is used then to extract concessions from the government, but they do not use it for education or economic development, for example, which would be practical demands. Instead, their demands often focus on more stringent application of Islamic law. For example, when in spring 2000 General Musharraf's government announced a new antiterrorist law banning "any group activity that employs threats or violence, that incites the public to religious hatred or that violently promotes any religious, ethnic or sectarian cause," the reaction among the public was overwhelmingly positive. But leaders of the religious parties affected by the legislation were uniformly negative, going so far as to accuse the government of "selling out to the West, undermining the Kashmir cause and even doing the bidding of India."[81] Crowds gathered in the streets and the government was forced to back down. Such concessions do have the effect of empowering people who otherwise feel disenfranchised from the power politics of Pakistan. However, again, the appeal is emotional, giving a sense of power, but no power measurable in practical terms—for example, no better education to allow greater economic competitiveness, no power to bring about changes that would improve their standard of living or that of future generations.

In fact, the longer economic, social, and real political development is put off, the more potent this emotional appeal becomes to those sectors of society without access to economic power or the intellectual or educational apparatus to figure out how to get it. It is in this context that many people in Pakistan are expressing fear of "Talibanization" in Pakistan. Just as in Iran, many educated people are experiencing growing alienation from the kind of Islamism that promises empowerment and freedom but does not deliver it. But in Pakistan a growing number of rural male students—those with minimal modern education—are being drawn to the more strident calls of Taliban-style blend of Islamist exclusivity and defensiveness combined with an ultratraditional social outlook. They believe that "Islam" was able to drive the Soviets from Afghanistan, and then to overthrow the corrupt warlords who succeeded them. Unconcerned about the economic or social conditions in Talibani Afghanistan, they look to greater "Islamization" as the answer to Pakistan's problems. The BBC reported from Peshawar in April 2001 that some 200,000 men had gathered for an international conference of the conservative Deoband School. According to the report,

> Conference organizers have demanded the expulsion of what they call Christian and Jewish forces from the Arabian peninsula. . . . The organizers said they want Muslim youth to be prepared to fight a war there. The call was echoed in a statement sent by . . . Osama bin Laden from his hide-out in neighbouring Afghanistan. . . ." and the group want their interpretations of Islamic law enforced in Pakistan.[82]

The U.S.-led campaign in Afghanistan following the September 11, 2001, attacks has in fact increased the popularity of the Taliban among the Islamized masses who understand only that "Islam" is under attack by "the West"—again. Islamist parties, the "Jamaats," foster the growing anti-Americanism Pakistan. However, concern about their "street power" is not a new phenomenon in Pakistan. In interviews I conducted during the summer of 2000, Pakistani students, professionals, and intellectuals complained that the leader of the Jamaat-i Islami Qazi Hussain Ahmad was being received in Washington, D.C., as a "moderate face" of Pakistan.[83] They said that the Jamaat-i Islami and other more traditional organizations in Pakistan do not represent Islam; instead, they accused the Islamist organizations in general of being autocratic in organization, manipulating the poor through xenophobic emotionalism, undermining Pakistan's foreign policy in Central Asia and the subcontinent by sending fighters to participate in insurgencies in these trouble spots and, in fact, collaborating in the destruction of democracy in Pakistan.

The latter two issues—the Kashmir conflict, and the crisis of democracy in Pakistan—were of particular concern to members of Pakistan's educated and professional classes. They pointed to the example of the Jamaats's highly coordinated demonstrations in spring 1999, when former prime minister Nawaz Sharif met Indian prime minister Atal Bihari Vajpayee in an effort to discuss a negotiated resolution to the critical—and potentially nuclear—conflict in Kashmir. A video made of bloody clashes with police during the demonstrations was circulated widely in order to raise sympathy for those who characterize compromise with India as a violation of religious principles, akin to making a pact with the devil himself. The Pakistan government, according to public statements by its leaders, has no desire to engage in conflict with India. The Kashmir dispute should be settled through negotiation.[84] The continued confrontation forces Pakistan to dedicate over half of its GDP to defense. These funds could be used far more constructively for education and development. Now Afghanistan is added to the list of their concerns. The anti-American demonstrations threaten the fragile stability of the state itself. There is significant concern that continued American attacks in Afghanistan could spread the popularity of the Taliban within the military, possibly sparking a civil war.

In more recent interviews, Pakistanis have expressed support for Kashmiris, Palestinians, Afghanis, and Muslims in Central Asia and elsewhere. However, what they long for, first and foremost, is stability, good governance, and development in Pakistan. What once was optimism about the ability of Islamist movements to achieve those goals, however, is fading into pessimism among some of the youth, while among a growing number of young men, it is being radicalized. Not surprisingly, the polarization in Pakistani society has only increased since the beginning of the Afghanistan war.

Conclusion

The characterization of distinctions between the two phases of political Islam presented here is thematic, not absolute. The examples are not meant to be exhaustive descriptions of the subject views. They have been chosen to highlight the discursive trends under discussion. There are many other examples (and counterexamples) that could have been chosen. For example, greater emphasis could have been given to the reform elements of Islamism, such as acknowledgment of the positive role of women in society. This would allow for more careful distinction between traditional (nonreformist) Islamic scholars and (reform-minded) Islamists.

The reason for pointing out differences in degrees of reliance on emotional/rational appeal, utopian/practical vision, and defensive/self-critical posture is to suggest a framework of analysis of contemporary Islamic movements that allows recognition of their dynamism and fluidity. Emotional, utopian, defensive attitudes are perfectly understandable when a community is under siege and struggling for its very survival. Such discourse can be very effective in certain circumstances and for achieving the goals of solidarity and self-sacrifice often considered necessary to achieve freedom. Other circumstances, I have argued, require greater reliance on rational, practical, and self-critical approaches. This framework allows one to disagree with those who discuss "the failure of political Islam," as Olivier Roy has titled his book. It shows that the failures discussed by Roy are not those of political Islam, as such. They are the failure to move beyond motivational discourse to the kind of practical analysis necessary for effective economic and political development in specific circumstances. The effectiveness of motivational discourse is found in consciousness-raising on a mass scale, appealing to a Muslim population's most deeply held values and calling upon them to be proud of those values, to rise up, to cast off the oppressors, and gain control of their destinies in order to implement those values. In fact, these were universal themes in the colonized (or virtually colonized) Muslim world; the country of origin of Islamist ideologues was not important. As we saw, for example, Egyptian and Pakistani Sunni Islamists were as popular as Iranian Shī'i Islamists even in a Muslim minority community like that of South Africa. But once a population effectively gains control of its destiny—once the revolution is successful, then practical strategies geared to specific regional circumstances are necessary. They must deal with problems that vary from community to community. Size and homogeneity of the population are significant factors, for example, as are levels of literacy, the presence or absence of an effective education system, the presence or absence of a functioning press, the presence or absence of natural resources and the degree of their development, the presence or absence of hostile neighbors, the strength and cohesiveness of the country's military, and the presence or absence of a traditional ruling or landed class. Continued reliance on revolutionary rhetoric will not provide the kind of programs necessary to address effectively such specific problems in specific contexts. They require critical rational analysis, and often a good deal of flexibility and cooperation with a previously demonized "other." Where Islamism has made this transition successfully, as shown in the example of Iran, it is proving remarkably effective. In cases where independence has been achieved but the transition in discourse has not taken place, the ideals of Islamism remain cherished but distant goals. In that context, the frustration resulting from economic, social, and political instability provides fertile ground for radicalization.

Notes

1. See, for example, Leonard Binder, *Islamic Liberalism: A Critique of Development Ideologies* (Chicago: University of Chicago Press, 1988); and Charles Kurzman, ed.,

Liberal Islam: A Sourcebook (New York: Oxford University Press, 1998). The term "fundamentalism," often used by Western journalists, will not be used in this discussion. It generally refers to religious movements defined by insistence that historic and scientific claims found in scripture are literally true and may not be contravened by information derived from other sources. Although there are fundamentalist Muslims in the world today, that term does not characterize contemporary Islamic movements in general. The significant movements in the modern Muslim world are more appropriately defined by their sociopolitical goals. Since their origins in the first half of the twentieth century, these movements have been characterized by their efforts to address colonialism and the problems of postcolonialism, including cultural alienation, economic stagnation, and political corruption. Because of the centrality of Islam to these efforts, ideologues of these movements often identify themselves as "Islamist." Western scholars of modern Islamic movements use that term (or "Islamism") interchangeably with the term "political Islam," because the subject movements aspire toward a sociopolitical system that is essentially Islamic. However, there has never been unanimity concerning the proper terminology for these movements, because the movements themselves are both varied and dynamic.

2. See, for example, Jamal al-Din al-Afghani, "Answer to Renan," in *An Islamic Response to Imperialism: Political and Religious Writings of Sayyid Jamal ad-Din 'al-Afghani*," Nikki R. Keddie, ed. (Berkeley: University of California, 1983), 181.

3. Syed Ameer Ali, *The Spirit of Islam: A History of the Evolution and Ideals of Islam* (London: Christophers, 1922), xvii.

4. As Farish Noor put it recently, "Much of the literature and pedagogic material produced by the Islamist leaders and thinkers today is filled with references to their enemies. Chief among those who are regarded as the 'enemies of Islam' are the Turkish nationalist Mustafa Kemal Ataturk and the Shah of Iran. In the Malaysian context, the Malaysian prime minister has also been added to this infamous list of un-Islamic and anti-Islamic scoundrels." Farish A. Noor, "How 'Secularism' Became a Dirty Word in Malaysia," msanews.mynet.net, 4 September 2000.

5. Quoted by Richard P. Mitchell, "The Society of the Muslim Brothers" (Ph.D. dissertation, Princeton University, 1960), 524.

6. Mitchell, "Society of the Muslim Brothers," 379.

7. Mitchell, "Society of the Muslim Brothers," 375.

8. Mitchell, "Society of the Muslim Brothers," 373.

9. Mitchell, "Society of the Muslim Brothers," 384.

10. Mitchell, "Society of the Muslim Brothers," 432. Farish Noor describes the "appeal of Islamist discourse as based on mythological constructions of some 'Golden Age' of Islam." See, Farish Noor, "How 'Secularism' Became a Dirty Word in Malaysia," msanews.mynet.net, 4 September 2000.

11. Quoted by Y. Y. Haddad, "Sayyid Qutb: Ideologue of Islamic Revival" in *Voices of Islamic Resurgence*, J. L. Esposito, ed. (New York: Oxford University Press, 1983), 73, from Sayyid Qutb, *Maarakat al-Islam wa'l-Rasmaliyyah*, translated by Haddad (Beirut: Dar al-Shuruq, 1975), 36.

12. Seyd Qutb, *Milestones* (Indianapolis, Ind.: American Trust Publications, 1990), 137–38.

13. Haddad, "Sayyid Qutb," 25–26.

14. Syed Qutb, *Islam: The True Religion*, Rafi Ahmed Fidai, tr. (Karachi: International Islamic Publishers, 1981), 15–26.

15. Quoted by Haddad, "Sayyid Qutb," 79, from Sayyid Qutb, *Fi Zilal al-Qur'an* (Beirut: Dar al-Shuruq, 1973–1974), ix, 499; cf. ix, 1433.
16. Qutb, *Maarakat al-Islam*, 66, translated by Haddad, *Voices of Islamic Resurgence*, 71.
17. Qur'an 26:69, quoted in Syed Qutb Shaheed, *Islam, the True Religion*, Rafi Ahmad Fidai, tr. (Karachi: International Islamic Publishers, 1981), 3.
18. Syed Qutb, *Islam the True Religion*, 42–43.
19. Syed Qutb, *This Religion of Islam* (hadha'd-din) (Kuwait: International Islamic Federation of Student Organizations, 1988), 49–64.
20. Syed Qutb Shaheed, *This Religion of Islam* (hadha'd-din), 98–99.
21. Syed Charles Adams, "Mawdudi and the Islamic State" in *Voices of Resurgent Islam*, Esposito, 101.
22. A. A. Mawdudi, *Purdah and the Status of Woman in Islam* (Lahore: Islamic Publications, 1993), 157.
23. A. A. Mawdudi, *Islamic Law and Constitution*, Khurshid Ahmad, ed. and tr. (Lahore: Islamic Publications, 1967), 53.
24. Mawdudi, *Islamic Law*, 113.
25. Mawdudi, *Islamic Law*, 148; cf. 158, 172.
26. Mawdudi, *Islamic Law*, 264. Quoted by Adams, "Mawdudi and the Islamic State," 122. See, also Adams's discussion of the lack of specificity in Mawdudi's writings on Islamic government, 123–28.
27. Quoted by Michael M. J. Fischer, "Imam Khomeini: Four Levels of Understanding," in Esposito, *Voices of Resurgent Islam*, 154, from *Zendigi-Nameh Imam Khomeini* (Teheran: Fifteenth of Khordad Publishers, n.d.), II: 38–43.
28. Imam Khomeini, *Islam and Revolution: Writings and Declarations of Imam Khomeini*, H. Algar, tr. and annotated (London: KPI, 1985), 187.
29. Khomeini, *Islam and Revolution*, 182–85.
30. Khomeini, *Islam and Revolution*, 210–11.
31. Richard W. Cottam, "Inside Revolutionary Iran," *The Middle East Journal* 43, no. 2 (Spring 1989): 168.
32. John L. Esposito and John O. Voll, *Islam and Democracy* (New York: Oxford University Press, 1996), 61.
33. Shireen T. Hunter, *Iran after Khomeini* (Washington, D.C.: CSIS, 1991), 1.
34. Esposito and Voll, *Islam and Democracy*, 61.
35. Statement by H. E. Seyyed Mohammad Khatami, president of the Islamic Republic of Iran and Chairman of the Eighth Session of the Islamic Summit Conference, Tehran, www.undp.org/missions/iran/new, 9 December 1997.
36. Mohammad Khatami, *Islam, Liberty and Development* (Binghamton, N.Y.: Institute of Global Cultural Studies, Binghamton University, 1998), 3.
37. Khatami, *Islam*, 4.
38. Khatami, *Islam*, 11.
39. Khatami, *Islam*, 40. The passage ends with the provision: ". . . unless religious leaders are among the Infallibles [the divinely-guided imams]."
40. Khatami, *Islam*, 5.
41. Khatami, *Islam*, 5.
42. Khatami, *Islam*, 32.
43. Khatami, *Islam*, 53.
44. Khatami, *Islam*, 54–55.

45. Khatami, *Islam*, 17, where he says that the idea that modernity "is a Western phenomenon, built through the dismantling and breaking of tradition" is "premature."
46. Khatami, *Islam*, 7.
47. Khatami, *Islam*, 14.
48. Khatami, *Islam*, 19.
49. Khatami, *Islam*, 9–10.
50. This view was also expressed by Palestinian intellectual Bandali al-Jawzi, *Min Ta'rikh al-Harakat al-Fikriyyah fi'l-Islam* (Jerusalem, 1928). See Tamara Sonn, *Interpreting Islam: Bandali Jawzi's Islamic Intellectual History* (New York: Oxford University Press, 1996).
51. Khatami, *Islam*, 8–9.
52. Khatami, *Islam*, 46.
53. Khatami, *Islam*, 60.
54. Khatami, *Islam*, 64.
55. Khatami, *Islam*.
56. Khatami, *Islam*, 65.
57. Khatami, *Islam*, 59.
58. Khatami, *Islam*, 15.
59. Khatami, *Islam*.
60. Khatami, *Islam*, 21.
61. Khatami, *Islam*, 44.
62. Khatami, *Islam*, 7.
63. Mohammad Khatami, *Hope and Challenge: The Iranian President Speaks* (Binghamton, N.Y.: Institute of Global Cultural Studies, Binghamton University, 1997), 77–78.
64. John Ward Anderson, "Iranian Village Creates Model of Democracy," *Washington Post*, 2 September 2001, A1, 24.
65. For history of Muslim populations in Southern Africa, see Y. DaCosta, "The Spatial Origins of the Early Cape Muslims, and the Diffusion of Islam to the Cape Colony," *Journal for Islamic Studies* 10, no. 3 (1990): 45–67; Achmat Davids, *The Mosques of the Bo-Kaap* (Athlone: South African Institute of Arabic and Islamic Research, 1980); Achmat Davids, *The History of the Tana Baru* (Cape Town: Committee for the Preservation of the Tana Baru, 1985); Fatima Meer, *Portrait of Indian South Africans* (Durban: Avon House, 1969).
66. For a survey of such organizations, see Farid Esack, *Qur'an, Liberation, and Pluralism* (Oxford: Oneworld, 1997), 20–30.
67. *Muslim News* (Cape Town, South Africa), 31 March 1961, 4.
68. See Tamara Sonn, "Islamic Studies in South Africa," *American Journal of Islamic Social Sciences* 11, no. 2 (Summer 1994): 273–81.
69. Tamara Sonn, "Islamic Studies in South Africa," 273–81.
70. According to Constitutional Assembly negotiators, as reported in personal communication from Farid Esack.
71. See for example, Robert Kaplan, *The Coming Anarchy: The Dreams of the Post Cold War* (New York: Random House, 2000). The phrase "failed state" is generally associated with Madeline Albright's description of Somalia in the early 1990s.
72. John Ward Anderson, "Iran's Conservatives Face a Growing Split," *Washington Post*, 2 June 2001, A13.
73. Anderson, "Iran's Conservatives."

74. Anderson, "Iran's Conservatives."

75. Sahibzada Masud-ul-Hassan Khan Sabri, *The Constitution of Pakistan, 1973* (Lahore: Publishers Emporium, 1994), 24–26.

76. Vali Nasr describes this process in his book about the *Jamaat-i Islami The Vanguard of the Islamic Revolution* (New York: Oxford University Press, 1994). He describes how Mawdudi bifurcated Pakistani society into those who agree with him—the *ahl-i sunnat*, and those who, because they disagreed the finality of traditional interpretations of Islam, were declared to be antireligious innovators—the *ahl-i bid'at*. Those who agreed with his interpretations of Islam were identified as "religious," and those who disagreed were denied their very religious identity. They were dismissed as "secularists"—even *kuffar* (unbelievers or heretics). Accordingly, Nasr describes how the Islamic Research Institute's reforms of human interpretations of Islamic principles were described as giving "a veneer of Islamization" to an irreligious ("secular") government, in particular, the institute's director, Fazlur Rahman, was said to have provided "an intellectual rationale for the essentially political campaign against the religious forces." In fact, Fazlur Rahman was a devout and committed Muslim who considered secularism equivalent to atheism. But like many other reform-minded devout Muslims, his voice was silenced in his homeland, precisely due to the pressure of the Jamaat. He resigned his position and lived the rest of his life in voluntary exile.

77. 1981 Amendment to the 1973 Constitution. See Sabri, *Constitution of Pakistan*, 158.

78. Sabri, *The Constitution of Pakistan*, 423–29.

79. This is not to deny the voluminous and qualify output of the Islamic Research Institute in Islamabad, particularly dealing with details of Islamic law and economics. The reference here is to the Islamization programs of the government and their lack of practical strategies to achieve their goals.

80. Sardar Fakhre Alam, Rashid Aziz Khan, and Hamid Ali Mirza, *General Elections Report, Vol. II: Comparative Statistics for General Elections 1988, 1990, 1993 & 1997* (Islamabad: Printing Corporation of Pakistan Press, n.d.), vi.

81. Pamela Constable, "In Pakistan, a Crusade Stumbles," *Washington Post*, 9 September 2001, A22.

82. Daoud Yaqub, "Deoband Gathering," www.washingtonpost.com, 10 April, 2001.

83. Nora Boustany, "Presenting a Moderate Face in Pakistan," *Washington Post*, 19 July 2000, A18.

84. Before the September 11, 2001, attacks in New York and Washington, the Pakistani Chief Executive Pervez Musharraf was involved in ongoing discussion with Indian Prime Minister Vajpayee of the countries' shared concerns. Significantly, these meetings took place outside Pakistan. The two leaders were scheduled to meet in New York in October 2001. The Jamaat-i Islami had expressed cautious support for the initiative, in return for political favors from the Musharraf government in the elections that were planned to return Pakistan to democracy. As of this writing, negotiations have been halted in the context of the Afghanistan war, although fighting continues in Kashmir.

Chapter 6

Hindu Revivalist Cultural Policies and Programs in India: A Critique

Santosh C. Saha

The legacy of cultural colonialism and recent modernization created an identity crisis for the Hindu Far Right or the Hindu revivalists, led mostly by urban-based middle classes, pushing them to search for new forms of self-definition. In seeking a new social order, they seemed to argue that in Indian liberal democracy the moral-cultural sphere had been neglected compared to the political and the economic. This study examines selected aspects of Hindu revivalist[1] cultural policies in the context of the political emergence of revivalist religio-political parties and groups in recent decades. I would examine the strength of "ethnic nationalism" upheld by such parties as the Hindu Mahasabha, the Jana Sangh, the Bharatiya Janata Party (BJP), the Vishwa Hindu Parishad (VHP), and behind them all, the Rashtriya Swayamsevak Sangh (National Volunteer Organization, or RSS), that were all profoundly attached to their epic heritage. It will be shown that their strategies of stigmatizing and emulating "threatening others," under the pretext of drawing inspiration from the ancient "golden age," proved to be an erroneous demonstration of cultural nationalism in India.[2] Theoretically, revivalists (also known as Hindu fundamentalists or Hindu militants) agreed with the alarmist claim of Samuel P. Huntington (1993), with his neo-Spenglerian thesis of the clash of civilizations, that competing civilizations dominated by religion would conflict, both politically and culturally. Seen from another perspective, the revivalists in India reasoned more in terms of the "Ethic of Divinity" (use of God's truth) than the "Ethic of Autonomy" (modern emphasis on the freedom of the individual to pursue diverse religious/cultural goals).[3]

Introduction

I would examine selected cultural aspects: (1) differences between earlier reformist cultural policies and those of the recent revivalists; (2) the revivalist educational philosophy; (3) Hindu women's status; and (4) the Muslim factor in culture, to conclude that the revivalist cultural policies and programs did not reach a crystallized form.

During the 1980s and 1990s, the revivalists, who wished to return the country to ancient Hindu social norms and religious values, gained strength and public support by their advocacy of stronger policies toward Kashmir, their demand for the destruction of the Ayodhya mosque and their call for the Uniform Civil Code. The BJP and the VHP saw in the Ayodhya conflict an opportunity to mobilize Hindus across the caste spectrum, especially those at the bottom of the caste hierarchy. In the early 1980s, the publicized conversion of a few hundred *Dalits* (untouchables, 160 million in 2001) to Islam in the Tamil Nadu state unleashed a Hindu campaign against further losses from the faith. In addition, the eclipse of the old socialist Congress Party at the state and national levels as well as economic reforms for globalization created tensions that were effectively exploited by all revivalist parties. Even the reconstituted and moderately tolerant reformist group, "Arya Samaj" (The Society of the Aryans), which was not supportive of the extreme revivalist ideals, recently declared, "The manifest destiny of western rationalism has been to supplement non-western cultures."[4] The Ram Rajya Parishad (RRP), essentially a regional party with its stronghold in Madhya Pradesh and Rajasthan, evoked in the popular mind the image of a golden age characterized by prosperity and social justice. Corruption of the society in the early 1990s occupied a fundamental place in the language of the Shiv Sena group in Madhya Pradesh and "everything" was thought by revivalists to be "adulterated." Grievances characterized the discourse of the Shiv Sena. The *Shiv Sainiks* spoke thus of "guts" and "blood," and of all social regressions. They wished to return to the ancient state of perceived relative peace and social harmony for permanent relief.[5] These revivalist views did not, of course, refer to specific historical events; they were purely ideological representations and as such were situated in the future. Culture, to the revivalists, meant not only inner or spiritual development against external developments, but also human needs that became associated with religion, language, family, and the state.

Research of the Western orientalists confirmed the revivalists' faith in the past achievements of Hindu civilization and culture. The nostalgic view of the orientalists was nurtured by generations of Hindu nationalists.[6] From the confrontation between two value systems, oriental and occidental, there arose the urge to define India's normative needs from within India's cultural repertoire. In a way, this was an attempt to seek answers to India's many problems in the broader context of religio-cultural revival. Basing their defense on a consensual view of traditional society, revivalists called for "Bharatiya Sanskriti and Maryada" (Hindu culture and pride).[7] Pandit Deendayal Upadhyaya was general secretary of the Jana Sangh and the formulator of "Integral Humanism" (1965). "Integral Humanism" was a cornerstone of socioeconomic reorganization on the basis of the Hindu ideal of *dharma* (virtue). Like Mahatma Gandhi, Deendayal Upadhyaya believed that national development must be consonant with its cultural traditions. One element of *dharma* was the adjustment of "individuals for a harmonious corporate existence."[8] Thus Hindu culture, with its core belief in Vedic virtues, as interpreted by the revivalist scholars and activists, remained the projected foundation of the Indian identity.

However, it was not a unified call from all revivalist parties. Cultural approaches were conflicting at times. Whereas the RSS called for a return to the "ancient traditions of the race," a corporate social organization, and a "cult of leadership," the pragmatic BJP leadership virtually accepted the norms of a liberal democracy. The RSS itself is now an enormous umbrella organization with many facets of cultural work, some of which do not receive the attention of the party's hierarchy.[9] The VHP was specifically set up in 1964 to forge a corporate Hindu identity to unite all Hindu sects in opposition to Islam. In contrast, the Jana Sangh had a broad and alternative secular culture with declared economic programs. The Shiv Sena's cultural project to restore a pristine rural setting in Bombay city in the mid-1990s was deeply political, and culture was used as a political tool. It extended the reach of politics to every sphere of society. Revivalist programs and cultural strategies greatly differed from each other's designs.

Culture as an Integrating Force

Culture is a dynamic variable, enormously potent and influential. When it is articulated in a manner aimed at achieving an objective, it releases the dormant energies of a community (religious group). It is thus comparable to energy and power, and has similar place vis-à-vis political programs.[10] The revivalists came to realize anew that the viability of the state and the political economy was necessarily dependent on moral-cultural assumptions and that the erosion of the moral-cultural consensus was of a serious magnitude.

The revivalist paradigm accords well with the proposition of Robert Nisbet (1953), a conservative American sociologist, who argues that the "artificial" power of the state and the natural authority of communities had been at odds.

Whereas the power of the state tended to be coercive and external, the authority of communities was internal in the sense that those following it believed in its legitimacy. Nisbet's "quest for community" was based on the premises that (a) the modern preoccupation with community was a manifestation of the decline of natural communities; (b) natural communities consisted of family, religious association, and local community; and (c) modern communities were created by the Western political state.[11] Although Nisbet was concerned with Western situations, his ideas had some similarities with the projects of a Hindu state. The revivalist forces seemed to argue that the projects of social reconstruction designed by social and political leaders for execution had simply done more harm than good.[12]

In India, the problem remained in the determination of the nature of the codes that would work for national unity, and historical investigations in this respect had been wide and unconvincing. Some historians argue that the national identity in India dissociated from the Aryan race and gravitated toward a common cultural purpose in which religion would play a pivotal role. W. Halbfass and R. Thapar are on the right track when they argue that traditionally, culture, not race, produced exclusion of communities in India.[13] The subaltern studies, on the other hand, submit that Hindu nationalism as a whole was based on a modern rationalist idea and Hindu reasoning was "entirely secular." Differing with what they called the "elite historiography" on India, the subaltern group, led by Ranajit Guha, Dipesh Chakravarty, Gyanendra Pandey, and Partha Chatterjee, call into question all three of the theoretical perspectives—modernization-secularization theory, Orientalist theory, and world-system theory because these theories pertain to a small segment of Indian social reality. The subaltern studies often focus on microscopic and regional issues to check "religious consciousness" that "informs political actions."[14] Unlike the Marxists and secularists, Ranajit Gupta and his subaltern historians resisted the analysis that sees religion simply as a displaced manifestation of human relationships.[15] This group has not made much progress in its treatment of religious consciousness, but it has highlighted the singular importance of the religious perspective in state formation.[16]

The revivalist literature has found a sympathetic analysis in Oswald Spengler, a spiritual reactionary. Spengler, in trying to define German identity, argues that the German nation was "neither linguistic nor political nor biological, but spiritual," and spirituality was the basis of German unity. Thus a revivalist scholar argues that the spiritual element was "more than religious," and by mystifying spiritual values, he devalues the other components of identity and unity.[17] The Hindu historians interpreted the ancient kingdom of Rama and the medieval regimes of the Rajputs and Shivaji as just and unified societies based on religious-social ethics. In this view, culture was the cementing force. However, Hindu histories virtually ignored the role of nonreligious elements in state building. The problem of the cultural interpretation of the orientalists such as Louis Dumont is that his exposition of hierarchy was, in his own words, "purely a matter of religious values."[18] His cultural connotation did not recognize other elements, including *artha* (power and gain), that were significant in keeping positive social relationships.

Benedict Anderson, a critic of Hindu hierarchical social order, argues that the revivalist cultural imagination was self-evident but cautions that it should not be read to mean false.[19] The revivalist concept of cohesion through culture was not false but misleading. Their central theme was that, instead of moving away from Hinduism, which was the source of India's culture, a "true nationalist" (revivalist) should explicitly ground politics in religion, not in laws and institutions. It is this religious idea known as *Hindutva* that remained political, and this political approach to religion and culture created confusion. The "New Religious Politics" (NRP) paradigm is perhaps an appropriate description of the nature of the cultural program of the *Hindutva* forces. Nikki R. Keddie of U.C.L.A. differentiates between religious nationalism (directed primarily against other religious communities) and conservative religious politics (directed primarily against internal enemies) and concludes that current Indian revivalism is "not based on monotheist scripturalism but on religious politics, conservatism, and populism."[20] The cultural thrust was indeed a populist movement that aimed at gaining political power in order to transform the state on the basis of the revivalist religio-political program.

The existing scholarly interpretations about the relevance of religio-cultural (non-secular) approaches have two opposing perceptions. One group of social scientists and historians have argued that secularism is essential for fostering ties between people of different communities in India. "It seems to be the most effective cementing force in this context."[21] Nasim Ansari of the G. B. Pant Institute in Allahabad in India argues that "a secular policy to contain excessive proliferation of places of worship is of utmost importance in a multi-religious society like India."[22] The other school of thought tends to support the significant role of religion-based culture in community building. Ashis Nandy of Nehru University in Delhi doubts the tenability of the secular ideology for tolerant political life.[23] Tapan Raychaudhuri of Oxford University is nearer the truth when he writes that the Westernized elites in India "refuse to acknowledge the centrality of religious values in the lives of our masses."[24] T. N. Madan, a noted social analyst and historian, likewise, applies his criticism to secularism, not just that strand of secularism, which does not tolerate religion. He adds that the hostility of secularism toward religion seems futile because religion is an integral part of life in India.[25] While admitting that both schools of ideas fail to do justice to the process of nation building, it may be legitimately argued that any vigorous antireligious stance disturbs many Indians. Benedict Anderson sees many other elements, such as languages, as equally important. He argues that those in the "last wave" of nationalisms have a larger array of tools with which to forge the imagined community.[26] However, the religion based cultural approach to nation building and cohesive life may not be helpful because too much emphasis on religion easily evokes strong counterarguments.

The pertinent question is: why were the defenders of the Hindu state so preoccupied with cultural values as the most important elements in maintaining cohesion in the social fabric as well as a foundational pillar of the projected state?

First, in their organicist (Deendayal Upadhyaya's "integral humanism") worldview, the revivalists elevated community over individuals; here the social order was built around the notion of human beings divided into fundamentally unequal castes. The worldview was based on the assumption of the homogeneity of the Hindu community, or at least the assumption that a general Hindu communal identity or mobilization would override intracommunity differences. This vision, in effect, was framed by the "Great Traditions" of Brahmanical and classical Hinduism (Vedas and Sanskritic texts), supposed to have the most enduring values. These traditions, obviously, ignored the popular "Little Traditions" that were supported by smaller gods and goddesses, village deities, regional rituals, and intense personal faiths.

Second, by the time India attained independence in 1947, the Brahmanical paradigm of social integration through the *"varna"* (caste) ideology lost its force. The integrative principle remained hierarchical, legitimizing social inequality. V. S. Naipaul's little mutinies in several regions among peasants and workers and a "national idea" in favor of centripetal forces were surfacing in the 1960s and 1970s at the same time. As disintegrating tendencies in Assam, Kashmir, the Punjab, and among the social lower castes and economic lower middle classes deepened, a sense of Pan-Indian nationalism was also growing. Accounts of India, especially the journalistic ones, mostly concentrated on the disintegrative tendencies. The Hindu revivalists, on the contrary, took up national stewardship and began to think in terms of national integration by means of cultural uniformity. A nation, in this view, was not just a cultural community; rather, it was a sovereign cultural community. The *Hindu Rashtra* (Hindu state) model moved from a religious versus cultural issue to an understanding of Hindu culture as Indian culture in national identity.[27] But this approach proved to be a cultural resurgence transforming into a "cultural aggrandizement," in the words of Chetan Bhatt, an Indian social scientist in Britain, because the revivalist evaluation unduly demonstrated the ancient culture to be the superlative one "in its intellect, philosophy, mysticism, science, humanity, knowledge, arts . . . and so on."[28] Also, in advancing their program for change through culture, the revivalists came in conflict directly not only with the agents of Westernization but also with other religious groups that had alternative or competing visions of the good society based on their perceptions of reality.

Third, the revivalists assumed that the historical course of society was "contingent" and hence could be created and changed by a set of religious people indoctrinated with particular undefined cultural values. It was believed that institutional spirituality could be an effective form to organizing consent among various groups within a particular religion.[29] Vinayak Damodhar Savarkar of the

Hindu Mahasabha wrote in the 1920s, "The concept of *Hindu Rashtra* is essentially cultural whereas the Congress and their like believe in a purely territorial-cum-political concept of a nation." But in defining the nation, he often moved from the territorial to the religious to the cultural planes to cover all the grounds he wished to see covered."[30] The Jana Sangh party twisted the concept of nationalism to include a new concept based on consciousness. The party recognized freedom of worship but was opposed to the practice of asking for special rights based on religion.[31] The implicit idea was that, once consciousness on the basis of one culture was accepted, religious discord would eventually disappear. In this view, the Congress party's communal considerations for the majority and minority were irrelevant.

Last, the revivalists argued that an integrated community based on some selected Hindu beliefs alone could form a sound basis for a state. Two foremost revivalists ideologues, Deendayal Upadhyaya and D. B. Thengadi, argued that the contract theory (Rousseau's General Will) could be applied to the state, but not to nation. In this perspective a nation was self-born and the state was only an institution. While European state building involved conflicts among cultural groups for supremacy, the Indian empires, according to the revivalist concept, were characterized by a kind of cultural syncretism that included a doctrine of nonantagonistic strata whose laws and customs preceded the state and were protected by good kings. However, as Indologists Rudolph and Rudolph cogently argue, the Hindu concept of *dharmasastras* (religious literally texts) emphasized compartmentalization of diversity rather than "homogenization."[32] There were two fallacies in the revivalist views. First, the revivalists were unaware that classical Hinduism spanned the spectrum from atheism to the crudest forms of animism. Second, the state remained a secular agency capable of pluralism in both political and sociocultural life. While socialism had been discarded, secularism tarnished, and nonviolence exploded, democratic practices remained firmly entrenched. New ideologies and unstable governments had only increased the popularity of democratic methods. The much-used slogan, "unity in the midst of diversity," remained valid.

(A) Differences between Early Reformist Cultural Policies and those of the Latter-Day Revivalists

Earlier reform movements and Hindu socio-political associations (1880–1912) endowed the independence struggle with strong spiritual and cultural undertones. The "Aryan Movement" of the *Arya Samaj* in the Punjab drew inspiration from the Pan-Indian enthusiasms of Max Muller, Oxford professor of Sanskrit. Theosophists in Calcutta, Bombay, and Pune felt the need of emphasizing moral norms and eradicating evils of caste-based society. Social reformers demanded an end to child marriages, although religious revivalists then resented any interference with existing customs. Contemporary revivalists subscribed to some of these elements. There were some similarities between the cultural ideas and programs of the Hindu reformist movements of the nineteenth and early twentieth centuries and those of the contemporary revivalists. In fact, both spread religious orthodoxy where heterodoxy had earlier prevailed. The historian Ashutosh Varshney argues that there had been a religious nationalist ideology (like the contemporary revivalism ideology) under which Hindu's perceived India to be a Hindu nation-state.[33] Neither the earlier reformists nor the latter-day Hindu activists admitted that they were leading a fundamentalist movement. Both the earlier and contemporary nationalist movements belonging to the main stream of Hinduism called for a sort of Hindu cultural renaissance in order to find the basis for a purified as well as unified nation. However, differences between the cultural policies of the two Hindu movements were considerable.

First, earlier socioreligious reformists, such as Raja Ram Mohan Ray (1772–1833), Keshav Chandra Sen (1838–1884), Swami Vivekananda (1863–1902), B. G. Tilak (1856–1920), and Gopal Krishna Gokhale (1866–1915), did not construct a notion of a religiously Hindu nation and had no globalized stance against internal "others." By restoring the self-confidence of Hindus in their religion and religious culture and quickening their sense of patriotism, Vivekananda combined politics with ethical values. The early social reformers did, however, ground Hindu spirituality in a systematic interpretation of the *Vedanta* (End of the Vedas) to transform Hindu culture in its encounter with Western materialistic culture.[34]

By contrast, since the 1930s revivalists such as Vinayak Damodar Savarkar, Deendayal Upadhyaya, Lal K. Advani, and Bal Thackray produced their own religious symbols with the intention to exclude other cultures. In Tamil Nadu, mostly women ran the Jan Kalyan movement. Later known as the Jan Kalyan political party, it articulated key ritual symbols to define Hindu culture. The women used "kunkumam," a red powder used on the head, to create a group identity. The movement's founder, Sri Jayendra Saraswati, made opportunities for the deployment of various key Hindu symbols, devotional music, and rituals to identify the caste-based Smarta community with the more extensive community of the nation. By virtue of their ownership of key elements of the cultural traditions that allegedly defined India, Smaratas as a community were supposedly "legitimate" cultural "representatives of the nation."[35]

The people's frustration over unemployment, severe political violence, and economic difficulties sought a new orientation in public policy. International fundamentalism, especially Islamic militancy, had aroused fear. Hindu revivalists began to use various visible symbols to defensively interpret Hindu culture as the ethical foundation for homogenous society. They expressed awareness through rituals and symbols, *pujas* (worship), and *yatras* (massive religious processions). Thousands of Hindus were attracted to cultural symbols to attain Indian unity (Hindu unity).[36] Even the supposedly godless cadre of Dravida Munnetra Kazagam (DMK), united to organize rituals such as the three *rathams* named *shakti, gynam,* and *depth* (power and knowledge) in Tamil Nadu. Leaving aside communism, the DMK's progressive federation in Madras was the only rationalistic philosophy in India, and unlike communism, it was of indigenous origin.

The Vishwa Hindu Parishad (World Hindu Council or VHP) was strongly allied with the BJP during the Ayodhya controversy. The VHP and other cultural groups made strategic use of selected sacred elements in Hindu culture— *trisul*, Rama, and chariot—for Hindu votes. Within the confines of the mass psyche, the revivalists embarked upon a zealous unification by means of symbols. *Harijan*, tribal people, as well as the lower-caste Hindus, who had strayed into other religions, were urged to reenter Hinduism. *Trisual*-wielding Shiv Senas, banding into self-defense groups, demanded an end of special privileges enjoyed by the religious minorities.[37] The Shiv Sena (King Shivaji's soldiers) Party combined religious militancy with regionalism. This new spirit arose from Mrs. Gandhi's "penchant," particularly in the last years of her rule, to woo Hindu society for purposes of political power. This brought a possibly dormant and disaggregated Hindu phenomenon out into the open.[38] In short, whereas earlier reformers/revivalists such as B. G. Tilak of Bombay and B. C. Pal of Bengal combined politics with ethical values, recent revivalists invented new symbols for popular appeal and political success. Equating Indian unity with Hindu cultural symbols—a logical but not a valid equation with large Muslim, Sikh, and Christian components—the revivalist parties urged the promotion of Hinduness in all aspects of national life for a cultural uniformity. This reinforced the forces of "Hindu nationalism" rather than Indian nationalism.

Second, unlike the earlier Brahmo Samaj (1828), the Arya Samaj (1875), and the Deccan Education Society (1880s), Hindu cultural groups such as the VHP became accumulative rather than reformist. Social reforms received less priority. The VHP became the primary carrier of Hindu values in the 1980s because the Rashtriya Swayamsevak Sangh (RSS), the parent body of several Hindu parties, decided to make it the main means of action after it had distanced itself from the Bharatiya Janata Party (Indian Peoples Party or BJP), which appeared to be more moderate. The VHP assembled items drawn from many sources and local traditions and then articulated these values by effective repetition and cumulative imagery,[39] and the party wished to spread Hindu values to make them relevant to the politically charged majority.[40] The secular state was forced to succumb to the pressure of the social authority of Hindu revivalism.

Third, unlike the earlier reformers, contemporary revivalists wanted the state apparatus to reflect Hinduism. They did not incorporate religious pluralism into their concept of secularism, as "secular politicians in India do today."[41] Madhav Sadashiv Golwalkar (1906–1973), an ascetic ex-school teacher and a former general secretary of the RSS, declared, "Political power shall only reflect the radiance of culture, integrity and power of the organized society . . . just as the moon reflects the radiance of the sun." He did not believe in altering the nature of the state in order to change the character of society but certainly hoped to cast the society as between a Hindu state and nation and predicted that eventually the distinction between the state and the society would disappear altogether with the assimilation of divergent cultures.[42]

Fourth, earlier reformists were pacifistic in their advocacy of the restoration of ancient Hindu culture and civilization. They desired to preserve some of the priceless legacies of Hindu culture by means of "Indological Orientalism," claiming that India's inherent cultural superiority would act as a spiritual corrective or supplement to a materialistic, overly rational, and harmful Western world.[43]

As opposed to this approach, contemporary revivalists became xenophobic against any outside religio-cultural influence. During the 1950s and 1960s, the Jana Sangh Party insisted that historically derived Hinduism had been a cultural force and that that force could achieve the ultimate ideal of "Hindu Sangathan" (unity). B. D. Graham argues that the ethical assumptions underlying this doctrine were activist because the Jana Sangh doctrine sharply conflicted with the quietist and devotional aspects of the *bhakti* (devotional religion) tradition. According to the *bhakti* movement, influenced by the Hindu-Muslim syncretic faith of Sufism, believers conceived of themselves as individuals involved in a personal relation to a particular form of divinity. As against this tradition, a contemporary revivalist was not a synthesizer but a creator of new values. More recently, exposed to the threats of the spread of Islam (12 percent), Christianity (2.4 percent), and Buddhism (0.7 percent), the VHP and the RSS developed a strong perception of vulnerability and as such projected a return to the past by borrowing from the "aggressors" (other religious groups) the aggressive cultural characteristics to which they ascribed their force. Swami Chinmayananda, the Bombay VHP leader, said, "If we do not organize ourselves, there will be no integration. . . . If we are not integrated despite the 82 percent of the population . . . our voices will never be heard."[44] Even the spread of neo-Buddhist influences among the schedule castes was the object of much cultural resentment.[45] The Bajrang Dal (VHP's violent youth wing), with Hanuman of King Rama's head as its religious symbol, resorted to cultural vandalism in October 1996 and destroyed works of the celebrated painter, Maqbool Fida Husain. In addition, they tore down priceless tapestries and paintings by artists on exhibition at an Ahmedabad art gallery.[46] In Varanasi, a Hindu holy city, the VHP members vandalized sets of Indo-Canadian filmmaker Deepa Mehta's new film, "Water," arguing that it degraded Indian culture. The film depicts the plight of widows abandoned by their families, who lived miserable lives in Varanasi and were at times forced into prostitution.[47]

In the same vein, contemporary revivalists regarded Gandhian nonviolence as an example of cultural impotence.[48] Notions of masculinity and Hinduism intertwined in the political identity of the Shiv Sena. Sikata Banerjee, a Bengali scholar, argues that masculinity should not automatically be associated with violence. However, she adds that over the past twenty-five years, scholars have demonstrated cultural links between masculinity and violence in the Euro-American tradition. Banerjee, in analyzing the nature of Shiv Sena's cultural nationalism, concludes that masculine Hinduism encompassed ideas of militarism linked to notions of manhood that made violence a likely consequence.[49] The paradigm, "we" versus "others," became a source of cultural emancipation. Thus, one of the textbooks, prepared by the Jana Sangh Party that ruled the Delhi Administration, narrated a story entitled *shashi balak* (courageous Hindu boy). In the story, King Shivaji of the Maratha people killed a Muslim when the Muslim was taking a cow to the slaughterhouse. This story of the violation of a Hindu cultural norm (killing a cow) was illustrated with a graphic sketch to good effect.[50] Violent means and practices were thus devised to encourage national pride and more effectively resist the cultural "offensive from outside." The clear and present danger approach demanded a staunch identification with the group, an evocation of group loyalty and assertiveness that showed no respect to toleration.

The cultural emancipators adopted a European cultural technique for the society's purification. The RSS ideologue, K. C. Sudershan, admitted that a tempered acceptance of civil "disorder" was inevitable and as such discipline had to be introduced. The technique of the Boy Scouts, founded in 1908, by General Baden-Powell with its emphasis on quasi-military discipline as the foundation for a life of service to the nation, was thought to be effective. The earlier nationalists condemned the movement as a thinly disguised prop of British imperialism. In contrast, the revivalist leaders in the RSS such as Keshav Baliram Hedgewar, the founder of the RSS, the core driving force of Hindu revivalism, took to the idea of military style disciplinary exercises as helpful in reawakening of the service spirit. The martial art spirit found a receptive audience when it was given political expression in the discourse of modern Indian politics.[51] Perhaps this Hindu violence for a Hindu nation was a modern manifestation of the "psychic" polarity between disciplined control and violent energy long recognized in Hindu religious culture.[52] Thus, Sudhir Kakar, a psychoanalyst, correctly argues that the search for cultural identity "is an unconscious human acquirement which becomes consciously salient" only when there was a perceived threat to its integrity. Violence was the result.[53]

Fifth, the nineteenth-century reformers had no concept of leadership in the sense of its manifest dictatorial role in the party. The contemporary revivalists accepted the destined role of their sociopolitical leaders as moral guides. The parties calculated that culture could be conveniently imparted through the agency of a mystic leader. For example, the leadership within the RSS exercised power by systematically employing the instruments of discipline, training, and surveillance. Although both Hedgewar and Golwalkar denied the relevance of a "leader," in essence the supreme guides were supreme in imparting values.[54] Golwalkar as the second "supreme leader" was less political than Hedgewar but gave the RSS a systematic cultural ideology that was followed by cultural activists.[55] Although Golwalkar held considerable discussions in the executive council, only he could make pronouncements. According to an insider, "he is an absolute dictator."[56] The Shiv Sena Party, which started as a nativist party in Bombay in the 1960s, often engaged in spectacular agitational campaigns for Hinduness (*Hindutva*) in accordance with the whims of its leader, Bal Thackray, a former journalist. Shiv Sena's ideology was largely produced and articulated by the "supremo," Thackray, whose rhetorical style, invocation of the martial spirit of the Marathas, and use of direct language with religious intonation demanded and obtained absolute loyalty from his party members.[57]

Sixth, earlier reformers and revivalists in the nineteenth century had accepted some liberal principles of the modernizing West. The Poona "Sarvajanik Sabha" (All People's Association) founded by a Chtipavan Brahman, Mahadev Govind Ranade (1842–1901), sought to borrow the self-governing ideals that were embodied in British society, literature, and law. This essentially emulative approach made Poona the foremost city in India in revolutionary cultural nationalism. Bombay's "Prathana Samaj" (Prayer Society), western India's version of Calcutta's "Brahmo Samaj," called for Western education and legal reforms. It also pleaded for the amelioration of the plight of Hindu widows through Western education.[58] In fact, older revivalism, as expressed by Swami Vivekananda, Annie Besant (1847–1933) of the Theosophical Society of India, and others, did not necessarily emulate bygone life styles but rather made a conscious attempt to use chosen elements of the past for functions that were largely secular and certainly futuristic. They considered the *shastras* (ancient religious rules and codes) amenable to progressive changes.[59] Dayanand Saraswati's (Arya Samaj) concept of the *Vedas*, his unorthodox interpretation of the *Samhitas* (religious texts), his theory of creation and of a universal golden age in pre-*Mahabharata* times, were all ideological tools for denouncing evil social customs. Indeed, Dayanand denied the validity of *jati* (caste) divisions and considered the *varnas* (caste division) a secular division of labor.[60]

In contrast, by upholding the *jati* (caste) system, revivalists kept the "outcastes" in a continuous inferior status. The leadership of the new movement upheld patriarchal norms and the "varna" caste system, going to the extent of beheading a *sudra* (untouchable) for practicing austerities and aspiring to heaven.[61] The revivalists noted that King Rama killed a pious non-Aryan King Sambuk for his crime of reading the Vedas, forbidden to *Sudras* (untouchables).[62] Ideologically, the BJP was against the caste system, a high-low status differentiation based on birth. Like the RSS, the party ignored caste differentiations. Hindu unity, the BJP argued, would wipe out differentiations based on birth. The BJP's contention was that (a) the upper class was not responsible for degrading the condition of the backward and lower castes, (b) the lower castes could improve their position by education and the inculcation of "good" values and behavior, and (c) the caste conflicts were made mainly by Congress for the purpose of electoral gains. In this view the differences were political and as such artificial.[63] With a little variation, the RSS leader Dattopant Thengadi argued that caste exploitation was the fault of the Brahmins, not of Hindu religion.[64] The Brahmins were the authors of authoritative scriptures, which formed the elements of what was sometimes called codified Hinduism.

Most revivalist leaders, however, accepted the reality of the caste system. This reality caused friction in contemporary society. Untouchable communities, which formed 20 percent of the population, formed in the early 1970s the "Dalit Panthers" (oppressed panthers). It was organized by a group of Buddhist converts from the Untouchables—poets, writers, and public figures—who launched a Gandhi-style civil disobedience in western India. The Dalit's rejection of Hinduism clearly showed how the element in the Hindu mélange, Brahmanism, became identified with Hinduism as a whole, and therefore, why groups like the Dalits rejected it.[65] The lower caste and tribes in India, being economically and socially oppressed and exploited, resorted to self-expression through other forms of religious identity. Troubled by the complex of "Brahamanisation," a lower-caste Hindu author, who has become critical of Brahmanical Hinduism, writes, *Why I am Not a Hindu*. The author Kancha Ilaiah argues that it was incorrect to assume that "everyone in India who is not a Muslim, a Christian, or a Sikh is a Hindu." He adds that traditionally the lower-caste people were considered outsiders in Brahmanic Hinduism. The revivalists, he justifiably concludes, advocated a "saffron-tilak" (religious mark on forehead) Hindu culture that demonstrated the upper-caste-class dominance. Here Brahmanisation meant the inclusion of lower castes into the *Hindutva* fold. To Ilaiah, *Hindutva* was more than communal; it was "casteist" as well.[66]

Seventh, earlier revivalists never concentrated on Rama as the most important image in restoring past glories. By contrast, during the last decade the votaries of Hinduness ideology floated a new model for cultural integration, that of "Rama-Bhakti" (devotion to Rama), which became a kind of litmus test for one's loyalty to the nation. Here, Rama became the founder of a new political institution, "chakravartin" (world-conqueror-ruler) who, after his diplomatic and martial successes in the south, came to Ayodhya to create a Hindu nation. The 1993 controversial exhibition, "Hum Sab Ayodhya" (We are all Ayodhya), at Faizabad in Uttar Pradesh was consciously designed to project a holistic vision of Ayodhya city (birthplace of Rama) through the ages. The Safdar Hashmi Memorial Trust (SAHMAT), a secular group linked with the communists, who preferred to demonstrate secularism in art, organized the exhibition. Since diverse visions and perceptions of Indian history were projected, the BJP instigated a campaign against an authentic picture of Rama and his wife Sita as siblings. Members of the VHP and Bajrang Dal disrupted the exhibition on August 12, 1993. Against the intention of the SAHMAT, *Hindutva* editorials became critical of the exhibition. An excerpt from an editorial in *The Tribune* was revealing in this connection. The editorial wrote, "Culture is a common heritage. Cultural and artistic movements are national-regional. That is why 'Hum Sab Ayodhya' is an eloquent expression. Rama is in all; all are in Rama. Ayodhya is in all of us and we are in Ayodhya." In this statement, a disturbing equation was declared: culture, nation, and Rama—all were one. In a communalized context, the Bajrang Dal and VHP sacrificed secularism. The exhibition became a platform for Hindu politics.[67] Several pro-Hinduness newspaper editorials veered toward a BJP endorsement of "Sri Rama." The historian Geeta Kapur argues that the exhibition was so "transparently secular" that the revivalists' attacks proved to be simply political, and that the Rama devotion was used for election purposes in Uttar Pradesh.[68] Here Rama was a cultural ("national") and not simply religious hero. "They alone are Indians who recognize the greatness of Rama." The message of nationalism and of religion assumed a particular importance during the propaganda generated in Ayodhya in the late 1980s.[69] It seems improbable that a heroic tale of love (king and queen), loss (loss of Sita), and recovery (recovery of Sita after the defeat of the demon King Ravana) from the classical past should be invoked to empower and give substance to the politics of the present. It proved to be the utopian impulses of social harmony "resonating in the symbol" of Rama, and as such led to homicidal ends in the 1990s (Ayodhya's religio-political crisis).[70]

The BJP and the VHP argued that India's vast spiritual, psychic in modern parlance, energies, largely dormant for centuries could be tapped by the symbol of Rama, as was evident in the 1920s when Gandhi moved millions by his talk of *Ramaraja*. To Gandhi, Rama stood for social justice. *Ramarajya,* Gandhi maintained, was a divine *raj*, the kingdom of God, and an ideal state where rulers looked after the welfare of all, disregarding any social, economic, religious, and political distinction. An ideal visionary for the BJP, Gandhi never desired a Hindu state. But in the revivalist discourse Rama was a victor defeating Ravana (demon king), the evil spirit in the south. "Gandhism both legitimized this thrust [religious thrust] and ensured that it would not take the extreme form of political demand for a Hindu state." In contrast, recent defenders of the Rama cult asked for a Hindu-dominated political state in which non-Hindus would not have any significant role.

Several observations may be made now. (A) Contemporary revivalists gave up the genuine social efforts of the earlier Hindu reformers. Calcutta's *Brahma Samaj* (Divine Society, 1828) desired to reform Hindusim by ridding it of caste and discrimination against women in public life. In contrast, the contemporary movements put emphasis on political awakening because of their immediate interest in controlling the government without concentrating on social work. (B) Hinduism was a religion that prided itself on its passivism, and on its ethic of an expansive love extended even to enemies (the whole world is friendly, a basic concept). The current revivalists embraced coercion as soon as the state enabled them. (C) More importantly, the attempt to bring all Hindus under one cultural umbrella had already sparked a controversy. Following B. R. Ambedkar, their charismatic leader, the lower castes, as well as many liberal and educated Hindus, defended the traditional-modern synthesis that Nehru formulated an Indian liberal democracy[71] catering to the social/economic needs of the general populace.

Demonstrations of differences do not allow us to make a legitimate statement that earlier reform movements were by all means more conducive to the growth of unified national identity. They made no serious attempts at collaboration between religious communities. Yet it is safe to admit that the contemporary revivalists brought forward Hindu beliefs and symbols as the focus in creating a national identity. Of course, the leading party, the BJP, despite many faults, remained committed to transform India into a liberal, modern, industrial, and military power with a united nation and a disciplined workforce. Nevertheless, the revivalist educational philosophy offered a unified platform.

(B) Revivalist Educational Philosophy and Programs

The revivalist educational orientation rejected the contemporary trend toward professional preparedness. They had no specific goals in favor of achievement-oriented tasks and thus totally disregarded the necessity for recognizing the existence of the specific needs themselves.[72] Philosophically, the revivalist parties had two broad goals.

First, Western-style educational setup and objectives were ignored. The first major thinker to grapple with the problem of modernity was Hegel; Hegel defined modernity, with a strong emphasis on individualism, as not having to seek legitimacy from the past. Hindu revivalists rejected his postulate on individualism because in their eyes the individualistic West had already suffered its debilitating consequences with respect to moral values. It was argued that before modernization in education took place, India had been capable of living off its own intellectual, educational, and economic resources.[73] Revivalists, who by the mid-1980s had won political respectability, envisioned a community opposed to a modern individualistic society. G. M. Jagtiani, a Bombay author, advises, "Hinduism should not divide one Hindu from the other Hindu."[74] This community needed to be constantly rejuvenated through religious education in order to prevent its dissolution at the cruel hands of modernizing forces.[75] Western "development education" for secular knowledge and individual enterprise appeared to be of little use in national unity.[76]

Second, English education incurred the wrath of the defenders of faith. The cultural ideology was not geared toward the creation of the modernist "civil society," nor was it intended to restore indigenous village schools. When the pro-*Hindutva* card lost its appeal in the elections in Bombay after the mid-1990s, Shiv Sena activists, for example, vandalized English billboards to make a statement against English, a colonial legacy, and for a national language, Marathi.[77]

This "national education" would displace "English education" (Lord Macaulay's educated clerk concept) and promote instead Hindu identity. Macaulay, a British administrator and essayist, created a certain mind-set in the Indian society that favored the Western model of education and created an educated elite class to serve the colonial administration. Indian educational reformers, especially Calcutta intellectuals, who were sympathetic to European education, faced new assumptions: that the patterns of reform meant Westernization, and that oriental civilizations were static and worthless. The educated elite then confronted a crisis of identity.[78] Gandhi's "Nai Talim" (New Education), a kind of constructive work program, was different from both Macaulay's model and the revivalist scheme. While Gandhi emphasized primary education with "bread labor," the contemporary revivalists sought moral education through the memorization of facts of the Hindu period, although the memorization of facts and imitating of great characters did nothing for critical thinking and analytical learning.[79] Besides these two general goals, they had some specific designs in education.

Hindu Moral Education

The cultural approach in formal education was not only to compete with Indian mainstream secular education, but also to subvert it from within. During the immediate postindependence era, revivalists as reformists sought to introduce religious teachings in schools in addition to secular courses of study. The Hindu Mahasabha president, Dr. Shyama Prasad Mookherjee of Bengal, an eloquent speaker, and a religious moderate, in his presidential address in Kanpur in December 1952, called for a "clear Hindu orientation in education." A former vice-chancellor of Calcutta University and a leading figure in the revivalist movement to impose Hindu ideology upon education spoke for both the Hindu Mahasabha and the Jana Sangh; Mookherjee gave an early orientation toward revived Sanskrit study as well as ancient Hindu values. He argued for "knowledge about *Upanishads, Bhagavat Gita, Ramayana* and *Mahabharata*," which would bring a "common cultural stream," a base for the foundation of the Hindu community.[80] The Hindu Mahasabha Party itself argued that students should be taught about the Indian contribution to the advancement of world civilization. The role of "great saints" in this respect should be emphasized[81] in order to change the features of Indian culture. There was, of course, no direct attack on the existing educational system.

By early 1980, the Jana Sangh and the RSS leaders began to argue that the pursuit of power without the proper Hindu ideology resulted in a high tolerance of corruption, inefficiency, and social conflict.[82] Moral education was the solution. The leaders argued that it was one thing, for instance, to know that rivers and mountains existed; and a much higher thing to know the spiritual causes, which had determined the distribution of land and water on the face of the earth. Like the Chinese Daoists, the revivalists believed that knowledge of all beings was to be attained mystically by intuition and spiritual illumination, rather than by scholarship and rationality. However, whereas Daoism protested against authoritarianism and the constructions of rituals, Hindu revivalism incorporated Brahmanical authority into the knowledge system.

The move toward the primacy of moral education was not new. Earlier in 1902, "The Dawn Society" was established with the specific aim of supplementing college education to compensate for its deficiency in "moral training," a euphemism for knowledge about religion and Hindu cultural traditions.[83] Later, the RSS's chief ideologue, M. S. Golwalkar, demanded purity of character through teachings in moral education for "national glory."[84] The educational goal was to control desires. "Timeless cultural essences" could be relived by controlling one's desires and libido.[85] Satya Pal Gulati, secretary of *Samrath Shiksha Samiti* in New Delhi, declared recently "education is not expected to merely impart information and culture but to build up character and personality."[86]

To build one's moral character, "Gurukuls" (teacher's abodes/schools) were planned in accordance with the Brahmanic traditions. Deendayal Upadhaya (Jana Sangh) and D. B. Thengadi (RSS) argued that in the *Gurukul*, Hindu primary education had well been imparted.[87] The spiritual East and the materialist West were innately different and this idea should be indoctrinated early in life.[88] Prime Minister Rajiv Gandhi, a former student at Imperial College in London, had formulated a comprehensive educational policy, popularly known as the "1986 policy," which provided more emphasis on scientific and technical education. During the 1997 elections, revivalist leaders attacked this policy. The BJP asked for "Indianising and spiritualizing school education," and called for compulsory Sanskrit teaching up to the secondary level. This new policy was supported not only in four Hindi belt states but also in Andhra Pradesh and the Punjab, both of which were ruled by BJP allies. In Rajasthan, a new textbook contained writings by Rajendra Singh, the RSS ideologue, who extolled the moral virtues of ancient India.[89] Angry reaction was inevitable. An educated *sudra* (lower caste) author writes, "Right from school up to college our Telegu textbooks were packed with these Hindu stories . . . but the lower castes do not find our lives reflected in their narratives." Upper-caste Hindu morals remained main themes in books.[90] Independent students' and teachers' organizations, as well as The National Council for Educational Research and Training, the federal agency responsible for enforcing the national curriculum, conveyed grave concern to the union government.[91] Later on, revivalist textbooks were withdrawn from school curriculum under intense public pressure.

Obviously there existed differences in strategies. To mold individual character the RSS relied on the physical culture of young men (not women), whereas the VHP admitted the role of religion as a major factor in shaping the moral character of all Hindus.[92] Both went ahead with their own formulations. Religious education and moral philosophy spread through the agencies of newly constructed Hindu schools. Hedgewar and his associates in the RSS believed that "character-building" through Hindu education was in itself sufficient to achieve its social and political objectives.[93] "Vidya Bharati" (RSS affiliated school system, 1997) was an all India apex body that coordinated the working of different provincial educational societies and facilitated the exchange of their mutual experiences and experiments. These societies ran about five hundred educational institutions, which were engaged in the task of imparting education to over 2 million students in the early 1990s.[94] Even in remote Port Blair, the capital of the Andaman Islands, there were RSS administered schools.[95] In the mid-1990s, over five thousand young *"sevavratis"* (full-time missionary teachers) worked for moral teaching all over Karnartak in such areas as social service, *yoga shikshana* (exercise), yoga therapy, personality development, and ecoconservation. Experts in various fields of training came from service organizations in Karnataka, including the VHP and *Rashtrothana Parishad*[96] (emerging board).

Other cultural nationalists set up their own schools to effect moral programs. The "Sanatan Dharma Sabha" (Eternal Religious Assembly) had about one hundred schools and colleges in 1991 under its wings but these were fairly autonomous.[97] In Karnatak, seven hundred VHP committees ran schools and hostels. In 1952, the RSS founded a primary school named *Saraswati* (Hindu goddess of learning) *Shishu Mandir* at Gorakhpur in U.P. to fill in "an ideological vacuum" and impart religious education using highly modern technology. This educational experiment in U.P. proved to be successful in attracting students, and so a new plan was drawn to open branch schools in every subdivision in the state after 1972.[98] "Corrupting" Western knowledge was ignored in favor of moral education, but when Western technical know-how was used it created confusion in the educational goals of the schools.[99] Hindu education thus stitched together two unrelated streams—Western know-how and Indian religious values.

This brand of moral education evolved into "social censorship" effected by the BJP's "culture police," who recently put vermilion marks on the foreheads of little schoolgirls, and imposed *"Saraswati Bandana"* (ritual knots) upon nonbelievers in Delhi and its neighborhood. The prestigious English daily, *The Statesman*, complained that the BJP had begun intruding into citizens' privacy. Mange Ram Geng, Delhi BJP president, insisted on wearing the "right dress."[100] In essence, a self-proclaimed moral superiority denied India's pluralistic and postindependence syncretic educational culture, and subverted modern educational planning for both private and government schools.

The Contents of Textbooks

Revivalist complaints against secular educational contents in books were many. The Orientalist concept of an Aryan community turned the "Hindu" period into a golden age as contrasted to the Muslim period, which was seen as an age of moral decline.[101] The "Overseas Friends of the BJP," mostly based in the United States and the United Kingdom, argued that texts in books should provide the "fact," i.e., the famous "Tajmahal" was in "reality" the "tejmahaly," an ancient Shiv temple, not a Muslim tomb. One nonresident author claimed that the term "Tajmahal" itself never occurred in any Moghul court paper or chronicle, because it was a Hindu temple.[102] A relatively "unknown" (self-styled) Hindu leader lamented that Karvela was a great king of "Utkal" (Orissa) who had carried the flag across the seas to Indonesia. But most Indian scholars, he continued, "did not hear his name."[103] Another complaint was that the history of the expansion of Indian "thought and culture" outside India did not have a special place in history textbooks.[104] Some argued that history books should state that the great Rajput defender, Rana Sanga, with only thirty thousand troops confronted Babar, the first Mughal emperor, who appeared with sixty thousand soldiers on the battlefield.[105] Akbar might have been a great ruler, but he was a "foreigner," remarked a BJP leader and a prominent revivalist ideologue, Govindacharya. "Who says Akbar was a great ruler?" a VHP volunteer asked in November 1990.[106] The high-ranking BJP and the RSS leaderships submitted that textbooks had not yet depicted that "crimes in this country have been committed in the name of Christianity and Islam."[107] The implicit line of thinking in these complaints was that all Hindu events must be recorded to depict Hindu history and glory for a forced resurgence in culture.

Particular complaints were made against the existing structure in child education. The revivalist "*Shishu Mandirs*" (Children's Schools System) put forth the concept of a "developed child." The Hindu system made provision for home education in Hindu basic manners, and then sent a child to a "*Shishu Mandir*." A "developed child," as trained in the *Sishu Mandir* educational system, would have an innate love for "*Bharat Mata*" (Mother India), an amicable nature, a spirit of dedication, the power of discrimination (*viveka*), and a keen thirst for learning ancient Sanskritic norms in order to play a role in building a strong Hindu community. Those children who thought of becoming doctors, architects, engineers, or lawyers, would lose "the central theme of education" of "a developed child,"[108] concluded the framers of the new educational program. Critics would argue that *Bharat Mata* has indeed been a loaded term, for not only is *Bharat* (India) a Sanskrit word, but the rallying cry of "*Mother India*" revealed that, ultimately, the revivalists were appealing to politics, not religion.

Another revivalist complaint was that Hindu revivalist leaders were not depicted as national leaders. Some suggested that the RSS founder Keshav Rao Hedgewar and his disciple M. Golwalkar must be depicted in books as "genuine national heroes" who gave new directions to *Hindutva* philosophy.[109] Some books written since 1992 for schools in Hindi-speaking areas labeled the Mughal kings as "foreigners and oppressors," seen by revivalist politicians as people for dominance.[110] After December 1993, the BJP governments in four northern states did not focus on development projects but on things like rewriting school textbooks to extol the glories of Hindu India and of ancient Sanskrit texts. Through resolutions, the Akhil Bharatiya Vidyarthi Parishad, the Jana Sangh's student wing, welcomed the changes made in the textbooks by U.P. and M.P.

governments to reflect "national values."[111] However, voters interested in economic conditions lost interest in the BJP, which became a political pariah, and no other party would form an alliance with the BJP for some time at the regional and central levels.[112] The party suffered electoral reverses in 1993 in H.P., M.P., and U.P. gains in Delhi and Rajasthan were not sufficient to compensate for the losses in the cradle of the *Sangh Parivar's* (Sangh family) cultural nationalism.[113]

Complaints against the existing secular system of education raised two related issues: the role of the partisan interests in the allocation of scholarly resources, and the political consequences of the new historical interpretations of Indian unity and public perception. However, neither the public allocation of funds nor the unity issue could easily be resolved because of the opposition mounted by secularists.

Nevertheless, contents in books were altered or rearranged to conform to revivalist educational ideology. In the late 1970s, the Janata Party's (the party had many members from the Jana Sangh) cultural fundamentalists challenged the Nehru government's secular cultural settlement by raising the textbook controversy. The Janata government encouraged the creation of, and helped to fund, the "Indian History and Cultural Society" to reflect the Hindu perspectives in books. The Society attracted a variety of members, including some sympathetic to the RSS.[114]

When the BJP-led central government became a reality in New Delhi in the late 1990s, in the wake of the collapse of the Congress rule and the chaos of coalition governments, the Indian Council for Historical Research (ICHR) came under the control of the Far Right. The Council was under the purview of the Human Resources Development Ministry, which was headed by Murli Manohar Joshi, a campaigner of the RSS cultural cause, and now a cabinet minister in Human Resources Development (HRD) in New Delhi. In 1998, Murli Manohar Joshi appointed new members to the Council who subscribed to the BJP's views on Ayodhya affairs. The ICHR had earlier published two volumes of the freedom struggle written by noted historians, K. N. Panikkar and Sumit Sarkar. The ICHR was pressured by the government to withdraw works of alleged leftist historians who gave little respect to the revivalist Hindu outlook. M. Venkaiah Naidu, a BJP member, claimed that the two volumes already published by the ICHR had undermined Mahatma Gandhi's role while they enhanced the role of the communists.[115] Incidentally, the World Archaeological Congress censured two important members of the reconstituted ICHR.[116]

Likewise, the Indian Council of Social Science Research (ICSSR), funded by the HRD ministry under Murli Manohar Joshi, faced a challenge from revivalist supporters. The ICSSR has been the premier agency promoting social science studies in the country. The Council has seven nominated RSS members who currently oppose Manohar Lal Sondhi's (chairman of the council) "liberal and pluralistic values." The council faces attacks from three quarters: (A) Leftist academics who support a Soviet style regimentation in scholarship and research, (B) India's bureaucrats who typically abhor independent intellectual pursuits, and (C) the RSS members who want to orient toward Hindu values. *Hundutva* sympathizers such as Saradindu Mukherji of Delhi University and J. K. Bajaj, director of Centre for Policy Studies, frequently imposed their opinion on textbook contents. In 1998, a prescribed book on India's economy was commissioned by the ICSSR. Edited by Surjeet Bhalla, it opposed "swadeshi economics." Indicative of the censorship of the RSS members, who had the support of Manohar Joshi (government minister), the book was not distributed.[117] Secular educationists could only helplessly cite Thomas Paine, who wrote, "When we are planning for posterity, we ought to remember that virtue is not hereditary."[118]

The Jana Sangh Party campaigned to discredit books written within a secular framework, and in fact, harassed several secular authors.[119] Most of the new RSS scholars wrote political science and history books for schools in the north. A RSS hard-liner, Gopeswar Dayal Mathur, headed the Rajasthan Secondary Education Board, which prescribed textbooks. The state education minister Gulab Chand Katara justified the RSS philosophy of moral values arguing that it was "just another school of thought."[120] Thus contents in textbooks were modified to further a Hindu cause.

Further Hindu Education

Several schemes were designed for a wider and broad-based education for the future citizens of the projected Hindu. This project was based on the assumption that indoctrinated members of society would contribute to the organicist base of the new nation.

First, new courses in higher education would include Hindu astrology, which attracted the attention of the revivalist administrators because many of them were fatalists. Recently, a central minister, Murli Manohar Joshi, argued for the inclusion of astrology in both graduate and undergraduate classes. Joshi, a former successful student in physics, informed the parliament that twenty-four universities had shown interest in the subject as part of further education. A strong believer in Hindu astrology, he noted that most cultural nationalists had faith in the subject and as such a new course introduction was in order.[121]

Second, the revivalists spread Hindu myths and stories among students by various means. To spread the god Rama's (Ram, Hindi word; Rama, Sanskrit) ideals, *Vidya Bharti* (education centers) schools taught yoga, music, and moral education. As part of its indoctrination program, school walls were invariably plastered with inspiring scenes from Hindu history and Hindu mythology.[122] The *Hindu Parishad* (central education body) tested students' knowledge of the *Mahabharata* and *Ramayana* and awarded gold and silver medals for excellence.[123] L. K. Advani and other top BJP leaders became "media-savvy manipulators" of Rama-related religious imagery. By the early 1990s, they had been given Pan-Indian exposure by the centrally administered T. V. (Doordarshan) to project a sense of resurgence of Brahmanic values.

Third, the Hindu media glorified ancient Hindu characters. In 1991, the BJP campaigned for the extension of a Sunday morning television serial glorifying the ancient political scientist and statesman, Kautilya (fourth century B.C.), who was the author of *Arthashastra*, a textbook on realpolitik. The media portrayal of Kautilya appeared to be a struggle by the BJP leadership against the secular Congress Party for the establishment of a kingdom with Hindu norms. The bureaucrats and politicians of the ruling Congress Party were challenged. In such a conflict, the formally educated secular civil servants were amenable to the revivalist ideology. The scholarly community of historians had few weapons to fend off political pressure.[124] This media depiction of *Hindutva's* ideology in further education helped the rapid rise of a Hindu revivalist hegemony in the early part of the 1990s, creating discord among communities.[125] The Nehruvian separation of politics and education was thus discarded from further education as well.

Assessment of Educational Strategies

Several deficiencies may be noted in the education programs of the revivalist educationists: (A) The revivalist educational ideology and historical perception set out to speak on behalf of the community in place of a Western-style nation of many cultures. The object of education was not only to instill pride but also to arouse hatred. The proposed educational program created a perception of an eternal contest between good and evil. The Hindu history of Ayodhya, for instance, appeared to be only a replay of this eternal conflict.[126] (B) The revivalist "knowledge" implied a selective restoration of older ideas and not an introduction of new information. Secular scholars have correctly argued that India's poverty, malnutrition, and above all, low productivity could not be solved without proper secular and technical education. It is relevant to note that truth-seeking education, unfettered by religious prejudices, have improved material conditions in countries such as South Korea, Malaysia, Taiwan, and Singapore. (C) The educational instruments of the "Sangh Parivar" (revivalist family of parties) simply united with pedagogical tools to promote a totalitarian and monochromatic ideological orientation.[127] (D) In the Tamil land in the south, there had been an attempt to reject the epic *Ramayana* because it was northern (Aryan) and anti-Dravidian. The attempt at national unity in the name of one Hinduism generated tensions not only between the upper and lower castes but also in center-state relations.[128] West Bengal, the Punjab, Kerala, and some other states did not conform to the ideals of Brahmanical education.

(C) Hindu Women's Status

In revivalist writing, there was no expression of the danger of the seductive wiles of women, which was common in the Indian literature. If a RSS worker decided to remain a bachelor, that was an indication of his loyalty to the party cause; avoidance of relations with the opposite sex was not to show disgust at women in general.[129] Most revivalists, however, defended the traditional social and economic lesser role of women on the ground that any status change would jeopardize the community's aspiration. The debatable issue in the revivalist discourse was the extent of the subordinate role of Hindu women. Did the revivalists ask for any kind of social and occupational "emancipation"?

The revivalist arguments had several assumptions: (A) The Hindu society controlled itself by internal governance and in this perspective the issue of the women's status was social and not economic, and (B) Hindu women were traditionally embedded in pristine nature. In fact, they were part of the supreme power represented by goddesses Kali or Durga. Women in this image had already supreme power. Third, the Western view of women in India as subjugated sprang from Western ignorance of Hindu traditions. Their methodology in studying women was inadequate. Therefore, the revivalists argued that the women's status debate should not be seen in terms of a struggle between the Enlightenment and superstition. How would a rational-secular discipline understand Hindu attitude toward women? The issue of cultural relativity was invoked, arguing that the Hindu cultural specificity required a special approach to women's rights issue.

I would argue that the revivalists not only subscribed to the traditional lower status but also created conditions for further subordination to implement new programs.

First, women were denied high public positions even though women were educationally equipped. Gerad Heuze (1992) has done two in-depth studies of Shiv Sena, an autonomous group in Chattisgarh in M.P., and his findings are revealing with respect to the status of women. The Shiv Sainiks there liked that their sisters would support the Shiv Sena movement, but the sisters "are never to be seen in public activities." This phenomenon contrasted with the regional culture in which women occupied public high positions in Delhi, the Punjab, and West Bengal. The Shiv Sainiks of Chattisgarh argued in the name of stability that women should not be given any significant role because "total chaos would follow, both in society and on the jobs." Women were to be exorcised, "as the living embodiment of the evil which gnaws at the substance of the country." This line of argument was in-line with traditional customs of the upper caste in M.P.[130]

The rationale for conformity with family traditions varied. Mridula Sinha, the president of the BJP's "Mahila Morcha" (Women's Brigade), stated that a woman's role in the family was to carry out the activities especially prescribed for women.[131] Therefore, women were given a limited public identity. To provide womanly "aloofness," the "Rashtra Sevika Samity" (The Patriotic Association of Women, henceforth called the *Samity*), the women's wing of the RSS established in 1936, provided intellectual and spiritual training for women, affirming their religiosity, and providing them access to a world of "knowledge and spirituality." However, the power of the family to make decisions regarding female members remained unthreatened.[132] Following the parent body's (RSS) guidance, the *Samity* was careful not to talk about separate women's rights.[133] Mrs. Apte of the group formulated the RSS view on gender by writing that "we (Rashtriya Sevika Samity female members) consider the women to be the navigator of the chariot of life. The man steers/drives, whereas the women navigates." The *Samity* consolidated the RSS's overall strategy of creating the new Hindu nation as an alternative civil society in which Hindu women would work as an auxiliary force not only of the RSS but also of the nation.[134] As a result, the persistence of the housewife ideology, the self-perception of the lace makers as petty commodity producers rather than as workers in an industry, for instance, was not only upheld by the structure of a provincial industry as such but also by the deliberate propagation and reinforcement of patriarchal norms in places of work.[135]

Others interpreted womanly "aloofness" differently. Unmindful of the contemporary earned higher social and public status of women in society, some revivalists argued "we have had a standard of gentle aloofness for women."[136] "Women are the solace and comfort of hearths and homes," Savarkar argued. So, Hindu "women should be given some sort of specialized training congenial to the temperament of women."[137] Ignoring social oppression of Hindu women, Golwalkar argued that women were predominantly mothers, who could help the Hindu cause most by rearing their children within the RSS framework of "samskaras" (family rituals and women's deference toward RSS leaders).[138]

Second, differences between men and women were emphasized in defense of the existing lower status of women. The *Samity* (society) allowed women to become leaders in their societies and associations, but decreed that the "deepest tradition of the role of women in Hindu society" must be maintained in relationship between men and women.[139] Whereas boys were allowed to dress as they liked, college girls were asked to uphold social traditions. The youth wing of the BJP that spearheaded the ruling coalition in U.P. urged the Surendra Nath College management in Kanpur to introduce a strict dress code imposed only on the college girls. Girls of the college, of course, protested the "regulations" on skirt dresses.[140] In fact, most revivalists sought a controlled situation for women's education simply because they were women. The best way to serve the nation was to develop a woman's inherent domestic skills and dedication as a mother. An "unidentified" revivalist scholar argued, "Our women receiving the same kind of education (as men's education) obtain the same mentality (men's mentality) of job hunting." So, "every girl should learn painting, sewing, embroidery, cooking, making various sweets in schools, and should (also) learn how to combine necessary vitamins from various vegetables and other foods."[141] He added that modern secular education made women forget their true duties, and transformed them into individualistic and self-centered entities. "Emancipation" through modern education made women "wage earning servants" and as such "objects of male desire."[142] The problem with idealizing differences was that it did not bring with it material rewards, higher wages, meaningful recognition, real rights, and any effective control.[143]

The BJP did not oppose women's educational, legal, and political rights that would accord them greater equality with men. The party nominated Deepika Chikalia, the actress who played the role of Sita, to run on a BJP ticket during the 1991 parliamentary elections. Throughout the campaign, her demeanor remained exactly the same as in the television series: unable to represent herself, she had to be represented.[144] Thus the secondary public role of women was maintained. Two reports by social scientists, Ratna Kapur and Brenda Cossman, found that for decades the RSS had sought a women's place within the confines of home. When a woman used uncharitable language against her own protector (man), that use was calculated as bitter shame. Kapur and Cossman concluded that this was a kind of "masterful manipulation" by the "Hindu Far Right."[145]

Third, the revivalists argued that westernizing "liberation" was irrelevant within the traditional family structure. The family and the society had accorded a high role to dutiful and self-sacrificing mothers. An additional role was ancillary to women's virtues. Thus, the RSS considered the women's liberation movement as "the worst enemies of women."[146] In a policy statement, some educated and highly placed Hindu women declared, "We maintain that the family must be maintained. Too much of freedom to woman would break the nuclear family and we resist this."[147] A social science textbook for high schools, issued by the BJP government in U.P. stated that reforms in Hindu personal laws, such as the Hindu Widow Remarriage Act, 1954, and the Hindu Marriage and Divorce Act, 1955, had led to "disorganization within the family." The revivalists argued that "progressive legislative measures" in favor of women had created "tension and strife in the family."[148]

Fourth, any public discourse on the women's status was discouraged. An angry but witty Hindu lower caste author has counterpoised the mother's status differently. Whereas a lower-caste mother is left alone because she "is gender-neutral" (a nonperson), the father's "atrocities against the mother cannot be discussed in Brahmin or Bania (business class) families . . . the more a wife puts up with her husband's atrocities, the more she is appreciated." As women were asked to adopt the sex and marriage code of the Brahmins or upper castes, the process of sanskritization was adhered to. Social scientists argued that "sanskritization" resulted in harshness toward women and the lower status of Hindu women was a consequence.[149] Amrita Basu, a Bengali social scientist in an American university, has found after her field researches in West Bengal that those Hindu women who had Sanskritic practices such as the rejection of widow remarriage and absolute devotion to male folks, tended to be timid. "The more the Sanskritzed the group," the greater deference women displayed.[150]

Inevitably, enlightened Hindu women did not agree with the revivalist strategies. Madhu Kishwar, the editor of *Manushi*, a women's journal seeking women's public rights, justifiably contends that "our cultural traditions have tremendous potential within them to combat reactionary and anti-women ideas." Gail Omvedt (1978) classifies women's rights into two movements— equality movements and liberation movements. If remnants of "feudal patriarchy" could be removed, argues Omvedt, Hindu women might attain social equality.[151] The first one was more relevant in Indian social movements, and the stark reality was that Hindu revivalists neglected the upward social mobility for women at great social and economic costs.

Most Indians, however, have little regard for the modernist tendency of providing absolute freedom given to women, although they accept the idea of equal education and status. After all, the Western style women's social liberation had contributed to the disintegration of the family system largely testifying to the revivalist claim that extreme liberation was not the solution to equality problem.

Sati and Emancipation

The acceptance of the idea of *sati* meant a lack of social equality. The *sati* tradition of self-burning mainly by the high-caste widow on husband's funeral pyre was irregularly practiced until it was banned by the British. In the Hindi belt, the revivalist activists supported the *sati* to reinforce the idea that a widow had no independent existence after her husbands' death. In 1987, when eighteen-year-old widow Roop Kanwar was being burnt on a funeral pyre in Rajasthan, following an obscure Hindu tradition of the *sati* sacrifice, hundreds of revivalists in and around Deorala village saw nothing horrific. "It was a Brahmanical culture that prevailed as far as the status of higher-caste women was concerned."[152] Liberal women's groups in the state claimed that it was illegal and pleaded those connected with it should be prosecuted for murder under Section 306 of the Indian Penal Code.

Nevertheless, the followers of Hindu parties donated about Rs. 30 lakh to a newly formed "*sati* committee" planning to erect a monument there. A Janata Party leader, Kalyan Singh Kalvi, as well as a BJP member of the state assembly, Hari Ram Khara, visited the spot to seek the *sati mata*'s (*sati mother's*) blessings. On another occasion, an orthodox Hindu woman explained that the *sati* "is morally right. It is in our Holy Books and Puranans . . . The wife dies with her husband in order to preserve her chastity and her devotion to her husband." Thirty-five percent of orthodox Hindu women believed that *sati* was a scripturally sanctioned act for the salvation of a woman's soul.[153]

Organized pro-*Hindutva* political parties supported the *sati* burning in Rajasthan. The Rajasthan branches of the Janata Party and BJP rallied to the cause of *sati* because they wanted to portray their party as allies of the local conservative Hindu majority, and to cast the ruling Congress party in the role of an "outsider." The Dharma Raksha Samity (Committee for the Defense of the Religion of s*ati*), with the support of seventy thousand defenders of the *sati*, observed the first anniversary of Roop Kanwar's *sati*.[154] A pro-*sati* group in the Marwari community that wielded explicit and implicit political force in all major northern cities allied with the Rajput groups defending the *sati*.[155] The Hindu Mahasabha Party spoke on the side of the pro-*sati* Rajputs, and the Vishwa Hindu Parishad (VHP), the main actor in the Ayodhya Mandir-Musjid affair concerning Rama's birthplace, remained officially silent.[156] The home minister of Rajasthan cleverly declared that *sati* was cruel in itself "but not the glorification of the *sati*, and that is why noted politicians sought *satimata*'s (goddess) blessings. Major business houses made regular contributions to the *sati* temple.[157] The myth of historical precedence of the act of *sati* was so strong that Roop Kanwar's self-sacrifice was endorsed by a *sankaracharya* (Hindu high priest), although there was no proof that Kanwar did the *sati* of her own free will. To the revivalists, it became women's identity issue because women were supposedly allowed to do certain things and to follow certain codes. It was a peculiar kind of empowerment.[158] The Rajasthan state government did not interfere to enforce the law against the *sati*. The patriarchal attitude of the state was prominently obvious in Roop Kanwar's *sati*. A new cultural concept, in which the development of so-called spiritual development against external developments prevailed, was fostered in the name of *sati*. From *sati* to infanticide (girls), it is always the woman who has been at the receiving end in a hidebound, feudal structure that worships manhood; contemporary revivalist idealists felt no obligation to improve the situation.

However, recent research and field surveys indicated that not a single progressive Indian thought that a woman had the right to do *sati*. To progressives, a person's choice by itself was often an insufficient moral consideration. They spoke of how *sati* ran counter to a woman's own interest.[159] Dr. Hemlata Prabhu, the woman principal of Canodia College in Jaipur rightly declared, "This is but one more form of glorifying crimes against women. It is not a religious issue."[160] Atal Behari Vajpayee denounced the glorification of the *sati*.

The newspaper of the Sarvadeshik Arya Pratinidhi Sabha (The Aryan International Association) and the Arya Samaj (Aryan Society) published articles on the *sati* of Rajasthan. The newspaper argued that there was no mention of *sati* in the Vedas. "The authors of the shastras (religious texts) forbid this system and said that it is a sin like suicide."[161] Referring to the Roop Kanwar case, a feminist Indian scholar, Veena Talwar Oldenburg (1994), in a contesting interpretation of the *satimata* (*sati* mother) myth rightly argues, "the *sati* myth cannot really qualify as the inspirational myth for *sati*."[162]

Several comments may be made at this stage in the debate. (A) The *sati* burning in Rajasthan legitimized the revivalist ideological belief system. Holy violence was as much a part of the modern revivalist world, and maltreatment of women was far from gone.[163] (B) The role of gender among revivalist parties was perplexing. While the *sati* issue involved defense of gender traditions, the RSS and some other Hindu cultural nationalists mobilized women in a partially modern manner on political occasions.[164] (C) Although revivalists did not condemn the *sati* burning, they had been vociferous over the issue of Muslim women's rights concerning divorce and alimony. (D) The revival of *sati* at Deorala village was more to assert Rajput identity and gain political clout than for any real religious sentiments. Two Indian social scientists correctly argue that the preconceived notion of *sati* was regressive and that was why Indian women "particularly fear religious fundamentalism."[165]

In sum, the revivalists ignored the emerging trends among the Hindu women. Westernization helped economic empowerment in recent decades. There is no definitive study about the adverse social effects of Western education among Hindu women. What is clear is that "education is also the strongest variable affecting women's own sense of well-being."[166] Education by itself has been the most likely means for women to achieve equality of opportunities. Leaving aside other related issues, the very fact that revivalists asked for more traditional education at the expense of modern education proved to be an obstruction in achieving an enhanced status. The revivalist argument that the women's status was social, not economic, seemed to be diversionary. Their acceptance of the predetermined sexual inequality provided a key to explaining the revivalist conservatism in other spheres as well.

(D) Muslim Factor in Culture

I would examine two aspects—protection of Hindu women against a perceived threat from the Muslims and Urdu language as a threat to national identity—arguing that the revivalist claims seemed to be misperceived.

The revivalist cultural history in respect to Muslims (135 million) reduced all of India's past to a two-fold statement: first, the civilizational glory of pre-Muslim India was unique and perfect; and second, the unceasing cultural degeneration had existed since the culturally different Muslims came to the subcontinent as invaders in the tenth century. The discourse concerning the recuperation of cultural values found supporters in the middle classes as well as the revivalists, and in its populist form the discourse created fears and prejudices about the Muslim other, the "cultural pollutant."[167]

Hindu Women and the Muslim Factor

A prominent "sevika" (volunteer), Kamlabehn of Gujarat, agreed with the RSS that Muslim identity was essentially embodied in the immoral Muslim male. She referred to the tragic Ahmedabad riot as simply "the 1969 riot," despite the fact that during the riot about fifteen hundred lives were lost and over thirty thousand people, mostly Muslims, were left homeless. The Jana Sangh that had succeeded in establishing its hold in Gujarat by the late 1960s played a leading role in the 1969 riots. The 1969 riots were aimed mainly to weaken Mrs. Indira

Gandhi's government that had tried to woo the minorities through its secular plank. However, the revivalists saw Muslims as both a political and cultural threat to Indian unity. Referring to the 1986 communal riots in Ahmedabad, Kamlabehn said, "They spill our blood. They rape our women. Let their blood be spilled, the bloody bastards. Just as Kali (Goddess) did not spare even one *raksha* (demon)." She constructed the anti-Muslim act as modeled upon Kali's ridding the world of evil in the form of demons in the religious text called *Devi Mahatmya*.[168] It may be recalled that child marriage was ostensibly evolved as a safeguard against Muslim invasions during which young Hindu girls were carried away as part of the booty.

The RSS Party claimed that Muslim women belonged to the same biological/cultural category of the Hindus but became culturally different (Muslims) only when Muslim men or their male family members abducted them for conversion. The RSS solution was to reabsorb them into the Hindu community by marriage to Hindu males. Some letters allegedly written by Muslim women after the 1985-1986 riots in Gujarat and elsewhere preferred Hindu men to Muslim men because the Muslim society was oppressive to women. Here, purification would be achieved through marriage of converted Muslim women to Hindu males. This was the "common sense" (RSS's word) solution to the purification process.[169] One outspoken exponent of the Nazi-style forced purification from the "unclean" Muslims was the young "sanasin" (renunciant) Sadhvi Rithambara, an active member of the VHP's "Marg Darshan Mandal" (Central Committee in the Women's Brigade). She was a daughter of a Punjabi farmer, lived in a hermitage in the holy city of Haridar, and was mainly instructed in the skill of oratory. Speaking on behalf of Hindu women she declared, "Muslims ridicule the Hindu culture." Rithambara argued that Hindu male valor (*purusharth*) could protect innocent Hindu women against "Muslim marauders." Her three-point program of reform in essence meant: voting BJP, reclaiming Sri Rama's birthplace in Ayodhya, and killing Muslims.[170] She acted like an infuriated political figure rather than an ascetic defender of faith. Rithambara remarked, "The state tells us Hindus to have only two or three children. But what about those who have six wives, 30-35 children and breed like mosquitoes and flies." Hindu women had the responsibility to impress the government to prevent polygamy among Muslims.[171] The argument against polygamy was not that it was detrimental to women, but rather that Muslim polygamists produced more children and thus Muslims multiplied more rapidly than Hindus. Revivalists thought the supposed danger of the greater number of Muslims a political fear, and not a cultural defense.[172]

Urdu Language and National Identity

The Urdu language issue was a complex issue. During the Muslim rule and thereafter, the residential areas, while often juxtaposed, remained self-contained; Urdu-speaking Indians lived in separate quarters."[173] This situation aggravated the division between communities. Muslim educated elites and regional politicians in U.P. and neighboring states contributed to the debate about Urdu. As the Muslim elites in the then United Provinces demanded that Urdu in Persian or Arabic script be the medium of instruction, the functions of language in the north thereby became transformed from their uses for religious discourse or for ordinary discourse into symbolic links among members of the same ethnic group (Muslim). The Muslim elites promoted the Urdu language in schools. In fact, Urdu remained a secondary symbol (Islam was the first) of the nationalist Muslim identity. Thus arose barriers to communications between communities.[174]

Most revivalists assumed that the Muslim culture had spelled out its adverse disintegrating influences through the agency of the Urdu language. The Turkish conquerors made Persian the language of culture in north India, and during the sixteenth century at the insistence of Raja Todarmal (Emperor Akbar's Revenue Minister), Persian was made the official language of the revenue department in place of *Hindavi* (Hindu language) and other Indian languages. This was to culminate in the Persianization/Arabization of *Hindavi* to make Urdu.[175] Urdu was written in the Arabic script. Because Urdu had links with foreign languages, the *Hindutva* forces denied its importance in society.

The first line of argument was that Urdu was not the result of the synthesis of the languages of various native ethnic groups who were themselves in the process of becoming merged into one people through Sanskritized Hindi. The Jana Sangh Party was engaged in election campaigns in Bihar, U.P., and M.P. in 1954. As part of political campaigns for electoral success, the party called for the removal of Urdu from the list of languages given in the Eighth Schedule of the Constitution of India. Deendayal Upadhyaya complained that Urdu was foreign in spirit. "It has no grass-roots and therefore people who claim to speak Urdu have no roots in the soil."[176] The Jana Sangh's central working committee argued that Urdu was "the language of no region in India" and had "foreign script and a foreign vocabulary," and as such was unacceptable for public and educational use.[177] The party manifesto demanded further that English or Urdu should not be offered a status of native languages. Thus the status of Urdu was an issue built into the rhetoric of politics at the state level in U.P., but at the level of individual districts and cities, job privileges enjoyed by Muslims were often the focus of envy and suspicion by Hindus. The Jana Sangh faced a dilemma. If the party exploited the communal tensions over Urdu, it ran the risk of being drawn into violence. If it ignored them, it could be accused of denying its stance on Hindi. This dilemma became acute during the Aligarh riots in U.P. in 1961[178] and the party remained defensive to avoid any political embarrassment. Recently, Girilal Jain, an author explaining the emergence of cultural revivalism, argues that Urdu being of foreign origin should have no place in communication.[179]

The revivalist argument that dismissed Urdu as a mere "dialect of Hindi" seems to be perverse. A noted linguist has clarified the status. Julia S. Falk has remarked, "Two systems of communication may be similar enough to be mutually intelligible, and yet they may be labeled as separate languages. The two systems, Dutch and German, are accepted as separate languages, rather than simply as dialects of a single language, primarily for political or nationalistic reasons."[180] Above all, Urdu, with its own script, had been an independent language used by millions of Indians. In fact, Urdu maintained its separate identity among good numbers of Indians not only in the north but also in large cities such as Hyderabad in central India.[181]

The second line of argument was that the Muslim conquerors imposed Urdu as the language of cultural imposition. An Indian author sympathetic to the revivalist cause complains that the Persianizing writers of Delhi, Lucknow, and Hyderabad, in the eighteenth and nineteenth centuries, caused a cultural revolution in the threatening spirit of Urdu. "Persianized Urdu" then played a role in producing a rival "cultural matrix which Persia itself could not have done." An instance of purification of languages was drawn from King Shivaji, the Maratha hero who had tried to replace Persian words with Sanskrit, an attempt that failed to outlast his lifetime.[182] Perhaps, Hindu traders and high middle classes expressed alarm at pockets of Muslim prosperity arising out of quick money earned in the Muslim Gulf and possible use of such funds to enter trades, which were the preserves of the Hindu traders as in Moradabad in U.P.

The third line of argument was that Urdu was not a separate language on its own. Balraj Madhok, a ranking RSS volunteer and a leader of the Jana Sangh, went so far as to argue that Urdu was not "a separate language"; it was a style of Hindi with a heavy admixture of Persian and Turkish words and phrases.[183] The claim that Hindi and Urdu were the same language appeared to be a political rather than a linguistic claim. It was submitted that Urdu in the Arabic script (modern Persian is written in Arabic script) in which it was written was not only foreign but also unscientific and difficult. The adoption of the *Dev-Nagri* (Sanskrit script) script for writing Urdu was necessary if Urdu was to be prevented from playing the disruptive role that it had played before, said Balraj Madhok. Thus, the use of Urdu in schools and public places should be limited.[184]

In sum, the cultural militant activity along with local communal riots fostered by both the communities drove the Muslim minority into the arms of equally militant and obscurantist Islamic ideologues. Consequently, Indian unity was fractured. On the other hand, the use of Sanskrit and Sanskritized Hindi along with rituals associated with these, in effect, meant continuation of the undue process of "sanskritization" of society. In his discussion of "Sanskritization," Professor M. N. Srinivas, a pioneer sociologist, concludes that the process was nothing but a Hindu maintenance of "the caste hierarchy" causing social friction.[185] If the Muslim community failed to live up to the nationalist harmonious spirit, that was no justification for the revivalists to foster a minority complex within the majority.

Conclusion

Critics would argue that the revivalist cultural nationalism as a foundational pillar of a unified community proved to be disruptive to everything that provided balance and security. Several major weaknesses in the revivalist cultural strategies may legitimately be affirmed.

First, the Brahmanical concept of Hindu cultural norms, with Sanskrit and Hindi as main languages, womanly aloofness as proofs of family values, and Muslims seen as cultural pollutants, etc., introduced new barriers to social harmony. Even before the coming of Islam and Christianity, Indian traditions had always been plural. Romila Thapar, the dean of the history of Hinduism, argues that historical sources revealed more complex pictures of Hinduism. Some precepts of the Vedas were challenged by more egalitarian practices, which opposed ritual sacrifices, caste hierarchy, and violence.[186] Although there was an Indian "style" of religiosity, the proponents of traditional syncretism exaggerated the degree of cultural unity that had existed in the past.[187] As Amartya Sen correctly argues, Hindu cultures contained considerable internal variations, and different attitudes might be entertained within the same vaguely defined culture. Indian (Hindu) traditions were often taken to be intimately associated with religion, and indeed in many ways they are, and yet Sanskrit and Pali have larger literatures on systematic atheism and agnosticism than perhaps in any other classical language.[188]

Second, Hindu revivalists emphasized the contrast between their spiritual heritage and Western materialism as part of the process of recovering their self-esteem. A Hindu scholar argues that revivalists needed to overcome the lopsidedness, which laid an undue emphasis on piety at the cost of two of the central Hindu goals of prosperity.[189] The starting point of the pluralism was the recognition of differences and hierarchy. The Indian nation was a community of bounded communities, and as such cultures were pluralistic. In this sense, a non-resident Indian in New York correctly observed, "The cultural awakening of Hindus is commendable, but its leaders would do a great service to our heritage if they worked for the eradication of caste hierarchy and inspired the positive affirmations of Vedic visions, rather than instigate people to demolish mosques, burn Bibles and engage in hate-mongering talk which are unworthy of the highest ideals of Hindu world views."[190]

Third, the revivalist formulation of culture was "cultural chauvinism." Here, every aspect—personality, contribution, and system of philosophy, historical period, and social organization—was reduced to a product of Hindu civilization, so that absolute contradictions and conflicts between philosophers and political thought would be erased. It was an unacceptable assertion that the Hindu culture discovered truths that were both "universal and transcendental" in all times.[191] Not only did most revivalists believe in Samuel Huntington's "clash of civilizations," but also concluded "we are in a clash of civilizations."

Fourth, Hindu revivalists had a populist cultural ideology that aimed at gaining political power in order to transform the central and provincial governments on the basis of their religio-political program. In reality they held predominantly conservative sociocultural views. For instance, they unjustifiably defended patriarchal views regarding the unequal social status of women. Virtually the entire revivalist approach to cultural policies was religious, but culture was more than religious values. Revivalists, as orientalists, noted the classical "essences" of ancient India. However, such formulations, as Ronald Inden has cogently shown in his *Imagining India*, were unreal. World-system theorizing clearly recognizes the significance of the religious perspective as an identifiable component in many antisystemic movements, but treats the perspective in a reductive fashion, as something other than what appears to be.[192] Actually, the cultural program of the revivalist was political, not religious. At its core lay a secular ideology of the state and a modern approach to party politics. Whereas Vinayak Damodar Savarkar had little to say about the content of religious traditions in building the Hindu state, Mahatma Gandhi, who Savarkar considered a danger to Hindu norms, spent his life redeploying these valued traditions in politics with a high degree of success.[193]

Fifth, the emergence of the BJP-led government in India did not mean an absolute victory for cultural nationalism. K. R. Malkani, the RSS ideologue and a former editor of the RSS publication, the *Organiser*, was inducted into the office of the BJP. His job included the image projection of the BJP. In a "hagiography" on the RSS, K. R. Malkani, in his examination of the extent of borrowings in culture, argues that imposition of an "alien" culture outside its heartland had so far failed. He cites an example from Indonesia where the reverence for Rama was said to be persistent in parts of the country in spite of the fact that the country has been largely Muslim dominated.[194]

Sixth, this chapter has never tried to minimize the genuine religious reform movements such as the Ramkrishna Vedanta Society and other Hindu organizations in various forms in contemporary India; nor have the main tenets of Hinduism been attacked. Secularists, with their many faults and corruptions, need not take pride in their modernist approach solely on the basis of their attitude. Ashis Nandy, a noted social psychologist of Delhi, has natural instincts against both Westernized modernity and Hindu cultural nationalists. Nandy correctly argues that revivalists as well as Anglophiles failed to understand the Indian ideal of spirituality. Whereas the Westernized elites largely ignored the Hindu social ethos, the revivalists, including "atheist" V. D. Savarkar, being Hindu "chauvinists" unsuccessfully tried to reconstruct a Hindu state. By doing so, the revivalists made the institutions of Hindus their main targets. Nandy concludes, rightly so, Hinduism was not an all-perfect antidote to Western cultural encroachment.[195] Deendayal's national *chiti* (inner reflective pure mind) as a foundational pillar of the Hindu state was a preserve of cultural autonomy capable of resisting cultural domination from outside, and proved to be otherworldly and tradition-ridden, and thus weak and backward-looking. When the cultural resistance fails to achieve its utopian goals because of its flawed image of indigenous society, there arises a new question: can there be nation building on the basis of uniformity in culture? The question of whether those propagating the new Hindu identity were embarked on its construction or merely on its articulation for others does not have a simple answer.

Last, cultural strategies failed to make any serious dent in Indian polity. The central dilemma of the BJP leadership (the main party in the central government) had been how to retain its militant core support based on the RSS and its cadre, while developing a wider and more centrist appeal in all aspects of life. The BJP distanced itself from the RSS's call to Christians and Muslims to Indianize their religions. The new president of the BJP, Bangari Laxman declared, "The BJP agenda is different from that of the RSS."[196] In fact, the BJP's pragmatic top leaders felt that the BJP was overreaching to a temporary upsurge of religious revivalism that was bound to die down. In this sense, cultural nationalists could not effectively carry out their programs for the creation of a Hindu *Rashtra*. Without being grounded in historical contexts, revivalist reflections on culture became abstract for any practical result. Their attempts to salvage and retrieve imagined national cultural traditions remained divisive. It is admitted that many Indians were recovering the language they felt most comfortable with the language of religious ties and identity, but the majority of Hindus were in favor of a secular state because modernity would likely bring efficiency and material prosperity without jeopardizing Hindu norms and valued traditions.

In sum, the fragmented character of Indian society might prevent the Hindu "community-in-the-making" from reaching a crystallized form but the very process itself was dangerous, regardless of what destination point it might try to reach.

Notes

1. In the "progressive" mind in India, a "revivalist" is a reactionary and secular-minded educated Indians did not always support a blind restoration of ancient values, as defined by traditionalists.

2. Anthony Smith, cited in Christophe Jaffrelot, *The Hindu Nationalist Movement in India* (New York: Columbia University Press, 1998), 5.

3. Lene Arnett Jensen, "Moral Divisions Within Countries between Orthodoxy and Progressivism: India and the United States," *Journal for the Scientific Study of Religion* 37, no. 1 (March 1998): 1.

4. J. E. Llewellyn, *The Legacy of Women's Uplift in India: Contemporary Women Leaders in the Arya Samaj* (New Delhi: Sage Publications, 1998), 184.

5. Jayanta K. Lal, *Hindutva: The Emergence of the Right* (Madras: Earthworm Books Ltd., 1995), 99; Gerad Heuze, "Shiv Sena and National Hinduism," *Economic and Political Weekly* (October 10, 1992): 2254.

6. R. C. Majumdar, *History of the Freedom Movement in India*, 3 (Calcutta: Firma K. L. Mukhopadhay, 1963), 320–28.

7. Richard G. Fox, "Gandhian Socialism and Hindu Nationalism: Cultural Domination in the World System," *Journal of Commonwealth and Comparative Politics* (November 1987): 235–36.

8. M. S. Golwalkar, *Bunch of Thoughts* (Bangalore, India: Jagaran Prakashan, 1980), 515–16.

9. An insider's history of the Sangh Parivar's internal has been depicted in Partha Chatterjee, *In the Belly of the Beast: The Hindu Supremacist RSS and BJP of India* (Delhi: Ajanta Books International, 1998).

10. For a good reading in culture and the state in India, see B. P. Singh, *India's Culture: The State, the Arts and Beyond* (Delhi: Oxford University Press, 1998), 48.

11. Robert Nisbet, *The Quest for Community: A Study in the Ethics of Order and Freedom* (New York: Oxford University Press, 1953).

12. See Arvind Sharma, *Hindu Scriptural Value System and the Economic Development of India* (New Delhi: Heritage, 1980). He notes that the *Rig Veda* does not deny the world. There is no trace of pessimism in the thoughts of the *Rig Veda*, 82. Indeed, Hindu codes of conduct had never been otherworldly always.

13. Christophe Jaffrelot, "The Idea of the Hindu Race," in *The Concept of Race in South Asia*, Peter Robb, ed. (Delhi: Oxford University Press, 1995), 343.

14. Gerald James Larson, *India's Agony Over Religion* (Albany: State University of New York), 41.

15. Dipesh Chakravarty, *Provincializing Europe: Postcolonial Thought and Historical Differences* (Princeton: Princeton University Press, 2000), 103.

16. Partha Chatterjee, "History and Nationalization of Hinduism," *Representing Hinduism*: 103–27; Larson, *India's Agony Over Religion*, 42.

17. Jay Dubashi, "Seculariss' Communal Syndrome: A Case Fit for Freudian Analysis," *Organiser* (July 1989): 2.

18. Louis Dumont, *Homo Hierarchicus: The Caste System and Its Implications* (Chicago: Chicago University Press, 1970), 107.

19. Walter K. Anderson, "Bharatiya Janata Party," in *The New Politics of the Rights: New Populist Parties and Movements in Established Democracies*, Betz and Immerfal, eds. (New York: St. Martin's Press, 1998), 228.

20. Nikki R. Keddie, "The New Religious Politics: Where, When, and Why Do Fundamentalism Appear?" *Comparative Studies in Society and History* 40, no. 4 (1998): 701.

21. David Fado, "The Struggle between Hindu and Secular Nationalism in India," www.utexas.edu/depts/das/.html/south.asia/sagar/fall (1994).

22. Fado, "Struggle between Hindu and Secular Nationalism," 3.

23. Ashis Nandy, "The Politics of Secularism and the Recovery of Religious Tolerance," in *Mirrors of Violence: Communities, Riots and Survivors in South Asia*, Veena Das, ed. (Delhi: Oxford University Press, 1990), 81.

24. Tapan Raychaudhuri, "Nehru and Western Dominance," in *The Legacy of Nehru: A Centennial Assessment*, D. R. SarDesai, et al., ed. (New Delhi: Promilla and Co., 1992), 286.

25. T. N. Madan, "Secularism in Its Place," *Journal of Asian Studies* 46 (November 1987): 748.

26. Fado, "Struggle between Hindu and Secular Nationalism," 6.

27. Ashutosh Varshney, "Contesting Meanings: India's National Identity: Hindu Nationalism and Politics of Anxiety," *Daedalus* 122, no. 3 (Summer 1993): 245. See also Ashutosh Varshney, *Democracy, Development and the Countryside: Urban-Rural Struggles in India* (Cambridge: Cambridge University Press, 1995), 230.

28. Chettan Bhatt, *Liberation and Purity: Race, New Religious Movements, and the Ethics of Postmodernity* (London: UCL Press, 1997), 226–27.

29. Lise Diane McKean, "Towards a Political Spirituality: Hindu Religious Organizations and Indian Nationalism", Ph.D. dissertation, University of Sydney, 1992), 37.

30. Jyoti Threhan, *Veer Savarkar: Thought and Action of Vinayak Damodar Savarkar* (New Delhi: Deep and Deep Publications, 1991), 128.

31. B. K. Kelkar, *Pandit Deendayal Upadhyaya: Ideology and Perception: Political Thought* (New Delhi: Suruchi Prakashan, 1988), 111.

32. L. I. Rudolph and S. H. Rudolph, "The Subcontinental Empire and the Regional Kingdom in Indian State Formation," in *Region and Nation in India*, P. Wallace, ed, (Delhi: Oxford University Press, 1985).

33. Varshney, "Contesting Meanings," 227–61.

34. Peter van der Veer, *Religious Nationalism: Hindus and Muslims* (Berkeley: University of California Press, 1994), 68; Tapan Raychaudhury, *Europe Reconsidered* (Delhi: Oxford University Press, 1988), 230.

35. Mary Hancock, "Hindu Culture . . . South India," *American Ethnologist*, 910.

36. "Cover Story," *India Today* (11 May 1986), 32.

37. "Cover Story," *India Today* (11 May 1986), 32.

38. Nirmal Mukherji and Ashis Banerji, "Neo-nationalism Symposium: The Hindus and Their Isms," *Seminar* (New Delhi, 1985), 27.

39. Sandria Freitag, cited in *Making India Hindu: Religion, Community, and the Politics of Democracy in India*, David Ludden, ed. (Delhi: Oxford University Press, 1996), 53.

40. BJP, *Bharatiya Janata Party Manifesto* (New Delhi: BJP Office, 1991), 29; Vishwa Hindu Parishad, "General Secretary's Report," in Souvenir volume of *Annual Meeting* (Allahabad, 1986), vii.

41. Paola Bacchetta, "Militant Hindu Nationalist Women Reimagine Themselves: Notes on Mechanisms of Expansion/Adjustment," *Journal of Women's History* (Winter 1999): 127.

42. M. S. Golwalkar, *We or Our Nationhood Defined* (Nagpur, India: Bharat Prakashan, 1939), 74; Prabha Dixit, "The Ideology of Hindu Nationalism," in *Political Thought in Modern India*, Thomas Pamtham and Kenneth L. Deutsch, eds. (New Delhi: Sage Publications, 1986), 140.

43. Samuel Huntington, "The Clash of Civilization?" *Foreign Affairs* 72, no. 3 (1993): 22–49; Edward Said, "What is Islam?" *New Statesman and Society* (10 February 1995), 32–34.

44. Christophe Jaffrelot, "The Vishva Hindu Parishad: Structures and Strategies," in *Religion, Globalization and Political Culture in the Third World*, Jeff Haynes, ed. (New York: St. Martin's Press, 1999), 198–99.

45. Mukherji, "Neo-nationalism Symposium," 27. Another strain of resentment has been noted among the women. See Bacchetta, "Militant Hindu Nationalist Women Reimagine Themselves," 125–47.

46. *India Abroad* (12 May 1998), 24.

47. Arvind Padmanavan and Liz Mahew, "Differing Views: Cultural Regeneration or Cultural Regression," *India Abroad*, March 17, 2000, 24.

48. Gerad Heuze, "Shiv Sena and National Hinduism," *Economic and Political Weekly* (October 10, 1992): 2254.

49. Sikata Banerjee, *Warriors in Politics: Hindu Nationalism, Violence, and the Shiv Sena in India* (Boulder, Colo.: Westview Press, 1999), 154–55.

50. K. K. Gangadharan, *Sociology of Revivalism: A Study of Indianization, Sanskritization and Golwalkarism* (New Delhi: Kalamkar Prakashan, 1970), 124.

51. Ainslie T. Embree, "The Function of the Rashtriya Swayamsevak Sangh: To Define the Hindu Nation," in *Accounting for Fundamentalisms: The Dynamic Character of Movements*, Martin E. Marty and R. Scott Appleby, eds. (Chicago: University of Chicago Press, 1994), 628.

52. Daniel Gold, "Rational Action and Uncontrolled Violence: Explaining Hindu Communalism," *Religion* 21 (1991): 365.

53. Sudhir Kakar, *The Colors of Violence: Cultural Identities, Religion, and Conflict* (Chicago: Chicago University Press, 1990), 144.

54. T. N. Madan, *Modern Myths, Locked Minds: Secularism and Fundamentalism in India* (Delhi: Oxford University Press, 1997), 277.

55. Robert Eric Frykenberg, "Hindu Fundamentalism and the Structural Stability of India," in *Fundamentalisms and the State: Remaking Polities, Economies, and Militance*, Martin E. Marty and R. Scott Appleby, eds. (Chicago: University of Chicago Press, 1993), 242.

56. Dina Nath, *RSS: Myth and Reality* (Sahibad, India: Vikas Publishers, 1980), 67; Jean Alonzo Curran, *Militant Hinduism in Indian Politics: A Study of the RSS*. (N. Y.: International Secretariat, Institute of Pacific Relations, 1951), 81.

57. Thomas Blom Hansen, "Recuperating Masculinity: Hindu Nationalism, Violence and the Exorcism of the Muslim Other," *Critique of Anthropolgy* 16, no. 2 (1996): 160.

58. Stanley Wolpert, *A New History of India* (New York: Oxford University Press, 2000), 252–53.

59. Amiya P. Sen, *Hindu Revivalism in Bengal, 1872–1905: Some Essays in Interpretation* (Bombay: Oxford University Press, 1993), 11.

60. Dayanand Saraswati, *Arya Dharma, Hindu Consciousness in 19th Century Punjab* (Delhi: Manohar, 1976), 214.

61. Suvira Jaiswal, "Semitizing Hinduism: Changing Paradigms of Brahmanical Integration," *Social Scientist* 19, no. 12 (December 1991): 30.

62. Anil K. Sarkar, "Stop Gloating about the Vedic Culture," *India Tribune*, April 21, 2001, 5.

63. Praful Bidwai, et al., *Religion, Religiosity and Communalism* (New Delhi: Manohar, 1996), 229.

64. Bidwai, *Religion, Religiosity*, 228.

65. Prasenjit Duara, "The New Politics of Hinduism," *Wilson Quarterly* (Summer 1991), 49.

66. Susie Tharu, "A Critique of *Hindutva*-Brahminism," *Economic and Political Weekly* (July 27, 1996): 2019.

67. Rustom Bharucha, *In the Name of the Secular: Contemporary Cultural Activism in India* (Delhi: Oxford University Press, 1998), 58–59.

68. Bharucha, *In the Name of the Secular*, 56–57; *The Tribune*, August 23, 1993); Geeta Kapur, "On the Exhibition," *MHSA* (New Delhi: SAHMAT, 1994).

69. Gyanendra Pandey, *Hindus and Others: The Question of Identity in India Today* (Delhi: Viking, 1993), 15.

70. Sheldon Pollock, "Ramayana and Political Imagination in India," *Journal of Asian Studies* 52, no. 2 (May 1993): 262–63.

71. Subrata K. Mitra, *Culture and Rationality: The Politics of Social Change in Post-Colonial India* (New Delhi: Sage, 1999), 395.

72. P. R. K. Rao, "Science and Technology as an Ideology," *Seminar* (Bombay, January 1982), 66.

73. Krishna Kumar, *Political Agenda of Education: A Study of Colonialist and Nationalist Ideas* (New Delhi: Sage Publications, 1991), 42–49.

74. Harjot Oberoi, "Mapping India Fundamentalism through Nationalism and Modernity," in *Fundamentalisms Comprehended*, Martin E. Marty and R. Scott Appleby, eds. (Chicago: Chicago University Press, 1995), 102.

75. Thomas Blom Hansen, "Controlled Emancipation: Women and Hindu Nationalism," in *Ethnicity, Gender and the Subversion of Nationalism*, Fina Wilson and Bodil Folke Frederiksen, eds. (London: Frank Cass, 1997), 83.

76. Krishna Kumar, *Social Character of Learning* (New Delhi: Sage Publications, 1989), 100. Kumar argues that even social studies have not been interdisciplinary in curriculum in the Third World.

77. Shiv Kumar, "Shiv Sena Activists Vandalized English Billboards," *India Abroad*, July 14, 2000, 8.

78. David Kopf, "Hermeneutics versus History," *Journal of Asian Studies* 39, no. 3 (May 1980): 505.

79. Ishwar C. Harris, *Gandhians in Contemporary India: The Vision and The Visionaries* (New York: The Edwin Mellen Press, 1998), 150.

80. Balraj Madhok, *Rationale of Hindu State* (Delhi: Indian Book Gallery, 1982), 119.

81. Gurudas M. Ahuja, *BJP and Indian Politics* (New Delhi: Ram Company, 1995), 130.

82. Walter Korfitz Anderson, "The Jana Sangh: Ideology and Organization in Party Behavior" (Ph.D. dissertation, Department of Political Science, University of Chicago, 1975), 6.

83. Kumar, *Political Agenda of Education*, 117.

84. Thomas Blom Hansen, "Recuperating Masculinity: Hindu Nationalism, Violence and the Exorcism of the Muslim Other," *Critique of Anthropology* 16, no. 2 (1996): 145; Golwalkar, *Bunch of Thoughts*, 65.

85. Hansen, "Recuperating Masculinity," 140.

86. Satya Pal Gulati cited in *Organiser* (November 12, 1978): 12.

87. Deendayal Upadhyaya and D. B. Thengadi, *The Integral Approach* (New Delhi: Deendayal Research Institute, 1979), 65; Sheldon Pollock, "From Discourse of Ritual to Discourse of Power in Sanskrit Culture," *Journal of Ritual Studies* 4 (1990): 315.

88. Richard Fox, ed., *Nationalist Ideologies and the Production of National Cultures* (Washington, D.C.: American Anthropological Association, 1990), 69.

89. Hasan Suroor and Suchitra Begal, "Nationalist Curriculum Prompts Walk-Outs," *The Times Educational Supplement* (November 20, 1998), 18.

90. Kancha Ilaiah, *Why I am not a Hindu: A Sudra Critique of Hindutva Philosophy, Culture and Political Economy* (Calcutta: Bhatkalan and Sen, 1996), 15.

91. Ilaiah, *Why I am not a Hindu*, 18.

92. Peter van der Veer, "Hindu Nationalism and the Discourse of Modernity," in *Accounting for Fundamentalism*, vol. 4, Marty and Appleby, eds., 655.

93. Anderson, "The Jana Sangh," 380.

94. "Vidhya Bharati," *Organiser* (November 10–12, 1978): 11.

95. P. Khanna, "Education: The RSS Way," *Ananda Bazar Patrika* (1 December 1991): 22–25.

96. H. V. Seshadri, ed., *RSS: A Vision in Action* (Bangalore, India: Jagaran Prakashana, 1988), 199.

97. Seshadri, *RSS*, 22.

98. "Shishu Mandirs Put Up an Impressive Show," *Organiser* (March 25, 1972): 15.

99. Tanika Sarkar, "Educating the Children of the Hindu Rashtra: Notes on RSS Schools," *South Asia Bulletin* 14, no. 2 (1994): 12.

100. Praful Bidwai, "BJP Ideology," *India Abroad*, October 6, 2000, 2.

101. T. Yayaraman, "Facing Up to Fraud," *Frontline*, February 12, 1993, 101.

102. P. N. Oak, a historian, cited at www.bighorn.dr.lucent.com.

103. M. S. Golwalkar, *Spotlights* (Bangalore: Sahitya Sindhu, 1974), 35.

104. Balraj Madhok, *Rationale of Hindu State* (Delhi: Indian Book Gallery, 1982), 119.

105. Gyanendra Pandey, *Hindus and Others: The Question of Identity in India Today* (Delhi: Viking, 1993), 10.

106. Pandey, *Hindus and Others*, 12.

107. Khanna, "Education: The RSS Way," 22.

108. "Shishu Mandirs and the Concept of Developed Child," *Organiser* (November 12, 1978): 12, 13.

109. Liz Matthew, "Publication of Books by Left Historians Withheld," *India Abroad*, February 25, 2000, 10.

110. Krishna Kumar, "Hindu Revivalism and Education in North-Central India," in *Fundamentalisms*, Marty and Appleby, eds., 555.

111. "Sangh Developing Bharatiya Model Acceptable to Modern Mind," *Organiser* (October 4, 1992): 11.

112. Ved Mehta, *Rajiv Gandhi and Rama's Kingdom* (New Haven: Yale University Press, 1994), 185.
113. Ramesh Thakur, *The Government and Politics of India* (New York: St. Martin's Press, 1995), 244.
114. Lloyd I. Rudolph, ed., *Cultural Policy in Delhi* (New Delhi: Chanakya Publications, 1984), 31.
115. Arvind Padmanabhan and Liz Mahew, "Differing Views," *India Abroad*, March 17, 2000, 24.
116. Francine R. Frankel, *Transforming India: Social and Political Dynamics of Democracy* (New Delhi: Oxford University Press, 2000), 401.
117. Ashok Malik, "One Man Barmy," *India Today*, May 14, 2001, 10.
118. *India Today* (14 May 2001), 12.
119. Oberoi, "Mapping," in *Fundamentalisms*, Marty and Appleby, eds., 104.
120. *The Times Educational Supplement*, November 20, 1998, 18.
121. Reporter, "Astrology in Higher Education," *Sangbad Bichitra* (Bengali News Organ, published in New York) April 16, 2001, 7.
122. Khanna, "Education: The RSS Way," 23.
123. Sarkar, "Educating the Children of the Hindu Rashtra," 11–14; "Cover Story," *India Today*, May 11, 1986, 34.
124. Rudolph, *Cultural Policy in India*, 17.
125. Kumar, "Hindu Revivalism and Education in North-Central India," 554.
126. Gyanendra Pandey, "The Appeal of Hindu History," in *Representing Hinduism: The Construction of Religious Traditions and National Identity*, Vasudha Dalmia and Heinrich von Stietencron, eds. (New Delhi: Sage Publications, 1995), 386.
127. Sarkar, "Educating the Children of the Hindu Rashtra," 12.
128. Victoria L. Farmer, "Depicting the Nation: Media Politics in Independent India," 267.
129. Embree, "The Function of the Rasahtriya Swayamsevak Sangh," 626.
130. Gerad Heuze, "Shiv Sena and National Hinduism," *Economic and Political Weekly* (October 3, 1992): 2190–91; Heuze, "Shiv Sena and National Hindusim," *Economic and Political Weekly* (October 10, 1992): 2253.
131. Ratna Kapur and Brenda Cossman, "Communilising Gender, Engendering Community," in *Women and Right-Wing Movements*, Tanika Sarkar and Urvashi Butalia, eds. (London: Zed Books, 1995), 91; Manini Chatterjee, "Stringent Sadhus: Contours of a Hindu Rashtra," *Frontline*, January 16–29, 1993: 21.
132. Kapur, "Communalising Gender," 118, n. 44.
133. Manini Chatterjee, "Strindent Sadhus: Contours of a Hindu Rastra," *Frontline*, January 16–29, 1993, 21–27.
134. Hansen, "Controlled Emancipation," 85.
135. Chandra Talpade Mohanty, et al., eds., *Third World Women and the Politics of Feminism* (Bloomington: Indiana University Press, 1991), 22, 315.
136. An Obscure Hindu, *Grave Danger to the Hindus: An Address* (Malabar: K. C. Bhalla, 1940), 239.
137. Dhananjay Keer, *Veer Savarkar* (Bombay: Popular Prakashan, 1966), 212.

138. Tanika Sarkar, "The Women as Communal Subject: Rastrasevika Samiti and Ram Janmabhomi Movement," *Economic and Political Weekly* 26 (August 31, 1991): 2057–58.

139. Embree, "The Function of the Rashtriya Swayamsevak Sangh," in *Accounting for Fundamentalisms*, 640–41; Tanika Sarkar, "Heroic Women," 187.

140. News Despatches, "Girls Resist Ban on Jeans, Skirts in College," *India Abroad* (10 March (March 10, 2000), 6.

141. An Obscure Hindu, *Grave Danger to the Hindus: An Address* (Malabar: Kerala: K.C. Bhalla, 1940), 234.

142. Hansen, "Controlled Emancipation," 87; See also L. Kelkar, *Amrit Bundi* (Pune, 1971). The book argues that women must not leave the house for reasons of education and work.

143. Meera Nanda, "Is Modern Science a Western, Patriarchal Myth? A Critique of the Populist Orthodoxy," *South Asia Bulletin* 11, nos. 1 & 3 (1991): 48.

144. Patricia Jeffery and Amrita Basu, eds., *Appropriating Gender: Women's Activism and Politicized Religion in South Asia* (New York: Routledge, 1998), 114.

145. Ratna Kapur and Brenda Cossman, cited in *The Legacy of Women's Uplift in India*, Llewellyn, 20.

146. K. R. Malkani, *The RSS Story* (Delhi: Impex India, 1980), 175.

147. Ratna Kapur and Brenda Cossman, "Communilising Gender: Engineering Community," in *Women and Right-Wing Movements*, Sarkar, 91, 98.

148. Kapur, "Communilising Gender," 104.

149. Ilaiah, *Why I am not a Hindu*, 9; M. N. Srinivas cited in *Women, Democracy and the Media: Cultural and Political Representations in the Indian Press*, Sonia Bathla (New Delhi: Sage, 1998), 76.

150. Amrita Basu, *Two Faces of Protest: Contrasting Modes of Women's Activism in India* (Berkeley: University of California Press, 1992), 111.

151. Ghashyam Shah, *Social Movements in India: A Review of the Literature* (New Delhi: Sage Publications, 1990), 131.

152. Bathla, *Women, Democracy and the Media*, 48.

153. *India Today*, October 15, 1987, 59.

154. John Stratton Hawley, ed., *Sati: the Blessing and the Curse: The Burning of Wives in India* (New York: Oxford University Press, 1994), 10.

155. John Stratton Hawley, ed., *Fundamentalism and Gender* (New York: Oxford University Press, 1994), 89.

156. Veena Talwar Oldenburg, "The Roop Kanwar Case: Feminist Responses," in Hawley, ed., *Sati: The Blessing and the Curse*, 9.

157. Bathla, *Women, Democracy and the Media*, n75.

158. Ratnabali Chatterjee cited in Madhusree Dutta, et al., eds., *The Nation, the State and Indian Identity* (Calcutta: Samya Publishers, 1996), 38.

159. Lene Arnette Jensen, "Moral Divisions Within Countries Between Orthodoxy and Progressivism: India and the United States," *Journal for the Scientific Study of Religion* (March 1998): 46.

160. Inderjit Badhwar, "Sati: A Pagan Sacrifice," *India Today*, October 15, 1987, 58–60.

161. Llewellyn, *The Legacy of Women's Uplift in India*, 48–50.

162. Veena Talwar Oldenburg, "The Roop Kanwar Case: Feminist Responses," Hawley, ed., *Sati*, 163.

163. Oldenburg, "The Roop Kanwar," 9.

164. Hawley, "Hinduism: Sati and Its Defenders," in *Fundamentalism and Gender*.

165. Veena Poonacha, "Hindutva's Hidden Agenda: Why Women Fear Religious Fundamentalism," *Economic and Political Weekly* (13 March 1993): 439.

166. Margaret Snyder, *Women: The Key to Ending Hunger*, The Hunger Project Papers, no 8 (August 1990), 9.

167. Thomas Blom Hansen, "Controlled Emancipation," in *Ethnicity, Gender and the Subversion of Nationalism*, Wilson and Fredericksen, eds., 8.

168. Paoloa Bacchetta, "All Our Goddesses are Armed," in Kamla Bhasin, et al., eds., *Against All Odds* (Delhi: Kali for Women, 1996), 149–50.

169. Paola Bacchetta, "Communal Property/Sexual Property: Representations of Muslim Women in a Hindu Nationalist Discourse," in *Forging Identities: Gender, Communities and the State in India*, Zoya Hasan, ed. (Boulder, Colo.: Westview Press, 1994), 217.

170. Kumkum Sangari, "Consent, Agency, and Rhetoric of Incitement," *Economic and Political Weekly* (May 1, 1993): 878.

171. Thomas Blom Hansen, "Recuperating Masculinity: Hindu Nationalism, Violence and the Exorism of the Muslim Other," *Critique of Anthropology* 16, no. 2 (1996): 155.

172. Leslie J. Calman, *Toward Empowerment: Women and Movement Politics in India* (Boulder, Colo.: Westview Press, 1992), 162.

173. Girilal Jain, *The Hindu Phenomenon* (New Delhi: UBS Publishers, 1994), 33.

174. Paul R. Brass, *Ethnicity and Nationalism* (New Delhi: Sage, 1991), 85.

175. Jain, *Hindu Phenomenon*, 31.

176. B. D. Graham, *Hindu Nationalism and Indian Politics: The Origins and Development of the Bharatiya Jana Sangh* (Cambridge: Cambridge University Press, 1990), 118.

177. Bharatiya Jana Sangh, *Documents* 21 (Delhi: Central Working Committee, May 8, 1954).

178. Sangh, *Documents* 21, 122.

179. Jain, *Hindu Phenomenon*, 33.

180. Amrit Rai, *A House Divided: The Origin and Development of Hindi/Hindavi* (Delhi: Oxford University Press, 1984), 286.

181. Rai, *A House Divided*, 286–87.

182. Ahmad, cited in "Reconversion to Hinduism through Suddhi," 64.

183. Balraj Madhok, *Rationale of Hindu State* (Delhi: Indian Book Gallery, 1982), 29.

184. Madhok, *Rationale of Hindu State*, 80.

185. M. N. Srinivas, *Caste in Modern India* (New Delhi: Asia Publishing House, 1962), 42.

186. Sudha Ratan, "Hindutva: The Shaping of a New 'Hindu' Identity," *Southeastern Political Review* 26, no. 1 (March 1998): 215.

187. Mark Juergensmeyer, "Hindu Nationalism and Human Rights," *Religious Diversity and Human Rights*, in Irene Blom, et al., eds. (New York: Columbia University Press, 1996), 258.

188. Amartya Sen, *Reason Before Identity* (Oxford: Oxford University Press, 1999), 24.

189. Jain, *Hindu Phenomenon*, 58.
190. V. V. Raman, "Bring Back the Glory of Hinduism," *India Abroad*, May 5, 2000, 3.
191. Bhatt, *Liberation and Purity*, 196.
192. Larson, *India's Agony Over Religion*, 42.
193. Suresh Sharma, cited in *Creating a Nationality*, 60.
194. Thomas Blom Hansen, "Globalisation and Nationalist Imagination: Hindutve's Promise of Equality through Difference," *Economic and Political Weekly* March 9, 1996: 609.
195. Swapan Dasgupta, "A Mind of His Own: A Rare Representation of Asish Nandy," *India Today*, March 15, 2001, 34; Vinay Lal, ed., *Dissenting Knowledges, Open Features* (New Delhi: Oxford University Press, 2001).
196. India Abroad News Service, "BJP Distances Itself from RSS," *India Abroad* October 27, 2000: 22.

Chapter 7

Perceiving Islam: The Causes and Consequences of Islamophobia in the Western Media

Zohair Husain and David M. Rosenbaum

Revolutionary Islamism is as feared and reviled today as reactionary Fascism and revolutionary Communism were in their heyday. Islamophobia and paranoia of the so-called green peril seems to dominate the influential Western mass media today just as the fear of German Nazi imperialism, the Soviet Communist "red menace," and the Chinese Communist "yellow peril" permeated the anti-Nazi and anti-Communist Western mass media in the twentieth century. However, the West's Islamophobia and Islamdom's distrust, fear, and antipathy toward the West are not new. This chapter will describe, analyze, and explain some of the principal reasons for and major consequences of the West's Islamophobia as well as the major reasons for Islamdom's distrust of, and antipathy toward, the West.

In the hours and days following the attacks on the Pentagon and World Trade Center, symbols of American military and economic preeminence, Americans were asking themselves, "Why do they hate us?" Trying to make sense of the biggest terrorist attack on American soil, they asked themselves: why did the terrorists strike at us? What conceivable grievances could they have? Do all Muslims hate us? Alternatively, were these criminal acts merely the work of a few zealots? Was the problem poverty or oppression? Alternatively, was Islam itself to blame for the national catastrophe of September 11, 2001?

Many Westerners today, if they possess any perception of Islam at all, often imagine it as a monstrous force stretching its arms over the face of the world. Revolutionary political Islam, or Revolutionary Islamism or Islamic fundamentalism, is as thoroughly feared in the West today as Soviet Communism was before it. Islam is seen as a monolithic force threatening not only the West's way of life but also its survival. Yet Western fear of the Islamic "threat" or the green peril[1] is rooted not in reality but in misperception and misunderstanding. Western politicians, scholars, and of course, the mass media habitually focus on the most sensational aspects of political Islam, and this by itself has contributed to a tragic distortion of Islam and of devout Muslims around the world. Islam is erroneously characterized as some force unto itself, both inconceivable to the Western mind and inherently opposed to the Western way of life.[2]

Clash of Western and Islamic Civilizations: Historical Roots

The notion that Islam, as a religious and cultural force in the world, stands somehow intrinsically opposed to all things Western is nothing new. Western scholars have for centuries weighed the "Islamic threat," wondering when again the Saracens would be at the gates of Vienna or threatening Paris. Western scholarly perception of Islam has historically been hostile. Islam is "other," alien; it is incomprehensible; it is hostile politically, militarily, and culturally to things Western. The clash between the Christian West and the Muslim world is more than a thousand years old. Islam's Prophet Muhammad himself faced vehement opposition to his mission not only from idol worshipers, but also from Jews and Christians. This conflict between the Christian West and the Muslim world intensified when Muslims conquered portions of Europe and the Holy Land and when the Muslim Ottoman Empire dismembered the Christian Byzantine Empire—the same fate, ironically, that later befell the Ottomans. Although the Crusaders themselves rarely were a picture of Christian unity in opposition to various Muslim empires,[3] the Crusades profoundly affected Western thinking about Islam. Even during the European Renaissance (1350–1650)—sparked in part by Muslims engaging not in war but in peaceful trade and commerce with Europe—and during the European Enlightenment of the eighteenth century, Islam continued to be maligned as a threat to Christendom or even as a threat to reason and rationality. The men of letters and guiding lights of the Enlightenment, while courageously debunking Christian Church propaganda, which had stigmatized Islam as a perverse hedonistic faith, were themselves particularly unenlightened about Islam, Muslims, and the Muslim world. Voltaire, one of the Enlightenment's prominent figures, for instance, wrote a play entitled *Fanati-*

cism, or the Prophet Muhammad and referred to Prophet Muhammad in his *Philosophical Dictionary* as "a brazen impostor who deceived imbeciles."[4] Meanwhile, the paintings of Jean-Auguste-Dominique Ingres portrayed Ottoman Turks lolling around in their harems with their female concubines and thereby conjured up and reinforced the distorted image of Muslims as permissive and promiscuous misogynists.

Christian Europeans had for centuries viewed Islam as a dangerous and threatening adversary both on the field of battle and in the realm of ideas. Indeed, "until Karl Marx and the rise of communism, the Prophet [Muhammad] organized and launched the only serious challenge to Western civilization...."[5] As Roman might ebbed in the fifth century, the Islamic empire rose in the seventh century as a formidable political, ideological, and military force threatening the very heart of Europe, at different times conquering Spain and southern Italy, central Europe, and southern France. Muslim powers represented an alarming thousand-year threat that not only enjoyed considerable military success against Europeans but posed an ideological challenge as well, winning converts away from Christianity by the tens of millions.[6] Nothing before or since—with the exception of Communism—has so alarmed the West as this steady westward push of a massive, relentless, and frequently victorious challenge.[7] Unable fully to subdue Muslim armies on the field of battle, Christian Europeans vilified Muslims and denigrated Islam, describing it as a monolithic essence, a faith founded on deception and clumsy plagiarism of Judaism and Christianity, and depicting its believers as frightful caricatures.

By the nineteenth century, advances in military and industrial technology favored the West. The Muslim world suffered gradual conquest by European military forces. Muslim economic and political power declined.[8] This eventual technological superiority of secular Western nation-states over the expansive but fragmented Muslim world ushered in an era of imperialism and colonialism. Western nations conquered, administered, and exploited the developing Muslim societies in spite of considerable opposition from the Muslims themselves. Western fear of Islam abated; the alleged "threat" of Islam had been tamed by superior Western technology. During the period of Western imperialism and colonialism, Muslims who dared challenge Western dominance were branded subversive agitators; they were hunted down and imprisoned or killed in their own lands. Even after gaining nominal independence from Western colonial rule in the twentieth century, the secular pro-Western nationalists who assumed power in these Muslim countries felt greater affinity with their former Western masters than with the people they governed.

In the closing decades of the twentieth century, the Western relationship with the Muslim world changed. States in the Muslim world were revealed as friends or foes through the prism of the Cold War. The intense ideological struggle between the West and the Communist bloc inspired greater American aid to strategically located and resource-rich Muslim countries to maintain pro-Western, anticommunist regimes. Whenever Islamists challenged the governing pro-Western secularists, they were suppressed with Western help. The Western mass media justified this suppression by branding them "Marxists," "Fundamentalists," or "terrorists."[9] No attempt was made to explore the meaning of these terms; the universal understanding of Westerners was that these revolutionaries were a threat to their interests, indeed to the Western way of life.[10] Thus, when authoritarian Muslim regimes' security forces, trained and equipped by the West, crushed opposition movements that threatened the status quo, the West either ignored the repression or applauded it as though the troublemakers had no right to revolt but were merely communist dupes. Law and order were to be preserved as a hedge against Soviet expansion, no matter the people's grievances.

Western interest in the Muslim world is sensible and appropriate today given the geostrategic interests of the West in the region, the region's possession of natural resources vitally important to the West, the sizable market that more than 1.2 billion Muslims present, and the history of Arab and Turkish Muslim armies conquering the Holy Land and parts of Europe. All this is coupled with modern Western ignorance, insensitivity, and misunderstanding of justifiable Muslim frustration. Moreover, Westerners are constantly reminded that Muslims, holding fast to the anchor of Islam as best they understand it, have often rejected modernization and secularization.

However, with the end of the Cold War and the conclusion of the Gulf War, Western interest in the Muslim world briefly declined. Incidents of terrorism, a common news item in the 1980s, seemed to abate. Oil prices were low. The troubled history of the Middle East seemed of little importance, and Westerners, particularly in the United States, turned their attention to domestic priorities. During the 1990s, however, radical Islamists were active. Defeat of the Soviets in Afghanistan, war with the Russians in Chechnya, and a hasty U.S. withdrawal from Somalia emboldened some Islamists who were preparing for another battle with the West.

Events such as the OAPEC oil embargo, the OPEC oil price explosion, the destruction of the U.S. Marine barracks in Lebanon, the Islamic Revolution in Iran, the Iranian hostage crisis, the kidnapping of American hostages in Lebanon, the assassination of Egypt's President Muhammad Anwar al-Sadat, and the Persian Gulf War, to name only a prominent few, briefly resurrected that sense of an Islamic threat" antithetical to U.S. interests. Yet nothing less than the attack on the Pentagon and the World Trade Center was required to rekindle Western interest in the Muslim world. The attack on the USS *Liberty* by Israeli aircraft in 1967 and the Jonathan Pollard Affair, in which case, an American Jew in U.S. navy intelligence handed over a significant amount of sensitive information about the Middle East to Israel: should these events have been described as evidence of a "Jewish threat"? Of course not, nor should acts of terrorism, even when carried out by Revolutionary Islamists, be considered signs of a "Muslim threat" or "Islamic threat." After the events of September 11, discussions of a "Muslim threat" or "Islamic terrorism" became commonplace. But Western concern about "Islamic rage," is by no means a new phenomenon. Immediately after the Cold War and the emasculation of communist ideology, Western scholars and policy-makers went fishing for a new adversary worthy of Western attention.

Although the ideological context within the Western world has shifted from a parochial and conservative Christian worldview to a secular and liberal worldview over the last three hundred years, deep-seated and negative perceptions of Islam fed by a millennium of anti-Muslim propaganda have tenaciously endured, and the Western image of Muslims and the Muslim world remains a distorted caricature of reality. But how has this image been conveyed and who is responsible for it? Insofar as most Westerners, including journalists, are poorly informed of the thousand-year history of clashes between the West and the Muslim world, the true descendants of the Crusader mentality are modern Western scholars and policy-makers, sometimes mistaken as "experts."

Samuel Huntington identified Islam as the West's new adversary in his 1993 article "The Clash of Civilizations." Relying heavily on works by Bernard Lewis—Professor Emeritus of Near Eastern Studies at Princeton University—Huntington described "Islam" in a fashion that assumed that such an entity could be comprehensible without reference to the myriad opinions and doctrinal viewpoints held by the world's 1.2 billion Muslims. Huntington's daring and compelling proposition turned out to be nothing more than a rehash of the Cold War paradigm, with Muslims filling in for the villain. Judith Miller's contention in a 1993 opinion piece for *Foreign Affairs* that Islam does indeed represent a threat to the West offers a similarly unimpressive view of the worldwide conspiracy of Islam against the West. But scholars like Lewis, Miller, and Huntington tread dangerous ground by promoting overly simplistic explanations of Islam. Their absurd reductionist perceptions of Islam as enemy convey nothing of the richness or nuance or complexity of Islam as a religious faith, whether today or during its long and eventful history. Their understanding of Islam as an entity that is at once quickly recognized as opposed to all things Western is in fact no understanding at all. It is a clumsy, prefabricated conspiracy theory that "ties together isolated events and trends." As Leon Hadar—an adjunct scholar at the Cato Institute in Washington, D.C.—notes, "all changes and instability in the post-Cold War Middle East and its peripheries are described as part of a grand scheme perpetrated by 'Islam International.'"[11]

Such a conception of Islam rests on a foundation of willful ignorance and lazy scholarship. It is not, for example, Bernard Lewis's contention that Revolutionary Islamists have perverted and mutilated Islam but rather that these fanatics who twist Islam into a means of attaining political power are in fact the true exemplars of what Islam is. Of course, it is no myth that individuals and organizations supporting particular forms of Islamic militancy against the West have, in fact, attacked Westerners and the West. The myth is that this violent activism is representative of Islam as a religion of 1.2 billion people, or for that matter, that the world's Muslims are somehow more dangerous than the world's Protestants or Hindus or Roman Catholics. Hardly unified, Islamic politics is better described as "a kaleidoscope producing shifting balances of power and overlapping ideological configurations" that defy central control.[12]

Tragically, it is the scholarship of oversimplification that informs the West about Islam. People predisposed to distrust what they do not understand readily embrace inaccurate shorthand explanations of a religion they know nothing about.[13] This is the understanding of Islam that gave us, in the days immediately following the 1995 Oklahoma City bombing, "experts" who claimed that it was the work of Islamic terrorists—a claim that proved wholly untrue.[14] This is the scholarship that inspired Newt Gingrich to denounce the "worldwide phenomenon of Islamic totalitarianism funded and largely directed by the state of Iran."[15] It is to such experts and political personalities that the Western mass media turn to understand the complexities of the Muslim world. What Americans know about Islam has been fed to them by the Western mass media, which is very little. The Western mass media served as the conduit through which medieval anti-Muslim propaganda and nineteenth-century Orientalist prejudice have been translated into modern Western anti-Muslim press. The preponderance of Western-born and educated reporters, editors, writers, and producers in the Western media establishes the apparatus by which the Western viewpoint prevails in news reporting. Although most reporters genuinely attempt to be objective in their interpretation of events, no person can erase his or her political socialization or deny his or her culture and the voice that a subconscious bias lends it. Given the inordinate influence the media wield in the West, negative images of Islam, however unrepresentative or dishonest, only reinforce ancient stereotypes.

Thus, a long and traumatic history of conflict between the Western world and the Muslim world has clouded Western and Muslim sensibilities with regard to one another. And just as many Muslims hastily decry the West and all things Western, so do many Westerners with comparable haste decry all things Islamic. Furthermore, the recent memory of the Cold War has only reinforced a Western us versus them worldview, lent credence by scholars like Huntington and Lewis. In the Muslim world, distrust, frustration, and resentment of the West run deep and is periodically manifested in acts of anti-Western protest and violence. Westerners, for whom the era of colonialism was largely beneficial, are insensitive to the feelings of downtrodden and persecuted Muslims. Westerners are inclined to think that Muslim demonstrations against Western hegemony in ostensibly sovereign Muslim states are a reflection of ingratitude, parochialism, and ignorance and, worse still, are irrational and barbaric outbursts of an Islamic threat.

Anti-Islamic Bias in the Western Mass Media

Unwilling to divine the wellspring of Muslim anger or ever to fathom its abyssal depths, the West has devised an alternate terminology that vilifies Muslims for actions or attitudes that Westerners praise in themselves. Armed Zionists in the Hagannah, Irgun, and Stern Gang, fighting often ferociously for the independent Jewish state of Israel, were referred to not as Jewish terrorists but as patriots, nationalists, commandos, guerrillas, the Jewish underground, and freedom fighters. Their struggle was treated with considerable sympathy in the context of a history of virulent Western anti-Semitism. Following the Holocaust, few Westerners in good conscience could deny the Jewish people their long-awaited homeland, where they might freely practice their religion, enjoy their own culture, and govern themselves. Consequently, their military activities were portrayed as an "independence struggle."

In contrast, the military activities of members of the Palestine Liberation Organization (PLO) were never called by the Western mass media a "liberation struggle" or seen in light of a similar history of injustice and victimization suffered by Palestinian Arabs. Until only recently, the Western mass media has referred to Palestinians only as "terrorists," so often that "terrorism" and Palestinian are nearly synonymous in the Western vocabulary. Unable to accept that Jews and Palestinians have both been persecuted, many Westerners have reduced a complex political situation into simple black and white. How easy the world is to understand when the "good guys" (the Israelis) engage in "counter-terrorism," "retaliation," "preemptive strikes," "commando raids," or an "iron-fist policy" against the "bad guys" (the Palestinians) who are always terrorists"; the Palestinian Authority, Hamas, and Hezbollah are forever branded as the instigators of violence who murder Israelis. Israeli bombing of Lebanese villages, always with civilian casualties was, in contrast, depicted by the mass media clinically and unfeelingly. When extremist Palestinians kill and wound Israelis, the Western mass media repeatedly depicts the bloody and gruesome scenes, and as a result, viewers are understandably shocked and furious. However, when the Israeli government unleashes awesome military firepower against Palestinian towns and refugee camps—thereby killing and wounding many innocent Palestinians and destroying their homes and farms—the Western mass media rarely shows us the dead, dying, maimed, homeless, or suffering Palestinians. The impression often left in viewers' minds is that Israel was merely targeting terrorists in its retaliation and, therefore, the Palestinians deserved it. There are also calls to both sides in the dispute to "end the cycle of violence."

This double standard in terminology occurs not only in the Arab-Israeli conflict but also throughout the world. In former Yugoslavia, the Western press rightly decried Serbian attacks on Bosnian and Kosovar Muslims but never made reference to them as "Christian terrorists," though the Serbs called themselves Christian soldiers defending Europe from the scourge of "Islamic fundamentalism." Religion is as central a feature in the conflict between the Serbs and the Bosnians as it is between the Arabs and the Israelis. Yet the Serbs are always called "nationalists," while the Palestinian Islamists are defamed as Islamic terrorists. When the Serbs committed genocide against Bosnian Muslims and Kosovars (Muslims of Kosovo), the Western mass media constantly referred to it as "ethnic cleansing," not genocide or mass murder of innocent Muslims. However, if Muslims had done the same thing, it would probably have been called Islamic terrorism or genocide.

The mass media ought to know that words have power. We must therefore empathize with the victims and try to end their victimization rather than accept the language of the aggressor and victimizer. Still, the press has convinced both itself and the public that only Muslims are "terrorists." Strangely, there are no "Christian" or "Jewish" terrorists! The Catholic Irish Republican Army, which has carried out attacks against Irish and English Protestants, was never called an organization of "Christian terrorists," nor is the Protestant Ulster Defence Association so termed, though it too carried out acts of terror against Catholics. In the United States, Christian antiabortion zealots firebombing health clinics are never portrayed as Christian terrorists, and for good reason. They are not acting as Christians or in the loving spirit of Christianity when engaging in acts of fanatical violence. Logically, then, the mass media should refrain from decrying Islamic terrorism. Moreover, the mass media should remember that kidnapping, incarcerating, and torturing innocent civilians of any religion, race, color, or nationality is totally reprehensible, whoever does it. Killing innocent civilians, of course, is heinous and barbaric no matter the perpetrator, whether it is the Israeli Defence Forces, the Mossad, the CIA, the Serbs, militant Hindu fundamentalists, the Palestinian Authority, Hamas, or Hezbollah. The selective perceptions of the Western mass media, however, cause many Westerners to condemn strongly the alleged crimes of their enemies while overlooking or rephrasing euphemistically the human rights abuses of their allies and friends.

Some Muslim observers of the Western mass media have declared its biases and prejudices indicative of a neocolonialist conspiracy against Islam. In general, however, there is an absence of malice in mass media coverage of Islam, though never a shortage of the prejudice, bias, and ignorance in the cultural baggage we all carry. Certain universal psychological factors, acting often subconsciously, work behind mass media misperception of Islam. Ingrained since birth with negative images of Islam, the ordinary Westerner is predisposed to maintaining and justifying certain convenient stereotypes. Stereotyping Muslims as harem-keeping oil-rich shaykhs, as angry mobs, or as fanatics and terrorists occurs for several reasons. First, such stereotypes are easy; they make actual thinking unnecessary. Instead of a thorough examination of Islam, instead of worrying about the many sects and schools of Islam that render it a faith as divided as Christianity, Islam is reduced to a few negative images. This, in turn, transforms the innocent Muslim into a convenient scapegoat for the ills of modern Western civilization.

The "greedy" and "ruthless" Muslims, for example, are blamed for rising oil prices and for the West's poor economic performance in the 1970s. Meanwhile, the West's inordinate demand for and self-imposed dependence on oil are not addressed. Someone else is always to blame, and our stereotypes of Muslims as avaricious oil rich shaykhs make them an easy target. The social and economic troubles of the United States in the 1970s become the fault of the Muslim world—a world predominantly of destitute urban workers, small farmers, and peasants who must pay the same prices for oil as do Westerners. Western stereotypes that portray Islam as a religion of fanatics reinforces the Muslim conviction that the West is determined to frustrate the Islamic quest for identity. Muslims point to the outpouring of Western sympathy for the aspirations and suffering of the Eastern Europeans and the Caucasians of the Baltic states (Lithuania, Latvia, and Estonia) and Russians and to Westerners's apparent indifference to what happens to Muslims in many parts of the world. Implicit is the attitude that Muslims are very different from "us," and probably even against "us" and our national interests. Western military intervention to stop Serbia from carrying out genocide in Kosovo represented a step in the right direction but was by no means an expression of Western support for Kosovar independence from Serbia. Western policy remains that Kosovo is unquestionably a part of Serbia. In the case of Chechnya, which the United States recognizes as part of the Russian Federation, sympathy for Chechens and opposition to Russian brutality in the region have enjoyed some play in the Western media. But even this lukewarm support ended entirely with the attacks on the Pentagon and World Trade Center. In any event, Western media support for the Chechens was likely more representative of residual Cold War fear of and opposition to Russia.

A process called *cognitive consistency*, which is based on the notion that human beings, by and large, resist change and prefer stability, perpetuates established stereotypes. When a person is used to a particular stereotype, when it is comfortable, he or she enjoys cognitive stability with regard to the subject of the stereotype. This saves him or her the mental effort and anguish of rethinking not only that stereotype but also his or her entire worldview. Cognitive consistency is thus the frequently subconscious effort human beings naturally make to avoid potentially contradictory perceptions. Whenever an image is inconsistent with one's established stereotype, one simply disregards the new information and the stereotype goes unaltered. Although the stereotypes are wrong, they become firmly entrenched at all levels of society—particularly in academia, where young scholars simply force new information to fit old perceptions and paradigms.[16] The *evoked set*, much like *cognitive consistency*, is another psychological process by which the West's perception of Islam, Muslims, and the Muslim world has been colored. Having grown accustomed to the Cold War and the difficulty of retrenching millions of people employed in the enormously influential military-industrial complex, Westerners have tended to recycle the obsolete Cold War, us-versus-them mentality and applied it to other trouble spots. Once upon a time, the "Reds" were our greatest adversary, and now by drawing an imperfect historical analogy, called an "evoked set," we believe that militant Revolutionary Islamism is an enemy comparable in every way to communism and thus must be at all costs contained and neutralized. Certainly Huntington's description of Islam as an entity that exists for apparently no reason other than to defy the West falls into this category.

The "blindness of the instant" concept also explains Western mass media misperceptions of the angry outbursts of some Muslims. Individuals tend to perceive and interpret unanticipated events out of historical context. In fact, they sometimes wholly disregard causality. Thus, the West, while rightly condemning Iranian hostage- taking in 1979, conveniently overlooked the prominent U.S. role over a period of decades in propping up the *shah*. Indeed, a long history of callous and shortsighted U.S. support for the tyrannical and unpopular *shah* contributed directly to the callous and shortsighted Iranian retaliation during the Islamic Revolution. The attack on September 11, 2001, which differs in that it is strongly pathological, does not excuse the United States from trying to determine the motivations of the attackers and potentially changing Western policy to prevent future attacks.

All the above tendencies are buttressed by the *black-white diabolical enemy image* that transforms "us" versus "them" into a sweeping good versus evil paradigm. The adversary is demonized and dehumanized. It becomes impossible to understand or empathize with "them." One disregards the possibility that this adversary may be just like "us," that "they" may be hoping for peace or spoiling for war for reasons that are readily explicable, provided we put ourselves in their place. Moreover, the *black-white diabolical enemy image* is compounded by its reciprocity. It is, like all the above-mentioned psychological processes of misperception, double-edged. All human beings are subject to their own parochial caprices. Just as some Westerners sense the Islamic threat as an evil best contained, so do some Muslims perceive Westernization and secularization as an evil best dismantled—whether personified by the Israeli state or by Western-supported puppet governments like that of the *shah* of Iran, President Hosni Mubarak of Egypt, or the late King Hussein of Jordan and the late King Hassan of Morocco. Moreover, this reciprocity of hostility lends itself to a *conflict spiral,* in which the perceived hostility of a foe is matched by hostility in return. The consequent cycle, the action-reaction syndrome, thereby reinforces untrue, unsavory, and unsympathetic stereotypes, generates reactionary policies, and undermines efforts to bring disputants together.[17] Like Sisyphus perpetually rolling the stone up the hill, the combatants expend everything in their struggle with one another, but it avails them nothing.

The persistence of stereotypes, related directly to the human need for cognitive consistency, haunts us today despite, or perhaps because of, the communications revolution, and the shrinking of our global village. Two hundred years ago militant Islamism was irrelevant to the newly created American republic. Islam was a distant, mysterious, but intriguing force that never intruded into an American's world. Now *everything* concerns us. During the 1980s and 1990s the Cable News Network (CNN) frequently carried stories dwelling on the Islamic threat. Today this fear of some universal and monolithic Islamic threat is not only perpetuated but is amplified far out of proportion to its reality by the Western media. Western reporters and journalists who cover and portray the Muslim world are either predisposed to condemn Islamism outright or totally unprepared to comprehend it. And with scholars like Huntington and Lewis informing Western journalists, no wonder that many consumers of Western media confidently proclaim the backwardness and barbarism of Islam and the cultural superiority of the West.

Imagine a world in which prominent scholars were better informed and more balanced in their discussions of Islam. The Western media, in an effort to say as much as possible in the least amount of time, would still lack the capacity to distinguish between Islam and criminally insane fanatics who purport to be God's warriors on Earth. Not all Muslims are militant and violent religious fanatics, nor for that matter, are all militant and violent religious fanatics, Muslims. Edward Said—the Palestinian-American professor of Literature at Columbia University—asks, when analyzing the September 11 attacks, why not "see parallels, admittedly less spectacular in their destructiveness, for Osama bin Laden and his followers in cults like the Branch Dravidians or the disciples of the Rev. Jim Jones at Guyana or the Japanese Aum Shinrikyo?"[18]

Westerners have been convinced that Osama bin Laden, Ayatollah Khomeini, and Saddam Hussein epitomize Islam—that these men are true representatives of the faith. Yet in truth, Islam is in spirit, as kind and gentle a faith as its two predecessors—Judaism and Christianity. The Revolutionary Islamist interpretation of Islam should be seen as the violent reaction to perceived Western (including American) imperialism and neocolonialism. Nor should anyone confuse the totality or essence of Christianity with the examples of David Koresh and Jim Jones. Nor are many radical fundamentalist Jews like Baruch Goldstein or Rabbi Meir Kahane (who founded the Jewish Defense League) representative of the totality of Judaism. Why then does much of the Western mass media take Osama bin Laden's crazed militant Islamism out of context or, worse still, label Islam and all devout Muslims as irrational zealots and fanatics? Islam is as diverse, rich, and meaningful a monotheistic and peaceful belief system as the monotheistic religions of Judaism and Christianity. There is just as much diversity in the worldview of Muslims as there is in the worldview of Jews, Christians, and members of other religious faiths.

Western mass media have also engendered a confusion of *Arab* with *Muslim*. Although as many as 10 percent of Arabs worldwide are Christians and Jews and although 80 percent of Muslims are non-Arabs, the West invariably equates all Arabs with Muslims—even such prominent non-Arab Persian Muslims like Ayatollah Khomeini are subject to this misconception. In the bombing campaign in Afghanistan, most Westerners were not aware that the Afghans are themselves not Arabs. Arabs in Afghanistan are foreigners. Perhaps the greatest misconception perpetrated by the Western mass media is that the Muslim world consists of wild and murderous people seething with inexplicable anti-Western rage. Camera crews went looking for a few Palestinians celebrating the September 11 attacks or a crowd of Pakistanis chanting their allegiance to Osama bin Laden and denouncing the West. Little mention was made of the many more Muslims who express no support for bin Laden and who sympathize with the victims of the attacks. Instead, 1.2 billion Muslims scattered the world over with different and unique historical backgrounds, cultures, traditions, and worldviews are conveniently reduced to a series of simple stereotypes immediately recognizable by the dimmest wits.

Western media rarely engage in a substantive examination or appraisal of the Muslim world. Instead, they often portray Muslims—whether in movies, news programs, or television sitcoms—as negative, one-dimensional caricatures and tend to represent them "in unqualified categorical and generic terms: one Muslim is therefore seen to be typical of all Muslims and of Islam in general."[19] Through the media looking glass, all Muslims are mysteriously transformed into oil shaykhs, terrorists, or uncivilized, bloodthirsty, book-burning, stone-throwing, placard-waving anti-Western mobs. Thus, Western media disregard Islam as a holistic religion in the objective sense and use it instead to describe all aspects of the diverse Muslim world, "reducing all aspects of Islam to a special malevolent and unthinking essence."[20] In the Western worldview, therefore, Islam becomes "them" in an easily understood "us" versus "them" equation.

All forms of the Western mass media are responsible for perpetuating certain ridiculous stereotypes of the Muslim. Television programs and Hollywood motion pictures have been instrumental in giving Westerners a distorted picture of Islam and its adherents. Given this alleged reputation for liberal and politically correct inclinations, one might expect that the Western mass media would know better. After all, the American mass media has taken great pains to eliminate most negative, unpleasant, and untrue stereotypes of Jews, African Americans, and Native Americans. Yet the Muslim "stock character" persists in movies and television. Far from eliminating such negative stereotypical characters, "Hollywood films preserve traditional stereotypes and television shows follow Hollywood's lead."[21] Indeed, "assiduous research has shown that there is hardly a prime-time television show without several episodes of patently racist and insulting caricatures of Muslims."[22] Western mass media depictions of Islam and of Muslims have been generally shallow, callous, and often racist. The Arab-Israeli conflict, for example, helped to popularize films such as "Exodus," depicting the founding of Israel. These films, instead of using drama to explain the conflict's complexities relied instead on creating an ambience reminiscent of World War II. In fact, "these movies present the Israeli-Arab conflict in much the same way as cowboys and Indians: the Arabs are always the bad guys, the Israelis, the good guys."[23]

Cinema stereotypes persisted during the 1970s. Several years after the murder of Israeli Olympic athletes by Palestinian extremists in Munich, the movie *Black Sunday* postulated an Arab attack on an American Superbowl crowd by means of a blimp.[24] OPEC price hikes in the late 1970s also engendered the film *Rollover* in which "the Arabs destroy the world financial system." As a star of *Rollover*, Jane Fonda, future wife of CNN founder Ted Turner, declared in an interview: Arabs "are unstable, they are fundamentalists, tyrants, anti-women, anti-free press."[25]

Perceiving Islam 183

During the 1980s and 1990s, popular Hollywood movies depicted Muslims solely as terrorists bent on humiliating or conquering the United States. The lesson that movies like *Navy SEALs, Iron Eagle, Delta Force, Invasion USA, Death before Dishonor, True Lies, Rules of Engagement,* and *Executive Decision*[26] teach is that diplomacy is worthless, seeing an adversary's point of view has no value. Instead, "violence serves as the main vehicle for plot development and plot resolution."[27] And in Hollywood, "it doesn't take long to figure out which side is going to win the shootout."[28] Not surprisingly, the spirit of these movies lived on not just in future films but in future U.S. relations with Iraq. By the early 1990s, Iraqi conscripts became the victims of ten years of Hollywood dehumanization.[29] Notwithstanding the impact of television and film depictions of Muslims on the Western image of Islam, the news media—both print and electronic—are the primary source of information in Western society and thus the greatest perpetrator of "Islamophobia." Television shows and motion pictures have portrayed Muslims negatively and simplistically not only because these media trade in comfortable and convenient stereotypes but because they too rely on the Western news media. Fictional television and movie depictions of Muslims are merely the popular cultural expression of Western antipathy toward "Islam." Humiliating stereotypes of Muslims constructed for entertainment provide a catharsis through which Western paranoia and "Islamophobia" is expressed and partly relieved. The news media is the instigator of that paranoia and "Islamophobia."

For the most part, the mass media have unintentionally fabricated the "threat of Islam" in the guise of extremist Revolutionary Islamism. The psychological motivations previously discussed facilitated this demonization of Islam and dehumanization of Muslims. But cognitive consistency and other such processes are alone not sufficient to explain the news media's bias in their coverage of Islam. Western media typically provide a simplistic, monochromatic picture of the Muslim world because of commercial constraints inherent in their operation. Journalists and reporters in the Western press, for example, tend to prefer sensational and exciting news events that will capture and hold the viewer's interest rather than slower-paced, more deliberate, more substantive stories—the kind that require time-consuming research and draw smaller audiences. The Muslim "types," which include terrorists, angry mobs, and oil-rich emirs, no matter how unrepresentative they are of Muslims at large, are common fixtures in news coverage of Islam and represent Islam to Westerners. Westerners will on television screens, perceive the inherent newsworthiness of isolated incidents in the Muslim world as typical fare. Hostage taking, bomb throwing, and rioting mobs chanting "Down with America" come to epitomize the Western view of "Islam." Western news media rely on inherently sensational events to attract viewers. Endless stories of planes taking off and landing every hour without incident will likely drive viewers and advertising dollars away, if it does not kill viewers with boredom first. Unfortunately, lacking an informed and intelligent picture of the Muslim world, Westerners are likely to mistake the act of terrorism or the crowd runs amuck for the everyday reality of Islam. Imagine Westerners's surprise if Muslims were to perceive the Los Angeles riots of 1992 as everyday reality all over the United States.

Certainly the great fault of the electronic news media is a lack of time and a consequent lack of depth. CNN's Headline News, for example, has only half an hour to explain important international events; and that brief thirty minutes must be shared with domestic news, business news, and sports and entertainment segments; add to that a hearty portion of commercials, and it is not surprising that the coverage of Islam and the Muslim world gets short shrift. Of course, viewers could eschew the sound bites and turn to more in-depth news coverage from, for example, National Public Radio's *All Things Considered*. But only a tiny fraction of the American population has time for news and analysis that is totally devoid of entertainment. We have patience only for the easily digestible, beautifully packaged, half-hour helping of network news. In addition, while such news is not inherently bad, it is demonstrably insufficient, and worse, most Western viewers are unaware of its limitations as a source of valuable or reliable information. ABC, CBS, NBC, CNN, and Fox promise to give us the world if we give them half an hour. However, the world they give us lacks depth and substance. Headline news has time enough only for the finely crafted headline—the story itself is sacrificed in Western haste.

The Western news media's inability and/or unwillingness to present an unbiased view of Islam, Muslims, and Muslim societies are a tragedy not only for Westerners who come away with a poor understanding of the Muslim world but for Muslims as well. The impact of the Western news media is felt around the world. During the Gulf War, that impact was magnified and compounded. Since the war, Muslims and Muslim nations, no longer strictly "the source of news . . . have become consumers of Western news."[30] Thus, the Muslim world is today "learning about itself by means of images, histories, and information manufactured in the West."[31] Muslims now are being emotionally and psychologically affected by watching Westerners vilify and belittle Islam, Muslims, and the Muslim world on television. This has, understandably, shaped Muslim perceptions of the West.[32]

The communications revolution that brought CNN into Muslim households during the 1990s has been accompanied by "an over-all Muslim delay in understanding the reasons for Muslim dependence" on the Western mass media; this delay "prevents their doing something about it."[33] Well-organized, well-funded, and assertive Israeli interest groups have had a positive impact on media coverage of Jews and Israel, while no effective organization of pro-Muslim sympathies has improved coverage of Islam, Muslims, and Muslim states. Muslims themselves share some of the blame for this misfortune. First, Muslims living in democratic Western nations who decry unfair and unfavorable media coverage have done little to redress the problem. They have remained relatively disorganized, parsimonious with their money, nonpolitical, and therefore, powerless. Second, authoritarian leaders of most Muslim countries, fearful of their own unsavory human rights, economic, and social records, are unwilling to provide access to the Western mass media within their own countries. Third, some of the blame falls on those oil-rich Muslim nations that possess the money but lack the interest or will to improve the Western media's depiction of Islam, Muslims, and the Muslim world.

The establishment of Al-Jazeera, the twenty-four-hour Arabic language news channel based in the tiny emirate of Qatar, was one response to Western media bias in its coverage of the Muslim world. Founded in 1996 with $140 million from the Qatari government, this Arab equivalent to CNN and Fox reaches 35 million viewers in the Muslim world. During the U.S. war in Afghanistan, Al-Jazeera was the sole foreign broadcaster allowed in Taliban-controlled territory. Osama bin Laden made use of the media outlet to supply videotapes of his denunciations of the West in the aftermath of the September 11 attacks. Al-Jazeera's anti-Western coverage of the conflict concerned Western policy-makers, but attempts by the Bush administration to stifle Al-Jazeera were viewed in the Muslim world as hypocritical, considering that many Muslims consider Western news media "fundamentally partisan and biased in their own right."[34] Al-Jazeera's anti-Western slant is best answered not by attempts to quash the network's independence (curbed somewhat by the channel's reliance on funding from the Qatari government) or to censor its message but by genuine Western attempts to convey the Western message to the Muslim world. That message can be persuasive to Muslims only insofar as it rejects blanket statements about Islam and terrorism that have no basis in reality.

Presently, Western fear of the "threat of Islam" is the overwhelming theme of Western media treatment of the Muslim world. Sensational and misleading information selectively perceived and transmitted by the news media could make Huntington's prophecy of a clash of civilizations self-fulfilling. While the West continues to portray Islam in a bad light and to give it a bad name, "the irony is that Western views of Islam on the whole prefer to associate Islam with what many Muslims themselves are opposed to in the current scene: punishment, autocracy, medieval modes of logic, theocracy."[35] Therefore, deliberate Western vilification of Islam, many Muslims reason, is nothing more than cultural imperialism, a Western-instigated and -funded conspiracy against them and their faith. Such views find a voice on Al-Jazeera.

Misperception is reciprocated by the Muslim world toward the West. Muslims are not immune to cognitive consistency and the black-white diabolical enemy image, by which the West is made into "the Great Satan." Just as the Westerner condemns "Islam" and its medievalism and barbarity, so does the Muslim condemn the "West" and its arrogance and consumerism? The conflict spiral of misperception soon becomes one of real hostility, increasingly difficult to defuse. And global Islamism and the Islamic revival both feed upon and fuel that conflict spiral. Real and perceived provocation by the West against "Islam" is answered with real and perceived hostility by frustrated and angry Muslims. Thus, the West and the Muslim world demonize each other, transforming the other into what each fears most. A political and cultural polarization occurs and the chasm separating "us" from "them" becomes evermore unbridgeable. The most radical demagogues rise to power spouting inflammatory religious rhetoric to win over the masses—and Islamic politics, militant or otherwise, takes on a more anti-Western temperament. Thus in response, the Western mass media, instead of denouncing the acts of a few radical and relatively parochial Muslims, begin ridiculing Islam, Muslims, the Muslim world, and a rich and varied civilization.

The Western Mass Media and the Iranian Revolution

Of all the upheavals gripping the Muslim world none has been more misread and misinterpreted by the Western mass media than the Iranian Revolution and the consequent hostage crisis in the twilight of the Carter presidency. The Western media totally misunderstood the motivations and dynamics animating the Iranian Revolution and therefore contributed to a conflict spiral and to policies implemented by both the United States and Iran that were shortsighted and often irrational. As the ultimate source of public information, the Western media blundered famously in its coverage of the Iranian Revolution specifically and Islam in general. The failure of the media rested not so much in its ignorance as in the failure to concede its ignorance to the viewer. With the revolution and the hostage crisis, suddenly every journalist and pseudointellectual was an expert on Islam and on the causes of the Iranian Revolution. In short, the media and its "experts" erred in "pretending that a great deal was known and in presenting a view of Iran's revolution that was dictated more by official Washington than by reality."[36]

In truth, the Iranian Revolution was a phenomenon of the United States's own making. It was the likeliest reaction to decades of senseless, short-term U.S. policy toward Iran. The ultimate success and ascendancy of the Revolutionary Islamist Ayatollah Khomeini over such Modernist Islamists as Mehdi Bazargan and Abdul Hassan Banisadr and Muslim Secularists as Shahpour Bakhtiar was partly made possible by a long history of Western interference and intervention in Iranian internal affairs. Holding the line against communist expansion at all costs—even the life, liberty, and happiness of the Iranian people—insured not only the revolution against the repressive *shah* but its decidedly anti-American temperament.

Yet both the Western media and Western policy-makers were surprised by the Iranian Revolution and by the overthrow of the "iron-fisted" *shah*. Only months before, the Western news media were assuring readers and viewers that the *shah* maintained full control of Iran and enjoyed widespread popular support. Even President Carter praised the *shah* as a beloved and enlightened leader. Most Westerners accepted this public relations spectacle, but the Iranian people were not only unconvinced but also incensed by favorable Western press coverage of the hated *shah*. When, for example, the *shah* in a last-ditch compromise move appointed Bakhtiar as prime minister and the new leader was lauded in the Western media, Bakhtiar found his position of authority in Iran abruptly untenable. The Iranian people did not trust the Western media. The government-controlled Iranian media was itself directly responsible for triggering the revolution when, in a "spectacular case of bad judgment," a story was planted which called into question the ancestry of opposition leader Ayatollah Khomeini. This false report sent Iranians into the streets to protest angrily but peacefully in defense of the *ayatollah's* honor.[37]

The consequent Iranian Revolution interested a Western mass media that sought to determine the motivations and ultimate intentions of the Iranian people. Conveniently overlooking a long history of U.S. support for a regime with a deplorable human rights record, the news media decided that the culprit behind "senseless" revolutionary upheaval was Islam, currently typified by "a disturbingly neurotic Iran," which was "writhing in self-provoked frenzy."[38] Unsatisfied even with the explanation that Muslims were insane and that their behavior was inexplicable, some journalists and scholars entertained the ridiculous idea that "the diabolism of communism" was acting "in natural alliance with the devilish PLO and the satanic Muslims."[39] Haunted by the Cold War paranoia that had cost the United States Iranian friendship in the first place, scholars, journalists, and policy-makers evoked the 1950s-era notion of a worldwide conspiracy of "them against us." Consequently, the media swallowed "the regime's and Washington's contention that the *shah*'s problems were wholly the work of Islamic reactionaries and Marxists," their alleged cooperation and their fictional friendship producing what the *Washington Post* described as "a poisonous brew."[40] In reality, however, the Shi'ah leadership in the vanguard of the Iranian Revolution succeeded and prevailed only "as a result of widespread disillusionment with Western reforms and Soviet Marxism—two of the main sources of opposition ideology in Iran for fifty years."[41] Moreover, the *mullahs* were equally happy to characterize the USSR as the Great Satan as they were to demonize the United States—particularly after the Soviet invasion of Afghanistan in December 1979. The belief that Soviet Marxism motivated the fervor and the rage of the Iranian Revolution was unsupported by the evidence. Indeed, by 1979 it had grown obvious that "alleged Marxist influence among oil workers [was] more a product of Western press panic than a reality in the oil fields."[42] Nevertheless, the Western mass media—in thrall to a Cold War worldview and to a historical ignorance of and antipathy to Islam—sustained the incredible fiction of a communist-PLO-Shi'ah conspiracy against the West.

The Western media perpetuated another popular myth that the Ayatollah Khomeini "had made the revolution instead of the other way around."[43] The Western media as usual simplified information to the extent that the simplification bore little resemblance to reality. The Western news media, immediately and unthinkingly reducing any event of consequence to the work of one man, determined that the aging *ayatollah* from Khomeini had cleverly "masterminded" the revolution entirely by himself from exile and was, therefore, "the man who brought down the *shah*" and who would send Iran hurtling into medieval barbarity.[44] The role of the Iranian people individually and *en masse* was, according to the Western mass media, inconsequential and irrelevant to the story of the Iranian Revolution. In fact, U.S. dislike of the revolution was first founded in that "single-minded media caricature of the Ayatollah Khomeini, a caricature that sends ethnocentric chills through Americans."[45] The news media by far preferred the simplicity of a story in which "our man in Tehran," the *shah*, was subverted and overthrown by a crazed *ayatollah*. In addition, if Khomeini was bad, then conversely, the *shah* must have been good, if the world as portrayed by the Western media is truly black and white.

Consequently, mass media depictions of the *shah* were shallow and misleading. The *shah* cleverly portrayed himself the sturdy dam containing the Red deluge, as well as the enlightened, benevolent, and paternalistic dictator, like a latter-day Peter the Great, introducing his ignorant, backward, and stubborn subjects to the bounties of modernization and secularization. Thus, the king on his Peacock Throne enjoyed decades of relatively favorable press at the expense of the truth. The impression he left with the Western mass media was strong and endearing. At his downfall, the Western media, long feted and pampered by an indulgent *shah*, depicted the ruler as a "saddened, tearful, and ill-treated sovereign whose ungrateful people, in mindless fashion, had driven him from his country."[46] Looking back, the media described, but never discredited, the *shah*'s rule as "stern" and "iron-fisted"—terms that are euphemisms for what was really going on in Iran—and, indeed, even appealing to law-and-order-minded Americans. Conversely, the press very rarely used unpalatable terms like "bloody" and "tyrannical," although they were equally appropriate descriptions of the *shah*'s rule.[47] Moreover, Iranians in opposition to the *shah* viewed Western media coverage with disappointment. They believed that the Western press had "misinterpreted and oversimplified their motives" while denying them "the legitimacy they believed their cause deserved."[48]

The American Hostage Crisis

The Western news media, however, did not turn definitively against the revolution until the seizure of U.S. diplomats in Iran by zealous Iranian students. The embassy takeover occurred in response to years of perceived interference, intervention, and abuse perpetrated by the United States against Iran. The mass media thought otherwise. American anchors and journalists—who were, after all, patriotic Americans—abandoned the pretense of objectivity in news coverage of Iran. They took personal offense at the taking of American hostages by Iranian militants. Their loyalties and their empathy rested fully with the hostages. In response to this Iranian attack on U.S. sovereignty, American reporters stigmatized the Iranian Revolution specifically, and Islam generally. Iran, in effect, "came to symbolize . . . American relations with the Muslim world."[49] In turn, Islam came to symbolize Iranian behavior. Blinded by the instant, unwilling to submit their attitudes to analysis, unable to escape the prison walls of their prejudices, Americans made the Iranian Revolution and the hostage crisis the basis on which Islam was reduced to a militant, monolithic, and anti-American menace of explosive passions. As far as the Western press was concerned, "resentment, suspicion, and contempt were characteristic of Islam."[50]

The vilification of Islam was pronounced, not only because the Iranian students had taken hostages in the name of their own national pride but also because vilification was so easy. The news media, trading in simple and convenient stereotypes and stock characters could translate the revolution and all its complexities into a cartoon in which unreasonable mobs of self-flagellating Muslims confronted all things decent and American. The Iranian Revolution was portrayed as Islam out of control—a threat, like communism, best contained. Consequently, "the media had a field day in attacking Iran, even using abusive language against its leader. . . . Any dissent from the view that Iran was solely to blame for the crisis was considered bordering on unpatriotism."[51]

Wondering aloud how Iranians could hold "America itself" hostage, the press delved into the perceived cause of the frustration of efforts to free the hostages. A plethora of five-minute reports purporting to explain Islam crossed American TV screens. The impression these reports left with most Americans, who knew little or nothing of the Islamic faith, was shallow at best, grossly inaccurate at worst. Islam itself became the enemy because the Western media could not and/or would not explain the depth of, or even the reasons behind, Iranian anger with the United States. Instead of explaining Iranian anger, news organizations invented "the ugly Muslim" and his or her "hatred of this country," thereby slandering Islam to make the us versus them equation add up simply and without reference to tiresome complexities. Islam was fictionalized into a force within which "murder, war, [and] protracted conflict involving special horrors" were praiseworthy and commonplace.[52] In addition, this force, Americans were informed, had set itself against Americans and their way of life and, hence, warranted only our enmity and disdain. And as Muslims likewise viewed the gross fallacies attributed to Islam by Western journalists, the realization increased throughout the Muslim world that the West had set itself against all Muslims and, hence, warranted only their enmity and disdain. It was cultural imperialism, many Muslim charged; and the Western model was further discredited as something inherently anti-Islamic.

Western Coverage of the Iran-Iraq War

Although "media antipathy towards the Iranian Revolution [was] a continuation of past hostility," Western media misperceptions of Iran ended neither with the consolidation of the Islamic regime nor with the peaceful resolution of the hostage crisis during the inauguration of Ronald Reagan. Instead, encouraged by an American public strongly against Iran, the Reagan administration embarked on policies meant to punish the Iranians. The mass media rarely questioned these policies even when they involved lending support to Saddam Hussein following the 1980 Iraqi invasion of Iran. Only when George Bush faced a stubborn and dangerous Saddam Hussein a decade later were those policies critically examined by the media. During the 1980s, however, anger with Iran was rooted so deeply in the American psyche that the press further demonized the Iranians even at the cost of coddling the ambitious tyrant of Baghdad.

When the Iraqi advance into Iran began to flounder and Iraqi armies suffered dramatic setbacks at Iranian hands less than five months after the initial invasion, the Western mass media began to consider the prospect of total Iranian victory over Iraq. News stories from Western correspondents in Tehran described the Iranian military forces repelling Iraqi invaders as "a barbaric and fanatical army on the rampage." Analysts in Washington, D.C., used such images "to conjure up an image of imminent danger to the globe that must be contained at any cost."[53] Consequently, in the eyes of many Muslims, "rather than appreciating the Islamic qualities which triumphed over Ba'athism, the readers of the western media once again prepared to accept and more likely welcome a concerted western attempt to destroy the Islamic Revolution."[54]

Perhaps the crowning error of the Western news media during the long Iran-Iraq War rested in coverage of the 1980 destruction of a commercial Iranian airliner by the USS *Vincennes*. To engage high-speed but easily outclassed Iranian gunboats operating within Iranian territorial waters, the *Vincennes* willfully and intentionally crossed "into Iranian waters, . . . in violation of international law;" however, the captain of the U.S. ship "was not paying attention to juridical niceties."[55] While pursuing the Iranian gunboats, the *Vincennes* picked up a radar blip that was initially and correctly identified as a commercial airliner. The 290 passengers and crew of Flight 655 had taken off from Iran's Bandar Abbas Airport heading for Dubai along a routine and prescheduled flight path from which it never deviated. Unfamiliar with Iranian flight schedules over Iranian territorial waters, the *Vincennes* now mistakenly identified the Iranian airbus as a possible F-14 Iranian air force jet fighter. The *Vincennes* fired on the plane; there were no survivors.

The destruction of Flight 655, empathy for the captain of the *Vincennes*, and discussion by some in the American mass media (especially on radio talk shows) that the Khomeini regime had intentionally sent the civilian airplane with dead Iranians on board to embarrass the United States, infuriated Iranians and "surely caused Iran to delay the release of the American hostages in Lebanon."[56] More important, it brought grief to the families of the innocent dead and reinforced the conviction among many Muslims around the world that the United States was "out to get them." Indeed, when the mass funeral for the victims was conducted in Tehran, "it was an article of faith in Iran that the Americans deliberately attacked the plane."[57]

Perceiving Islam

The Pentagon and White House, while expressing remorse, explained the tragedy solely in terms of a technical error and praised the captain of the *Vincennes* for his commendable service to his country. And the press in its initial coverage of the event engaged in no investigative journalism or critical analysis. It should be emphasized, however, that the American news media is not necessarily subservient to the U.S. government; it is often a prisoner, rather, of its own ethnocentric worldview. Consequently, "the news stories about the U.S. downing of an Iranian plane called it a technical problem while the Soviet downing of a Korean Jet (Flight 007 in 1983) was portrayed as a moral outrage."[58]

The 1983 Soviet attack on Korean Airlines Flight 007 was branded "Murder in the Air" by *Newsweek* magazine. In contrast, for a situation with eerily similar circumstances, but with roles reversed, *Newsweek* on its July 18, 1988, cover laid no blame but merely "promised to disclose, about Iran Air, 'Why It Happened.'"[59] The press blamed the government of the USSR at every level for the KAL disaster while shifting the blame for the U.S. attack on the Iranian plane either to technical error or, worse yet, on (nonexistent) Iranian provocation. The underlying tone in the Western media was that the Iranians had somehow been asking for it. The Western media described victims of the KAL tragedy as "innocent human beings" who could tell "269 tales of personal poignancy." Discussion of the Iranian victims was bloodless and sterile, as though the *Vincennes* had inadvertently swatted a fly.[60] While the attack on the KAL was described as "brutal" and "barbaric" by the U.S. media, the U.S. attack on Iran Air was "fatal" but "understandable."[61] In fact, one retired navy captain insisted, "the Iranian airliner was placed in a dangerous situation that was created by its own government."[62]

Newsweek took four years to determine that the attack on the Iranian airbus was only superficially the result of technical error. Despite Pentagon assertions to the contrary, *Newsweek* determined that the *Vincennes* was in Iranian coastal waters in clear violation of international law—just as Iran had been by taking American diplomats hostage. Muslims around the world, distressed by the United States's nonchalant attitude to Muslim deaths, were further inclined to see the Western mass media as yet another tentacle of the imperialist leviathan. The mass media's reporting was hypocritical but not devious or conspiratorial. In short, "news organizations shape their reports to elicit favorable reactions from readers and viewers, and the anticipated reactions of the public also affect the rhetoric and actions of political elites, who are the primary 'sponsors' of news frames."[63] The opinions of the public, the media, and the policy-makers were thus founded on the basis of conformity.

The mutual derision and distrust sowed by the mass media coverage of Iran's Islamic Revolution, Khomeini's Islamic regime, the Iran-Iraq War, and the 444 days that Americans were held hostage in Tehran surfaced again with the Rushdie controversy in the late 1980s. The war of words between the two worlds—the Western and the Muslim—was rejoined.

The Rushdie Controversy

"The author of *The Satanic Verses* book, which is against Islam, the Prophet and the Koran, and all those involved in its publication who were aware of its content, are sentenced to death."[64] With this declaration, Iran's Ayatollah Khomeini baited the West, gave the Revolutionary Islamists and Traditionalist Islamists a new issue with which to attack Western animosity toward Islam, polarized the Muslim world, and made Salman Rushdie's novel an international best seller, in nations where it was not banned.

Born a Muslim, Rushdie was no longer practicing his faith when he wrote *The Satanic Verses*. He was educated in Britain, where he resided until driven into hiding by Khomeini's death sentence. His 1988 novel, *The Satanic Verses*, was roundly condemned throughout the Muslim world as an affront to Islam. However, the eighty-eight-year-old Ayatollah Khomeini more than anyone, thrust the Rushdie controversy onto the world stage, polarizing world opinion, and contributing to a confrontation of rhetoric between Islam and the West.

The Muslim world was justifiably galled by Rushdie's inflammatory book. The very title, *The Satanic Verses*, questions the validity of the Qur'an as Holy Scripture. Rushdie consciously impugns the Qur'an and imputes upon it satanic overtones—that it is the work of the Devil. Likewise, the second part of the book is entitled "Mahound," a derogatory name for Muhammad given by medieval Christians to discredit Islam. "Mahound" is an intentional caricature of Muhammad insofar as Rushdie parallels the life of the fictional "Mahound" with the life of Muhammad. Moreover, Rushdie insinuates that Muhammad manufactured the Qur'an for his own benefit under satanic influence and, thus, that the holiest book of Islam is not the revealed Word of God. Hence, the "businessman-turned-prophet" is portrayed as a fake, and Islam a work of clever forgery. Along the way, Rushdie gratuitously names twelve prostitutes after Muhammad's wives and thereby even further infuriates Muslims. In essence, "to devout Muslims, this book challenged and even violated the centrality of their beliefs, the very words of God, the integrity of their religious doctrine, and the image and dignity of the person of prophet Muhammad."[65] Harvard professor William Graham explains "it's as if you took the Bible, and in the middle of the Sermon on the Mount, you showed Jesus fantasizing copulation with whores."[66]

It is a testament to the Western media's culturally myopic worldview that, upon publication of *The Satanic Verses*, the Muslim world's vehemently negative reaction was unanticipated and totally misperceived. Immediately, calls came from Muslim communities to ban Rushdie's novel, and many developing nations obliged—among them Egypt, Saudi Arabia, Pakistan, India, and South Africa.

To Westerners and Muslims alike, the Rushdie controversy warranted outrage, but for different reasons. Westerners, particularly those in the liberal media, viewed Muslim attempts at censorship as at least unseemly, at most an affront to principles of freedom of speech and expression. Islamists viewed

Perceiving Islam 193

Western defense of Rushdie as the continuation of a fifteen-hundred-year-old cultural crusade against Islam. Above all, the Rushdie controversy became a rallying cry of Revolutionary Islamists to reject all things Western. The West, meanwhile, watched in horror as Muslims in Britain staged book-burnings and protestors marched on the American Cultural Center in Islamabad, Pakistan, throwing stones, roughing up a few Americans, and demanding Rushdie's death. For the West, the coup de grace came February 14, 1989, with Khomeini's "Valentine's Day" death sentence.

Sadly, the West responded to these unreasonable emotional outbursts with a few of its own. Western commentators and politicians heralded Rushdie's "inalienable" right to offend even 1 billion Muslims, while the Western news media, with an eye to the sensational, portrayed all Muslims as primitive religious fanatics burning books, donning shrouds, and proposing to hunt Rushdie down and "send him to Hell."

Death threats aside, Muslim calls for censorship of *The Satanic Verses* are easily explicable. Since Muslims identify themselves not according to the nation-state, as Westerners do, but according to the *ummah*, according to Islam and its community of believers, the charge against Rushdie of cultural treason is reasonable, while suppression of his book, which represents an obscene attack on that community, is understandable.[67] If, after all, the United States can plot to kill Fidel Castro of Cuba, Ngo Dinh Diem of South Vietnam, Rafael Leonidas Trujillo of the Dominican Republic, and Muammar al-Qadaffi of Libya; if it can overthrow Jacobo Arbenz Guzman of Guatemala, Salvador Allende of Chile, and Muhammad Mossadeq of Iran; and if it can invade Panama, Granada, and Iraq in the name of "democracy" and "human rights," why cannot the Muslim world in the name of the Qur'an, which "is the ultimate constitution of the community of believers,"[68] prohibit publication of Rushdie's libelous book, given that permitting publication is analogous to inciting a riot? Indeed, for the sake of the public order in predominantly Muslim countries, banning Rushdie's book is not a repressive act; it is a responsible act. If "American political morality expects its citizens to be ready to 'uphold, protect and defend the Constitution of the United States'"[69] against enemies foreign and domestic, how can the West deny the right of Muslims to uphold, protect, and defend the integrity of the Qur'an? Western media bent on insulting the villain of the day, never addressed these questions. Instead, the news media turned to simple stereotypes in which once again "Islam is reduced to terrorism and fundamentalism and now, alas, [was] seen to be acting accordingly, in the ghastly violence prescribed by the Ayatollah Khomeini."[70]

Both Britain and the United States, whose staunch defense of individual freedoms is admirable, consistently censor information whether for reasons of national security (i.e., Britain's ban of the book *Spycatcher*) or to avoid unduly offending minority groups. Although the latter form of censorship is practiced less by government than by private corporations and interest groups, it is still censorship. Moreover, thoughtful censorship in a free society is not necessarily harmful so long as reasonable limits are observed. Likewise, the "political correctness" fad currently sweeping U.S. campuses is based on gagging individuals who might otherwise give offense to women and minorities. In sum, this is all characteristic of the struggle between individual and corporate rights.

Muslims naturally wonder why censorship of culturally treasonous material is commonplace in the West (see if you can find a legally displayed swastika in Germany) while the reasonable concerns and requests of Muslims are either ignored or deemed unreasonable. Meanwhile, Rushdie wins literary awards, more for pity than for merit. Thus, the Muslim world rightly perceives Western hostility toward Islam. The West bestows upon Rushdie the right to blaspheme Islam and slander its 1.2 billion believers, in fact congratulates him for it, while the right of those 1.2 billion believers to apply their community standards against Rushdie's heretical, hate-inspiring book is denied.

In contrast, when Irish singer Sinead O'Connor tore up a photograph of Pope John Paul II on an airing of *Saturday Night Live* in 1992, press sympathy was clearly for millions of rightly offended American Catholics. No mention was ever made of O'Connor's right to free speech while a mob cheered on a steamroller as it crushed hundreds of O'Connor CDs—a picture analogous to the burning of Rushdie's book by a handful of Muslims in different parts of the world.

There was no question in the Muslim world, or even in the West, that Rushdie maligned Islam. However, there was a question among Muslims regarding what constituted an appropriate response to Rushdie's blasphemy. While the Western mass media characterized riots, book-burning, and death sentences as the universal reaction of Muslims to *The Satanic Verses*, this was simply not the case. And while all Muslims justly condemned Rushdie's book, not all demanded Rushdie's death.

Many Muslims openly supported Khomeini's death edict and made comments that truly shocked Western sensibilities and therefore enjoyed great exposure in the mass media. According to one zealot: "I think we should kill Salman Rushdie's whole family. . . . His body should be chopped into little pieces and sent to all Islamic countries as a warning to those who would insult our religion."[71] But many more Muslims, offered no such publicity in the Western mass media, regretted and repudiated the *Ayatollah's* actions: "[Rushdie] should never have said those things against the prophet. . . . But it is also not right to call for his death."[72] In addition, in India, where the Rushdie book had been banned, prominent Muslims denounced Khomeini's death sentence and felt that the anti-Rushdie movement had been co-opted by the Iranian *ayatollah*.[73] Furthermore, they conceded "this ban has made the book more popular. Just ignoring it would have been better for Muslims."[74] Another Muslim expressed similar misgivings about the Rushdie uproar: "It has set back Islam. It conveys to non-Muslims a picture of Islam that is barbaric, rabid, and extreme."[75]

Few Muslims felt any warmth or sympathy for Rushdie's partly self-imposed plight, and many Westerners were similarly inclined to denounce

Rushdie's insensitivity. Former president Jimmy Carter, for example, insisted, "while Rushdie's First Amendment freedoms are important, we have tended to promote him and his book with little acknowledgment that it is a direct insult to those millions of Muslims whose sacred beliefs have been violated."[76] Rushdie had insulted the most sacred beliefs of Islam. Nevertheless, the news media refused to acknowledge the contention that blasphemy and apostasy were at the heart of Muslim anger. Instead, a story was widely disseminated that Khomeini's death sentence was no better than a cynical effort to prop up the floundering Iranian Revolution, not a measure to defend the integrity of Islam. Western journalists perceived hidden motives behind Khomeini's death threats, particularly in statements the *ayatollah* made indicating that, "the dispute over *The Satanic Verses* proved that it was pointless [for Muslims] to pursue moderate policies."[77]

There is little doubt that Khomeini's behavior can be partly attributed to his falling stature in the Muslim world by 1989. His nation was in economic shambles and social decline; he had been forced by prolonged and bloody stalemate to accept a cease-fire with sworn enemy Iraq; and Khomeini's own probable successors had begun to decry the failures and shortcomings of the Islamic Revolution. By seizing the anti-Rushdie banner from those who first unfurled it and making it his own, the aging *ayatollah* sought to stoke the smouldering embers of the Islamic Revolution in Iran and reassert himself and his brand of militant Islamism on the Muslim world.[78]

Unfortunately, many analysts seized upon this interpretation of the *Ayatollah's* actions as though Rushdie's blasphemy was irrelevant to the story or as though 1.2 billion offended Muslims were the brainwashed minions of the Shi'ah *imam*. The Rushdie controversy was symptomatic of the ever-widening chasm of perception between the West and the Muslim world. When, on February 12, 1989, enraged Muslims marched on the American Cultural Center in Islamabad, Pakistan, they "carried placards attacking Zionism as well as Rushdie's book and its publisher."[79] Evidently, the Rushdie book represented only the latest in a series of perceived Western-instigated affronts to Muslims and their faith. Just as the West had used the Rushdie controversy to vilify Islam and to ridicule its alleged "medievalism," so did Islamists on the same basis justify their rejection of Westernization and secularization as evils inherently incompatible with the "straight path" of Islam? The Rushdie controversy did not occur in a vacuum but must be considered in the context of Islamic politics insofar as, "given the interrelatedness of culture, religion, and politics in the Muslim world, the reactions to [*The Satanic Verses*] have taken on understandably explicit political forms."[80] In fact, the Rushdie controversy represents "the spark which set alight an explosive mixture already present."[81] Thus, Revolutionary Islamists, like Khomeini, utilized the Rushdie book to galvanize mass support against Western influence generally, and against the Muslim secularists and Modernist Islamists specifically. By extrapolation then, the Rushdie controversy is not merely a manifestation of Revolutionary Islamism but a positive contribution to its strength and popularity.

The Gulf War

The 1990 Iraqi invasion of Kuwait and the subsequent U.S.-led Operation Desert Storm were of profound significance in the short history of Western news media coverage of Islam and Muslims. Of course, Operation Desert Storm was not an explicitly anti-Muslim crusade, nor was it portrayed as such, primarily because Kuwait itself was a Muslim nation and other Muslim countries, including Saudi Arabia and Egypt, fought with the U.S. coalition to expel Iraqi forces from Kuwait. Yet there remained an undercurrent of anti-Muslim sentiment that affected Western public opinion to the war.

This war, called the first "media war" because of the round-the-clock coverage it received, was both brief and, at least from the Western perspective, bloodless. Support for the war was based primarily on propaganda generated by the exiled rulers of Kuwait, who made a media spectacle of terrible atrocities committed by the occupying Iraqi forces in Kuwait. Recognizing the willingness of the Western mass media to serve as a conduit for Iraqi atrocity stories, the Kuwaiti government hired the public relations firm Hill and Knowlton. In October 1990, Hill and Knowlton provided the U.S. House of Representatives with a witness to the Iraqi invasion who claimed that Iraqi soldiers had removed babies from incubators and had let them die on the hospital floor. As it turned out, the "witness" was, in fact, the daughter of the Kuwaiti ambassador to the United States. She had not been in Kuwait during the invasion and had witnessed no atrocities committed in Kuwait by Iraqi forces. But before the Western news media became aware of the shaky credibility of the story's teller, the story itself had been accepted, like so many other xenophobic rumors, by the Western public and by Western policy-makers, including U.S. Senators who referred to the incubator atrocity in support of war against Iraq. In fact, ABC discovered, some years after the war, that Hill and Knowlton had used focus groups to determine which atrocities would most upset Americans: they discovered that baby atrocity stories were effective.[82]

The Hill and Knowlton firm played a significant role in galvanizing U.S. support for war against Iraq. Prior to their campaign of atrocity stories, public opinion was opposed to possible war, and Congress was inclined against military intervention.[83] The Hill and Knowlton media blitz, however, tipped the scales of public opinion toward war. The Western mass media sold viewers on the likelihood of war and the Bush administration's prosecution of that war. Atrocity stories circulated, although many were exaggerations or simply untrue, with the Western media's connivance. Douglas Kellner, professor of Philosophy at the University of Texas at Austin, argues: "The media which repeated these lies without skepticism or inquiry also revealed itself to be a naïve instrument of

U.S. (government) propaganda."[84] In reality, however, both the Western news media and U.S. policy-makers turned out to be the naïve instruments of the Kuwaiti government through the offices of the public relations firm Hill and Knowlton.

There is no question, however, that Western news media were largely uncritical of the U.S. government's prosecution of the war. When U.S. deployment of troops in the region began, the news media agreed to limitations on access to soldiers in the field by accepting the press pool system. Coalition military forces restricted media access by organizing journalists into pools "that were taken to sights selected by the military itself, and then reporters were allowed to interview troops with their military 'minders' present."[85] The pool system had been adopted by the U.S. military, partly due to British success with such a pool system in the Falkland Islands war and partly because the media had enjoyed virtually unrestricted access to the field in Vietnam. Unflattering media reports in Vietnam, so the military believed, had undermined Western public support for the war. The U.S. government saw to it that it wouldn't happen again; their control of the media during the Gulf War "was unprecedented in the history of U.S. warfare."[86] Moreover, "press and video coverage were also subject to censorship, so that, in effect, the military tightly controlled press coverage of the U.S. military deployment in the Gulf and then the action in the Gulf War."[87]

The imposition of press pools was not necessary to keep the Western media under control. The very fact that journalists were so accommodating to the military's use of pools was evidence enough that the pools themselves were a formality. Critics of the Western media have claimed "[in] its framing of the 'national debate,' the media cooperated with the government in limiting public understanding of the conflict."[88] The media acted almost as another branch of the armed services or a government department. The Western news outlets were quick to report sensational stories, sometimes untrue. Months or years later, more in-depth Western reports would reveal the falsity of those initial stories. However, it was too late—the damage had been done. Of course, Western media skepticism and criticism is unlikely in times of war—the journalists are almost universally American or European in background and are likely to be patriotic in the face of war or crisis. Thus, there is good reason to expect that "when the United States undertakes an especially dramatic foreign policy action, such as the bombing of another country, the media tend to be compliant mouthpieces of administration policy."[89] Unfortunately, it is at precisely these times that the Muslim world is most likely exposed to Western news accounts. In addition, these accounts necessarily do not reflect the anger and resentment of the Muslim world toward the West. Rather, they tend to demonize the Muslim world and thus alienate non-Western news consumers. This apparent connivance of Western media with Western governments was further reinforced by the tendency of U.S. and U.K. reporters to identify themselves with government policies and coalition forces by using the words we and our in Gulf War coverage.[90] This blurring of distinction has been more pronounced during the recent "war on terror."

Other media critics point out that Western public opinion supporting war with Iraq was based on popular Western anti-Arab and anti-Muslim cultural stereotypes. Although ostensibly coming to the defense of an Arab country against Iraq, the U.S. public was swayed "by media employment of culturally acceptable anti-Arab images."[91] The Western mass media did not offer balanced perspectives of the buildup to war or the war itself. Instead, it relied on traditional and commonplace references from popular culture. Attacks on the character and humanity of Saddam Hussein, which were largely true, unfortunately were "accompanied by commonplace images of other Arabs—including U.S. allies—as incompetent, weak, self-centered, and incapable of diplomacy in their own region."[92] Interestingly, these fearsome caricatures of Iraqis and other Arabs were accompanied by a second commonplace: "the righteousness of a civilized Western world courageously defended by U.S. soldiers."[93]

The Western media's use of these disparaging stereotypes was made considerably easier by their uncritical reporting of stage-managed press briefings in which footage of the war was presented in a way more evocative of a video game than a conflict in which people were dying. The use of so-called smart bombs that, at least in footage supplied by the U.S. military, could strike targets with exacting precision was presented by Western media in a manner that convinced many that this was the reality of the Gulf War. Images of collateral damage (i.e., civilian casualties) appeared on occasion but were downplayed as the regrettable exception rather than the rule. Grainy footage of laser-guided bombs striking Iraqi air force buildings emphasized an impression of the Gulf War as a "clean" war that would upset few Western sensibilities; the technology permitted the coalition "to provide good family entertainment without offending the viewing public."[94]

Apart from being a misleading portrayal of the war's realities, at least for those civilians and soldiers under the bombs, the footage removed any possibility of empathy for victims. The war was "an attack on things—weapons, transporters, bridges, buildings—but not on people."[95] But it was because Westerners were not subjected to the horrors that this war visited on Iraqi civilians and soldiers—who, incidentally, wanted nothing to do with a conflict with the world's remaining superpower—that Western stereotypes of Muslims could go undisturbed. Western minds could remain untroubled by the realization that these were fellow human beings and their suffering, even if not their culture was real. Such feelings of empathy for the avowed enemy would have been counterproductive to the task at hand, which from the U.S. government's point of view was not only to cripple Saddam's power to make war on U.S. allies but to win U.S. public support.

Ultimately, the most significant casualty in the Gulf War was public opinion in the Muslim world.[96] Anti-U.S. demonstrations against the war in Algeria, Egypt (which was a coalition partner), Libya, Mauritania, Morocco, Sudan, Tunisia, and Yemen received scant attention in the Western news media. Although the United States was able to find allies in the governments of many Muslim countries, the populations themselves seemed at best wary of U.S. intervention in the Gulf and objected to the U.S. military presence in Saudi Arabia. In fact, it was this very objection that motivated Osama bin Laden to denounce the United States and carry on a *jihad* against the West that ultimately culminated in the attacks on New York and Washington, D.C.

The War on Terror

On September 11, 2001, Revolutionary Islamists, most probably trained by the al-Qaeda terrorist network led by Osama bin Laden in Afghanistan, destroyed the twin towers of the World Trade Center in New York City and destroyed a portion of the Pentagon building in Washington, D.C. Western media coverage began that morning, and as bin Laden's connection to the attacks became clear, war became inevitable. But the war was to be a very different one. The al-Qaeda network was not a nation-state but an affiliation of militant Revolutionary Islamists, headquartered in Afghanistan but spread among terrorist cells in many other countries both in the West and in the Muslim world. The attacks were devastating to the West, not so much in terms of their actual physical impact, as psychologically.

In the days immediately following the attacks on the United States, Western media reporting was thoughtful in a way it had avoided before. The overwhelming response was one of terrible sadness and reflection on the loss of life. Calls for revenge were relatively muted, particularly given that in the first several days little was known about the perpetrators or their motives. Throughout the country—indeed, throughout the West—there were outbursts of anti-Muslim violence. However, this ignorant racist violence was often misdirected; victims in the United States included Sikhs, who aren't Muslims but wear turbans. Additionally, the Western media was quick to carry extensive reports on anti-Muslim attacks in the West. The media reported on statements made by President Bush and other national and local leaders who warned Americans not to attack Muslim immigrants or Muslim Americans. Newspaper editorials around the country urged restraint and cautioned Americans "not to repeat the tragic injustice that occurred when we detained Japanese Americans during World War II, just because of their race."[97] Even Western popular culture resisted the urge to renew Arab and Muslim bashing and adhered instead to more conscientious programming, intended not to inflame passions but to calm fears and raise money for victims.

Amnesty International also warned of the danger of xenophobia and applauded steps taken to avert it. In its annual report, the organization noted, "there is a danger that as the world's political leaders focus on combating 'terrorism' from abroad, a climate is engendered in which racism and xenophobia can flourish."[98] The report also listed hate crimes in the aftermath of the attack committed in the United States and other Western countries against Muslims and people mistaken for Muslims. Like the victims in the World Trade Center towers and the Pentagon, these Muslims were similarly "victims of an attack carried out in the name of Islam."[99]

In the following weeks, Western news media focused increasingly on Osama bin Laden's connection to the terror attack. Bin Laden's ties with the Taliban regime governing 90 percent of Afghanistan were close enough that the West turned to the Taliban leadership and demanded it turn over bin Laden and his chief lieutenants. Even Pakistan, which had nurtured the Taliban, made it clear to the Taliban leadership that the regime would be attacked by a new U.S. coalition of primarily Western powers if the Taliban failed to comply with the West's demands. This, in fact, is precisely what happened. The bombing campaign against Afghanistan's ruling Taliban began within a month of the attacks on the United States. The Taliban crumbled within another month, and members of al-Qaeda fled or were taken prisoner by various Afghan factions that opposed the Taliban. The Western media's role in all this was primarily one of support for Western action and a patriotism that tended to defer to the U.S. government. This was predictable and not necessarily inappropriate, given the magnitude of the attacks on New York and Washington, D.C., and the willingness, shared by most Americans, Europeans, and Russians, to root out al-Qaeda whatever the cost.

Owing to the Taliban regime's quick collapse, the Western bombing campaign was briefer than anticipated. But in spite of the campaign's short duration, public opinion in the Muslim world, while often sympathetic with the United States, was opposed to what most Muslims viewed as the futility and devastation of a Western bombing campaign against impoverished Afghanistan. Al-Jazeera's anti-Western coverage of the bombing campaign, which began on October 7, finally motivated U.S. policy-makers to find a way to convince Muslims around the world that the bombing of Afghanistan was not a crusade against Islam. In an October Gallup poll in Pakistan, percent of Pakistanis supported or sympathized with the Taliban. Only 3 percent sided with the United States.[100] Demonstrations and street violence in Pakistan underscored the anti-Western leanings of many Pakistanis, despite their government's support of the Western campaign against the Taliban.[101]

What the Western media has failed to explain to most Westerners is how deeply resentful the Muslim world is toward the West, and toward the U.S. in particular. While many moderate Muslims view the attacks on the United States as tragic and un-Islamic, they themselves have been critical of U.S. foreign policy and could not comfortably support the West's bombing of Afghanistan—a fellow Muslim nation.[102]

Although President Bush and other Western leaders insisted that the war on terror was not a war on Islam, many Muslims thought differently. Many in the Muslim world see the war on terror as just another phase in an ongoing Western crusade against Muslims. The Russian war in Chechnya is seen as one phase, the Western bombing of the pharmaceutical plant in Sudan, another. Moreover, Western sanctions against Iraq, which have devastated the Iraqi people but have failed to topple Saddam Hussein, are cited as a form of Western genocide against Arabs and Muslims. Many Muslims view Western military support for the Saudi monarchy and Western military presence in Saudi Arabia as an imperialist occupation of Islam's two holiest cities, Makkah and Madinah. Finally, many Muslims consider the West's long-standing support for Israel as Western hostility to Muslims and support for Israeli occupation of Islam's third holiest city, Jerusalem. Bin Laden's entire appeal to militant Muslims is based on this list of complaints. Whether these complaints are fair or have merit is irrelevant; what is relevant is that many rational and reasonable Muslims who would never harm anyone are incensed by what they see as a Western conspiracy against all Muslims. For these moderates, as much as for the Revolutionary Islamists, it all adds up to a Western crusade.

Still, Western media and policy-makers are mystified by the fear and hostility found in public opinion in Muslim countries. While Western leaders explain that the terrorists "hate us" because of our freedoms and our democracy and propose to explain those concepts more vigorously to Muslims around the world, the Western media fails to note that most Muslims already long for such freedoms but have been deprived of them by their own governments—governments often supported by or allied with the West. On this basis alone, our protestations that we stand for democracy and civil liberties strike Muslims as hypocritical. The terrorists may list opposition to democracy and freedom as one among their list of grievances against the West; certainly the Taliban were not great democrats even in the eyes of most Muslims.

But there is one thing that most Muslims can agree with Samuel Huntington about: the West is at war with Islam. The Western mass media have conveyed this impression successfully to a generation of both Western and Muslim viewers, and the damage will be difficult to undo. Western ignorance was the cause of this recklessly simplistic distortion of Islam in the Western mass media; those media conveyed this distortion to Muslims around the world; they have responded to our apparent hostility with a hostility of their own—hostility more dangerous because it is also a reaction to endemic problems of poverty and oppression. Consequently, TV channels like Al-Jazeera will continue enjoying popularity in the Muslim world, and Western viewpoints, once filtered through our own media, will now be interpreted by journalists who themselves are certain of the Western crusade against Islam.

Conclusion

Western news media coverage of Islam and the Muslim world is decidedly one-sided and usually echoes the policy and the rhetoric of Western governments.

Consequently, Muslims who oppose Western policy find themselves and their worldviews at odds with the Western press and are thereby convinced that "the media is as much an arm of imperialism as the Sixth Fleet, nuclear weapons, [or] gunboat diplomacy."[103] However, any collusion between the Western press and Western policy-makers is the result not of a tacit alliance or imperialist conspiracy. Instead, Westerners, whether making policy or writing news stories, share an identical view of the Muslim world. Thus, "it is this worldview, projected in the Press, which finds its tangible expression in Western foreign policies."[104]

Images and consequent opinions about Islam are channeled through our media within the context of the unspoken and unchallenged presumptions of Westerners. Such presumptions, perpetually reinforced by a culturally parochial and myopic media, stand as the framework beyond which nothing exists and within which all things operate—public opinion, media coverage, and policy making. This unassailable framework of presumptions is held aloft by an automatically self-reinforcing cycle in which "news and views are put forward by the media, opinion polls reflect the media's news and views, published polls are then highlighted by the same media to indicate 'public opinion' and naturally, the White House responds to this public opinion."[105] The media, therefore, do not engender consistent foreign policy; indeed, they undermine consistency. Foreign policy becomes merely "responses to the 'drama of the moment,'" a drama highlighted briefly by media that jump from one unrelated issue to another.[106]

The attention span of the consumer of news is typically short and has been rendered shorter still by Western news media. Policy, therefore, consists primarily of quick fixes and knee-jerk reactions to problems and provocations. Washington policy-makers learned that patience and persistent diplomacy is the recipe for electoral disaster. When Jimmy Carter refrained from applying military force against the Khomeini regime during the hostage crisis and as the crisis dragged on for more than a year, his political fate was sealed despite the eventual success of his diplomatic efforts. Ronald Reagan and George Bush, in contrast, wasted no time employing force to address international problems, and Western media heralded military action against countries like Granada, Libya, Panama, Iran, Iraq, and Afghanistan—so long as it was marked by conspicuous success and lasted only briefly. Easy and instant psychic gratification, demanded by the media and the public, is thus the standard by which foreign policy is made.

Having established a direct connection between media images and foreign policy in the West and examined how the press has projected Islamophobia into Western and Muslim cultural and political consciousness, we should consider the implications of that projection on foreign policy and on the perception of policy-makers. This unending cycle, the sound bites of "McNews" fueling the engine of "McPolicy," has empowered Revolutionary Islamists in that critical attacks on Islam and Muslims are only likely to strengthen radical Islamist trends. Whether such attacks are conducted by the media or by the military is irrelevant . . . the result is identical.[107]

Notes

1. The color green is a symbol of Islam.

2. We talk about "the West" and "Islam" as though history, politics, and culture can be reduced to these terms and yet remain comprehensible. However, these are the words that are used to frame most discussions, whether scholarly or journalistic, of Western and Muslim encounters with one another. Of course these terms are inadequate and misleading, and this chapter specifically addresses the gross oversimplification that necessarily results when using the word "Islam" to convey the complexities and contradictions of the Muslim world. We leave it to the reader to understand the equivalent argument: that talking about "the West" is equally inadequate.

3. The Fourth Crusade, led by Doge Dandolo of Venice, involved no skirmishes with Muslims in the Holy Land. Instead, it ended when the Crusaders sacked the Christian city of Constantinople in the thirteenth century.

4. Voltaire, *The Portable Voltaire*, Ben Ray Redman, ed. (New York: Viking Press, 1961), 187.

5. Fathi Osman, "Ayatullah Khomeini: A Genuine 'Alim-Leader' in the Contemporary World," *The Minaret* 10, no. 3 (Summer 1989): 19–20.

6. Osman, "Ayatullah Khomeini," 19–20.

7. Osman, "Ayatullah Khomeini."

8. Yvonne Yazbeck Haddad, *Contemporary Islam and the Challenge of History* (Albany: State University of New York Press, 1982), xiii.

9. Of course, the Soviets did likewise. As an ideology firmly and openly committed to atheism, communism necessarily was incompatible with Islamism, and the suppression of Muslim religious expression in Central Asia was but the mildest form of Soviet oppression of Islam. The more severe form was displayed in the Soviet occupation of Afghanistan.

10. Of course, when Revolutionary Islamists were in active opposition to the Communist regime of Afghanistan during the 1980s, Western media and policy-makers were quick to use the term freedom fighters, rather than fundamentalist fanatics or Islamic terrorists.

11. Leon T. Hadar, "What Green Peril?" in *Taking Sides: Clashing Views on Controversial Issues in World Politics*, 5th ed., John T. Rourke, ed. (Guilford: Dushkin, 1994), 101.

12. Hadar, "What Green Peril?"

13. Edward W. Said's excellent critique of the Huntington article appears in "The Clash of Ignorance," *The Nation* (22 October 2001): 11–13. Another critique of both Lewis's and Huntington's views can be found in John L. Esposito, *The Islamic Threat: Myth or Reality?* 3rd ed. (New York: Oxford University Press, 1999), 219–22.

14. Greg Noakes, "Muslims and the American Press," in *Muslims on the Americanization Path?* Yvonne Yazbeck Haddad and John L. Esposito, eds. (Oxford: Oxford University Press, 2000), 289–90.

15. Newt Gingrich quoted in Esposito, *The Islamic Threat*, 213.

16. William Montgomery Watt, *Muslim-Christian Encounters: Perceptions and Misperceptions* (New York: Routledge, 1991), 111.

17. For a concise discussion of these psychological processes, see Bruce Russet and Harvey Starr, *World Politics: The Menu for Choice*, 4th ed. (New York: W. H. Freeman), 274–79; Also see: Ralph K. White, *Nobody Wanted War: Misperception in Vietnam and Other Wars*, rev. ed. (New York: Doubleday, 1968); John G. Stoessinger, *Why Nations*

Go to War? 7th ed. (New York: St. Martin's Press, 1998).

18. Said, "The Clash of Ignorance," 12.

19. Edward W. Said, *Covering Islam: How the Media and the Experts Determine How We See the Rest of the World* (New York: Pantheon Books, 1981), 69.

20. Said, *Covering Islam*, 8.

21. Jack G. Shaheen, *The TV Arab* (Bowling Green, Wis.: Bowling Green State University Popular Press, 1984), 5.

22. Said, *Covering Islam*, 69.

23. Laurence Michalak, "Cruel and Unusual: Negative Images of Arabs in American Popular Culture," *ADC Issues* (January 1984): 14–16.

24. Michael Parenti, *Make-Believe Media: The Politics of Entertainment* (New York: St. Martin's Press, 1992), 30.

25. Parenti, *Make-Believe Media*.

26. For a complete listing of Hollywood movies that slander Arabs and Muslims, see Jack G. Shaheen, *Reel Bad Arabs: How Hollywood Vilifies a People* (New York: Olive Branch Press, 2001).

27. Parenti, *Make-Believe Media*, 31–32.

28. William Claiborne, "Hollywood's Mideast Policy," *Washington Post*, July 14, 1986, 29.

29. Parenti, *Make-Believe Media*, 31–32.

30. Said, *Covering Islam*, 52.

31. Said, *Covering Islam*.

32. Said, *Covering Islam*.

33. Said, *Covering Islam*, 62.

34. Joel Campagna, "Between Two Worlds: Qatar's Al-Jazeera Satellite Channel Faces Conflicting Expectations," www.cpi.org/Briefings/2001/aljazeera_oct01.html.

35. Said, *Covering Islam*, 64.

36. William A. Dorman and Mansour Farhang, *The U.S. Press and Iran: Foreign Policy and the Journalism of Deference* (Berkeley and Los Angeles: University of California Press, 1987), 179.

37. Dorman and Farhang, *U.S. Press and Iran*.

38. Edward W. Said, "Inside Islam," *Harper's*, January 1981, 27.

39. Edward W. Said, "Islam Rising," *Columbia Journalism Review* (March/April 1980): 26.

40. Dorman and Farhang,, *U..S. Press and Iran*, 153.

41. Dorman and Farhang,, *U.S. Press and Iran*, 171.

42. William A. Dorman and Mansour Farhang, "Nobody Lost Iran," *Politics Today*, May–June 1979, 37.

43. Dorman and Farhang, *U.S. Press and Iran*, 160.

44. Dorman and Farhang, *U.S. Press and Iran*, 160–61.

45. Dorman and Farhang, "Nobody Lost Iran," 37.

46. Dorman and Farhang, "Nobody Lost Iran," 163.

47. Dorman and Farhang, "Nobody Lost Iran," 164.

48. William A. Dorman and Ehsan Omeed, "Reporting Iran the Shah's Way," *Columbia Press Review* (January–February 1979): 27.

49. Said, *Covering Islam*, 77.

50. Said, "Inside Islam," 20.

51. Mushahid Hussain, "How Western Media Didn't Report Islam," unpublished

paper, August 15, 1980, 26.
52. Said, *Covering Islam,* 79.
53. Iqbal Asaria, "Media Proves Mightier than the Sword and Penetrates Islamic Defenses," *Crescent International* 11, no. 4 (May 1–15, 1982): 4.
54. Asaria, "Media Proves Mightier than the Sword."
55. John Barry and Roger Charles, "Sea of Lies," *Newsweek* (13 July 1992): 33.
56. Barry and Charles, "Sea of Lies," 29.
57. Barry and Charles, "Sea of Lies," 39.
58. Robert M. Entman, "Framing U.S. Coverage of International News: Contrasts in Narratives of the KAL and Iran Air Incidents," *Journal of Communication* 41, no. 4 (Autumn 1991): 6.
59. Entman, "Framing U.S. Coverage of International News," 11.
60. Entman, "Framing U.S. Coverage of International News," 17.
61. Entman, "Framing U.S. Coverage of International News," 19.
62. Quoted in "The Navy Returns Fire," letters to *Newsweek* (August 3, 1993): 8.
63. Entman, "Framing U.S. Coverage of International News," 7.
64. Quoted in Russel Watson, et al., "A Satanic Fury," *Newsweek* (February 27, 1989) 34.
65. Mahmood Monshipouri, "The Islamic World's Reaction to the Satanic Verses: Cultural Relativism Revisited," *Journal of Third World Studies* 3, no. 1 (Spring 1991): 205.
66. Quoted in Donna Foote, "At Stake: The Freedom to Imagine," *Newsweek* (27 February 1989): 37.
67. Ali Mazrui, *The Satanic Verses or a Satanic Novel? The Moral Dilemmas of the Rushdie Affair* (Greenpoint, N.Y.: Committee of Muslim Scholars and Leaders of North America, 1989), 6.
68. Mazrui, *The Satanic Verses,* 10.
69. Mazrui, *The Satanic Verses,* 6.
70. Edward W. Said quoted in Lis Appignanesi and Sara Maitland, eds., *The Rushdie File* (Syracuse, N.Y.: Syracuse University Press, 1990), 165.
71. Quoted in Watson, "A Satanic Fury," 35–36.
72. Quoted in Sheila Tefft, "Muslims Debate Rushdie Uproar," *Christian Science Monitor,* February 27, 1989, 3.
73. Tefft, "Muslims Debate Rushdie Uproar."
74. Tefft, "Muslims Debate Rushdie Uproar."
75. Quoted in John Hughes, "Authors, Death Threats, and Islam," *Christian Science Monitor,* February 22, 1989, 18.
76. Jimmy Carter quoted in *The Rushdie File,* 237.
77. Youssef M. Ibrahim, "Khomeini Assails Western Response to Rushdie Affair," *New York Times,* February 22, 1989, 1.
78. Alex Efty, "Khomeini Aimed his 'Verses' Attack to Stop Liberal Trends," *Birmingham News,* February 26, 1989, 5A.
79. Barbara Crossette, "Muslims Storm U.S. Mission in Pakistan," *New York Times,* February 13, 1989, 12.
80. Monshipouri, "The Islamic World's Reaction," 205.
81. Watt, *Muslim-Christian Encounters,* 121.
82. Douglas Kellner, The Persian Gulf TV War (Boulder, Colo.: Westview Press, 1992), 67–69.

83. Kellner, *Persian Gulf TV War*, 70.
84. Kellner, *Persian Gulf TV War*, 71.
85. Kellner, *Persian Gulf TV War*, 80.
86. Kellner, *Persian Gulf TV War*, 81.
87. Kellner, *Persian Gulf TV War*, 80.
88. Lee Wigle Artz and Mark A. Pollock, "Limiting the Options: Anti-Arab Images in the U.S. Media Coverage of the Persian Gulf Crisis," in *The U.S. Media and the Middle East: Image and Perception*, Yahya R. Kamalipour, ed. (Westport, Conn.: Praeger, 1997), 120.
89. Douglas Kellner, "The U.S. Media and the 1993 War against Iraq," in *U.S. Media and the Middle East*, Kamalipour, 117.
90. Kellner, *Persian Gulf TV War*, 87.
91. Artz, "Limiting the Options," 119.
92. Artz, "Limiting the Options," 120.
93. Artz, "Limiting the Options."
94. Haim Bresheeth, "The New World Order," in *The Gulf War and the New World Order*, Haim Bresheeth and Nira Yuval-Davis, eds. (London: Zed Books, 1991), 252.
95. Martin Shaw and Roy Carr-Hill, "Public Opinion and Media Coverage in Britain," in *Triumph of the Image: The Media's War in the Persian Gulf—A Global Perspective,* Hamid Mowlana, George Gerbner, and Herbert I. Schiller, eds. (Boulder, Colo.: Westview Press, 1992), 146.
96. Khawla Matter, "Western Media: Guilty until Proved Innocent," in Mowlana, Gerbner, and Schiller, eds., *Triumph of the Image*, 104.
97. Amital Etzioni, "A Proud American Moment," *Christian Science Monitor*, October 11, 2001, 1.
98. Peter Ford, "Xenophobia Follows U.S. Terror," *Christian Science Monitor*, October 11, 2001, 1
99. Ford, "Xenophobia Follows U.S. Terror."
100. Francine Kiefer and Ann Scott Tyson, "In War of Words, U.S. Lags Behind," *Christian Science Monitor*, October 17, 2001.
101. The Pakistani population, while sympathizing with the Taliban, was generally unwilling to take to the streets or challenge the authority of the Musharraf government to side with the West.
102. Peter Ford, "Listening for Islam's Silent Majority," *Christian Science Monitor*, November 5, 2001, 1.
103. "Tehran Insists on Playing Host to Hostile Media," *Crescent International*, April 16–30, 1982, 2.
104. Mushahid Hussain, "American Mass Media Coverage of Islam," unpublished paper, 1980, 14.
105. Hussain, "American Mass Media Coverage of Islam," 14–15.
106. Hussain, "American Mass Media Coverage of Islam," 15.
107. Watt, *Muslim Christian Encounters*, 124.

Chapter 8

Democracy vs. Fundamentalism: Religious Politics of the Bharatiya Janata Party in India

Krishna K. Tummala

> The idea that there are one people in possession of the truth, one answer to the world's ills or one solution to humanity's needs has done untold harm throughout history.
>
> Kofi Annan, UN Secretary-General, 2000

Fundamentalism, understood as an uncompromising stance, and democracy defined as a government by consensus and compromise, is by its very nature antithetical. Religious fundamentalism as an incontrovertible faith in a purportedly secular state is even more unacceptable. Insofar as democracy is understood as majority rule with minority rights guaranteed, there is no place for a minority, or even a majority for that matter, to let its own private writ run large. History shows that when a logrolling majority party or a dictatorship had tried unilaterally to impose its own dictum, the results had been disastrous. Any number of contemporary examples can be cited: the Taliban in Afghanistan (which was routed out in 2001); Ayatollah Khomeini's fundamentalism in Iran (against which reformist President Mohammad Khatami is now fighting), General Zia-ul Haq's Islamization in Pakistan.

There are, however, mechanisms in a democratic system that moderate such factious fundamentalist stances. James Madison wrote in *The Federalist* papers: "By a faction, I understand a number of citizens, whether amounting to a majority or a minority of the whole, who are united and actuated by some common impulse of passion, or of interest, adverse to the rights of other citizens, or to the permanent and aggregate interests of the community." Were such a faction a minority, the majority would take care of it by curbing its ambition. If it were to be a majority, then what? The answer is of course the republican form of government where the representative principle, with its "tendency to break and control the violence of a faction," will take care of the problem.[1]

One can also invoke the great Aristotelian sense of "proportion"—the value of the mean which is defined as the ethical good—a single point between the many points of excess and deficiency.[2] George Sabine comments that the best form of government in one sense is not an ideal at all. "It is merely the best practicable average which results from avoiding the extremes in democracy and oligarchy that experience has shown to be dangerous."[3]

Further, in a secular state, the state itself does not profess any particular religion though its populace is free to practice any or every religion. This also means a government in power will poorly serve the nation by professing a particular religion, particularly in a virulent form, by putting it on its agenda for popular consumption. This type of fundamentalism, again one expects, will be curbed by the representative principle. It is also hoped that political parties would keep away from exploiting religious sentiments.

India is a secular democracy under its Constitution adopted in 1949. Yet, its political parties have not always kept their distance from religion. In fact, they all have used religion, one way, or the other, for partisan advantage and for electoral gain, and even to legitimize their very existence and power. The country now has a government at the Centre (as the federal government commonly is known) run by a coalition—the National Democratic Alliance (NDA), whose major partner is the Hindu nationalist *Bharatiya Janata Party* (BJP). Consequently, the issue of religious fundamentalism keeps raising its ugly head from time to time. This paper proposes that not only the representative form of government, but also the very nature of a coalition government, would come as a welcome relief as they both serve as moderating influences. The political mediating process, certainly through free and fair elections, is expected to moderate fundamentalist views—be they economic, political, or religious. The paper also cautions against the use of religious fundamentalism for partisan gain. India is the world's largest working democracy in which all the concomitant political institutions have taken root and are working. The basic admonition is to avoid extreme positions so that the democratic form as well as process will be preserved.

To facilitate this discussion, the paper is divided into several sections. The first deals with the nature of the Indian state. The second explicates the BJP's religious politics by the use of the Ram janmabhumi issue while showing that party is not alone in its exploitation of religion for political gain. The third examines coalition politics as a check against the pressures of its constituents on the BJP. The fourth explains the events around March 15, 2002, and the simultaneous fiasco in Gujarat. The final section reflects some conclusions.

Secular India

India is a multireligious society dominated by the Hindu population (82 percent); its Muslim population (12.12 percent) constitutes the second largest congregation in the world. The rest are Christians (2.34 percent), Sikhs (1.94 percent), Buddhists (0.76 percent), Jains (0.4 percent), and others (0.4 percent).[4] Indian history is replete with interreligious conflicts in the form of Muslim rulers and Hindu Rajas fighting each other. Yet, some Muslim rulers, and the great Mughal ruler Akbar himself, were known for their love of Hinduism. The British however, in their (in) famous *divide et imperia* (divide and rule) principle, kept the Hindus and Muslims apart and against each other (see below).

Members of the Constituent Assembly, while writing the Indian Constitution, were very much exercised by the issue of religious freedom.[5] With regard to secularism, "Preliminary Notes on Fundamental Rights" read thus:

> The State in the Indian Union . . . shall be entirely a secular institution. It shall have or maintain no official religion or established church; and shall observe absolute neutrality in matters of religious belief, worship, or observance. All public institutions, maintained, aided, or supported in any way by the State shall observe the same policy of absolute neutrality in matters of religious worship, belief, or observance.[6]

Further, while assuring that when any property of a religious establishment was taken over by the Government, a "reasonable and appropriate" compensation would be made, the document went on to say: "Without prejudice to the existing property in land or other form, acquired by way of gift and owned and held by any religious body, corporation, temple, mosque, church, synagogue, dargha or any other religious institution no property real or personal, shall be alienated to, or owned or held by any such religious body, authority or institution. Nor shall any such property held by any such religious order, corporation or organization be exempt from any taxation, fees, dues or other charges levied by the Union, Provincial, State or Local Governing Authority."[7] Article VI of the Draft Constitution, however, also contained the caution" . . . that the economic, financial or political activities associated with religious worship shall not be deemed to be included in the right to profess or practise religion."[8]

The debates in the Constituent Assembly on these clauses shed some light on what was intended. For example, K. T. Shah took exception to the expression "morality," when it was stated that freedom of conscience and religion be subject to "public order, morality, or health." He contended that morality is a "very vague term. Its connotation changes substantially from time to time." He also recalled several historical instances when essential freedoms of thought or expression were curtailed in the name of morality, and concluded thus: "In a land of many religions, with differing conceptions of morality, different customs, usages and ideals it would be extremely difficult to get unanimity in what constitutes morality. Champions of the established order would find much in the new thought at any time, which might be considered by them as open to objection on grounds of public morality. If this is not to degenerate into a tyranny of the majority, it is necessary either to define more clearly what is meant by the term 'morality,' or to drop this exception altogether."[9] However, without any further definition, the term "morality" was retained in the new Constitution as a commendable precept.

Another member, Raj Kumari Amrit Kaur, objected to the recommendations of the Minorities Subcommittee to include the phrase "free practice of religion," in that it might bar not only future social legislation but also invalidate previous legislation (mostly pertaining to Hindu religion) such as the Widow Remarriage Act, the Sarada Act (prohibiting child marriages), or the prohibition of sati (immolation of the widow on the funeral pyre of her husband). She also contended that this "will keep alive communal strife."[10] In meeting with such objections, the Constituent Assembly incorporated the following language: "The freedom of religious practice guaranteed . . . shall not debar the State from enacting laws for the purpose of social welfare and reform and for the throwing open Hindu religious institutions of a public character to any class or section of Hindus."[11]

In its Preamble, the Constitution declared India as a "Sovereign Democratic Republic." This was changed in 1976 (by the Forty-Second Amendment) to read a "Sovereign Socialist Secular Democratic Republic." It also substituted the words "unity and integrity of the Nation," for the original "unity of the nation." Thus, besides the reiteration of the socialist nature, secularism and the integrity of the nation were emphasized, consequent to several fissiparous tendencies, communal agitations, and alleged antinational activities.[12]

Part III of the Constitution dealing with Fundamental Rights contains provisions pertaining to the secular nature of India. Article 15 (1) and (2) decree that the state shall not discriminate on the basis of religion, among others. A similar ban on discrimination in public employment is placed by Article 16 (2). Article 25 confers freedom of conscience and the right to freely "profess, practise and propagate religion," subject only to "public order, morality and health." Article 26 permits every religious denomination "to establish and maintain institutions for religious and charitable purposes," and "to manage its own affairs in matters of religion." No person can be compelled to pay taxes meant for the specific purpose of promoting or maintaining any particular religion or its denomination (Article 27). Article 28 prohibits religious instruction in any educational institution that is solely funded by the state. (Those institutions established under an endowment or trust that are receiving aid, or being administered by the state, are exempt from such a prohibition.) Article 29 bars denial of admission into any educational institution on the basis of religion, while Article 30 guarantees the right to minorities (including religious) to establish and administer their own educational institutions.

Yet, the word "secular" must be understood properly. The *American Heritage Dictionary* defines the word "secular" as "of pertaining to the temporal rather than to the spiritual; not specifically pertaining to religion or to a religious body." This formal western meaning must be distinguished from the informal non-Western meaning which connotes a state that accords equal protection and respect for all religions.[13] This inclusive and pluralist meaning of secularism is more pertinent to an India whose people are largely religious, even superstitious (as opposed to the scientific and rational temperament).[14] Thus, within the context of India, a secular state is neither antireligious, nor irreligious; it guarantees religious freedom to all its citizens without proclaiming a state religion.[15] It is within this secular framework one needs to understand the use of religion, particularly by the BJP when it stresses *Hindutva*—a Hindu state, as highlighted by the Ram janmabhumi issue. To provide a proper perspective, it is important here to make a brief sketch of the antecedents, beliefs, and political ambitions of the BJP, and the Ram temple at Ayodhya.

The BJP and Religious Politics

The Indian National Congress (INC), which was in the forefront of the national movement, did represent several elements of the Indian society. It had not only several traditionalist Hindus, but also Muslim representatives including Maulana Abul Kalam Azad and Rafi Ahmad Kidwai. While several of the Western educated and secular-minded Hindu leaders such as Jawaharlal Nehru (the first prime minister) took exception to the backward-looking Hindu traditionalists, a few such as Rajendra Prasad (who would be the first president of India) and Sardar Vallabhai Patel (first Home Minister), gave yeoman service to the cause of independent India. Others found themselves affiliated with either the Hindu Mahasabha or the Rashtriya Swayamsevak Sangh (RSS).

The Hindu Mahasabha, under the leadership of V. D. Savarkar, took interest in party politics and general elections as a rival to both the Congress Party and the Muslim League. However, having made no significant impact, it fizzled. On the other hand, the RSS continued as a social movement with its brotherhood— the *sangh pariwar*—looking to the promotion of a *Hindu Rashtra* (Hindu nation). When on January 30, 1948, Mahatma Gandhi was assassinated by a Nadhuram Godse who was connected to both Hindu Mahasabha and the RSS, both groups were temporarily banned.[16]

Shyam Prasad Mookerji, who succeeded Savarkar as president of Hindu Mahasabha, resigned from the party and became a minister in the Nehru Cabinet of the Congress Party. But, in April 1950, he resigned arguing that the Indian government was too lenient in settling some financial and other disputes with Pakistan, and started rallying the traditionalist Hindu leaders toward the idea of a new party. Thus came into existence the Bharatiya Jana Sangh (commonly known as Jana Sangh) on October 21, 1951, under the presidency of Mookerji and with the support of the RSS. The party, while supporting liberal economic and social policies, promised special aid to backward classes. It refused, however, to recognize minorities based on religion. It went further to state that a reunited India would be its goal—a hope that some cherish even today (see below).

The Jana Sangh had its initial strength largely in the Hindi-belt comprising the northern States of U.P., Madhya Pradesh (M.P.), Rajasthan, the Punjab, and Delhi. Although it carried some weight in the coalition State governments, by 1970 it had lost whatever clout it had. Later it joined with other opposition parties against Indira Gandhi's Congress (I) government at the Centre and was suppressed during the national Emergency of 1975–1977. In January 1977, as the Emergency was lifted and the nation went to the polls, the party became part of the newly created opposition Janata Party, which came to power in the Centre as well as in some States. But in the 1980 general elections, the Janata Party was soundly beaten by Congress (I). Consequently, former members of the Jana Sangh asserted their own independence from the Janata Party and formed the new BJP in April 1980.[17]

Among the plethora of political parties in India, the BJP is (as was its predecessor the Jana Sangh) the only communal party (apart from the former Muslim League). It is important to note here that while the BJP is a political party, its components, the RSS and Vishwa Hindu Parishad (VHP is a more militant subgroup of the RSS) are not. Both, however, backed the BJP in its quest for political power. The RSS leaders even acted as major arbiters in leadership struggles within the BJP. Thus, the distinction between the pronouncements of these three units cannot always easily be made, and at times certain cognitive dissonance occurs as to where precisely the BJP stands on the various issues. To this day, the RSS continues to be the spiritual mentor of the BJP, and during the BJP presidency of Murali Manohar Joshi the distinction between the BJP and VHP was largely blurred.

Hindu nationalism is the creed of all these groups. Some of its initial substance was provided by Savarkar, the Maharashtrian nationalist, in his 1934 book *Essentials of Hindutva*. To him, culture and territory were unmistakably intertwined. To be a Hindu one has to accept India as the fatherland. Though the Muslims do that, he nonetheless believed that they would be looking outside of

Democracy vs. Fundamentalism

India for their spiritual guidance. For followers of Savarkar, the Indian subcontinent is one geographic unit and its partition into India and Pakistan is an unacceptable mistake.

Continuing the Hindu nationalist tradition, the BJP stands for a Hindu nation. The party's plank is consequently stated thus: Article 370 of the Constitution of India which confers special status on the only Muslim majority State, Jammu and Kashmir, and the Muslim personal law—the Shari'a—are considered by the BJP as no more than attempts at appeasing the Muslim minority. The party contends that if the Muslims are to be part of India, they ought to be treated on par with the rest of the Indians with a single civil law, uniformly applied.[18] The BJP's Hindu nationalism went even further to object the use of English language insofar as it is identified with the British colonial masters. Similarly, Urdu language is opposed, as it happens to be the language of the Muslim minority. So is its demand against cow slaughter, an animal sacred to the Hindus, but eaten by the Muslims.[19] All this is read as anti-Muslim, and by many southern Indians as some sort of Hindi (a northern language) imperialism.

In general, the BJP is against preferential treatment of minorities. Despite the fact that the 1989 BJP election manifesto talked of continuing the "reservation" of public service positions for Scheduled Castes and Tribes on a quota basis, top leaders of the BJP have not altogether repudiated the RSS Guru Golwalkar's theory propounded in 1939 that minorities in India must live at the "mercy" of "the national Hindu race," or "quit the country at their sweet will."[20]

As already mentioned, the party could not make major inroads into the political arena till recently. Why was this so? As B. D. Graham suggests, the answer is "that it failed to transcend the limitations of its origins. Its close initial ties with the Hindi-speaking heartland were, in the long run, a serious disadvantage; from the outset, the party was preoccupied with northern issues such as the promotion of Hindi, the defense of refugee interests, and energetic resistance to Pakistan. In addition, its interpretation of Hinduism was restrictive and exclusive; its doctrines were inspired by an activist version of Hindu nationalism, and indirectly, by the values of Brahmanism rather the devotional and quietist values of popular Hinduism."[21] But these are the very values that the BJP has come to exploit for political advantage of late. In particular, the party made good use of the Ram janmabhumi issue.

A fictional character (though for the masses, led by the fundamentalists, a real person), King Rama (often simply Ram), the main character of the Hindu epic Ramayan (known as the *adi kavya*—the very original literary treatise), is held by the Hindus as an ideal person, and a revered God.[22] In the Hindu cosmology, according to fundamentalist belief, Ram lived during *treta yuga*, the second of four *yugas*—ages.[23] Tradition is that the Gupta king, Vikramaditya, built a temple for Ram in the city of Ayodhya which was considered to be the latter's birthplace; hence in Hindi, Ram janmabhumi. (Ayodhya is on the bank of the holy river Sarayu, about 120 kilometers from Lucknow, the capitol of the State of U.P.) It is also believed that the temple was destroyed by the Mughal ruler Babar, who built a mosque over it in 1528—the Babri Masjid, or the Babar mosque. However, despite the presence of the mosque, the Hindus did not stop worshiping there, and the Ramanandi sadhus dominated the worship as well as the spiritual life in Ayodhya ever since. It should, however, also be noted that in fact no attempt was made by the Muslim rulers—the nawabs—to suppress Hinduism altogether. In fact, they depended much upon Hindu and Muslim collaboration.[24] Similarly, there was no attempt at removing the mosque even after the downfall of the Mughal empire.

As the influence of the British rose, Muslims of Ayodhya in 1855 claimed that there was another mosque within the compound of adjacent Hindu temple–Hanumangarhi, and that it should be opened for their worship. This led to a bitter battle, which was won by the nagas (a largely military Shaivite Hindu group). Subsequently, a Commission was appointed by the British, composed of both Hindus and Muslims, which decided that there was no basis for the Muslim claim. The following year, the British put up a railing around the Babri mosque so that Muslims could continue to worship there. The Hindus also continued to make their offerings outside the mosque on a raised platform. Later, consequent to the anti-cow slaughter movement led by the Hindus, there were serious conflicts in 1912 and 1934 between the Hindus and Muslims, particularly during the Muslim festival of Bakr-id.

In postindependent India, on the night of December 22–23, 1949, an idol of Ram appeared mysteriously in the mosque despite the presence of armed guards posted there. Because the Hindu attempt at worshiping the Muslims considered Ram there as an act defiling their own religion, riots broke out. Consequently, both religious groups were banned from entering the complex. While both groups went to court seeking permission to enter the complex for worship, the Commissioner of Faizabad ordered the District Magistrate to remove the idol from the complex. The Magistrate, a Hindu (so was the Commissioner), but a supporter of the more militant Hindu group, the RSS, refused, and were removed from office (through forced retirement). Thus, the idol remained in the mosque; and an idol needs worship.

This cause was taken up by a Ram janmabhumi Seva Committee, and permission was accorded for worship once every year on the night of December 22–23. This arrangement remained intact until October 6, 1984, when the Ram janmabhumi issue was rekindled with the *Ram Janmabhumi Mukti Yajna* (liberally translated as worship to liberate the birthplace of Rama) led by the VHP. It was no doubt "a religious procession with an activist aspect," as Peter van Der Veer observed.[25] One cannot mistake the timing; the 1985 general elections were to take place shortly thereafter. The attempt was to pressure the politicians to resolve the issue of the mosque and temple. But the Yajna's efforts were obscured as Prime Minister Indira Gandhi was assassinated by her Sikh guards on October 31, 1984. The resulting violence was aimed at the Sikh community, which has been agitating for a separate Sikh nation—Khalisthan (see below), and the dispute between Hindus and Muslims took a back seat, at least for the time. But on February 14, 1986, the District and Sessions Judge of Faizabad ordered the opening of the complex for Hindu worship on a technicality that the previous decision to close it was made not by a judicial authority but by an administrator. So far, however, no one has decided whether the complex rightfully houses a mosque or a temple. Turning to Ram janmabhumi politics, with only two members in the *Lok Sabha* (lower House of Parliament), the BJP had little or no political pretensions until 1989 when it won 82 of the 225 seats it contested acquiring 11.4 percent of the total vote. It has been gaining in strength since. There are several reasons for this. One is the changing political scene in India as minority governments started coming into vogue while the Congress (I) strength began declining. The second is the exploitation of the religious sentiments of the majority Hindu community, which was already turning not only against Muslims but also against the Hindu minorities—the former because of traditional enmity, and the latter due to the new extension of privileges in the form of further "reservation" of positions in public service for the Other Backward Classes (OBCs) by the V. P. Singh government in 1990.[26] Third, in May 1986, Ashok Singhal, the *mahamantri* (chief organizer) of the VHP laid out a four-point program to (i) bring all Hindus under one umbrella organization to further their cause; (ii) ban proselytizing by other religions; (iii) promote Sanskrit language uniformly in India; and (iv) to back only those political candidates who support the Hindu cause.[27]

Fourth, and more importantly, was the use of the Ram janmabhumi issue. In the 1989 elections, the BJP not only worked with Janata Dal to defeat Congress (I), but also worked with the VHP to build a Ram temple in Ayodhya. In its Palampur National Executive Committee meeting (June 9–11, 1989), the BJP resolved:

> The National Executive of the Bharatiya Janata Party regards the current debate on the Ram Janma Bhoomi issue as one which has dramatically highlighted the callous unconcern which the Congress Party in particular, and the other political parties in general, betray towards the sentiments of the overwhelming majority in this country—the Hindus. . . . The sentiments of the people must be respected and the Rama Janmasthan handed over to the Hindus.[28]

Given that posture, the BJP was outraged by the V. P. Singh government's decision in 1990 to implement the Mandal Commission report (pertaining to "reservations" for the the OBCs. When the BJP leader, L. K. Advani, joined the Ayodhya movement and started on a 10,000-kilometer trek—the *rath yatra* (chariot pilgrimage)—from Somanath to Ayodhya, Singh ordered his arrest. This led the BJP to withdraw its support, and the Singh government collapsed leading to general elections the following year. Thus the BJP not only got national attention but also showed that it could flex its political muscles.

In 1990, Mulayam Singh Yadav, chief minister of U.P., brutally put down the *kar sevaks* (Hindu devotees) resulting in twenty-six deaths and a Hindu backlash in that State particularly, and in the Hindi-belt in general. This gave further political impetus to the BJP, which, in its 1991 Manifesto, quite openly offered, to the electorate Ram with Roti (Roti meaning bread). Contesting as many as 479 seats, the BJP won 119 seats to the *Lok Sabha* with 19.9 percent of total votes, and became the largest opposition group in Parliament for the first time in its existence. Later its leader, Atal Bihari Vajpayee, was recognized as the leader of the opposition in Parliament. The BJP had finally arrived politically.

The BJP also came out strong enough in four Hindi-belt States—U.P., M.P., Rajasthan, and Himachal Pradesh (H.P.)—to form governments. Noteworthy is the fact that the government of U.P. (the State where the Ayodhya complex is) was captured by the BJP, which gave a new strength and a greater demand for the temple in Ayodhya. On October 11, 1991, the BJP government of Kalyan Singh bought 2.77 acres of land around the Ram janmabhumi complex to develop it for the "public purpose" of tourism. But many feared that the government would hand over that land to the VHP to build the temple that they have been demanding. While as many as 53 percent of those polled in the nation were willing to have both a temple and a mosque in the complex, by July–August, 1992, the VHP *kar sevaks* embarked on a foundation east of the complex for the temple.[29] The Kalyan Singh government remained as a spectator despite the fact that it gave an undertaking to the National Integration Council that it would guarantee the protection of the disputed structures in the complex.

Many thought that it was time that the U.P. government be dismissed under the Emergency Powers, and save the situation.[30] Surprisingly, Congress (I) prime minister, P. V. Narasimha Rao, did not act. Even within his own party, his rival Arjun Singh, charged that Rao and the BJP were working hand in glove. As a devout Hindu, Rao could not have taken on a Hindu party without being charged as anti-Hindu. Surely, he must have been wary of risking his less than comfortable majority in the *Lok Sabha*. (In fact, in July 1991 he survived a no-confidence motion in the *Lok Sabha* with a majority of 267 to 215, given the fractured opposition.) Quite possibly, he was not prepared to make the BJP and its supporters martyrs by using repressive measures. Alternatively, he might even have believed that by letting the BJP have its way, he could get all the secular forces galvanized. In any case, Prime Minister Rao demonstrated his usual procrastination until the end.

On November 28, 1992, the Supreme Court of India accepted the U.P. government undertaking that no construction will be allowed within the complex, but permitted singing of Hindu hymns, and appointed a Senior Judge of the Allahabad High Court as an "observer," with the charge that he should report daily to the Supreme Court on the activities at the complex. Several security forces were sent by the Centre to Faizabad to meet any contingency. And the U.P. government promised that it would prevent *kar sevaks* from flouting the Supreme Court orders. But the same day those orders were passed in favor of building a temple.

On December 6, 1992, while all the top brass of the BJP, VHP, and RSS were addressing a meeting just a couple of hundred feet away from the complex, the mob got the better of it and razed the Babri mosque to the ground, and installed a Ram deity in a makeshift structure.[31] It is important to note that the district magistrate (who is the chief official in charge of the judiciary as well as law and order) was also present at the scene, but remained as a spectator. Practically nothing was done by either the U.P. State government or the Centre to prevent the atrocity. Neither of the governments could deny that it was unaware of the possible destruction. After all, the Intelligence Bureau of the Central government warned twice at the meetings of the Cabinet Committee on Political Affairs on November 19 and 22, 1992, that the intent of the movement was to demolish the mosque. The prime minister called it an "utter perfidy," and a "betrayal" by the BJP-VHP combined for having not prevented the destruction of the mosque, contrary to their previous assurances. The Supreme Court said that "the majesty of rule of law" was given short shrift as the U.P. government failed to prevent the mobs. The media thought it as a "witness of the burial of a secular dream," and "religious fanaticism at its ugliest."[32] The world watched in horror, and with contempt. However, the BJP thought, "It was a liberation—a sweeping away of cobwebs."[33] (A Commission of Inquiry is still investigating whether there was a BJP "conspiracy" to demolish the temple at the time of this writing.)

The day following the demolition of the mosque, five religious organizations—three Hindu (the RSS, VHP, and Bajrang Dal) and two Muslim (the Islamic Sevak Sangh and the Jamait-i-Islam)—were banned under the Unlawful Activities (prevention) Act of 1967.[34] This was followed by the dismissal of the other three BJP governments of Sunderlal Patwa in M.P., Shanta Kumar in H.P., and of Bhairon Singh Shekawat in Rajasthan, under the Emergency Powers. In less than an hour after the demolition, however, Kalyan Singh resigned as chief minister of U.P. These dismissals had nothing to do with the maintenance (or the lack thereof) of law and order. The concern was that the BJP governments (what with their connections with the RSS) might not carry out the ban order of the religious groups.[35] Later the Government of India by Ordinance took over 67.7 acres of land at the complex, and on January 7, 1993, the president of India asked the Supreme Court of India to see whether there was a temple before the mosque was built. Thus, the BJP not only gained prominence, but it placed the Ram janmabhumi issue squarely on the national agenda. However, it should be noted that the BJP is neither alone, nor is the first, to use religion for political advantage.

Reference was already made about the British efforts at driving a wedge between majority Hindus and minority Muslims. The partition of the State of Bengal was one of the first such moves. Although the British announced the partition under the pretext that Bengal was too large a State to be administered conveniently, the real intent was altogether different. In an official note of 1904, the then home secretary, H. H. Risley said: "Bengal united is a power. Bengal divided will pull several different ways. That is what the Congress leaders feel:

their apprehensions are perfectly correct and they form one of the great merits of the scheme. . . . (O)ne of our main objectives is to split up and thereby to weaken a solid body of opponents to our rule."[36]

The 1909 Minto-Marley reforms even went so far as to provide for separate electorates for the people of these two religions.[37] (Separate electorates were later created for the Sikhs in 1919, and for the Indian Christians and Anglo-Indians in 1935.) While the Indian National Congress, started in 1885, led the national movement against the British rule, and when several Muslims advocated a joint Hindu-Muslim political action for independence, the British instead set up some Muslim reactionaries such as Nawab Salimullah, who with 1.14 million Rupees sanctioned by the governor of Bengal, Sir Bampfydle Fuller, founded the Muslim League which demanded, and succeeded, in partitioning India in 1947 into two separate countries: a majority Hindu India and a majority Muslim Pakistan. This religious divide continues even today.

Since independence, besides the Assamese opposition to Bengali Muslim immigrants, and the earlier Naga separatist movement helped by Christian missionaries in the North Eastern Frontier Agency (NEFA), there have been two formidable threats to the Union of India based on religion: one in Kashmir, and the other in the Punjab. The Kashmir problem has been a continuous one ever since the partition of India resulting in two wars (in 1948 and 1965) and the Kargil conflict of 1999 with Pakistan. At the time of independence, the ruler of Kashmir, who happened to be a Hindu with a predominantly Muslim population, had not acceded to the Indian Union until part of the State was overrun by Pakhtoon tribals supported by Pakistan (which came to be known as Azad Kashmir).[38] Since 1989, the Islamization process of General Zia ul-Haque, religious militancy took hold in Pakistan. Consequently, Muslim insurgency demanding independence for Kashmir has been on the rise, which is met by the Indian forces resulting in the death of nearly fifty thousand people, largely Muslims, so far.[39] To be fair, it also should be noted that many Hindus, particularly the *pundits*—the priestly class, have been either killed or displaced from Jammu in particular.[40] With the Taliban and al Qaeda driven out of Afghanistan after the invasion by the United States in 2001, many of them moved into Pakistan and into Kashmir leading to further fears of communal conflict among the Hindus and Muslims in that State. Thus, Kashmir remains an intractable problem.

The Sikhs in the Punjab began demanding a separate nation—Khalisthan. Their cause took a militant turn subsequent to the assault by the Indian army on their Golden Temple in Amritsar on orders by the then Congress (I) prime minister, Indira Gandhi, in June 1984. The Akali Dal (the major Sikh religious party) itself based its demand for communal and political identity on religious grounds.[41] Sikhism subscribes to the doctrine of *miri-piri*, which in essence connotes the indivisibility of the spiritual and temporal. Thus, the political activity of Darbara Sahib (the Golden Temple) is nothing new. Given that, the 1956 attempts of the Congress Government at the Centre (which purportedly subscribed to secularism) failed to remove the Akali Dal from the political arena and con-

Democracy vs. Fundamentalism

fine it to moral, religious, and educational activities.[42] Later, Prime Minister Indira Gandhi tried to divide the Akali Dal by promoting the head of the Damdami Taksal, Sant Jarnail Singh Bhindranwale, a populist demagogue and revivalist as a political persona, who later turned out to be her own nemesis. (He was killed during the army assault on the Golden Temple.) After Indira Gandhi's assassination, her son, Rajiv Gandhi, succeeded as prime minister, and later reached the Rajiv-Longowal Accord on July 24, 1985. With the later election of Congress (I) Chief Minister Beant Singh, the demand for secession and the violence subsided in the Punjab.

But it is the BJP that has gotten the most mileage by using the religious card, as already seen. This is not to say that the Ram janmabhumi issue is no more than a political ploy for the BJP; it in fact is an article of faith with them. Its commitment is unwavering in this regard as they reiterate in their white paper of April 1993 that the Ayodhya agitation ". . . is a continuation of the unremitting struggle of the Hindus to repossess their holy place desecrated by the invaders."[43]

That the Ram janmabhumi issue helped the BJP in its quest for political power is undeniable. L. K. Advani, former President of the BJP, deputy prime minister, and home minister in the present Vajpayee's National Democratic Alliance (NDA) government, himself admitted by saying: "Had we not taken the Ram janmabhumi movement forward we would not have arrived at the place we are now."[44] Kashbhau Thakre, president of the BJP, addressing the party's National Council in May 1998, claimed that India is "one nation, one people and one culture," and went on to give a less than religious cover to the slogan *Hindutva* by calling it "cultural nationalism." One must, however, take the thought back with some trepidation to Jan Sangh and to RSS, and the latter's founder M. S. Golwalkar who wrote the following in 1939:

> In Hinduism (land of the Hindus before the Muslim invasions and the coming of the Europeans) exists and must needs exist the ancient Hindu nation and nothing else but the Hindu nation. . . . So long, however, as they (Muslim and other non-Hindus) maintain their special, religious and cultural differences, they cannot but (be) only foreigners. . . . There are only two courses open to the foreign elements, either to merge themselves in the national race and adopt its culture, or to live at the sweet will of the national race. . . . The non-Hindu people in Hindustan must either adopt the Hindu culture and language, must learn to respect and hold in reverence Hindu religion . . . in one word, they must cease to be foreigners, or may stay in the country, wholly subordinate to the Hindu nation, claiming nothing, deserving no privileges, far less any preferential treatment—not even citizens' rights. . . . In this country, Hindus alone are the Nation and the Muslims and others, if not actual antinational, are at least outside the body of the Nation.[45]

The intolerance of the Hindu nationalists toward non-Hindus may be seen from the argument that Sonia Gandhi (an Italian by birth)—widow of one prime minister (Rajiv Gandhi) and the daughter-in-law of another (Indira Gandhi), and the current president of Congress (I) and leader of opposition in Parliament—is not qualified to be the prime minister of India.[46] The January 1999 killing of the Australian missionary Gordon Staines and his two sons who had been serving lepers in Orissa by Dara Singh, who is a Hindu fanatic with the Hindu militant Bajrang Dal connections is yet another example. However, a 1999 official commission of inquiry concluded that no organized Hindu group was behind the murders. After all, when Vajpayee apologized for the destruction of the Babri mosque (beyond the brief of the RSS), he was virtually censured by the BJP National Executive Council, which led to his offer of resignation (which of course was not accepted). Advani himself stated that he was not ashamed of the destruction of the mosque in Ayodhya, except he was for removing it by "due process of law"; instead some hotheads destroyed it. Hence his advocacy to continue the ideological stance of the BJP.[47] Soon after the demolition of the mosque in Ayodhya, it was claimed that the next to go would be the structures in Kashi and Mathura, the two other prominent Hindu religious cities. The BJP leaders while not denying it only said that these structures are not on the "agenda immediately."[48]

Coalition Politics

Yet, the political ground realities are not propitious to push this religious fundamentalism in that the BJP cannot by itself form a government now. This also means that it has to moderate its stance to be able to forge alliances (against the once dominant Congress-I Party) with other parties that subscribe to secularism, even if it were lip sympathy.[49] Vajpayee's first BJP government in 1996 lasted a mere thirteen days as it had only 160 members of the coalition strength of 195 with four other parties (out of the total 545 seats in the *Lok Sabha*). His second government came to office in May 1998, with the support of fifteen different parties serving for thirteen months. The third time around, the BJP entered into the National Democratic Alliance (NDA) with twenty-four parties and came to power with a total strength of 297 (later, with others joining, the strength went up to 303). To get there, all the fundamental facets of the 1998 BJP Manifesto— abrogation of special status of Kashmir under Article 370, maintenance of uniform civil law code, abolition of the Minority Commission, banning cow slaughter and the export of beef—were dropped in the 1999 NDA agenda. Such a moderation dictated by political necessities, not surprisingly, is considered by the VHP and RSS as a loss in faith and dilution of ideology.

Thus, the BJP had to contend with internal dissension while trying to keep the coalition together. To this end, the party lives, like Janus, with two faces. While Home Minister Advani to some extent, and the education minister, Murali Manohar Joshi, to a large extent, shows the orthodox face of the party and its constituents, Prime Minister Vajpayee projects the moderate face of the BJP and its coalition. The NDA partners so far have successfully come in the way of the BJP and its constituents pushing their ideological agenda.

Any number of examples can be cited in this regard. Education Minister Joshi, who was a professor of Physics but an ardent RSS man, wants to rewrite school textbooks to embellish *Hindutva*. As many as twelve State governments controlled by parties which are also part of the NDA have opposed such "saffronization" (the color of the BJP) of education.[50] Similarly, the National Council of Educational Research and Training (NCERT) was accused of doctoring history textbooks, while Joshi and his compatriots claim that all they are trying to do is to rid the books of bias that crept in previously. (It should be noted that during the Indira Gandhi regime, the same NCERT did demonstrate a decided leftist bias.) Reminiscent of a reactionary attempt, much to the delight of his detractors and the chagrin of scientific-minded people, Joshi, through the University Grants Commission (UGC), even approved a new curriculum in astrology in over twenty universities when most universities in the country are suffering from paucity of funds to run their regular curricula. Apart from the existing Departments of Religion, it was also decided to offer separate higher degrees in the nitty-gritty Vedic rituals, and train Hindu priests. Then the cultural affairs minister, Anant Kumar, pressed hard the Archeological Survey of India (ASI) to carry out futile explorations in the small town of Chitrakoot on the border of M.P. and U.P. In an effort to find evidence to establish any possible connection between that town and Lord Ram, who was supposed to have journeyed there while he was in exile (as the epic Ramayana says), he was supposed to have instructed: *kuch nikalo* (pull something out).[51] Even the Hindu gurus, who formerly kept themselves preoccupied with religious matters, now may be seen jumping into the political fray as seen by the claim of Kanchi Kamakoti Sankaracharya Jayendra Saraswati that the VHP effort at building the Ram temple in Ayodhya was a "rightful religious movement and not politically motivated."[52]

The Ideas of March 2002 and the Gujarat Fiasco

In January 2002, the VHP marched on New Delhi demanding that Prime Minister Vajpayee allow them to start building the Ram temple in Ayodhya. He did not accede. In turn, the VHP gave notice that no matter what, they would start building the temple on March 15, 2002, which happened to be an important Hindu festival day, *Mahashiva ratri*. This fundamentalist stubbornness, countered by the need to keep the NDA coalition together, led the BJP President Jana Krishnamoorti to distance the party by stating that it had no commitment toward building the temple. The discomfort of the BJP was only compounded by the fact that four states—U.P., Uttarnachal, Punjab, and Manipur—went to the polls at the end of February. BJP lost all including the crucial state of U.P. where it gained only 88 seats (as against the previous 158).[53] It lost control of its stronghold, Delhi municipality, too, by gaining only 17 of the 134 seats. During this election, the BJP was on the horns of a dilemma: it could neither altogether stop the VHP, and thus appear to be unsympathetic to the Ram janmabhumi issue, nor allow them to go ahead and thus risk being attacked for being a communal party by everyone including some of its NDA partners. Thus, it appeared to be having it both ways by not condemning the VHP, but also not allowing the construction of the temple either by only putting off the issue through a referral to the Law Ministry (which later ruled against the VHP).

The VHP itself kept shifting its stand. First, the March 12 deadline was to commence building the temple. "The temple will be constructed at any date around March 12. We cannot wait beyond a point. Now, it will be a fight to finish," said the VHP international secretary general, Pravin Bhai Togadia. Its international working president Ashok Singhal said that the deadline was for the handing over of forty-seven acres of land around the complex that the government was holding as a trustee. The chief of the Ram Janam Bhumi Nyas (Trust), Mahant Paramhans Ramchandra Das, did not join the protest march to Delhi organized by the VHP saying that there were too many unnecessary security arrangements made, and that he would instead work for the removal of the government, if the government were not to clear the hurdles in the way of the construction of the temple. Others wanted to launch a *dharma yudha* (religious war) to build the temple without reference to any court decision.[54] Both Singhal and Das later moved the deadline to March 15 when they would start moving crafted stones to the complex as a token of construction. The RSS itself is aware that the temple issue might cause a rift between the BJP and the NDA coalition partners and thus worried about the possibility of the government's downfall. For them a government, which is sympathetic to the cause of Hinduism and the Ram temple, is preferable to waging an all-out demand for the temple. Thus, they wanted to mediate and even ask the VHP to cool down, but were snubbed with the latter saying that they do not care whether the government stays or falls.

It should be noted here that for the entire clamor, the VHP, however, might not even have any legal standing with regard to the decision to build, or not to build, a temple. Such a decision is said to be the domain of Mahant Jyotidas of Nirmohi Akhara, the seminary among the original petitioners. In addition, five of the seven Akhara heads are said to be anti-VHP.[55]

Added to this muddle is the dispute on the land itself. Of the sixty-seven acres of land acquired by the Narasimha Rao government in January 1993 (as seen above), forty-three acres are claimed by the Trust as its own. However, it appears that the Kalyan Singh government in U.P. only leased it eight months prior to the demolition of the Babri mosque to build a Ram Katha park. The park was never built; instead the mosque was demolished.[56] There are as many as four civil suits pending regarding the ownership of the total sixty-seven acres, and the Supreme Court in the past made it clear that this issue must first be resolved. The government of India also asked the Court for a ruling on whether there indeed was a Hindu temple in the complex, and whether the Muslims had a right over the land. The Supreme Court in 1994 in its turn sent back the issue of ownership to the (U.P.) Allahabad High Court for their determination (which is yet to come), and permitted offering prayers at the temple. These conflicting stances were summed by Venkaiah Naidu, rural development minister and the BJP leader thus: "VHP is an independent organization. It is a *dharmik* (religious) organization. They are following their own agenda. We are duty bound by the NDA agenda—the coalition *dharma*."[57]

As the threat of more communal violence grew subsequent to the Gujarat tragedy (see below), both Prime Minister Vajpayee, and Interior Minister Advani (who in the late 1980s led the temple issue), declared that they would not allow the building of the temple, but would abide by the Court's decision. It is quite possible that they might be concerned that any confrontation with regard to the temple might be construed as Hindu terrorism by a world, which is trying to come to grips with the September 11, 2001, disasters in the United States. Moreover, allowing the VHP to start its activity would have led to a massive communal conflagration that could have far-reaching reactions and major law and order problems, not limited to the downfall of the governments itself. For itself, the VHP might have thought that this is their last chance to get their fundamentalist religious agenda carried through when the BJP is in power, which, according to them, came to office with their assistance. But they may not have appreciated that the BJP is bound by the NDA coalition politics, and cannot serve their cause, which of course has been the BJP's cause too. The first signs of a certain climb down came from the VHP, which said that they would abide by the Court decision, but would like to go through only a symbolic *puja* (offering) on March.

As soon as this announcement was made, two Muslims went to the Supreme Court petitioning that this activity be stopped. The Court on March 13 assented, perhaps taking into consideration the deteriorating law and order situation in Gujarat (see below), which had the potential of spreading to the rest of the country. The Court also put on hold any handing over of the forty-three acres of land to the Trust, but referred the matter to a larger Bench. Just as the VHP was miffed, the All-India Muslim Personal Law Board expressed its approval of the decision. What is intriguing in this context is that the government of India's attorney general, Soli Sorabjee, argued that symbolic religious ceremonies be permitted. Once again, the duplicity of the BJP is seen when it made the astonishing announcement that he was acting on his own and it was not necessarily the stand of the government. The fact, however, remains that the NDA partners were not consulted in this context, which made them livid.

More bizarre was what followed. The Trust President Parmahans, who a few days before declared that he would commit suicide (which Hindu religion does not permit) if he were not allowed to do the symbolic *puja*, instead took to a small procession and handed over two carved pillars. One, this happened outside of the disputed land, and two more intriguingly, the gift was accepted by Shatrughan Singh, a central government observer, and an official of the Ayodhya cell in the Prime Minister's Office (PMO). Thus, once again the BJP showed its dual face. The opposition parties cried wolf. *Times of India*, a respected Indian English daily, captured the essence of it all when its banner read: "VHP victorious, Open furious, government ambiguous."[58] The crisis however passed, for now, but the issue remains. What the Courts would say, how the VHP and other fundamentalists behave, and how the BJP reacts to whatever might happen are imponderables at this time.

Another test to the BJP came in Gujarat on February 27, when a train load of Hindu devotees returning from Ayodhya were attacked and the train itself was set on fire by a Muslim mob in Godhra, killing fifty-eight people. The communal tinder box was lit resulting in the death of nearly seven-hundred people, mostly Muslims, and with around fifty-six said to have been displaced initially.[59] The greatest irony was that this had to happen in the State where the apostle of peace, Mahatma Gandhi, was born. Beyond the tragedy, the problem for the BJP was that the State's chief minister, Narendra Mody, is its party man who was accused by the opposition of doing nothing to stop the carnage at best, or encouraging the Hindus against Muslims at worst. Even some of the members of the NDA, demanded that the Mody government be dismissed (under Article 356), but the Vajpayee government not only did not yield, but went on to absolve Mody of any responsibility.

There indeed were some other apologists for Mody. For example, while disputing that his government was not actively dealing with the communal trouble and the consequent deteriorating law and order situation, *India Today* wrote that as of May, ". . . the police fired 8,465 rounds of bullets and 11,690 rounds of tear-gas shells. As many as 98 people died in police firing in the first three days alone. . . . As many as 168 persons have died in police firing so far, the highest in Gujarat history. Police arrested 33,563 people."[60] The point that is missed is not what was done subsequent to the riots, but that the situation in the first place was allowed by the Mody government to deteriorate, for which he ought to take responsibility. Whether there was any complicity of his government in this communal mayhem by fomenting the Hindu mobs is a matter yet to be judged. The National Human Rights Commission (NHRC), however, charged Mody with "comprehensive failure."[61]

Religious fires are still burning four months after the train disaster. Not so ironically, the play that is being staged currently with wide appeal in Gujarat is *Anandmath*, which was written twenty-five years after the Sepoy Mutiny of 1857, with only two themes: support the British and hate the Muslims.[62] Togadia, the VHP international general secretary, went on to declare that "(w)hat is happening in Gujarat is not communal riots but people's answer to Islamic jehad."[63]

At the National Executive meeting of the BJP on April 12, 2002, in Goa, Mody offered his resignation suggesting that the party decide on the direction it and the country ought to take following the electoral losses of February. The party rejected the offer. While some compared his role during the Godra riots to that of Slobodan Milosvic's genocide in Bosnia, some of the hard-core Hindu priests began offering prayers for Mody's well-being. Contrarily, senior vice president of the VHP, Acharya Girija Kishore, went on even to give some gratuitous advice to Muslims that they stop eating beef as a mark of respect for the Hindu sentiments. Ironically, not many voices of criticism were heard when the only Hindu king in the world, while visiting India in late June 2002, offered a buffalo and other assorted small animals to Hindu deities.[64]

An even critical political challenge and an opportunity for the BJP came in U.P., when it lost in the February elections and no other party got a majority. The claim of Mulayam Singh Yadav, leader of the Samajwadi Party, to form the government was not heard despite the fact he won the largest plurality with 145 seats (out of the total 399). The governor of the State left the legislative Assembly in a limbo while inordinately delaying inviting anyone else to form a government. The delay of course provided the time and opportunity to forge alliances. This also coincided with a no-confidence motion raised in Parliament against the Vajpayee government for its inaction in Gujarat. One of his cabinet ministers, Ram Vilas Paswan (Minister for Coal), in fact, resigned in protest. Some of the NDA partners (such as the Telugu Desam Party—TDP, with twenty-eight votes) declared that they would not support the Vajpayee government, and others opposed it outright (such as Lok Janashakti with four members and Trinamool Congress with nine members). Thus, Vajpayee needed some help. The Bahujana Samajwadi Party (BSP) of Mayawati, which came out Second in the U.P. elections (with eighty-nine seats against the eighty-eight seats of the BJP), had thirteen members in Parliament, and garnering their support would serve the BJP under the circumstances. Yet, it is important to note that while the BSP is a *dalit* (lower-caste/oppressed people) party, the BJP, as already seen, is considered the upper caste party against which the BSP fights. Such a philosophical difference did not, however, in the past hinder alliances between them. Mayawati, leader of the BSP, served as chief minister of U.P. twice before, both times with the BJP support, the first in 1995 lasting for four months, and the second in 1997 for six months. Now for the third time, a deal was again struck, and the BJP supported Mayawati who became the Chief Minister of U.P.[65] Noteworthy is that the deal between the two was struck just a day before the *Lok Sabha* was to start the debate on the no-confidence motion in Parliament.

Vajpayee himself won the vote of confidence handily (281 to 194 out of a total of 542 members) in the *Lok Sabha*. But when the matter came for discussion in the Rajya Sabha (the upper House) where it appeared that he would lose, Vajpayee joined the opposition in passing a resolution that his government would intervene in the governance of Gujarat under Article 355, and not under Article 356.[66] Thus, both the BSP and BJP had their political cake and ate it, too. In addition, it was all politics as usual.

The election of the speaker of *Lok Sabha* further illustrates political opportunism as well as the play of religion. The incumbent, who belonged to the TDP died in an airplane crash, and that party was offered the position again. Some claimed that Vajpayee is throwing some sobs to retain the support of the claimed that Vajpayee is throwing some sobs to retain the support of the TDP (during the no-confidence vote, as discussed above). The TDP declined the offer.[67] Instead, Manohar Joshi, the Minister for Heavy Industries, was elected. He is a member of the NDA, and belongs to Shiv Sena, a more militant Hindu nationalist party than the BJP. He is also a close follower of Bal Thackery, the Shiv Sena leader. It is well known that the latter at one time claimed that he would run the former's government "by remote control," despite the fact that Thackery had not held an elected public office.

In the thick of these developments, an exasperated Prime Minister Vajpayee, a moderate himself, was reported to have said in a speech at the party executive meeting in Goa that Islam is an intolerant religion. He angrily denied it stating that he was quoted out of context, and reaffirmed that India is a multi-religious society and everyone is free to follow any religion.[68]

Conclusion

It is apparent that while religion has played, and continues to play, its part in politics within the context of a secular polity, Hinduism as an article of faith was used by the BJP for great partisan advantage. There is no denying that the BJP and its core constituents (the VHP, RSS, and Bajrang Dal) are emboldened enough to push for a *Hindu rashtra* (Hindu state/rule). While they had not openly declared that India ought to be a Hindu theocracy, there is little doubt as to where their hearts are. Their entire idiom is not only Hindu but also Sanskriti and even Brahmanic—the latter particularly leading critics to argue often that BJP is an upper-caste (Brahmin) party.

For the BJP, the Ram janmabhumi issue came like a Godsend, so to speak, and certainly as a political blessing. A basic religious issue has been turned into an opportunistic partisan pawn, with the distinction between mythology and reality often blurred, or deliberately ignored. In addition, the government itself, unable to deal with the controversy, kept passing the buck on, by seeking judicial intervention. Divine issues now have become matters of jurisprudence leading some of the Hindu fundamentalists to argue that the courts should have no say in the matter which ought to be decided in Parliament.

While the VHP itself cannot claim to be a major force, either politically or religiously, it certainly proved to be very vocal in pushing its Hindu religious fundamentalism and serving the political purposes of the BJP. In the process secularism ceased to be a constitutional precept, and ended up as a political slogan.

Two important appointments in June 2002 lead one to believe that the BJP and the Ram janmabhumi issue will remain active on the political scene. For one, L. K. Advani, the home minister, has been elevated to the position of deputy prime minister, showing the hardliner BJP face as a counterweight to the moderate stance of Prime Minister Vajpayee.[69] For another, Vinay Katiyar, once the head of the hard-line Hindu group, Bajrang Dal, was appointed as president of the BJP unit in U.P. Everyone knows that, for him, the Ayodhya issue is a battle cry.

There is no doubt that religion and occult are an integral part of Indian life. Religious leaders—all the so-called Godmen and Godwomen—wield a considerable influence, command a large following (the more powerful a politician, the higher the civil servant and the wealthier a person, the greater is his or her connection with these), and have even come to play crucial roles in politics. (Names such as Dhirendra Brahmachary, Chadraswamy, and now the Shakaracharyas are very familiar in India for this reason.) State-sponsored orthodox and pseudo-religious ceremonies, bordering on the occult, have become quite common.[70]

In a society where religion and social life are so intermeshed that it is hard to distinguish one from the other, any effort to delink religion and politics through the passage of a law will not have much support. In fact, the Congress (I) admitted as much when they stopped introducing a proposed measure in 1993 (after the destruction of the mosque).[71] Although the claim made by Advani that "separating religion from politics would distance politics from ethics and morality,"[72] is debatable, one cannot but be dismayed, and even indignant, at the way religion is exploited for political gain. The very morality of such actions is highly questionable. What is paradoxical, and almost abhorrent, is that religion is used continuously for secular political reasons.

While for now the coalition *dharma* (as seen above) moderates the fundamentalist stance, if indeed the BJP were to succeed in pushing its *Hindutva* on India, and capture the government on its own eventually, what would happen to all the minorities who constitute over 18 percent of the population? In the height of tensions between India and Pakistan since the war against terrorists that the United States is waging in Afghanistan from October 2001, Advani made the comment: "If the two Germanies can come together, history will find some way some day of rejoining India and Pakistan of their own free choice."[73] The theme is repeated. While Advani proclaims that "we accept Pakistan as a sovereign country," he also envisions a confederation of India and Pakistan.[74] While this might be dismissed as idle talk or even a pious wish, the inflammatory rhetoric cannot be missed by the Muslims who fear that they may be pushed out (however outlandish the possibility might be), or worse, the BJP is harboring the notion of conquering Pakistan. Similarly, in March, the Akhil Bharatiya Pratinidhi Sabha—the RSS policy-making body—made the following charitable threat: "Let the Moslems understand that their real safety lies in the goodwill of the majority."[75] While there is no reason to doubt any religious group's patriotism, one can see the dangerous confusion against which the first prime minister of India, Jawaharlal Nehru, cautioned: "The communalism of a majority community is apt to be taken for nationalism."[76]

It is important to note that Muslims are not only part of the nation, but also that they have occupied important public offices and provided yeoman service to both the state and the society. Hindu nationalists might be discomfited to know that the script for the famous television series, *Mahabharat*, was written after all by a Muslim, Rahi Masoom Raza. Other illustrious Muslim personalities include Zakir Hussain, president of India, and several cabinet ministers, governors, justices and so on. A. P. J. Abdul Kalam, once scientific advisor to a prime minister, a man of impeccable academic credentials as a nuclear scientist, who received the highest civilian award—Bharat Rathna—from the Government of India, is a Muslim. In May 2002, he was also the nominee of the NDA for the office of the president of India (since elected President). But religion crept in once again when people criticized his nomination—a Muslim, and that too a nuclear scientist—to this high office (though ceremonial) at a time when the world went into the hysteria of a possible nuclear war between India and Pakistan over the Kashmir terrorist issue. Some interpreted this as a cynical political exploitation of religion by the BJP government for political ends. It is noteworthy, however, that Kalam is supported by all but the left parties. In addition, when asked whether his nomination was because of the fact that he is a Muslim, he deadpanned by saying: "Really? . . . I have always regarded myself as an Indian."[77]

For many of the orthodox, reason seems to have run its course; faith has become the watchword, occasionally bordering on the bizarre. For example, Acharya Girija Kishore, a VHP operator, said that should the government fulfill the long-standing VHP demand of declaring a war on Pakistan, the sants (religious leaders) would postpone construction of the (Ram) temple.[78] The BJP coalition partner in the state of Mahrashtra, Shiv Sena, similarly keeps bringing up issues, such as its opposition to even Valentine cards, as an assault on Hindu religion. All this raises more serious questions as articulated by Milton Viorst: "Has Enlightenment, with its worship of reason, run its course, leaving behind a sense of emptiness that can be filled only by primitive faith? Do the masses feel that technology has made them increasingly powerless, persuading them to turn for relief to an exigent God? Has modern society so depersonalized human affairs that mankind requires stringent religious practice to give meaning to life?"[79] These of course are mind-boggling questions demanding sane responses.

Several future scenarios can be painted. It is quite possible by now that the Hindu fundamentalists, the VHP in particular, may have thought that this is the last chance for them to push the Hindu agenda while their cohort the BJP is in power, though in a coalition. Alternatively, they are so intoxicated with their religion that they are ready to push it, no matter what. The BJP itself may have been tired of the VHP demands, as may be seen from Prime Minister Vajpayee complaining that he cannot run the government while the VHP keeps pulling the rug under him. It is also possible that the party may be feeling chastised by the world's concern over terrorism. It is doubtful, however, whether the other parties in the coalition, and in particular the Congress (I) in opposition, can succeed in stopping this religious fundamentalism for long. For they already know and may take a cue, just as the BJP might once more, that religion after all has always the potential of getting votes.

While, indeed, the BJP and its cohorts seem to be on a collision course with regard to the Ram temple issue, it is equally important to note that political pragmatism comes in as a savior, in a way. To keep in power, until at least it can stand on its own feet, the BJP will have to live like Janus, talking religion to satisfy its faithful and singing secularism as a political tool to retain the coalition in tact. The same coalition governments that are criticized for inaction and their transient nature due to the internal pressures among the disparate partners, have, after all, been a blessing in keeping fundamentalism at bay. Thus, for the future of India and religious tolerance, a lot depends upon the political parties and their leaders. This is only more so in case of the BJP, which claimed a moral high ground all along, but lost its innocence with the Gujarat issue and its support to Mayawati of the BSP to form a coalition government in U.P. The leaders of the nation can either let the country down the slippery slope, or stop the rut and try to move it on the developmental path. If only they can rise over the petty electoral politics, and look toward the nation, religious fundamentalism will have played its course. One can only hope that they will rise above the low politics, become statesmen, and preach the real Gandhian *Rama Rajya* concept of tolerance of all religions. It is also expected that the political parties subscribing to secularism would thwart any attempts of imposing Hindu religious fundamentalism just as the non-Hindi belt electorate should indeed act as a check.

Over half a century after independence, it is wise and useful to recall what Raj Kumari Amrit Kaur said on March 20, 1947: "There is no gainsaying the fact that foreign domination has been one of the main causes, if not the main cause, of creating internal dissensions between the two major communities. Now that the foreign power is definitely leaving, it behooves us more than ever before to turn the searchlight inwards. . . . (I)t cannot be denied that the foreign rulers sowed whatever seeds of dissension, the soil that nourished them and has allowed them to assume the menacing aspect they now bear is ours. The greater fault, therefore, is ours."[80]

Acknowledgment

I would like to express my deep sense of appreciation to Jon S. T. Quah, Editor, *Asian Journal of Political Science*, for allowing me to use some preliminary thoughts on the subject, which appeared in an article long ago. I thank the two anonymous referees and my colleagues Aruna N. Michie and Prasad V. Biderkota, for their valuable comments, which only improved this draft. However, I take full responsibility for any shortcomings here.

Notes

1. Alexander Hamilton, James Madison, and John Jay, *The Federalist: Or the New Constitution* (New York: E. F. Dutton & Co., Inc, 1948), 42.
2. See Ernest Barker, trans. and ed., *The Politics of Aristotle* (New York: Oxford University Press, 1974), 180.
3. George H. Sabine, *A History of Political Thought* (London: George G. Harrap & Co., Ltd., 1937), 107.
4. While the 2001 census data are not available, and there is no reason to believe that the ratios may have changed dramatically, the 1991 census figures may be seen at www.censusindia.net/religion.
5. See the discussion in Krishna K. Tummala, "Religion and Politics in India," *Asian Journal of Political Science* 1, no. 2 (December 1993): 57–76.
6. See B. Shiva Rao, et al., eds., *The Framing of India's Constitution: Select Documents* II (New Delhi: The Indian Institute of Public Administration, 1967), 50.
7. Rao, *Framing of India's Constitution*, 52.
8. Rao, *Framing of India's Constitution*, 76.
9. Rao, *Framing of India's Constitution*, 157.
10. Yet another member, Alladi Krishnaswami Ayyar, had similar misgivings. Rao, *Framing of India's Constitution*, 213.
11. This in effect became section (2) (b) of Article 5 in the new Constitution. The reference to "Hindu" here as including the Sikhs, Jains, and Buddhists, was also added as Explanation II to the same Article. Rao, *Framing of India's Constitution*, 302.
12. These changes, among others, were made consequent to the recommendations of the Swaran Singh Committee. Whether the Preamble can be amended, and what purpose does the addition of the words "secular socialist," and "integrity" serve, are highly debatable, and debated, topics. For example, see N. A. Palkhivala, *We, the People: India, the Largest Democracy* (Bombay: Strand Book Stall, 1984), 195–202.
13. See the distinction in Ashis Nandy, "The Politics of Secularism and the Recovery of Religious Tolerance," *Alternatives* 13 (1988): 180–81.
14. The preoccupation of the Indian mind with occult is well known. Even presidents and prime ministers of India have been known to consult astrologers and visit places of religious worship before filing their nomination papers for election. The Sports Authority of India, a government of India entity, performed *havan* (roughly exorcism) in 1989 when a football player and a gymnast died while attending training camps at the Jawaharlal Nehru Stadium in New Delhi. Religious ceremonies are regularly held seeking rain or to avoid a drought or some other catastrophe, real or perceived, or for the health of this or that important persona.
15. A whole host of issues stem out of this paradox of "a secular state that did not provide any formal role for religion in public affairs was superimposed on a society in which religion was a vital interpersonal bond." See Subrata Kumar Mitra, "Desecularising the State: Religion and Politics in India after Independence," *Comparative Studies in Society and History* 33 (October 1991): 755–77.
16. Consequent to the assassination, the government of India declared that no organization that would preach violence and communal hatred would be tolerated. Accordingly, the RSS was banned on February 4, 1948 (lifted on July 12, 1949).
17. For an exposition of the fortunes of the BJP since its beginning, see B. D. Graham, *Hindu Nationalism and Indian Politics* (Cambridge: Cambridge University Press, 1990).

18. When in the Shah Bano case the Supreme Court of India ruled that the Muslim personal law was unacceptable, the Indian Parliament passed an amendment reiterating the Shari'a as the personal law of the Muslims. The BJP opposes this in earnestness. For an insightful explanation of this case, see Nawab B. Mody, "The Press in India: The Shah Bano Judgement and Its Aftermath," *Asian Survey* 27, no. 8 (August 1987): 935–53.

19. Their demand is based on Article 48 of the Constitution which suggests that steps be taken to prohibit "the slaughter of cows, calves and other milch draught cattle." It should however, be noted that this Article is part of the Directive Principles of State Policy which are not justiciable in a court of law.

20. See the responses of Atal Behari Vajpayee in *The Hindu International Edition* January 23, 1993, 10. For an explanation of "reservations" policy, see Tummala, "Policy of Preference: Lessons from India, the United States and South Africa," *Public Administration Review (PAR)* 59, no. 6 (November–December 1999): 495–508.

21. Graham, *Hindu Nationalism*, 253.

22. Ramayan is one of the three Hindu epics. The other two are the Mahabharat and the Bhagavadgita, although the latter is part of the former.

23. According to Hindu belief, the universe will have four yugas: *Krita*, *Treta*, *Dwapara*, and *Kali yuga*, each in a declining moral and physical stature than the previous one. The last, *Kali yuga*, the current one, started in 3102 B.C. and will last for a total of 432,000 years, at the end of which the world will be destroyed. After some lapse of time, the cycle will start all over again with the first, *Krita yuga*.

24. See Richard Barnett, *North India between Empires: Awadh, the Mughals and the British, 1720–1801* (Berkeley: University of California Press, 1980).

25. See Peter van Der Veer, "'God Must be Liberated!' A Hindu Liberation Movement in Ayodhya," *Modern Asian Studies* 21, no. 2 (April 1987): 291.

26. See Tummala, "Policy of Preference."

27. See *India Today* (October 31, 1989), 15.

28. Quoted by Amrita Basu, "The dialectics of Hindu nationalism," in *The Success of India's Democracy*, Atul Kohli, ed. (New York: Cambridge University Press, 2001), 169.

29. "Politics of Opportunism," *India Today* (August 15, 1992), 14–21.

30. For an explanation of the use of Emergency Powers, and a case study of the dismissal of a duly elected opposition State government by the Centre, see Tummala, "India's Federalism Under Stress," *Asian Survey* 37, no. 6 (June 1992): 538–53.

31. For an explanation of the politics and the events leading to the demolition of the Babri mosque and the Rama janmabhumi issue, see Tummala, "Religion and Politics in India," *Asian Journal of Political Science* 1, no. 2 (December 1993): 57–76.

32. See, for example, the relevant stories: "A Nation's Shame," in *India Today* (December 31, 1992): 14–28; *The Hindu International Edition*, December 12, 1992, 1, and its editorial on 8.

33. They wrote: "For a handful—those in government, in political parties, and in large sections of the English press . . . what had happened was 'national shame,' it was 'madness,' it was 'barbaric.' For the rest of the country it was a liberation—a sweeping away of cobwebs." See BJP's *White Paper on Ayodhya & The Rama Temple Movement* (New Delhi: Bharatiya Janata Party, April 1993), 2.

34. It should be noted here that, under law, the ban itself was subject to referral for adjudication to a tribunal within thirty days, and the tribunal has six months to give its decision. In June 1993, the Allahabad High Court lifted the ban on the RSS till the tribunal made its findings known. And on June 6, 1993, the tribunal itself quashed the order banning the RSS and Bajrang Dal, but retained the ban on the VHP and the Islamic Sevak

Sangh. (The status of Jamait-i-Islam is not clear.) See *The Hindu International Edition*, May 29, 1993, 5, and June 6, 1993, 1.

35. The dismissal of the Patwa government in the State of M.P. was challenged in the court of law as an unconstitutional exercise of the Emergency Powers by the central government. And for the first time in the history of independent India, the M.P. High Court set aside the dismissal. But the prime minister declared that there is no way of restoring Patwa to office. See K. Tummala, "The Indian Union and the Emergency Powers," *International Journal of Political Science* 17, no. 4 (October 1996): 373–84; also, "Constitutional Government and Politics in India: The Case of Uttar Pradesh," *Asian Journal of Political Science* 6, no. 2 (December 1998): 79–97.

36. As quoted in Oroon K. Ghosh, *How India Won Freedom* (Delhi: Ajanta Publications, 1989), 51.

37. Both Mahatma Gandhi and Jawaharlal Nehru thought that this resulted in the destruction of unity in India. The Mahatma thought these reforms were. . . "our undoing. Had it not been for separate electorates . . . we should have settled our differences." Nehru said: "A political barrier was created round them (Muslims), isolating them from the rest of India and reversing the unifying and amalgamating process which had been going on for centuries." Quoted in V. D. Mahajan, *Constitutional Development and the National Movement in India* (New Delhi: S. Chand & Company Ltd., 1986), 62.

38. The only other ruler who refused to join the Indian Union, the Nizam of Hyderabad, a Muslim ruling a majority Hindu population right in the middle of India, was forced by a military action to join the Union by 1948. For a fascinating account, see V. P. Menon, *The Story of the Integration of the Indian States* (Bombay: Orient Longmans, 1961).

39. See Pankaj Mishra, "Death in Kashmir," *The New York Review*, September 21, 2000, 40.

40. Tarun Vijay, the editor of *Panchjanya*, a BJP organ, claimed that during the last twenty years more than fifty thousand Hindus were killed, and as many as two hundred thousand were driven out of their homes. See his guest column, "Stop Secular Talibanism," *India Today*, 25 March, 2002: 16. The numbers quoted, however, are not official, and cannot easily be verified, but the fact remains that untold numbers belonging to both religions died and suffered immensely.

41. The early demands of the Akali Dal for a separate State out of the territories of the Punjab are retold in Baldev Raj Nayar, *Minority Politics in the Punjab* (Princeton, N. J.: Princeton University Press, 1966).

42. See the analysis of Joyce Pettigrew, "In Search of a New Kingdom of Lahore," *Pacific Affairs* 60, no. 1 (Spring 1987), 1–25.

43. BJP's White Paper, 159. For a good account of the rise of Hindu nationalism see, Thomas Blom Hansen, *The Saffron Wave: Democracy and Hindu Nationalism in Modern India* (Princeton: Princeton University Press, 1999).

44. Quoted in Deepshikha Ghosh, "Ram temple issue helped BJP's rise to power: Advani," www.rediff.com.news/2001/oct/21bjp1.htm.

45. Quoted in Paul Dettman, *India Changes Course: Golden Jubilee to Millennium* (London: Praeger, 2001), 53–54.

46. This argument is often justified by showing that even in a mature democracy such as that of the United States, no one other than a native-born is qualified to be the president. It should, however, also be noted that people of Indian origin occupied the high political office of prime minister in foreign countries such as Fiji Islands and Mauritius.

47. See *The Hindu International Edition*, January 23, 1993, 4.

48. *India Today*, 15 June 1993, 40.

49. For the dynamics of this kind of coalition and the consequent inaction of the governments, see K. Tummala, "The Indian Administrator in the New Millennium," *Asian Journal of Political Science* 9, no.1 (June 2001): 49–65.

50. See the story in *The Indian Express* www.indian-express.com/fe20010903, September 2, 2001. In fact, the Supreme Court of India issued an order on March 1, 2002, staying the implementation of the National Curriculum Framework for Secondary Education (NCFSE). It was disputed that the Curriculum was designed without consulting the apex education body, the Central Advisory Board of Education (CABE). See www.timesofindia.inditimes.com, March 1, 2002.

51. See www.timesofinida.indiatimes.com, September 9, 2001.

52. www.news.sify.com/content, June 25, 2001.

53. As no party could muster enough strength to form a government, the State was placed under the president rule. Under Article 356 of the Indian Constitution, a duly elected Sate government can be dismissed, and the administration taken over by the Centre when there is a breakdown in constitutional machinery. In this case, the governor of the State left the newly elected legislative assembly in a limbo, but let the Centre take over. For the use and misuse of this power, see Tummala, "The Indian Union."

54. www.ndtv.com, January 21, 2002.

55. See *India Today*, March 18, 2002: 35.

56. For details of the dispute see www.indian-express.com, March 9, 2002.

57. www.expressindia.com, February 11, 2002.

58. www.timesofindia.indiatime, March 15, 2002.

59. www.news.bbc.co.uk, March 7, 2002.

60. "Gujarat: Facts & Reality," *India Today*, May 6, 2002: 23.

61. See www.hindustantimes.com, 31 May 2002.

62. The play, *Anandmath*, was written by an unabashed Hindu protagonist and paradoxically a supporter of the British, Bankim Chandra Chatterjee, during 1882–1885. Not ironically, the national song of India since independence, *vande mataram* (obeisance to the motherland) was also written by the same person. At the time of adoption of that song, several, including the Noble laureate, Rabindranath Tagore, opposed it in vain, having criticized it for being terribly chauvinist.

63. www.expressindia.com, April 1, 2002.

64. King Gyanendra of Nepal came to India in late May 2002, and offered a buffalo at the Kamakshi temple in Guahati, and five other assorted animals at the Kali temple in Benares. To save the situation, and certainly the face of the King himself, it was reported that the priests sacrificed the animals by slaughtering them after the King left the temples. See www.expressindia.com, June 28, 2002. It should be noted here that not eating beef, as the Hindus worship the cow, is a matter of conventional wisdom and tradition. No scriptures can be quoted to the effect that cows shall not be eaten. Contrarily, it is known that some Hindu kings of lore did sacrifice their horses after the *ashvamedha yaga*, and fed them to their priests.

65. Mayawati, when asked to prove her strength in the assembly, actually came out with the support of 270 to 180.

66. While Article 356 allows the Centre to dismiss a duly elected State government when it is satisfied that there is a breakdown of constitutional machinery in the State, Article 355 only enjoins that the Centre should "ensure that the government of every State is carried on in accordance with the provisions of the Constitution." In other words,

under the latter Article the Centre can instruct the State government as to how to run its business.

67. It was also reported that a Cabinet berth was offered to Mamata Banerjee, leader of Trinamool Congress, who kept moving in and out of the coalition to suit her own convenience, in return for her support. See Aarti Jerath, "Partners back off as PM waves sops list," www.indian-express.com, March 14, 2002. When the no-confidence motion came for voting, while the TDP abstained, the Trinamool Congress in fact voted for the Vajpayee government under the pretext of stability.

68. See "Vajpayee clarifies remarks on Muslims," www.hindustantimes. com, April 14, 2002. His original remarks may be seen in "How Vajpayee Ended up as the Hindutva Choir Boy," *India Today*, 29 April 2002: 15–16.

69. The position of deputy prime minister is nothing new. After all, six others occupied that position since independence. But the symbolism of elevating Advani nearly three years after the present government came into power, and before elections in Jammu and Kashmir held in October 2002, must not only be of symbolic importance but also a matter of political strategy.

70. See "Cajoling the Clouds," *India Today*, August 15, 1993, 20; also, "The Gurus for the 90s," *India Today*, July 31, 1993: 50–56.

71. *The Hindu International Edition*, September 4, 1993, 4.

72. *The Hindu International Edition*, 17 July 1993, 3.

73. Quoted in *India Today*, January 28, 2002, 9.

74. See *India Today*, February 4, 2002, 20.

75. See *India Today*, April 8, 2002, 21.

76. Quoted in "Saffron Quicksand," Cover story, *India Today*, March 25, 2002, 19.

77. See the interview with him in *India Today*, June 24, 2002: 19.

78. Quoted in *India Today*, February 4, 2002, 30.

79. Milton Viorst, *In the Shadow of the Prophet* (Boulder, Colo.: Westview Press, 2001), 19.

80. Memorandum to the Subcommittee on Minorities during the debates of the Constituent Assembly. See Rao, *Framing of India's Constitution*, 309–10.

Chapter 9

Ethnicity and Religion in Israeli Politics: Emergence of the Shas Party

Jacob Abadi

The existence of ethnic parties is not a new phenomenon in Israeli politics. However, with the exception of the religious Shas Party that in the 1999 elections managed to gain 430,000 votes and seventeen seats in the fifteenth Knesset, such parties had little success. Shas (Sephardi Torah Guardians) became the third largest party after the right wing opposition Likud, leaving behind older religious parties such as the National Religious Party (NRP), Agudat Yisrael, and Degel Hatorah.[1]

Shas represents many voters of oriental (Sephardi) descent in Israel. While its meteoric rise to power is a source of encouragement and pride to many Sephardim, the party's critics are numerous. The secular segments of the Israeli society regard it as a backward party that turns its back on Western values and capitalizes on Sephardi discontent against the Ashkenazi (European) establishment by encouraging ethnic discontent. Moreover, many of its secular critics regard it as a party that uses its political leverage in order to obtain benefits for its constituency, which include exemption from military service to young men attending its yeshivas and supporting them at the public's expense. Many Israelis regard the party's struggle for allocation of bigger resources for its religious education as blackmail. The 28,400 young men and women currently enrolled in the party's educational network constitute 2 percent of all Israel's students. The party's success in obtaining NIS 21 billion to educate its students led many Israelis to describe its maneuvers to obtain the funds as extortion.[2]

To most Israelis, the black coats, hats, and *tsitsiyot* (fringes sewn to the four corners of the small prayer shawl worn under the shirt) hanging over the pants of Shas's men are reminiscent of the Ashkenazi religious yeshiva men who remained clad like their ancestors who lived in the ghettos of Europe. This traditional image of the party's followers stands in stark contrast to that of the new Israeli, which the founders of Labor Zionism sought to create.

Shas's leaders had often argued that the Sephardim suffered discrimination only because of their ethnic origin. The purpose of this essay is to demonstrate that the argument often raised by Shas's leaders that Labor Zionism's quest for a new Jewish identity was a calculated attempt to discriminate against the Sephardim is inaccurate. It argues that in the process of creating such identity, not only the Sephardim but also all ethnic groups were subjects of discrimination by the Labor movement. Another argument presented here is that territorial maximalism never loomed large in Shas's agenda, and that matters of religious education, health, and social welfare were of prime concern for the ordinary Shas's voter. Shas's leaders preferred cooperation with the Labor Party despite the fact that they had much more in common with the Likud. Even the fact that many of their voters were pro-Likud did not dissuade them from cooperating with the Labor party. Shas's leaders had a keen sense of pragmatism and their political moves were dictated not by high principles of territorial maximalism or the sanctity of the land of Israel, but by the number of concessions which the ruling coalition, whether Labor or Likud, was willing to make to their party's cause. By and large, Shas did not truly represent the political views of its constituency, most of which held hawkish views about the occupied territories and the Middle East peace process.

It was largely due to its charismatic leadership that the party maintained a remarkable sense of discipline until the late 1990s, when one of its prominent leaders, Aryeh Deri was convicted of financial fraud that led to intense struggle over the succession. All along, Shas was torn by dissension among its leaders and followers, some of which remained loyal to the Likud while others supported Labor. However, the party's competition with the Likud was far more intense than with Labor because both Shas and the Likud remained convinced that they were competing for the same votes. That Shas continued to grow despite the dissension within its ranks was in large measure due to the fact that its members shared a common hatred toward the Ashkenazi establishment, which ignored their needs. Shas drew its strength from the Sephardim who felt discriminated against by the Ashkenazi establishment. This sentiment remained a powerful unifying factor. The lack of major ideological disputes within the party was due to the fact that virtually all Shas's followers accepted Rabbi Ovadia Yosef as the movement's spiritual father. In addition, the party's founders sought to establish a movement whose main purpose is to fight for Sephardi rights. Consequently, religious issues remained secondary on the party's agenda.

The Origins and the Objectives of the Shas

Initially, the founders of Labor Zionism were opposed not only to ethnic parties, but also to those dominated by rabbis and clerics.[3] Such attitude on the part of the secular establishment led by Mapai, which became the major party in the Labor coalition and remained in power for the first three decades of the Jewish state, was hardly conducive to the establishment of religious parties based on ethnicity. Sociological studies had proven beyond a shadow of a doubt that Mapai's founders established a highly controlled political system in which they remained the leaders and deliberately discouraged young people, whether Ashkenazim or Sephardim, from becoming involved in politics and assuming positions of power. Like their Ashkenazi counterparts, who were not trained or encouraged to assume positions of power, the young Sephardim remained alienated from the rigid political system established by the Labor movement.[4]

Yonathan Shapiro, a Tel Aviv University sociology professor attributed the rise of the right wing Likud Party in 1977, under Menachem Begin's leadership, to the fact that it managed to capture the votes of these disgruntled Sephardim without changing its symbols and myths. However, the fact that the Sephardim found it difficult to rise to positions of leadership was not entirely the fault of the Labor establishment. During the early years of Israel's existence the state's bureaucracy expanded by leaps and bounds. However, by the 1950s and 1960s, there was an unprecedented rise in the free professions. In order to enter these professions, or to enter the bureaucracy, there was a need for academic degrees, which the older population could achieve with greater ease, while the newcomers were faced with difficulties. Many of the newcomers, who were immigrants of Asian and African origins, were in no position to obtain such degrees. Consequently, the conflict between the older European immigrants and the new ones who came from Asia and Africa was translated into ethnic differences in which the former called themselves Ashkenazim while the latter called themselves Sephardim. Naturally, the better-educated Ashkenazim regarded the Sephardim as inferior. Consequently, the latter found it difficult to extricate them from that status.[5] By the later 1970s, it became evident that the Sephardim became disenchanted with the Labor movement.[6] However, they did not yet contemplate the formation of an ethnic party. Statistical evidence suggests that Shas's rise to power did not result from a specific desire to establish an ethnic party.[7]

Shas began its electoral campaign in the elections for the eleventh Knesset in 1984, when it gained four seats. In less than ten years the party became the third largest in the country. Its 41 percent growth gave it seventeen seats in the Knesset in 1999. Thus Shas became a force to reckon with in Israeli politics. Gone were the days when Mapai could construct a coalition without necessarily relying on the support of the religious parties. Shas's rise to power led to reaction among the secular segments in Israel and the 1999 elections, which resulted in an unprecedented victory for Shas also gave rise to the Shinui (Change) Party, whose platform called for opposition to clericalism and religious influence. Shinui advocated separation of religion and state thus intensifying a debate among many whether or not such separation is appropriate for Israel. Many remained convinced that such separation was not feasible. For example, Shlomo Sharan, a Tel Aviv University psychology professor was among those who argued that the Jewish religion is inseparable from the Jewish nation.[8]

Shas gained power because many Sephardim felt discriminated against, not only by the secular establishment, but also by the NRP and Agudat Yisrael.[9] Although Agudat Yisrael provided education to many Sephardim, Shas's founders felt that they were discriminated against.[10] With the decline of Labor Zionist ideology and Mapai's fall from power in 1977, an ideological void was created in Israel. Labor Zionism did not manage to offer a renewed vision for the state, nor did Likud offer a meaningful secular ideology. It was this void that allowed Shas to grow.

Shas's rise to such prominence constituted a triumph to the religious Sephardi communities in Israel. The party's triumph was due to a complex set of reasons. Soon after their arrival in the country, many Sephardim became well versed in the Torah and the Jewish tradition. Thousands of young Sephardim were absorbed in the religious camp through their attendance in yeshivas, many of which were established by Ashkenazim. Some of the students continued their studies in high yeshivas such as the prestigious *Porat Yosef* in the Jewish Quarter in Jerusalem. Sephardi Judaism was highly influenced by the religious practices of the Lithuanian yeshivas, where Rabbi Eliezer Schach was the dominant figure. Shas's leaders found it impossible to detach them from Schach, even when his views stood in stark contrast to those of Yosef, their mentor.[11]

The Ashkenazi yeshivas were famous for their high learning standards and thereby attracted many young Sephardim. However, the Ashkenazi institutions that absorbed the Sephardi students evinced a sense of superiority toward them. Moreover, the religious Ashkenazi community preferred to establish separate Ashkenazi and Sephardi institutions under the pretext that the Ashkenazi prayer style was different from that of the Sephardim. The most prominent Ashkenazi yeshivas set quota of Sephardi students eligible to enroll. Moreover, Agudat Yisrael avoided nominating Sephardi Knesset members from within its ranks. In addition, even when agreements were reached with that party to include Sephardi Knesset members these were ignored. This attitude did not remain confined to politics. Orthodox Ashkenazim avoided marrying off their children to Sephardim. Marriage with Sephardim was allowed only to repenting or slightly handicapped Ashkenazim. The attitude of the Ashkenazi elite toward the Sephardim was paternalistic and often condescending. Rabbi Schach himself had stated on several occasions that the Sephardim "are not mature enough for leadership."[12] Moreover, he did not encourage prominent Sephardim to become members of the Council of Torah sages that were under his control.

The discrimination against the Sephardim manifested itself in the political realm as well. Many remembered former Labor's prime minister Golda Meir's handling of the Black Panthers, whose Sephardi members protested the government's generosity toward the Soviet Jews who immigrated to Israel in the early 1970s, while they were left at the margins of the society, with little help or encouragement. Her statement that the Black Panthers were "not nice" remained ingrained in the minds of many Sephardim who later voted for Begin who identified with their needs.[13] This trend intensified and even those who voted for Shas made it clear that they preferred a Likud prime minister.[14]

The position of the Sephardim in the IDF (Israel Defense Forces) did not fare any better. Former Labor's Prime Minister Shimon Peres's argument that the IDF recruit officers according to their talent[15] was hardly convincing when most officers were of Ashkenazi origin. The Likud was just as negligent in meeting Sephardi demands. Prime Minister Yitzhak Shamir's statement at the First Conference of the Sephardi Federation in Israel, on May 19, 1987, that the discrimination against the Sephardim had virtually disappeared had left his listeners skeptical.[16]

Sephardi attitude during the first years of the state's formation was submissive. The Sephardim were thankful for the religious education, which the religious Ashkenazi establishment provided their children and thus saved them from poverty and crime. However, gradually their self-confidence increased and they began demanding equality by establishing their own educational institutions. However, it was not before 1983 that they began contemplating the formation of independent political institutions. They began in the municipal level in Jerusalem. The immediate reason for their rage was that the "Independent Education" network in charge of religious instruction discriminated against them by not appropriating sufficient funds. The political discrimination intensified the discontent. Former head of Shas in the Jerusalem municipality Nissim Zeev, recalled a discussion he had had with Avraham Kachila, who held the portfolio of planning and construction in Jerusalem. According to Zeev, when he came to ask for funds for the establishment of a network of schools for Sephardi girls, Kachila said, "you will get budgets when you have political power."[17] This is what led Zeev to establish a new political movement called the Union of Torah Observant Sephardim or Shas.

The newly established Shas Party ran in the 1983 municipal elections. In order to increase the new party's appeal Zeev convinced Yosef's eldest son, Rabbi Ya'acov Yosef to join the party. Already in the first election Shas managed to have three representatives in the city council, one of which was Yosef's son. At the same time, other Shas's candidates ran for offices in smaller towns, and some were elected members in their councils. However, the overriding factor for Shas's rise to power was Yosef's anger over his dismissal from his position as Israel's chief rabbi in the 1983 elections.[18] Many Sephardim regarded this as an insult and a slap in the face.

The Stature and Influence of Rabbi Ovadia Yosef

Born in Baghdad in 1920, Yosef is considered one of the most illustrious sages of modern times. His phenomenal memory and knowledge of the Hebrew Scriptures earned him the admiration of the Sephardim. Yosef did not hide his knowledge and did not refrain from speaking his mind on matters affecting the *Halacha* or Jewish law. He expressed his opinion on controversial matters such as whether or not to recognize the Falasha immigrants from Ethiopia, or the Karaites, as Jews. Yosef later denounced the discrimination of the Ashkenazi establishment against the Sephardim. Such a daring attitude allowed him to rise quickly within the rabbinical hierarchy in Israel. During his twenties he served as the deputy of Cairo's chief rabbi, and when the State of Israel was formed he was nominated as Petach Tikvah's chief rabbi. Later he became the head of the prestigious Yeshiva of Rabbi Yitzhak Nissim.

In 1960, Yosef ran for the office of Israel's chief rabbi but lost. In 1968, he was elected Tel Aviv's chief rabbi, and at the age of fifty-three he was nominated Israel's chief rabbi. Yosef regarded the Sephardi method of learning as different from the Ashkenazi in that it placed emphasis on knowledge of the Talmud that facilitates decision making in matters relating to the *Halacha*, whereas the Ashkenazi method did not require actual knowledge of the Talmudic text and therefore did not lend itself to practical interpretation. He therefore encouraged the establishment of yeshivas with high learning standards. His position allowed him to criticize and even belittle the Ashkenazi learning method. Moreover, he argued that even the Ashkenazim should go by the Sephardi tradition since they came to Israel to stay there permanently and therefore ought to act according to the local custom.

Basing his judgments on Rabbi Joseph Caro's *Shulhan Arukh* (The Prepared Table), which he regards as one of the main foundations of the *Halacha*, Yosef determined Jewish rules of conduct in a manner which many rabbis, both Ashkenazi and Sephardi, regarded as unorthodox. Thus for example, he determined that it was permissible for Jews to marry Karaites, and rejected the notion that in Jerusalem the Jewish Sabbath begins eighteen minutes before it begins in Tel Aviv. He was determined to embark on a cultural revolution aimed at restoring the pride that the Sephardim had in their religious heritage. Thus the political slogan *leha'hazir atarah le'yoshna* (to return the crown of Judaism to its rightful place) was adopted by Shas, and Yosef frequently used it to express his determination that Sephardi customs must be maintained. He told his followers not to be ashamed of their heritage arguing that some of the greatest sages in the history of Judaism were of Sephardi origin. He frequently mentioned prominent Sephardi names such as Maimonedes, Alfassi, Caro, and others, arguing that the

Sephardim are not inherently inferior and that their current position in the Israeli society is an outcome of Ashkenazi discrimination practices.

The Ashkenazi religious establishment was not pleased with Yosef's overconfidence and rejected his interpretation of the *Halacha*, arguing that although Yosef was well versed in it, his analytical ability was limited.[19] However, realizing that he wielded considerable influence in their yeshivas as well, his Ashkenazi rivals had to tone down their criticism. But once the rift between the Lithuanian religious leaders and their erstwhile Sephardi protégés became final, the criticism intensified.

Yosef's aspiration to obtain a lifetime nomination as Israel's chief rabbi did not materialize because Justice Minister Moshe Nissim did not forget that Yosef replaced his father as the chief rabbi. It was during that time that Yosef invited Deri for private lessons in Judaic studies. Together they conceived of a plan to exploit Shas's electoral triumph in order to turn it into a formidable force. This is how Shas became a national party in the elections to the eleventh Knesset that took place in 1984. Shas earned 64,000 votes and obtained four seats. Unlike other parties, Shas did not draft a political platform. Asked why his party refrained from drafting a political platform, one of the movement's leaders, Rabbi Yitzhak Peretz said, "We had opponents of all kinds who were waiting for us to make a slip. We were hesitant about inserting planks that might enable our opponents to misinterpret deliberately for their own advantage. . . . But in any case our platform is 3,500 years old and well-known: the Tora is our platform."[20]

Ideological differences have never loomed large within Shas. There is a considerable consensus among the party's religious members that Shas should be committed to preserve the Jewish tradition and they generally agree that the Torah is its platform. The fact that the Sephardim accept Yosef as the ultimate authority on the *Halacha* reinforced this consensus and reduced ideological disputes to a minimum. As for the party's secular members, their main concern is to see it fighting for the interests of the downtrodden Sephardim. The controversies within Shas relate not to matters of ideology, but to the ways and means by which it should pursue its practical goal of promoting the Sephardi cause. When Rabbi Yosef Kadourie capitalized on the religious sentiments and the superstitions prevalent among the Sephardim in order to attract more voters for the party, Yosef was furious. However, his disapproval of Kadourie's use of talismans in the party's election campaigns was primarily motivated by personal rivalry and should not be regarded as an ideological difference of opinion.

Yosef's reservations regarding the peace process are influenced by his negative attitude toward the Ashkenazi ruling elite. He has often criticized the Labor Party's position in the peace process as weak and indecisive. He never stated clearly his attitude toward Israel's boundaries. The fact that the number of Sephardim in the settlements of the West Bank remained small is a testimony to the fact the integrity of the State of Israel remained secondary on his party's agenda. However, Yosef's position reflected the conviction of most Shas's voters; that Jews have the right to settle in every part of their ancient homeland and that Jerusalem must remain the eternal capital of the Jewish State.

Competition for power among Shas leaders occupied much of their energy and they rarely preoccupied themselves with doctrinal issues or theological controversies. Shas's achievement was due to a campaign waged by Yosef and his protégé Deri, and not to its original founders, Zeev and his comrades from Jerusalem. Consequently, Zeev remained bitter that the leadership was stolen from him but was unable to challenge Yosef whose prestige soared among the Sephardim.

The Secrets of the Movement's Success

What made Shas such a formidable force in the electoral campaigns was the fact that it managed to gain considerable control over much of Israel's religious educational system. Shas's leaders had often boasted that their party's main concern was education and welfare.[21] Shas operated two educational networks, one called *Ma'ayan Ha'Khinukh Ha'Torati* (The Spring of Torah Education), and *El HaMa'ayan* (To the Spring), both established in 1985. The number of students attending *Ma'ayan Ha'Khinukh Ha'Torati* increased from a few hundred in 1985, to fifteen thousand in 2000. In addition, several thousand attended its kindergartens. No educational institution could boast such an increase. *El HaMa'ayan* was created because of the state's failure to cope with problems of poverty, crime, and drugs in underdeveloped towns such as Ofakim in southern Israel. By 1990, this network had nearly a thousand clubs in crime-ridden neighborhoods, among poor Sephardi families, most of which were secular.[22]

In 1999, eighty thousand young men and women attended the *El HaMa'ayan*'s extracurricular activities. This network became active in a variety of social and religious activities, including Torah and Talmud lessons, which its teachers gave in Sephardi communities throughout the country.[23] In addition, Shas established smaller networks that operated with considerable independence, but were tied to its nationwide educational system. However, Shas's tendency to allow many of its followers to open a school cost the party considerable loss of resources and led to major deficits. The upshot was that its leaders were compelled to allow the Treasury and the Ministry of Education to interfere in their financial and educational affairs. Thus Shas was compelled to increase the size of the classes under its jurisdiction and agreed to the principle of receiving funds based on the number of students instead of classes.[24]

In addition to educational activities, Shas operated day care centers for children and summer camps for the youth. It provided Torah lessons for women and began operating a charity organization whose aim was to provide help to the needy. In order to finance its grassroots charity activities Shas began soliciting help from the business community. Shas managed to raise funds from non-religious organizations and individuals. It expanded its charity activities to rural areas and promoted the cause of the agricultural communities in Israel. As part of its strategy to become involved in as many activities as possible, in 1994 Shas joined a coalition with Chaim Ramon and the left-of-center Meretz Party, to form the joint Ram faction in the elections to the Histadrut (The General Federation of Labor). The Ram faction won the election for the Histadrut and thus enhanced Shas's image as a welfare party.[25]

Shas's entry to positions of power within the Histadrut allowed it to expand its influence to other realms. For example, it obtained considerable influence in the Histadrut's *Mish'an* network of nursery homes. Thanks to its membership in the Histadrut, it also managed to establish its own publication *Yom LeYom*. In addition, Shas managed to obtain the directorship of the Histadrut's welfare division, which enabled it to solidify its position as a welfare party. Shas's position in the Histadrut also allowed it to control youth organizations that were traditionally under the purview of the Labor movement.

Although Shas's rise to power was due to the discriminatory feeling that the Sephardim harbored toward the Ashkenazi establishment, and to the fact that Yosef was frustrated by what he considered an insult to his honor, the party's success was due to general trends that prevailed in the Israeli society since the fall of the Labor Party in 1977, and to the impressive progress made by the Sephardim in the Israeli society. During the first years of the state's existence, Labor's goal was to turn the country into a "melting pot" of all ethnic groups.[26] All groups were expected to fit one model. This was part of Israel's first prime minister David Ben Gurion's vision in which the state and its institutions were meant to transform all Jewish ethnic groups who came from the Diaspora into one Israeli nation, with a distinct identity. Therefore, the state's institutions, and the IDF in particular, were established with this goal in mind. The tendency to ignore the individual characteristics of the ethnic groups was quite pronounced in Israel despite repeated statements by Labor politicians that they had respect for the uniqueness of each ethnic group.[27] Initially, these groups defied the new Jewish model.[28] Already prior to the establishment of the state, the religious Mizrahi faction within the Zionist movement was bent on fighting against the intention to forge a "national cultural." Therefore, its leaders seceded from the movement and established the Agudat Yisrael Party.[29]

So powerful was the impact of the melting pot concept that the Yemenite Jews who immigrated to Israel shortly after the establishment of the state had to fight for their right to maintain their religion and traditional practices.[30] The melting pot ideal became unpopular partly because of the erosion of the Labor Zionist ideology, which manifested itself clearly with the Labor Party's defeat in the 1977 election. It was largely due to the support of the frustrated Sephardim that the Likud party under Begin's leadership came to power.[31]

The rise of the Likud ushered in a new epoch in Israel's history. The melting pot concept was discarded in favor of ethnic pride. The Sephardim began expressing their unique cultural characteristics. This trend found its expression not only in the political arena, but also in education, music, and art. Many reverted to the Sephardi pronunciation of the Hebrew language and Sephardi music became popular. Sephardi family customs received greater attention and many began tracing the meaning of their family names and their genealogical background. This phenomenon began with the founding of the Tami movement by Aaron Abu-Hatzaira in the 1981 elections. Tami members later supported Shas, saying that its goal was to revert to the authentic character of Sephardi Judaism that became corroded in the Israeli melting pot. Despite the fact that they held "dovish" views, many of them said that they preferred Shas above any Ashkenazi party.

Shas appealed to the common Sephardim since most of them remained attached to tradition and the party's message were not alien to them. Many believed that at last Sephardi Jewry would regain its respectful place in Israeli society. It was this aspect of Shas program, more than the struggle against the social and economic discrimination, with which they identified. Many Sephardim had already managed to improve their economic conditions. They were seeking to promote their image as a distinct ethnic group, proud of its traditional heritage and not identified with crime and social decay. In addition to this powerful symbolic message, Shas had charismatic leaders of high caliber such as Yosef, Peretz, and Deri. There is little wonder therefore, that Shas remained powerful despite the indictment of some of its prominent members such as Yair Levy, Raphael Pinhasi, and Deri, who became the most powerful political figure in the movement. Instead of blaming their leaders for their involvement in financial scandals, Shas's supporters vented their anger against the Ashkenazi establishment. They believed that Shas constituted a nuisance to the Ashkenazim and therefore became convinced that it was indeed worthwhile to give it their vote. Shas had skillfully used the accusation against Deri in order to gain greater support from the Sephardim. Its 1999 election campaign poster carried the words "He is Innocent!"

Shas's success was not only due to its involvement in education and other aspects of daily life, but also due to the popular nature of such activities. Such grassroots activities, which included maintenance of educational institutions and cheap transportation to them, endeared the movement in the eyes of many low-income families. Moreover, the establishment of afternoon clubs for children gained Shas much respect as a movement whose purpose was to occupy children in the afternoon hours and thus prevent them from committing crimes. Unlike the clinics established by the Labor movement, those established by Shas were free from cumbersome bureaucracies. Their emphasis was not on bureaucratic matters but on the ability to address the personal problems of their clients. The tuition and fees in Shas institutions were far more flexible than those that belonged to the Labor movement. Clients were often allowed to pay their debts by installments and sometimes by providing nonmonetary services to the institution. Such arrangement gave Shas clients an intimate connection with these institutions.

Commenting on the attitude of many downtrodden Shas voters who continued to support Deri despite his indictment, Dr. Yossi Dahan, an Open University sociologist and founder of Keshet charity organization said, "These are people who live on the margins, who've seen the ugliest sides of Israel. They have no reason to be loyal to abstractions like democracy and the rule of law, because democracy and the rule of law never worked for them."[32] It is the personal contact that made Shas much more successful than David Levy's Gesher Party, both of which were after the Sephardi vote. According to Haifa University sociologist Sammy Smooha, Shas won because of its presence in the development towns and the poverty-stricken neighborhoods, while Gesher had no educational and welfare institutions there.[33] In his book *Hama'ayan Hamitgaber*, Aryeh Dayan attributed Shas's victory to the services, which it provided at the grassroots level, and to Deri's indictment. Shas's triumph came at the expense of the Likud because Shas fought against the Russian immigrants' party Yisrael Ba'aliya over the Interior Ministry portfolio and thus alienated many Russians who voted for Barak.[34]

Shas has two main groups. Its hard core includes graduates of Ashkenazi yeshivas whose level of education is as strict as other yeshiva graduates.[35] The second group includes traditional Sephardim who are only partially observant and normally reside in secular neighborhoods. Unlike the Ashkenazi religious parties that showed little or no tolerance toward the partially observant, Shas catered to their need and made strenuous efforts to attract them. Some of Shas Knesset members are in fact former secular politicians who turned religious. Shas's involvement in religious education created unexpected problems since its schools demanded that parents adhere to norms of religious tradition and modesty, which parents were often unwilling to accept. Moreover, many reject the tendency of the religious schools to teach Judaic studies at the expense of secular and practical subjects, which they consider essential in order to prepare their children for professional careers. Shas approached the problem by establishing different kinds of schools to fit parental demands. In many neighborhoods, parents could find schools that emphasize Judaic studies side by side with schools that offer more secular education.

Shas's schools are established not by the officials in charge of the educational system, but by local residents who decide to establish a school and then apply to *Ma'ayan Ha'Khinukh Ha-Torati* for support. Such approach provides the school founders with considerable autonomy, while leaving the school under Shas's control. By contrast, the Ashkenazi educational system failed to keep all educational institutions under its purview. Shas's leaders seem to understand that side by side with their emphasis on Judaic studies they have to establish vocational schools in order to meet the demands of many Sephardi parents with little incentive to provide religious education to their children.

As Shas came closer to the traditional Sephardi population it detached itself from the Ashkenazi religious circles and from Schach's authority. For many years, Schach was considered the main patron of the religious Sephardi Jews and he was the one to encourage the Ashkenazi yeshivas to open their doors to them. He was also the one to encourage them to establish an independent movement. While Yosef guided them in routine matters, Schach guided them in major political principles. In 1984, Schach, who was disenchanted with Agudat Yisrael, encouraged both Ashkenazi and Sephardi yeshiva students to vote for Shas.

The conflict between Yosef and Schach occurred in 1988, when the latter left Agudat Yisrael to form Degel Hatorah and encouraged the Lithuanians to vote for it. This was a serious blow to Shas because it no longer had the Lithuanian vote. Even Deri admitted that he voted for Degel Hatorah.[36] All these events led Shas to intensify its efforts to increase its size and to obtain greater independence.

Although Israel has no regional elections, Shas Knesset members represent all regions. In this manner Shas managed to establish an intimate link between the Knesset member and his constituency. Candidates were carefully selected from the various Sephardi communities. After the 1984 elections, four Knesset members represented the Moroccan, Iraqi, Yemenite, and Afghani ethnic groups.[37]

Shas's success was also due to the scholarly caliber of its leaders. Their expertise in the Torah and the *Halacha* provided them legitimacy in the eyes of their voters. The two personalities providing spiritual support for the Shas movement are Yosef and Kadourie. The tension between the two had manifested itself on numerous occasions. Nevertheless, the conflict did not tarnish Yosef's image as the ultimate spiritual leader in the movement. Moreover, Yosef's charisma within Shas allowed him to embark on a policy of alignment with left-of-center parties, without causing significant opposition among the party's numerous hawkish members who harbor contempt toward these parties. Yosef was a "dove" compared to other Shas leaders, but he was often tactless and his comments annoyed many, including some of his supporters. He made coarse comments about leading personalities, both in the Likud and the left-wing parties. The personalities, which became targets of his criticism, include former prime minister Yitzhak Shamir, former state comptroller Miriam Ben-Porat, Meretz leader Shulamit Alloni, Ashkenazi Chief Rabbi Shlomo Goren and others. He once described Ben Gurion as "wicked" and compared the arch-secular education minister Yossi Sarid to Satan and Amalek, the Biblical enemy of the people of Israel.[38] Yosef resented Sarid for forcing Shas to accept a financial recovery plan for its school system, which demanded outside supervision and new accounting methods to show whether the party made effective use of the funds allocated to it. Once he even went to the extent of asking Shas's followers to pray for Sarid's death.[39]

Criticizing Prime Minister Ehud Barak's peace initiative, Yosef went to the extent of saying that the Holocaust victims were "sinners." He said that they were reincarnated souls seeking redemption from past sins. He also said that Barak lacked sense for dealing with the Arabs whom he described as "snakes."

This comment triggered a bitter response from Shinui's leaders as well as from Palestinian officials. These remarks were embarrassing to Shas's leaders who found them hard to explain. After considerable pressure, Yosef found it necessary to retract his remarks about the Holocaust victims, but refused to admit that his remarks about the Arabs were tactless.[40]

Shortly after Shas won fame as a national party in 1984, Peretz became its undisputed leader. He was the one to demand the release from prison of members of the Jewish terrorist underground that terrorized the Arabs in the occupied territories and planned to destroy the Al-Aqsa Mosque in Jerusalem. He also sought to exclude women from the cabinet and even went to the extent of identifying with the ultra militant Rabbi Meir Kahane who dismissed democracy as inconsistent with the *Halacha*.[41]

The need to attract voters from among the religious population in Israel led Labor politicians to express concern about the Sephardim's predicament.[42] However, Shas managed to be ahead of the game. It made good use of primitive popular religion methods in order to gain the support of the downtrodden in the Sephardi communities. During the 1996 election campaign, Kadourie distributed talismans to all those who promised to vote for Shas. This practice continued on a lesser scale in the 1999 elections. It triggered critical response from seculars of all parties who criticized Shas for capitalizing on the ignorance and the primitiveness of the Sephardim. Even Yosef had reservations about the wisdom of using such methods.

Labor or Likud?

Initially, Mapai regarded itself as a secular party and dealt with the religious parties mostly when it needed their support in order to form coalitions. In return, it made minimal concessions to their demands in matters such as observance of the Sabbath and Jewish dietary laws. As for the right-wing Herut Party, its leaders struggled to bridge between the *Halacha* and the demands of modern life. However, frequent contradictions resulted in inconsistency in the party's approach.[43]

One of the issues that split Shas apart and threatened to destroy unity among its ranks was whether to support Likud or Labor. The majority of Shas's rank and file is sympathetic to the Likud. Like their Likud counterparts, many Shas followers subscribe to territorial maximalism, despite the fact that they reject Gush Emunim's notion that the integrity of the Land of Israel is a *sine qua non* for the Jewish people's redemption.[44] However, unlike Gush Emunim, Shas's followers have rarely taken part in militant settlement activities.[45]

By right, Shas's leaders had to identify more closely with Likud because their constituency holds maximalist views regarding the integrity of the Land of Israel. Moreover, most of the Sephardim harbor an aversion to Labor, which they regard as an elitist party that discriminated against them during most of the country's history.[46]

Explaining their attitude, Yosef said that most of them hate Labor because it neglected their interests and failed to provide them religious education. However, despite his rhetoric, Yosef was motivated by pragmatic considerations that led him to ignore the wishes of most of his voters. He repeatedly said that despite such sentiments he decided in favor of supporting Labor because it offered Shas much more than the Likud did. Yosef boasted that Shas managed to obtain the Ministry of Religious Affairs and received Labor's promise to accept his interpretation on the question of '*Who is a Jew.*' As for the Likud, he said, "they offered us less . . . because they thought they had us in their pocket."[47]

Initially, Shas's aversion toward Labor benefited the Likud and the alliance between the two seemed natural. By refusing to join a Labor-led coalition Shas helped the Likud and brought about a national unity government in which prime ministers of the two major parties alternated: Labor in 1984–1986 followed by that of the Likud in 1986–1988. It was only in 1990 that Shimon Peres of the Labor Party managed to attract Shas and Agudat Yisrael and thus ended the national unity government.

The Likud's failure to offer greater benefits to Shas stemmed from its confidence that most Sephardim, who voted for it in past elections, would remain loyal to it in the future. The fact that former populist Likud leader Menachem Begin acquired a status of a demigod among the Sephardim led many of the party's leaders to believe that Sephardi loyalty to them was unquestionable. The leaders of the Likud Party were far less experienced than their rivals in the Labor Party, who were in power for nearly thirty years and who were accustomed to dealing with the religious partners of their coalitions by offering them greater benefits. Moreover, the Likud failed to understand the importance that Yosef attached to his party's cultural revolution and its constant dependence on funds.

Like his mentor, Deri tended to side with Labor. Both Yosef and Deri concluded that in order to continue their cultural revolution they needed funds, and Labor's record in this respect was superior to that of the Likud. In the beginning, Shas's leaders followed the prevailing sentiments within their party and instructed their followers to vote for Likud. However, the pragmatic tendencies within Shas prevailed and its leaders changed their strategy. Whereas in 1984 they instructed their voters to vote for the Likud, in 1988 they did not commit themselves to supporting any of the major parties.[48]

Sociology Professor Menachem Friedman argued that the support that Shas gave the Likud in the early years was due to Schach's overwhelming influence. Although Yosef is the nominal spiritual leader of the movement, Schach remained the ultimate authority because the entire Sephardi elite owes ultimate allegiance to him. Almost all Sephardi youngsters studied in Lithuanian yeshivas prior to the establishment of the state. Schach called upon Shas's voters to support the Likud because he was convinced that only Shamir was in a position to give up territory as part of an overall peace agreement. In addition, once Schach made his opinion known, Shas followed through.[49]

Although both Yosef and Deri became Labor's advocates, they were unwilling to alienate their right-wing supporters, some of whom had once threatened to harm Yosef physically if he decided to support Labor. Shas's leaders played their cards with remarkable skill. Even the hawkish Peretz said once that although his heart continues to be with the Likud, "my brain tells me to support Labour."[50] But the most pragmatic and most calculating was Deri himself. Deri's pragmatism becomes all the more obvious from his negotiation methods. In October 1989, he negotiated an agreement with Histadrut Secretary General Yisrael Kessar regarding Shas's support for Labor in the elections to the Histadrut. He explained that he did not wish to run against Kessar, not only due to the cost of the campaign, but also because he wanted to secure influence for Shas within the Histadrut. Deri never concealed his preference for Labor, which he believes had laid the foundations for the State of Israel. He also subscribed to the idea that the "land for peace" formula was anchored in the *Halacha*. All along, he remained practical and refused to stick to entrenched ideological positions.[51]

Yosef's preference for Labor became obvious in the August 1989, when he declared that according to the *Halacha* trading land for peace is permissible. His statement created such anxiety in the Likud, whose leaders' motto was "peace for peace," that Shamir sent an urgent message begging him not to rule publicly in favor of trading land for peace.[52]

In March 1990, the Labor Party attempted to bring down the National Unity Government under Shamir and to form a narrow coalition under its leadership. Believing that in a narrow coalition Shas could have a chance to increase its power, Deri reached an agreement with Peres that in the newly created government he would become finance minister. Shas instructed its Knesset members not to attend the no confidence vote, which the Labor Party initiated and thereby felled the government. However, Schach had a surprise for them. He was reluctant to support a Labor-led coalition and instructed his followers to vote for the Likud. Consequently, Peretz accused Deri of betrayal and tended his resignation from the movement. The Likud was outraged at Shas's behavior. One Likud minister was quoted to have said, "the Likud chose to put Shas betrayal on the record, in the hope that in the next elections it would be 'punished' by its voters, many of whom might well return to the Likud ranks."[53]

Yosef's dovish attitude toward the peace process triggered strong reaction not only from his supporters in Israel but also from American Jews. Rabbi Alexander Shindler remarked that the outrageous pampering of Shas have caused a diminution of American support for the peace process.[54] The powerful Syrian Jewish community in New York was enraged over the part that Yosef and his party played in the government's fall. Many of the community's members were disappointed by Yosef's support for U.S. Secretary of State James Baker's plan, which according to them meant giving up Jerusalem to the Arabs. In an interview to *The Jerusalem Post*, on March 28, 1990, Dr. Joseph Faur, a leader of the Syrian community said that Yosef acted more like a politician than a rabbi. He said that there were rumors that the CIA had secretly contributed $4.5 million to Shas in an attempt to influence Yosef's position on the peace process, and that the rabbi instructed his party to adjust its position accordingly.[55]

Shas supported Rabin's plan to hold a referendum on the future of the Golan Heights. However, its leaders argued that their main concern was for the safety of the settlers of Judea and Samaria.[56] Yosef's views about the Golan Heights were diametrically opposed to those of other influential rabbis within the movement, such as Yosef Kadourie and Rabbi Moshe Maiya, who insisted that the Golan Heights must be under Israeli control. However, Shas's politicians continued to insist that their leaders were unanimous regarding the issue.[57]

The rivalry with the Likud intensified in the wake of Shas's attempt to fell the government. A Shas' official said that his party would regard the Likud as an adversary with whom it must compete for the same pool of voters.[58] Like its defunct predecessor, Tami, Shas tried to undermine the Likud in order to lure the voters to its ranks. However, unlike Tami, Shas managed to build a solid institutional infrastructure and proved adept at using its position and influence in order to attract votes. Another Shas's source told *The Jerusalem Post*, "We will beat the Likud."[59] Explaining Deri's strategy, Dayan said that Deri wanted his party to remain in the opposition and thereby take away votes from the Likud.[60]

It is not clear whether Shas benefited from the Likud's loss of votes. When Shas won four seats in the Knesset in 1984, the combined Likud and the non-religious right dropped from fifty-one to forty-seven seats in the Knesset. According to one commentator, the benefactors were other ultra-right-wing religious lists such as Morasha that won two seats, and Rabbi Meir Kahane's Kach Party that won one seat. The one seat accounted for by Israel's small swinging vote that leaned toward Labor after the unpopular war in Lebanon. The 1984 campaign resulted from the Ashkenazi-Sephardi conflict within the religious Aguda camp and Shas votes came from within the ultra-Orthodox community and not from the Likud. Shas gains in the 1988 elections came from the voters of the defunct Tami Party as well as from the NRP. It is therefore possible to assume that Shas gained from Sephardi dissatisfaction with the Zionist religious camp in 1988, just as it gained from Sephardi dissatisfaction with the non-Zionist camp in 1984.[61]

Shas remained determined to act independently and in 1992, it was the only religious party that agreed to join the Labor-Meretz coalition under Rabin. This was Yosef's way of expressing his disappointment from the Likud and its Ashkenazi supporters. The upshot was that Shas alienated itself from many of its Likud sympathizers.

Shas's leaders became confident about their ability to influence the Labor Party. They reacted to Rabin's attempt to persuade Shas to reenter his coalition, or at least not to vote against it saying, "Rabin treated Yosef with such deference that he revealed to him details on defense and foreign affairs that are not even

Ethnicity and Religion in Israeli Politics 251

known to some of the most senior ministers."[62] According to a source in Shas, Yosef had complete control over Rabin. Yosef's attitude toward Rabin was somewhat paternalistic. He once said, "Rabin makes no trouble. He does whatever I tell him and he does it with love, respect, and courtesy." While Yosef felt confident about his ability to influence Rabin he expressed resentment against Schach's influence on his party. He once said that Schach pushed him to join the coalition despite the fact that Alloni of the Meretz Party was awarded the education portfolio. He explained that he eventually decided to join the Labor coalition because Shas was getting "financing from Rabin for 400 classes in the Shas school system and each class is worth NIS 300,000."[63]

Shas's preference for Labor continued. However, its leaders sought to make the most out of their bargaining power and increased their demands in the 1999 election campaign. As a reward for his party's entry into the Labor coalition, Deri demanded that Ehud Barak support two bills introduced by the religious parties. The first was aimed at preventing Reform and Conservative rabbis from converting non-Jews, and the second sought to ban Reform and Conservative membership in religious councils.[64]

Shas's popularity among the Sephardim increased to such an extent that its leaders became virtually immune from criticism or accusations of wrongdoing. Yosef's tactless remarks enraged many officials in both the Likud and the Labor Parties. Yet in the eyes of his supporters Yosef could do no wrong. Even the news about corruption within Shas did not have serious consequences for its future. Shas could always claim that the accusations stemmed from discrimination and from the desire of the Ashkenazi elite to discredit the Sephardim. In March 1999, Deri was accused of taking bribes and condemned to four years imprisonment.[65] Responding to Deri's investigation on corruption charges, Shas Knesset member Shlomo Dayan accused the police of discrimination. He said that Deri was an easy target because he is Sephardi.[66] Labor - Shas relations soured in the wake of Attorney General Elyakim Rubinstein's reports regarding Deri's involvement in a financial scandal. Shas's leaders said that they would never again align with Labor because of what it has done to Deri. Shas embarked on an elite bashing campaign and Deri slammed the country's founders. Worried about their survival, Labor leaders like Peres, Barak, Ramon, and others prostrated themselves before Yosef and all criticized Rubinstein's report as unfair because it indicted Deri while acquitting others.[67]

Following the 1999 elections, there was an intense debate about whether or not to include Shas in a Labor coalition headed by Barak.[68] Many Labor voters objected to Shas's entry, arguing that it capitalized on poverty and was bent on creating a generation of yeshiva students drawing stipends from the state. The opponents included many kibbutzim members. Both Meretz and Shinui told Barak that if Shas entered the coalition they would stay out of it. Yet many within the secular left argued that for tactical reasons Shas had to be included in the coalition. Some argued that Shas's inclusion would bring it more popularity. Others said that including Shas would have a salutary effect on the peace process since Yosef adopted a moderate stand on the issue of territorial concessions to the Palestinians. Yet others said that keeping such a large constituency out of the coalition was unthinkable. There were also the Russian immigrants who were displeased with Shas's tactics. Barak was in a serious dilemma. He set conditions on Shas's entry, saying that the party must relinquish the interior ministry portfolio and respect the law, and that Deri should not take part in the coalition negotiations.[69]

This issue constituted a dilemma not only for Barak but also for Shas, which became divided over it. Deri, Interior Minister Eli Suissa, and Josef's son, David pressured the party to stay in the opposition. However, Labor and Social Affairs Minister Eli Yishai, Yosef's son, Moshe, and his wife Yehudit, were all in favor of joining the coalition. Fearing that another Shas politician might replace him if the party joined the coalition, Deri exerted pressure on Yosef to stay out. Aware of the need to stay in the coalition in order to enable his party to continue its cultural revolution, which depended on continued funding from the government, Yosef was forced to sacrifice his protégé.[70]

The discipline within Shas, which had been tight for over fifteen years showed disquieting signs of weakness after Deri's resignation. Yosef concluded that Deri was a liability for Shas, and Deri decided to fight back. Deri's alleged willingness to act as a mediator in a financial scandal involving the Lithuanian Itri Yeshiva frightened Yosef who thought that Deri was dragging him into a conflict with the Lithuanian yeshiva world. Therefore, he decided that Deri was even a greater liability than he previously thought. The event led to intense struggle over the leadership. While Yosef supported Yishai, Deri wanted to promote the candidacy of Yosef's son, David Yosef. Officials within Shas commented on the struggle saying that the Likud was delighted to see Shas torn because it felt that many of its votes were lost to Shas. They also argued that Labor was interested in Shas's fall from grace because Shas remained its only competitor.[71]

Deri was succeeded by Yishai who did not enjoy much popularity among Shas's voters but managed to remain in power due to the support of his mentor, Yosef who said in one of the party's conventions, "Elie is my choice, and whoever goes against him is going against me."[72] Another likely candidate for leadership was Shlomo Benizri. However, Benizri was the protégé of Rabbi Reuven Elbaz, the head of a religious school's network *Or Hahayim*, whose relationship with Yosef was tense. Even when Benizri was put on Shas's Knesset list he was passed over.[73] Thus Yishai became the uncontested candidate for leadership.[74]

Critics of Shas

Shas has many critics most of which are in the left wing in the Israeli political spectrum. These include members of the kibbutzim, secular parties such as One Israel (Labor), Meretz, and Shinui. In addition, many Likud members resent

Shas for its alignment with Labor and for tempting Likud supporters by capitalizing of the Sephardi feelings of inferiority.

Many critics see Shas as a reactionary party whose practices constitute a danger to democracy. One commentator argued that the Sephardim were discriminated against during the early days of the state. He said, however, that in the 1980s the two major parties began representing Sephardi interests. Therefore, he concluded that these professional ethnic-cum-religious parties became not only anachronistic, but also nests for corruption. He warned that although the return to traditional ways as opposed to modernity has positive aspects, a rush back to the ways of the past could lead to violation of the state law by those who believe that their actions are guided by a higher authority. He concluded by saying, "It is not by chance that the political corruption scandals of the past decade have been linked nearly exclusively with the haredi (ultra religious) parties."[75] One editorial blamed Shas for favoritism and nepotism. Reacting to the nomination of a Shas crony as the chairman of Israel's communications agency Bezek, the writer said, "The party's candidate of Bezek ... is a son of one of the "Tora Sages," the rabbinical association which spiritually guides the party. Unfortunately, this familial relationship seems to be his only qualification for the job."[76]

Another observer criticized Yosef's consent to join the Labor coalition, saying that it was contradictory to the democratic procedures because he did not adhere to the prevailing opinion within Shas and thus misrepresented these voters. Labor lured Shas with payments and thus obtained its collaboration, in March 1990, in the attempt to overthrow the National Unity Government and again in the 1992 elections. After receiving illegal payments, Shas helped Labor to form the most antireligious coalition conceivable.[77]

Shas's politicians became adept at arm-twisting and threats. In September 1994, the party threatened to join those who opposed Rabin on the Golan issue, if he failed to remove the obstacles, which Meretz put on Shas's return to the coalition. Shas exploited the opportunity to pressure Rabin when his government depended on it to obtain a minimal Knesset majority on the Golan issue. It was not the Golan issue that made Shas so recalcitrant but its demand for legislation that would circumvent the rulings of the High Court of Justice on religious affairs. Rabin yielded to Shas's demands despite opposition from Meretz. In order to achieve his aim Deri used the tactic of linking his party's religious demands with the Golan issue. He warned that Shas's "electorate is militant and does not like territorial concessions. Agreeing to them is difficult for us, but we are ready to make sacrifices for the maintenance of the Jewish character of this society." Responding to his ultimatum that Shas would join the opponents of withdrawal from the Golan if Rabin failed to convince Meretz to remove its objection to Shas entry into the coalition, Alloni referred to the ultimatum as "a transparent act of political extortion to further religious coercion." When Labor sources argued that Deri was using such tactics in order to end his trial for corruption, Deri called such insinuations "malicious character assassination, which calls to doubt the value of dealing with Labor." Shas's critics include not only political parties like Meretz but also organizations and individuals such as Israel Women's Network chairman Alice Shalvi, who called on Rabin not to yield to the "unfair pressure being applied by Shas." She added, "Peace is invaluable, but we will continue to live in this country after peace is reached. . . . The coalition agreement Shas is demanding will make this life unbearable, since it will not allow any reform in marriage and divorce, women's rights to their body, human rights and religious pluralism."[78]

Critics argued that Shas had capitalized on the misery of many of its followers who inhabit poor neighborhoods. Indeed, it was there that Shas established its low-tuition schools, clubs, and charity organizations, which offered its followers the warmth that they did not have under the Labor or Likud governments. Yosef's determination to protect his protégé, Deri, despite the corruption charges and his alleged embezzlement of funds, caused much fury in the secular camp. Moreover, the claim made by Shas's supporters that Yosef should not be asked to provide testimony, triggered a critical response from many who warned that religious leaders placed themselves above the law.[79] One critic argued that Shas thrived on adversity. He wondered why Shas remained popular despite the corruption charges against some of its officials and the opposition, the Ashkenazi religious establishment. He also mentioned the fact that Shas alienated its constituency by supporting the Oslo accords and joining a government with Labor and Meretz. The writer attributed Deri's success to the fact that he understands his voters and stated that "He has no shame in playing the 'ethnic card'; he plays it well, and plays it to the hilt."[80]

Deri's critics regard him as a rabble-rouser who accuses his opponents of ethnic bias in order to achieve his aims. One commentator argued that if Deri was to become Israel's prime minister many of his followers would be allowed to avoid military service, the police would turn a blind eye to corruption, family planning would be discouraged, poverty would increase, and ignorance of Western culture would triumph.[81]

Deri was under severe criticism not only for his involvement in financial scandals but also for his views. Many criticized his view regarding discrimination against the Sephardim. One critic called both Deri and his mentor Yosef racist agitators. He argued that Schach and his collaborators from Agudat Yisrael established Shas in order to steal votes from the Likud. In this manner they sought to silence the Sephardi politicians. The writer argued that during the early days of the Jewish State all immigrants were treated with disdain by the Zionist movement whose aim was to create a new Israel with a distinct identity. Moreover, he argued that prior to the establishment of the state the Sephardim who immigrated from Spain and Portugal were the elite who regarded the Ashkenazim and all those who did not come from Spain with contempt.[82] Above all, Shas was criticized for its opportunism. Indeed, Shas's opportunism manifested itself on several occasions. In an interview with David Landau and Haim Shapiro of *The Jerusalem Post* Yosef said, "God guided us in our decision making." However, Shas's behavior was motivated not so much by divine guidance as by pragmatism. It was the need for funds to continue his party's cultural revolution that guided Yosef's decision. According to Shinui's Knesset member Yosef Partizky, 70 percent of all the financial support given by Labor and Social Affairs Ministry in 1999, went to the yeshivas. He told reporters, "There are unemployed, poor, handicapped, and what have you, and the Labor and Social Affairs Ministry takes the money and sends it to yeshivot."[83]

Many regard Shas's bargaining methods as arm-twisting and blackmail. The fact that Shas managed to bargain effectively with the Ministry of Education became obvious to all.[84] Even more distasteful in the eyes of critics was the fact that Shas's spokesmen tend to accuse their opponents of racism whenever they fail to obtain their objectives. In December 1999, Finance Minister Avraham Shohat managed to solicit the support of United Torah Judaism (UTJ) and the NRP for his proposed budget and thus rendered the Shas vote unnecessary. When the Knesset Finance Committee approved the vote, on December 26, 1999, Shas's Knesset members expressed their outrage. Deputy Finance Minister Nissim Dahan said that Shas was bypassed because of racism.[85] Even more distressing in the eyes of Shas's secular critics was the fact that Deri remained popular after his conviction.[86]

Shas alienated many secular voters, including Sephardim when it decided to shorten the daylight-saving time and thus reduced the number of days in which Israelis could enjoy outdoor activities. Shas's leaders insisted that summer-time ends before the pre–High Holy Day daily penitentiary prayers, saying that it forces them to rise earlier for prayers and leave insufficient time to pray before work. However, their secular critics regarded their attempt as a political maneuver aimed at proving their point. The economic editor of the daily *Ha'aretz*, commented by saying, "The haredi [religious] war is political in essence. They want to prove that they are stronger than their [Labor] predecessors Ehud Barak and Haim Ramon. They will shorten daylight saving on us, even if it does not serve the interests of their own people."[87]

Shas has not changed its tactics. It continues to exploit the most basic beliefs of the Sephardim in the power of their holy men and capitalizes on their discrimination complex.[88] Shas left Barak's coalition in July 2000, because Barak did not consult its leaders regarding his plans to move the peace process forward. It endorsed the candidacy of Moshe Katzav, a Sephardi who ran against Peres as candidate to the presidency. And even after Deri's indictment, the party's popularity continues to soar.

Conclusion

This chapter has explored the origins of the Shas movement and its development to the present day. The chapter's main argument has been that although there were other ethnic parties in the earlier days of the Jewish state, Shas was the most successful. Shas's success was largely due to the metamorphosis that had taken place in the Israeli society. By the 1970s, Mapai lost its vitality. Its appeal was tarnished and its socialist Zionist ideology became obsolete.[89] The Likud, which came to power in 1977, remained preoccupied with territorial maximalism and did little to address the social and economic concerns of the Sephardim.

Both Labor and Likud failed to reach the voters through grassroots social and economic activities. The basic needs of the Sephardim for education and social welfare programs were not met. This state of affairs allowed Shas to emerge. As a party whose ideology is deeply anchored in Jewish tradition Shas provided an attractive alternative for many Sephardim searching for identity. Despite the fact that most of Shas's voters hold hawkish views regarding the Israeli-Arab conflict, the issue of whether or not to agree to territorial compromise does not loom large in the party's agenda. Many Sephardim left the Likud and joined Shas. However, despite the fact that both the Likud and Shas feel that they are competing for the Sephardi vote, there is no evidence to suggest that Shas increased its size by attracting former Likud supporters. Ironically, despite the fact that many Shas's voters identify with the Likud's struggle to maintain the integrity of the Land of Israel, Shas leaders had shown preference to Labor. This was largely because Shas's main concern is to continue and intensify its cultural revolution, which attracted many votes and turned it into a formidable force. Shas's leaders concluded that aligning with Labor was more beneficial to them. Indeed, they managed to obtain more concessions from Labor governments. This also explains why Yosef adopted a dovish attitude toward the peace process. The willingness to prefer Labor above Likud was adopted by both Yosef and Deri, his protégé.

Deri's imprisonment enraged his supporters within the party and made it more difficult for Yishai to contemplate joining Barak's coalition.[90] The Al-Aqsa Intifada which erupted in the West Bank and Gaza in September 2000, and Barak's negotiations with the Likud to form a national unity government convinced Yishai to join Barak's coalition but not without alienating many of Deri's supporters. Shas's leaders had so far demonstrated a remarkable sense of pragmatism. They agreed to extend their support to Barak's shaky coalition if he would drop his plans for a "civil revolution" designed to reduce the influence of the religious parties. And although Yosef said that Barak's government was incapable of dealing with the disturbances in the West Bank and Gaza, he promised to support the peace process after the violence ebbed.[91]

By the end of 2000, Shas's leaders became even more aggressive than they had been in the past. Barak's coalition was torn by dissent not only over the issue land transfers to the Palestinians but also over Shas's demand for more funds for its educational institutions.[92]

The Council of Torah Sages called upon Benjamin Netanyahu of the Likud Party to run for prime minister and urged the Sephardim to support him. This was the first time that the council has openly supported a potential candidate for the premiership at an early stage. Shas supported Netanyahu by sponsoring an amendment designed to enable him to run even if the Knesset did not dissolve. However, Shas's support for Netanyahu was not unqualified. Sources in Shas stated that the members of the Council of Torah Sages were displeased with his attempt to pressure them to support early elections. Moreover, Shas did not accept Netanyahu's claim that a stable government would be impossible with the existing Knesset. Benizri argued that Netanyahu was still in a position to set up either a unity government or a right-wing coalition with sixty-three members. However, Shas remained flexible and Yishai made it clear that if Netanyahu decided not to run Shas would support Ariel Sharon. Again, Shas sought to support whichever candidate offered it the most. It received a handsome gift for its support for a Likud candidate. Prior to the elections, Yishai made it clear that while the Council of Torah Sages was debating whether or not to endorse a Likud member as prime minister, his party would utilize the NIS 6.5 million in state funds that it was due to receive for such endorsement.[93] When the Knesset voted for Israel's new president in the summer of 2002, Shas supported Katzav who ran against Peres. Its leaders boasted that all its seventeen Knesset members voted for Katzav. Rabbi Yitzhak Kadourie said that Katzav was favored by the heavens and called on Shas's legislators to support his candidacy.[94] Shas's leaders had no hesitation in this matter. Not only because Katzav is a Sephardi but also because Peres is the most maligned figures in Israeli politics and very unpopular among the Sephardim.

In his analysis of church-state relations in Western countries, Ervin Birnbaum concluded that in the struggle between the states and the religious establishments the former gained the upper hand, and that a *modus vivendi*, based on a compromise between the secular and the spiritual authorities was achieved. He argued that adherence to the status quo would not save the religious establishment in Israel if its leaders persist in maintaining ultraconservative and reactionary positions. Moreover, religious interference in secular affairs would cause the religious establishment to lose part of its influence as a spiritual entity.[95]

Shas is unlikely to lose its appeal unless other leading parties with a new ideology accompanied by efforts to become involved in education, health care, and other matters affecting the daily life of the citizens comes to power. In the meantime, the secular parties must take into consideration the growing popularity of the religious Sephardi community. Politicians and political commentators were right to argue that given the political instability and the fact that the coalitions rest on shaky foundations, both Labor and Likud would have to treat Shas with greater respect. Former Knesset speaker Shevah Weiss argued that the growing number of the Sephardim makes it imperative to take Shas seriously. He argued that there are some 1.1 million Jews of North African descent, and they account for some 600,000 voters. In the 1999 elections, Shas captured 430,000 votes and seventeen seats, receiving 90 percent of its votes from this group. In a similar manner, former police minister Moshe Shahal argued that respecting Shas could ease the tension between Shas and Meretz. He recommended that Barak let Shas leaders participate in his peace negotiations in order to demonstrate respect to their opinion, as Begin had done. Similarly, *Jerusalem Post*'s political commentator Yoel Marcus recommended that Barak involve Shas in the diplomatic process and treat it as the second largest party in his coalition and not as a party of parasites and robbers.[96] Barak was impatient with Shas and was unwilling to meet its demands. Shas was particularly dismayed at the fact that shortly after Deri was escorted to his jail the cabinet adopted a plan to dismantle the ministry of religious affairs. Even among the Likud there are reservations about Shas's methods and the feeling that it has taken away many votes that should have gone to the Likud still persist.

Shas's negative image among the non-Sephardi public is justified largely. While many Israelis identify with the party's goal to restore Sephardi pride, they often criticize its methods. The tendency of Shas's leaders to change their loyalty from Likud to Labor, depending on material benefits and political concessions rather than on high ideological principles, contributes to the negative image, which their party has acquired. This negative view is reinforced by the physical appearance of many Shas members who wear the traditional dress of the nonproductive Jews of the Diaspora and whose sole purpose is to study the Torah at the public's expense. Shas's efforts to obtain exemptions from military service for many of its yeshiva students angers many Israelis. Moreover, the Israeli public resents Shas's excessive tendency to use the ethnic card in order to promote its goals. Finally, the corruption within the party's ranks and its leaders' involvement in financial scandals contributed significantly to its negative image. If Shas is to continue its spectacular growth and perpetuate its popularity its leaders must avoid confrontations and be willing to reach compromises with the secular segments of the Israeli society. In addition, they must maintain stricter discipline within the party, eliminate corruption in their ranks, and avoid blaming their political opponents of discrimination whenever their demands are not met.

Notes

1. The Likud is a right-wing party that emerged from the Revisionist wing of the Zionist movement. It began as the Herut party that later merged with other right-of-center parties to form the Likud, which came to power in 1977, after being in the opposition for twenty-nine years. The NRP was in existence long before the Jewish state was established. It played an important role in the Zionist movement and had been aligned with the Labor movement since the mid-1930. Agudat Yisrael was formed by Orthodox Jews who did not wish to cooperate with the secular Zionists, and Degel Hatorah is a faction established by Rabbi Eliezer Schach within Agudat Yisrael.

2. Arie Caspi, "Les religieux plutot victimes que beneficiares du systeme educatif," *Courrier International*, January 27 to February 2, 2000, n. 482, 32. The estimated value of the new Israeli shekel at that time was 25 cents.

3. Theodore Herzl, the founder of political Zionism believed that rabbis should be confined to their religious sphere "like soldiers to barracks." Amnon Rubinstein, *The Zionist Dream Revisited: From Herzl to Gush Emunim and Back* (New York: Schoken, 1984), 16.

4. Yonathan Shapiro, *An Elite Without Successors: Generations of Political Leaders in Israel* [Hebrew] (Tel Aviv: Sifriyat Poalim, 1984), 79.

5. Yonathan Shapiro, *Chosen to Command: The Road to Power of the Herut Party—A Socio-Political Interpretation* [Hebrew] (Tel Aviv: Am Oved, 1989), 179–81.

6. Shimon Peres told one of his Labor colleagues "Polls indicate that we are losing the Sephardim. They are going to the Likud." Cited in Michael Bar Zohar, *Facing a Cruel Mirror: Israel's Moment of Truth* [Hebrew] (Tel Aviv: Yediot Aharonot, 1990), 117.

7. A survey conducted in April 1981, three years before the party's establishment, showed that 79 percent among the Ashkenazim thought that the ideal party that they would like to see in power should be neither Ashkenazi nor Sephardi. Among the Sephardim the number was 74 percent. Only 20 percent among the Sephardim were in favor of a Sephardi Party, and 6 percent were in favor of an Ashkenazi Party. Michal Shamir and Asher Arian, "Ethnic Voting in the 1981 Elections," *Medinah u-Mimshal beYahasim Benleumiyim* [Hebrew] 19–20, no. 7 (Spring 1982): 93, 101.

8. Shlomo Sharan, "Why Separation of Religion from the State is Inappropriate for Israel," *Nativ* [Hebrew] 12, no. 6 (November 1999): 33.

9. Dan Horowitz and Moshe Lissak, *Trouble in Utopia: The Overburdened Polity of Israel* [Hebrew] (Tel Aviv: Am Oved, 1990), 99, 103, 230.

10. One of Shas's leaders, Rabbi Nissim Zeev had once told *Jerusalem Post's* correspondent Abraham Rabinovich, "They got our votes . . . but they gave us nothing." "Rising Star: The Post's Abraham Rabinovich Examines the Origins of the Movement," *Jerusalem Post*, April 13, 1984.

11. Yair Sheleg, *The New Religious Jews: Recent Developments Among Observant Jews in Israel* [Hebrew] (Jerusalem: Keter, 2000), 221.

12. Sheleg, *New Religious Jews*, 222.

13. Meron Medzini, *The Proud Jewess: Golda Meir and the Vision of Israel* [Hebrew] (Jerusalem: Edanim, 1990), 394–95.

14. Shmuel Sandler, "Rabin and the Religious Parties: The Limits of Power Sharing," in *Israel Under Rabin*, Robert O. Freedman, ed. (Boulder, Colo.: Westview Press, 1995), 177–78.

15. Shimon Peres and Haggai Eshed, *Now-Tomorrow* [Hebrew] (Jerusalem: Mabat, 1978), 45.

16. *The Prime Minister Speaks: Addresses by Yitzhak Shamir, 1893–1990* [Hebrew] (Tel Aviv: Yair, 1990), 64–65.

17. Sheleg, *New Religious Jews*, 222.

18. Menachem Rahat, *The Spirit and the Power: How did Shas Won Israeli Politics* [Hebrew] (Tel Aviv: Alpha Tikshoret, 1998), 32–34.

19. Sheleg, *New Religious Jews*, 225.

20. "The Tora is our Platform: The Post's Aryeh Rubinstein Talks to Shas Leader Yitzhak Peretz," *Jerusalem Post*, August 3, 1984.

21. David Zev Harris, "The Reluctant Prince," *Jerusalem Post*, August 20, 1999.

22. Dan Izenberg, "Shas Seeks to Win Favour with Clubs for Disadvantaged," *Jerusalem Post*, January 26, 1990.

23. Larry Derfner, "Running on 'Good Works,'" *Jerusalem Post*, October 23, 1998.
24. Sheleg, *New Religious Jews*, 227–28.
25. It is both interesting and constructive to compare the grassroots activities of Shas with those of the Hizballah (Party of God) in Lebanon. Both parties emerged in an attempt to improve the lot of one segment of the population which felt left behind. The Shas sought to promote the welfare of the Sephardim while the Hizballah sought to promote the welfare of the downtrodden Shi'a population of Lebanon. Both parties managed to gain political power and their popularity grew.
26. The desire to "create" a new Israeli was prevalent in religious Zionism as well. As one of the founders of the religious kibbutz movements explained, "When a nation returns to its homeland and wants to prepare it toward political and economic independence, to dry up its marshes and to make its deserts bloom, it cannot do so without changing the patterns of life that became ingrained in the nation and the Diaspora. It needs—and must—build everything anew, otherwise it cannot fulfill its duty . . . it has to establish a society that contains some of the eternal elements of Israel's Torah as well as some of the achievements of the new epoch. Such amalgamation dictates the establishment of a new society that hitherto did not exist." Cited in Dov Schwartz, *Religious Zionism between Logic and Messianism* [Hebrew] (Tel Aviv: Am Oved, 1999), 27.
27. The distrust that the Sephardim had toward the politicians of the Labor Party manifested itself clearly on June 6, 1981, when Shimon Peres, who returned from peace negotiations with Morocco's King Hassan II, addressed North African Jews in Sacher Park on the occasion of the traditional Moroccan Mimouna holiday. When Likud Prime Minister Menachem Begin addressed the crowd he was greeted with great enthusiasm that verged on frenzy. But when Peres came to deliver his speech he was greeted with a salvo of tomatoes and was forced to leave the stage. Matti Golan, *Shimon Peres: A Biography* (New York: St. Martin's Press, 1982), 253.
28. Aviezer Ravitzky, *Freedom Inscribed: Diverse Voices of the Jewish Religious Thought* [Hebrew] (Tel Aviv: Am Oved, 1999), 271–72.
29. Eliezer Don-Yehiya, "The Solution of the 'Status Quo' in the Realm of Religion and State in Israel," *Medinah u-Mimshal beYahasim Benleumiyim* 1, no. 1 (Summer 1971): 101.
30. Zvi Zamert, "On the Unbearable Lightness of Blaming Ben-Gurion and the 'Religiose,'" *Medinah u-Mimshal beYahasim Benleumiyim*, vol. 41–42 (Summer 1997), 221.
31. *Chosen to Command*, 183.
32. Larry Derfner, "An A-to-Z Party," *Jerusalem Post*, August 1, 1997.
33. Herb Keinon, "Who Can Wave the Banner Higher," *Jerusalem Post*, January 2, 1998.
34. Herb Keinon, "Those Unsinkable Shasniks: Anatomy of a Victory," *Jerusalem Post*, May 20, 1999.
35. Haim Shapiro, "Shas: Family Feuds," *Jerusalem Post*, May 10, 1991.
36. Sheleg, *New Religious Jews*, 241.
37. Eliezer Don-Yehiya, "Religiosity and Ethnicity in Israeli Politics: The Religious Parties and the Elections to the 12th Knesset," *Medinah u-Mimshal beYahasim Benleumiyim* 32 (1990): 36.
38. Michael Arnold, "Guardian of the Torah," *Jerusalem Post*, March 31, 2000.
39. Arie Dayan, "Israel: Entre ultras de tous bords, un fosse toujours plus large," *Courrier International*, no. 493 (April 13–19, 2000), 27.
40. "Rabbi Labels Holocaust Victims as 'Sinners,'" *Jerusalem Post*, August 7, 2000.

41. Bernard Avishai, *The Tragedy of Zionism: Revolution and Democracy in the Land of Israel* (New York: Farrar, Straus, Giroux, 1985), 330.

42. *Yediot Aharonot* (Tel Aviv), November 24, 1995.

43. Uri Milstein, "Ideological Views of the Israeli Political Parties in Religion-State Relations," *Medinah u-Mimshal beYahasim Benleumiyim* 7 (Spring 1975): 99.

44. Gush Emunim was a movement of young settlers, mainly of Ashkenazi origin. It was established shortly after the Six Day War of 1967, by Moshe Levinger; a disciple of the revered Rabbi Tzvi Yehuda Kook. The movement's purpose was to establish settlements in the West Bank and they have constantly defied the government's orders to evacuate them. The group originated from the NRP and it exerted considerable influence on Likud and Labor both of which yielded to their demands.

45. For a detailed analysis of Gush Emunim's methods see Ehud Shprinzak, *Every Man Whatsoever Is Right in His Own eyes: Illegalism in the Israeli Society* [Hebrew] (Tel Aviv: Sifriyat Poalim, 1986), 121–45.

46. This partially explains the negative attitude, which Shas had toward the peace process. Shas's followers tied their resentment against the Ashkenazim to their reservations about the peace process. Deri himself had done so when he said that "Peace is for the rich Ashkenazim." He and his followers argued that the Ashkenazi establishment's quest for peace stemmed from its desire to further its economic interest. Yoram Peri, "The Assassination: Causes, Meaning, Outcomes," in *The Assassination of Yitzhak Rabin,* Yoram Peri, ed. (Stanford, Calif.: Stanford University Press, 2000), 32. So intense was the hatred toward the Ashkenazim that Rabin became a target of vilification by Shas's leaders. The party's organ *Yom Le'Yom* reported that the party's secretary Zvi Ya'akobson attacked the chief rabbis who ordered the reading of parts of the Mishna and Psalms on Rabin's memorial day. Yoram Peri, "Rabin: Between Memorial and Denial," in Peri, *Assassination of Yitzhak Rabin*, 348.

47. "God Guides Us in Our Decision-Making: Rabbi Ovadia Yosef Talks to David Landau and Haim Shapiro," *Jerusalem Post*, November 18, 1988.

48. David Makovsky, "Deri's Diplomatic Debut," *Jerusalem Post*, July 21, 1989.

49. Haim Shapiro, "The Collapse of Haredi Hegemony," *Jerusalem Post*, April 27, 1990.

50. Peretz was aware of the fact that Labor has been much more willing to meet Shas's demands. Dan Petreanu and Michal Yudelman, "Orthodox Parties Torn Over Labour," *Jerusalem Post*, October 16, 1989.

51. Susan Hattis Rolef, "A Breath of Fresh Air," *Jerusalem Post*, October 22, 1989.

52. Gershom Gorenberg, "On Trading Land for Peace and Religious Parties," *Jerusalem Post*, August 17, 1989.

53. Sarah Honig, "Shas Stance Promises Uphill Battle for Likud," *Jerusalem Post*, March 16, 1990.

54. Abba Eban, "Rabin-Rewards and Agonies," *Jerusalem Post*, October 14, 1994.

55. Haim Shapiro, "New York's Syrian Jews Angry over Role of Shas and Yosef in Gov't Fall," *Jerusalem Post*, March 29, 1990.

56. Herb Keinon, "Deri: Shas Ready for Referendum, but not for Coalition," *Jerusalem Post*, January 19, 1994.

57. David Zev Harris, "Waiting for Rav Ovadia," *Jerusalem Post*, December 24, 1999.

58. Sarah Honig, "Axes to Grind with the Likud," *Jerusalem Post*, March 19, 1990.

59. Honig, "Axes to Grind with the Likud;" David Zev Harris, "World View Apart," *Jerusalem Post*, October 1, 1999.
60. Cited in Herb Keinon, "The Schools that Shas Built," *Jerusalem Post*, September 24, 1999.
61. Ron Kampeas, "Conventional Wisdom and Shas," *Jerusalem Post*, March 29, 1990.
62. Sarah Honig, "Shas: Rabin Met with Ovadia Yosef about Golan," *Jerusalem Post*, January 27, 1994.
63. Sarah Honig, "Tape Depicts Rabin as Servant of Shas," *Jerusalem Post*, November 3, 1994.
64. Dan Izenberg, "Barak's Conversion Dilemma," *Jerusalem Post*, October 24, 1997.
65. Deri's sentence was later commuted to three years. *Jewish Chronicle* (London), July 14, 2000.
66. In a Gallup survey of public opinion regarding the Deri affair, five hundred Israelis were asked whether they thought that there was any connection between Deri's Sephardi ethnicity and the fact that he was the only candidate for possible indictment in the Bar-On affair. Nearly two-thirds of those identified as Sephardi, 64.8 percent saw no connection as compared to 18.9 percent who did see one. The rest either would not answer or did not know. Of the non-Sephardi interviewees, 74.9 percent saw no connection and 11.7 percent did see one. The overall figures were: No connection 70.6 percent; connection 14.6 percent. Michal Yudelman and Sarah Honig, "Shas MK: Police Show Ethnic Bias," *Jerusalem Post*, September 4, 1990; Moshe Kohn, "Finger-Pointers, Quakers and Hoodlums," *Jerusalem Post*, May 23, 1997.
67. Michal Yudelman, "A Festival of Political Correctness," *Jerusalem Post*, May 2, 1997.
68. Shortly prior to the 1999 elections the Labor Party renamed itself Yisrael Achat (One Israel).
69. Larry Derfner, "The Shas Dilemma," *Jerusalem Post*, May 28, 1999.
70. Herb Keinon, "Forced to Choose," *Jerusalem Post*, June 4, 1999.
71. Herb Keinon, "The War of Succession," *Jerusalem Post*, June 25, 1999.
72. Sheleg, *New Religious Jews*, 245.
73. Herb Keinon, "The Indomitable King of Shas," *Jerusalem Post*, March 19, 1999.
74. "The Reluctant Prince," *Jerusalem Post*, June 29, 2000.
75. Yosef Goell, "The Menacing Face of Ethnicity," *Jerusalem Post*, September 7, 1990.
76. Editorial, "The Shas Mess," *Jerusalem Post*, May 7, 1991.
77. Howard Grief, "Labor and Shas—On Party Corruption and Electoral Fraud," *Nativ* [Hebrew] 6, no. 5 (September 1993): 40, 42, 43.
78. Sarah Honig, "Shas Issues Ultimatum on Joint Coalition," *Jerusalem Post*, September 25, 1994.
79. Amotsa Asa-El, "On Jewish Catholicism," *Jerusalem Post*, March 14, 1997.
80. Herb Keinon, "Aryeh Deri, Superstar," *Jerusalem Post*, March 7, 1977.
81. Amotza Asa-El, "Tiger Deri's Lost Worlds," *Jerusalem Post*, May 2, 1997.
82. Moshe Kohn, "A Racist Vision," *Jerusalem Post*, January 30, 1998.
83. Nina Gilbert, "Crusader in the Knesset," *Jerusalem Post*, January 14, 2000.
84. According to Ne'eman Committee nominated by the Ministry of Education, the average number of pupils in Shas's schools is 125 compared to 387 in state and state-

religious schools. The class size is twenty compared to twenty-nine, and the number of pupil to teacher ratio is thirteen compared to nineteen. The committee agreed to help Shas on the proviso that it takes retrenchment steps such as closing some schools, combining others, and adopting stringent control systems. While the Ministry of Education insisted on payment per child, Shas demanded payment per class since many of its schools have small classes. The attitude of the Ministry of Education was that Shas's schools should be treated in the same fashion as other schools. Shas' officials insist that they should be treated as other independent religious schools. Aryeh Dean Cohen, "The Feud over Funding," *Jerusalem Post*, September 24, 1999.

85. Eli Groner and David Zev Harris, "Shohat's Deals Hurt Shas," *Jerusalem Post*, December 27, 1999.

86. Larry Derfner, "Convicted, but Still in Demand," *Jerusalem Post*, April 23, 1999.

87. Michal Yudelman, "The Avengers Ride into Battle with the Media," *Jerusalem Post*, February 7, 1997.

88. Matt Rees, "Miracle Campaign," *Time* (September 11, 2000): 40.

89. This is a process, which according to Maurice Duverger usually occurs in left-wing parties. Maurice Duverger, *Political Parties* (London: Croom Helm, 1986), 16–18.

90. Amotza Asa-El, "Shas Reaches Crossroads as Deri Starts Serving Time," *Jerusalem Post North American Edition*, September 8, 2000.

91. Deborah Sontag, "Barak Gets a Breather as He Tries to Form a Unity Government," *New York Times*, October 30, 2000.

92. "In face of renewed tension, Barak demands end to violence," May 19, 2000.

93. *Ha'aretz Special for the On-Line Edition*, www2haaretz.co.il/special/elections 2001-e/f/342759.asp (December 19, 2000).

94. "Rocking Israel: Barak Survives One Challenge, is Faced With Another,"

95. Ervin Birnbaum, "The Religious-Secular Confrontation: A Lesson for Israel," *Nativ* [Hebrew] 12, no. 6 (November 1999): 30–31.

96. Herb Keinon, "Elections Again," *Jerusalem Post*, June 16, 2000.

Chapter 10

Contesting Historiographies in South Asia: The Islamization of Pakistani Social Studies Textbooks

Yvette Claire Rosser

> If it is not anti-Indianism, then in what other terms could we possibly render Pakistani-Muslim nationalism? . . . The "ideology of Pakistan" as defined to students at every school and college in the country is nothing except anti-Indianism. In every walk of life in Pakistan—from academia to journalism, from sports to bureaucracy—a vast majority of people have been inculcated with fantastic anti-India notions. . . . Phrases like the "Hindu mentality" and "devious Indian psyche" are part of the daily military talk. . . . Anti-Indianism, in short, runs deep in Pakistani state and society. It is a state of mind that cannot be switched off. . . . People have no other alternative frame of reference in which to define Pakistani nationalism.
>
> Najum Mushtaq[1]

Assuming teleological imperatives of national identity formation inherent in social studies curricula—that history textbooks are narrated with the intent of developing students into patriotic, productive citizens—this paper highlights oppositional interpretations of history found in a selection of school textbooks from the Indian Subcontinent, with particular attention to the development of the

Pakistan Studies curriculum, a required course for all students in that country. Examples from state-sponsored social studies textbooks used in classrooms in India, Pakistan, and Bangladesh can illustrate the appropriation and application of historiography to create and reinforce a national philosophy or ideology. Textbooks represent a product constantly in need of revision. They are the result of social and political pushes and pulls, pressures rising from larger issues of state building and identity formation. Within each country historical interpretations have become codified, predetermined, and concretized. In this highly charged atmosphere, where history is seen as a powerful tool to mold a nation's youth, interpretations of historical events are isolated and manipulated, heroes and villains exchange places across the borders of neighboring countries, an antinomy of point of view renders interpretation-laden facts from the vast legacy of shared historical events mutually exclusive. Selective history often distorts and disconnects historical moments from their context and biography becomes hagiography when social science discourse is based on nationalist interpretations and ethnically or religiously driven political mandates.

Ideology is often more important than historiography in secondary level social studies textbooks. Sometimes the influence is overt, as in the discourse of chauvinistic Islamic nationalism that pervades *Pakistani Studies* textbooks, a narrative based on "Islamization"[2]—an indoctrination strategy institutionalized during the decade of General Zia-ul Haq's military rule.

The modern nation-state invokes images of ancestral blood ties and historical legacies to the land blessed by God across generations. Students in Pakistan, India, and Bangladesh are also subject to this agenda inherent in social studies curricula.[3]

Pakistan and Bangladesh emerged from the rupture of the Indian Nationalist movement as separate nations; each must deal with a past which created it but of which it is not now a political part. Writing or rewriting one's own history is seen as an enterprise that will help to create a bright future for the citizens and in particular, ensure the continuation of the nation-state or at least the present government's perspective of nationalism. Educators and bureaucrats are charged with creating, updating, and promoting paradigms to accomplish a transfer of various incarnations of patriotic identity to the next generation.

Several important questions are raised. Whose history is valued and reproduced in service to the social order or state? How and why are historical events appropriated and imbued with often-diametrical interpretations? Nationalized historical trajectories claim ownership of particular views of the past, but is the official version of the historical record believed "as fact" by subnational groups? Is there a displacement between history as official nationalized narrative and history as folklore?

Though this paper deals with textbooks published by the central government, it is with a caveat that I present the rhetoric in textbooks as central to the process of identity formation in a nation such as Pakistan. Not only is there tension between official history manufactured in Islamabad and the historical perspectives of regional ethnic groups such as Sindhis and Balouchis, but it is essential to keep in mind that in countries where large numbers of people are illiterate or semiliterate, textbooks and educational institutions are not the only medium through which citizens develop nationalist sentiments and historical grounding, or the lack thereof. The views of subnational groups who question the dominant historiographical narrative and nurture their own interpretations of the past will be introduced. This discussion of social studies curriculum and textbooks in South Asia draws examples from materials published since independence in 1947.

Pakistan Studies: Propaganda of a "Failed State"

All students in Pakistan are required to take courses called Pakistan Studies and must pass standardized tests based on that curriculum. Pakistani Studies is a compulsory subject in all secondary schools and colleges. There are numerous textbooks published under this title for the ninth class to the BA level. In general, the curriculum is a composite of patriotic discourses, justification of the Two-Nation Theory, hagiographies of Muslim heroes, and polemics about the superiority of Islamic principals over Hinduism. The rubric in these textbooks must be learned by rote in order for students to pass the required exam.

Many students in Pakistan dislike this required course. A student at a women's college in Lahore told me that "Pak Studies classes were usually scheduled at five or six in the afternoon" and "hardly any students attend," choosing instead to spend their time studying for "important classes such as Math or Urdu or English" which are held in the morning. "Besides," the student continued, "we've covered the Pak Studies material year after year, it's just the same Lucknow Pact, Two-Nation Theory . . . we don't have to study for the test, the Ideology of Pakistan has been drilled into us."

Textbooks in Pakistan must first be approved by the Curriculum Wing of the Ministry of Education in Islamabad after which they are published by the provincial textbook boards located at Jamshoro in Sindh, Quetta in Balouchistan, Lahore in Panjab,[4] and Peshawar in the North West Frontier Province (NWFP). The social studies curriculum in Pakistan, as both product and propagator of the "Ideology of Pakistan," derives its legitimacy from a narrow set of directives. The textbooks authored and altered during the eleven years of General Zia-ul Haq's military rule between 1977 and 1988, are still in use in most schools. They are decidedly antidemocratic.

When discussing General Zia's lasting influence on the teaching of social studies in Pakistan, a principal at a woman's college in Lahore told me a joke which she said was well known among intellectuals in the country, "General Zia—May He Rest in Pieces." Indeed, after his airplane exploded in the sky, the pieces of his body were never found. There are, however, bits and pieces of Zia-ul Haq's body-politic littered across the Pakistani psychological, educational, political, and military landscape.

Objective scholars warned that the textbooks in Pakistan were fomenting hatred and encouraging fundamentalism. For several decades, textbooks in not only Pakistan, but many Islamic nations, have promoted a radically restrictive brand of Islamic exclusivism, and exported that perspective to other nations as in the case of Pakistani born Taliban and their negative impact on Afghani society. In March 2001, an article by this author appeared in *The Friday Times*, a weekly newspaper published in Lahore, Pakistan. In that article I warned of the imminent blowback of America's foreign policies, in the 1980s in South Asia.[5]

The story manufactured to further Zia's "Be Pakistani/Buy Pakistani" worldview is presented through a myopic lens of hypernationalism and the politicized use of Islam. According to Dr. Inayat Magsi, a Sindhi psychiatrist, "[When Civics classes teach negative values] the result is a xenophobic and paranoid acceptance of authoritarianism and the denial of cultural differences and regional ethnic identities." In the past few decades, social studies textbooks in Pakistan have been used as locations to articulate the hatred that Pakistani policy-makers have attempted to inculcate toward their Hindu neighbors. *Pakistani Studies* textbooks are an active site for negatively representing India and othering the Subcontinent's Hindu past.

Many textbooks published in Pakistan under the title *Pakistani Studies* are particularly prone to the omissions, embellishments, and elisions that often characterize historical narratives designed for secondary level social studies classes. During the time of General Zia-ul Haq, social studies, comprised of history and geography, were replaced by Pakistani Studies, which was made a compulsory subject for all students from the ninth grade[6] through the first year of college including engineering and medical schools. Curriculum changes, institutionalized during Zia's Islamization campaign, required that all students also take a series of courses under the title Islamiyat, the study of Islamic tenants and memorization of Quranic verses. Committees were formed under Zia's guidance to systematically edit the textbooks. The University Grants Commission (UGC) issued a directive in 1983 that textbook writers were:

> To demonstrate that the basis of Pakistan is not to be founded in racial, linguistic, or geographical factors, but, rather, in the shared experience of a common religion. To get students to know and appreciate the Ideology of Pakistan, and to popularize it with slogans. To guide students towards the ultimate goal of Pakistan—the creation of a completely Islamized State.[7]

Pervez Hoodbhoy and A. H. Nayyar commence with a near prophetic comment regarding the inevitable and eventual blowback from General Zia's efforts to Islamize the educational system, "the full impact of which will probably be felt by the turn of the century, when the present generation of school children attains maturity."[8] Nayyar and Hoodbhoy explain that the UGC's directives centered on four themes:

1. The ideology of Pakistan, both as a historical force that motivated the movement for Pakistan as well as its raison d'être
2. The depiction of Jinnah as a man of orthodox religious views who sought the creation of a theocratic state
3. A move to establish the ulama as genuine heroes of the Pakistan movement
4. An emphasis on ritualistic Islam, together with the rejection of interpretations of the religion and generation of communal antagonism.[9]

This manufactured view of the past narrates Pakistan's emergence as an independent country: in just seven short years, under the enlightened guidance of Mohammed Ali Jinnah, Quaid-e-Azam, the father of the country, Pakistan rose from the strife and oppression of religious communalism in Hindu-dominated India to join the comity of modern nations. Nayyar and Hoodbhoy explain, "The 'recasting' of Pakistani history [has been] used to 'endow the nation with a historic destiny.'"[10] The story of Pakistan's past is intentionally written to be distinct from and often in direct contrast with interpretations of history found in India.

For most Indians, Pakistan is still seen as invalid, created without any real legacy of participation in the freedom struggle, without any sacrifice for the nation. Partition continues to be considered a terrible mistake, albeit, one that Indians must deal with diplomatically and sometimes militarily. Rather than a heroic leader of the oppressed South Asian Muslims, Jinnah is seen as almost Hitleresque, a ghostly messianic figure whipping up a false nationalism and leading a paper organization that had no clearly defined concept for the actual form of Pakistan. Obviously, the interpretation of historical events leading to the British leaving India and the Partition of the Subcontinent are narrated from absolutely contrasting approaches and completely contrary angles.

Light of God/Love of Plunder Schism: Dichotomies of Discourse

A comparison of several key historical events as represented in textbooks in Pakistan with parallel narrations in Indian textbooks reveals a dichotomy of discourse where guiding principals of interpretation are quite oppositional. Chronologically speaking, the first event that can be utilized to illuminate these poles of interpretation is the treatment of the conquest of Sindh in 712 C.E. by an Arab army under the leadership of Muhammad-bin-Qasim. *Pakistani Studies* textbooks appropriate bin-Qasim as fuel for nationalist inspired discourses, portraying him as the initial Islamizing agent, who less than a century after the death of the Prophet Mohammed started a movement that transformed the Subcontinent. On the other hand, Indian textbooks, though "appreciative of the cultural and scientific consequences of contact at this time with what is generally perceived as the 'highly civilized' [Arab] world," consider that Arabs had a minimal impact on the history of the Subcontinent. In *Medieval India: A History Textbook for Class XI*, Satish Chandra treats the "Arab invasion of Sind (sic) as a localized affair."[11]

In *Social Studies for Class VI*,[12] published by the Sindh Textbook Board, the story of the Arab's march up the Indus is narrated with a flourish as the first moment of Pakistan ushering in a new era and the glorious ascendancy of Islam on Pakistani soil. This textbook explains to the young sixth-grade class children of Sindh, "The Muslims knew that the people of South Asia were infidels and they kept thousands of idols in their temples." The Sindhi king, Raja Dahir, is described as cruel and despotic. "The non-Brahmans who were tired of the cruelties of Raja Dahir, joined hands with Muhammad-bin-Qasim because of his good treatment." According to this historical orientation,

> The conquest of Sindh opened a new chapter in the history of South Asia. Muslims had everlasting effects on their existence in the region. . . . For the first time the people of Sindh were introduced to Islam, its political system, and way of the government. The people here had seen only the atrocities of the Hindu Rajas. . . . The people of Sindh were so much impressed by the benevolence of Muslims that they regarded Muhammad-bin-Qasim as their savior. . . . Research and Analysis Wing is the Indian intelligence agency Muhammad-bin-Qasim stayed in Sindh for over three years. On his departure from Sindh, the local people were overwhelmed with grief.[13]

What is not mentioned in the textbooks is the fact that Arab armies attacked Sindh sixteen times prior to 712, but failed to overcome the "Hindu Rajas." When I was in Hyderabad, Sindh, I discussed the contents of this textbook with several Sindhis, who assured me that they told their children an alternative version of this story, where Raja Dahir is in fact referred to as a local ethnic hero. Several informants told me that any "good Sindhi knows the real history. In several cities in ancient Sindh, Muhammad-bin-Qasim beheaded every male over the age of eighteen and he sent tens of thousands of Sindhi women to the harems of the Abbassid Dynasty." They also explained that the impact of these textbooks was minimal because, though the back cover indicated twenty thousand copies were printed annually, "due to corruption, fewer than five thousand were ever printed and distributed."[14]

Though I cannot surmise what percentage of Sindhis may have reason to disassociate their identity from Arabization brought by Muhammad-bin-Qasim, it is true that they are often sensitive about their position vis-à-vis Pakistani society. Sindhis see a rupture between the expectations of a free homeland promised by the Muslim League and the repercussions of centralized politicized policies emanating from Islamabad, which have left them disempowered and impoverished in their own land. Three decades after calling for the creation of Pakistan in 1939, G. M. Syed, the grandfather of Sindh nationalism, called on Indira Gandhi during the Bangladesh war of independence, to send troops to

Sindh and free it from Pakistani exploitation, creating "Sindhudesh." He spent the rest of his life under house arrest. Sindhi and other subnational perspectives of history will be mentioned again later in this chapter.

As my friend and mentor, Dr. Inayatullah in Islamabad wrote to me in a personal e-mail communication,

> For last fifty years the history in Pakistan has come to be written from a purely "national perspective" and mainly by scholars belonging to two dominant ethnic groups, Punjabi and Mohajir. As a result their perspective considerably shapes historical consciousness of Pakistanis. What the historians of smaller provinces think of critical issues in writing history such as the role of religion and provincial struggles for independence in the creation of Pakistan is not sufficiently known to Pakistan's academic community. Absence of this perspective has also implications for policy-making. The demand of smaller provinces for regional peace in South Asia and equitable local development is not sufficiently appreciated and incorporated in national policies.

Eliding and Eclipsing: Victim or Villain

Historiography and hagiography are frequently interchangeable in the Pakistani social studies curriculum that juxtaposes the contributions of two heroes—the young Arab general, Muhammad-bin-Qasim and Sultan Mahmud, the Turkish-speaking military leader from the Ghaznavi dynasty in eastern Afghanistan. Mahmud Ghaznavi's multiple iconoclastic incursions into the Subcontinent began in Peshawar in 1001 culminating with the infamous sacking of the Somnath Temple in 1025. These two prominent figures are placed on pedestals used as stepping-stones toward the inevitable unfolding of the Ideology of Pakistan coming to closure with the near deification of the father of the nation, Mohammed Ali Jinnah. The standard *Pakistani Studies* textbook contracts the three centuries between Muhammad-bin-Qasim and Mahmud Ghaznavi, the great-grandfathers of the Pakistan movement. Muhammad Ghori's exploits, especially his defeat of Prithvi Raj Chauhan in 1192 are included, where after the tale is taken up again when Babar defeats Ibrahim Lodi at the Battle of Panipat in 1526.

The central narrative of the nation glides and elides through the descendants of Babar and is approached with renewed enthusiasm beginning with the reign of Aurangzeb in the late seventeenth century. This guided version of Pakistani history moves quickly to the rebellion of 1857, which British historians refer to as the "Sepoy Mutiny" but Indians and Pakistanis call the "First War of Liberation." Hindu-Muslim conflicts during Aurangzeb's era, 1658–1707, brief mention of the military victories against the British of Tipu Sultan who ruled Mysore from 1782–1799, along with the violent uprising in 1857 are implicated as the underlying inspirations for the growth of the Pakistan movement that came to fruition in 1939. Besides references to the establishment of Aligarh Muslim

University in 1875, the rest is apparently superfluous as far as Muslim identity constructs are concerned. The narration of the Freedom movement focuses mostly on betrayals by the Hindus and double-dealings by various British delegations.

In most Pakistani textbooks the Delhi Sultanate is almost disregarded and the nearly five hundred years between Mahmud Ghaznavi's multiple invasions and the establishment of Babar's Moghul dynasty in 1526 are collapsed. Muhammad-bin-Qasim is lauded as a kindhearted young prince and beneficent warrior, welcomed and beloved by the Brahmin-weary Sindhis while Mahmud Ghaznavi is defended and promoted in Pakistani textbooks as a crusader for the one true religion.[15]

Pakistani historians are often critical of Euro-American and Indian social scientists who generally discuss Mahmud Ghaznavi in terms of plunder, explaining that his numerous expeditions into India were motivated by economic considerations rather than religion. In contrast, most *Pakistan Studies* textbooks describe Mahmud as a warrior with a religious mission whose main objective was to bring the "light of Islam" to the pagans of the Subcontinent by waging a "holy jihad."[16] *Our World, for Class IV*, describes Mahmud's invasions into India,

> There was a temple in India during those times, Somnath. The biggest idol/statue in that temple was also called Somnath. This temple had so much treasure in it that no royal treasure could even come near it. All the Hindu rajas used to get together in this temple and think about ways to fight the Muslims. After covering the desert of Rajputana, Mahmud came right in front of Somnath temple. Hindus got panicky. All of them tried to do their best but couldn't succeed. The fort was conquered. The priests begged him not to destroy the Somnath idol but he said that he wanted to be remembered as Mahmud who destroyed the idol and not the one who sold it. He blew the idol into pieces. This success was a source of happiness for the whole Muslim world.[17]

J. Husain, in her Oxford University Press textbook, *The Illustrated History of Pakistan*, used in elite schools, deals with the Ghaznavi incursions from a less ideological perspective than is usually found in government textbooks. She discusses economic imperatives for Mahmud's plunderings of temples, but concludes that he "left the greatest monument of all: the gift of Islam."[18] Several of the government textbooks I have reviewed complained about the presumed negative treatment that Mahmud receives in British/Westernized and Indian versions of the events.

As such defensive postures in Pakistan suggest, the tendency in Indian textbooks is to treat Mahmud Ghaznavi as a plunderer, dismissing his religious motivations. Shatish Chandra states that Mahmud's "love of plunder went side by side with the defense of Islam."[19] In the following passage from Romila Thapar's NCERT textbook, Mahmud's religious motivations are considered, though only by coincidence,

> [Mahmud] had heard that there was much gold and jewelry kept in the big temples in India, so he destroyed the temples and took away the gold and jewelry. ... Destroying temples had another advantage. He could claim, as he did, that he had obtained religious merit by destroying images.[20]

These oppositional viewpoints regarding Mahmud Ghaznavi are characterized by ironic motivations. In India, textbooks published between the mid-1960s and the late 1990s by the National Centre for Educational Research and Training (NCERT) were intended to be culturally neutral, guided by the Nehruvian school of secular socialism. As such, they were reticent to give too much weight to "jihad" and the religiously inspired perspective since many Indians are quite sensitive concerning the legacy of forced conversions. In 1989, the West Bengal Secondary Board under a Marxist government, issued a circular dated April 28, 1989 (number "Syl/89/1"), which recommended the deletion of most discussions about the Medieval Period because it was too controversial. They included in the circular a column of politically correct perspectives that promoted the perspective that "Muslim rule should never attract any criticism. Destruction of temples by Muslim rulers and invaders should not be mentioned."[21] In contrast, Pakistani textbooks proudly proclaim that Mahmud rode into the Subcontinent under the "flag of Islam" to convert the "pagans of India."

The communal writing of history in Pakistan, where the mandate is to produce patriotic Pakistanis who are also practicing orthodox Islam, is in sharp opposition with the textbooks published by the NCERT in New Delhi, where the stated goal of social studies education is national integration promoted through pluralism and democracy. For four decades, textbooks in India, published by NCERT, in an effort to follow their mandate to include Muslim sentiments in their historical analyses, preferred to talk about economic motivations so as not to cast Mahmud as an iconoclast bent on conversions. Dr. Arjun Dev, Department Head of Social Studies at NCERT for many years, explained to me, "We are very careful not to write anything that could be construed as defamatory against Islam or any religion."[22] It is obvious that "the 'Pakistan ideology,'" on the one hand, and post-Independence resolutions to promote national integration in India, on the other, "have shaped the preoccupations, and sometimes the logic, of textbook writers in both countries."[23]

In India, the secular-leftists who authored NCERT textbooks for nearly forty years reasoned that iconoclastic motivations for conquest would seem far more negative and insulting to the Hindus of India than an economic analysis, which was considered more palatable to their sensitivities. They believe that religious interpretations of historical events breed communal hatreds. Yet this very orientation—masking the religious motivations—is offensive to many Pakistanis, who hail Mahmud's iconoclasm as the duty of a good Muslim and an integral aspect of the establishment of Islam in India, and thus the eventual birth of Pakistan.

An economic interpretation that discounts the jihad perspective is also repugnant to the more Hinducentric historians, such as those promoted by the

Bharatiya Janata Party (BJP) government associated with the Sangh Parivar—social and political groups that emphasize the essential Hinduness of Indian culture and civilization. These "Hindu nationalist" scholars assert that the "Marxist inspired" NCERT textbooks "whitewash the violence of the Medieval Period" and thereby cause resentment on the part of the majority Hindu population and denial on the part of the Muslim minority because the facts have been decontextualized. These nationalist historians argue that "Muslims in India should be encouraged to be patriotic citizens." They should disown the "temple desecrations that were perpetrated by Islamic invaders and distance themselves philosophically and politically from historical atrocities committed by their ancestors."[24] These Hinducentric intellectuals think that Indians of Muslim heritage should not take pride in a legacy that defaced and destroyed the symbols and institutions of Indic culture. Hindu nationalists hold that it is better to provide opportunities for the citizens of the country to understand the history of the nation in which they live than to let them be lulled into false pride of iconoclasm and religiously driven violence based on a legacy of conquest. These polarized perspectives reveal the complexities inherent in the narration and interpretation of controversial historical events.

As nation-states evolve and adapt to changing circumstances they often struggle to explain dynamic cultural influences by identifying and embracing new social variables as well as changing international realities, then narrating these within the expanding perimeters of their official histories. History by committee or consensus is not easy to write, history by decree is another matter. Historical narratives are never etched in stone, they can change dramatically from year to year. Demands to change historical interpretations can be and often are violence prone. Nationalism is a hot topic to die for. The need to give voice to all groups of citizens brings us back to the question of who determines whose voices are given agency. This dilemma was highlighted in the 1990 British National Curriculum reforms, which like the U.S. History Standards of 1995, were criticized as too multicultural. The British curriculum tried to deal with this problem by attempting to "impart knowledge of the diversity of cultures within Britain," and teach South Asia Studies "from their own perspective."[25] However, it is impossible to identify a collective South Asian "perspective." A history curriculum that is reflective of multiple strands of historiography in the Subcontinent is a highly unlikely, and at best, would be a polarized and multi-perspective compilation.

The Akbar Aurangzeb Axis

Contestatory points of view are evident in the polarity between the treatments of the ecumenical, syncretistic Mughul emperor Akbar and his orthodox grandson Aurangzeb. It seems logical that Pakistani textbooks would delve at length on the "Medieval Period' of Islamic ascendancy in South Asia as part of their historical legacy. What is "surprising, given the opportunity it would present for capitalizing on a 'golden age' of Mughul glory," is the discursive treatment of information provided about this period in the standard *Pakistan Studies* textbook. Avril Powell explains this as the "pre-occupation of the syllabus . . . with the final 'fulfillment' stage of the "Two Nations" premise through the creation of Pakistan in the mid-twentieth century."[26]

The Mughul Emperor Akbar, in NCERT authored textbooks, is portrayed as a just and truly Indian ruler, the father of national integration. This is in direct contrast to the perception of Pakistani historians and curriculum writers who see Akbar as harmful to the ultimate interests of Muslims in the Subcontinent. Most Indian and Western treatments represent Akbar's reign as "a high peak of cultural assimilation and religious harmony."[27] While Pakistani historians see Akbar's religious theories as apostasy, Indian textbooks represent him as the first truly "Indian" ruler, who along with the Emperor Ashoka Maurya before him in the second century B.C.E, personified the liberal, Pan-Indian leader. In her textbook, *Medieval India*, Romila Thapar states, "Akbar's great dream was that India should be united as one country. People should forget their differences of region and religion and think of themselves only as the people of India."[28] That this eminent historian falls into the trap of presentism to analyze the past can perhaps be forgiven since she is using a voice aimed at children.

Mubarak Ali, a progressive historian living in Lahore, asserts that Akbar has been systematically eliminated from most textbooks in Pakistan in order to "divert attention away from his 'misplaced' policies."[29] Where they exist, discussions of Akbar are short and superficial, such as in *Social Studies for Class VI*,[30] in which his name is simply listed, but events of his life not elaborated. In *Pakistani Studies for Class IX–X*,[31] Akbar's name is not even listed among the Muslim rulers of India; and in *Pakistani Studies for Secondary Classes*,[32] he is not mentioned in the text along with other famous Islamic figures, a list that includes Mahmud Ghaznavi, Babur, Humayun, Shah Jahan, and Aurangzeb. Akbar, the son of Humayun and the father of Shah Jahan, ruled India for over five decades, longer than any of his predecessors or descendants, who nonetheless find mention in the textbooks. Akbar's father, Humayun, whose solitary year of rather dubious rulership was terminated when "he tripped, light headed from a pipe or two of opium, cracking his head on the stone stairs of his private astronomical observatory, and as one chronicler put it, 'stumbled out of life as he had stumbled in,'"[33] finds at least cursory mention in Pakistani textbooks that ironically often fail to include even the name of his more famous, accomplished, and sober son, Akbar.

This Mughul king, often redundantly called "Akbar the Great,"[34] expanded his domain across a larger area of India than the Mauryan dynasty. However, in discussions of this seminal regime that firmly established the Mughul Empire on India soil, Pakistani textbooks, though necessarily brief in their presentation due to space limitations inherent in a chronological march through the millennia, are almost unanimously silent about Akbar. This omission is an amazing hiccup of historiography in which fifty-five very essential years are simply eliminated. Typical of most treatments, in *Pakistani Studies*[35] written by Rabbini and Sayyid, Akbar is mentioned only while discussing Shaikh Ahmad Sirhindi, who according to Mubarak Ali, "is projected as a hero challenging Akbar's religious policy and restoring Islamic values in India."[36] This perspective of Akbar's "misguided policies" are derived in part from I. H. Qureshi's interpretation of Mughul history as articulated in his magna opus, *The Muslim Community of the Indo-Pakistan Subcontinent*[37] and also in his book about Akbar in which he states,

> It can be seriously contented if he possessed wisdom of the highest order. If he had, he would not have sought to weaken Islam and the Muslim community of the Subcontinent. At least he would have refrained from interfering with the established principals of Islam. Even Vincent Smith, who narrates Akbar's aberrations from Islam with relish, concludes that "the whole scheme was the outcome of ridiculous vanity, a monstrous growth of unrestrained autocracy. . . ." How can it then be asserted that Akbar possessed wisdom in the highest degree?[38]

By the time Akbar's orthodox grandson had killed his brothers and imprisoned his father, just one generation later, Akbar was already perceived as a quasiheretic.[39] The Medieval historian, K. S. Lal in Delhi told me, "The Muslim chronicler, Khafi Khan, a contemporary of Aurangzeb, does not mention Akbar, though he names Babar, Shah Jahan, and the rest, but not Akbar."[40]

I. H. Qureshi, as well as K. K. Aziz and A. H. Dani are Pakistan's preeminent historians who, in footnoted articulate style, grounded their arguments in the Two-Nation Theory, thus creating a post-Partition intellectual milieu within which educators and bureaucrats could inscribe the face of a new nation. References to historical precedence are essential to justify and develop new definitions of nationalism. In this politically dynamic scenario, heroes were created and recreated, villains exchanged or expunged, and entire eras deemed meaningless. I. H. Qureshi taught at St. Stephen's College and at the University of Delhi before Partition. A. H. Dani received a Ph.D. in Sanskrit from Benares Hindu University in the late 1930s. Both scholars, who had spent years contemplating the vast historical legacy of their forefathers and the land of their birth, suddenly found themselves in need of a new narrative, a compulsion to create a past for a nation in which they had just been reborn.

According to a well-known Indian historian living in Delhi, Mushirul Hasan, "on reaching Pakistan [these India trained scholars had to] rewrite their own histories." They constructed "a different past altogether, one that was at variance with their earlier explorations [and began] to search for heroes and martyrs, involve new symbols and traditions, and discover milestones . . . for the historical antecedents of Pakistan." Much of A. H. Dani's work focuses on the Central Asian roots of Pakistan, though as a scholar he does not dismiss the bedrock of Indic influences in Pakistani culture. Qureshi and Dani were patronized by both Ayub Khan and Zia-ul Haq. They were instrumental in constructing a past for their new nation that would set it apart from Indic Civilization.

> The issue was not just the defense of Partition, or Independence from Pakistan's vantage point, but also a different reading of the past involving, among other things, the rejection of a diverse but vibrant composite-cultural and intellectual legacy.[41]

In order to legitimize Pakistan as a Muslim homeland, historians had to nurture the "image of the Muslims as a monolithic entity, acting in unison and committed to specifically Islamic values and norms."[42]

In this capacity, tendencies which led to cultural accommodation or spiritual syncretism between Hindus and Muslims, that could have preempted and perhaps prevented the call for Pakistan, came to be criticized as agents working against the interests of the Two-Nation Theory. *Deen-i-Ilahi*, the religion created by Akbar and Bhakti movements, which opened a spiritual space where Sufis (Islamic mystics) and Hindus could find common metaphors and experiences of God, were seen as dangerous forces that almost subsumed Indian Islam. These syntegrationist energies are roundly rejected by I. H. Qureshi as threats to true Islam. Akbar is therefore interpreted as dubiously Islamic, whereas his grandson, Aurangzeb, inspired by the orthodoxy of scholars such as Shaikh Ahmad Sirhindi, is credited with saving Indian Islam from being swallowed up yet another monist subsect of Hinduism.

Using the past selectively, passages from the writings of Indian Muslim scholars and chroniclers were appropriated where they seemed to support the eventual establishment of a Muslim nation. In the search for ideological validation, Pakistani historians reached into the past to own leading Muslim intellectuals of eighteenth- and nineteenth-century North India, such as Sir Syed Ahmad Khan, Shah Waliullah, and Syed Ahmad Barelwi, highlighting their ideas wherever they could be construed to support the Two-Nation Theory.

Aurangzeb, like Mahmud Ghaznavi, has earned a similarly controversial place in the hotly contested historical record of the Subcontinent. According to Zafar, "[Aurangzeb] reversed the policies of Akbar and made a genuine effort to give the State an Islamic orientation. Under Aurangzeb the Pakistan spirit gathered in strength."[43]

Though J. Husain in part blames Aurangzeb for the decline of the Mughul Empire, she ultimately acts as his apologist, explaining that he was caught in "a 'vicious circle' set in motion by Akbar's misplaced 'religious adventurism,'" which then precipitated "an 'opposite reaction' characterized in Aurangzeb's reign by 'anti-Hindu policies,'" which in their turn created a Hindu backlash. She defends Aurangzeb against his critics while pointing to the sharply divergent historical interpretations of this controversial figure,

> Because of Aurangzeb's religious fervor, historians tend to judge him according to their own religious leanings. Hindu and Christian historians often present

Aurangzeb's religious policies as the main cause of the disintegration of the Mughul Empire, while some Muslim historians try to completely ignore the negative effects of these policies.[44]

Elisions of time found in the historical narrative in Pakistan are not isolated to the Sultanate or Moghul periods. Such leaps began to appear in textbooks in the early years of the Islamic Republic that traced Pakistani history from the life of the Prophet Mohammed to the life of Mohammad Ali Jinnah. In a 1975 social studies textbook for grade eight,[45] the first unit covers the history of the Subcontinent, highlighting selected events leading directly to the creation of Pakistan. After several chapters on various invaders who introduced Islam into India, followed by several chapters on British colonialism, there are chapters focusing on the Muslim League and events central to the emergence of Pakistan such as the Lucknow Pact and the Lahore Declaration. Two historical characters who are invariably included in the story of Pakistan are the educator, Sir Sayyid Ahmed Khan, and Mohammad Iqbal, the poet.

The second unit in this 1975 eighth grade textbook is titled "Islamic History," narrating the story of the birth of Islam and the life of the Prophet. The final chapter, superimposed at the end of this unit on Islamic history, is titled, "The Pak-India War." This chapter, concerning the 1965 war, was not included in the original 1968 version of this textbook but simply tacked onto the 1975 edition, during Bhutto's regime to counter Pakistan's failure to prevent the breakup of the country in 1971. This chapter provided an opportunity to humiliate India whom Bhutto and most Pakistanis blamed for bifurcating the nation. Historical events had caught up with the Pakistani social studies curriculum, where contemporary warfare and political polemics were pasted at the end of a unit on the history of Islam, an ideologically significant placement in an otherwise illogical chronological progression. Including the 1965 war at the end of this unit created a connection between the life of the Prophet and the heroic acts of the brave Pakistani soldiers who were martyred defending the fatherland from India's "unprovoked attack on September 6, 1965."[46]

Selected events and charismatic characters in the long history of the Indian Subcontinent are interpreted differently and imbued with diametrically opposed meanings and motivations in school textbooks designed to teach nationalist allegiance. In Pakistan, the inevitability of a separate Muslim nation in the Subcontinent is supported by the belief that Hindus and Muslims in South Asia had always constituted distinct and irreconcilably separate communities. The official Indian curriculum, even the new one under the BJP, in sharp contrast to the Pakistani position, argues that the divide and rule policies of the British created communalism, which was not inherent in the interaction of Hindus and Muslims, and that communalism "has its roots in the modern colonial socio-economic political structure."[47] If the nature of a nation's social studies curriculum is, in varying degrees, determined by "the creation, preservation, or merely the 'understanding' of the twentieth-century 'nation' and its culture, then . . . what each syllabus will then encompass over time and space is . . . predetermined by such objectives."[48] In Pakistan, according to Avril Powell "ideology has . . . made a myth of history in the portrayal of . . . national heroes."[49] Where "nation-building agendas . . . take a priority over disinterested academic study, history becomes a medium for transmitting goals for the future."[50] In this uncritical milieu, commonly acknowledged "facts" of the past, such as the reign of Akbar or Operation Gibraltar, are twisted to fit into a predetermined mold.

Whose History? Whose Nation?

An analysis of civics education in Pakistan must be situated in several theoretically grounded questions: How do power relations between an increasingly politicized clergy and unstable, militarized governmental institutions impact the telling of history and the transmission of nationalism? Whose stories are valorized and reproduced in service to the social order or state and whose are discounted and demonized? How is Islam incorporated into the civics curriculum, designed to impart both piety and patriotism? How do Islamic historiographical methodologies and perspectives interface with the impetus towards nationalism and modernity?

The heritage of the geographical area of modern-day Pakistan is epitomized by the confluence of cultures. Graves excavated at prehistoric Indus Valley sites dating from the second millennia B.C.E produced skulls of peoples from diverse racial origins including Mediterranean, Proto-Australoid, Dravidian, and Mongoloid. Regional languages also reflect this amalgam of cultural influences: Urdu, created by the superimposition of Persian/Arabic vocabulary on Sanskritic /Prakritic forms; Balouch, an Indo-Iranian language, Sindhi, with Sanskrit roots, also shows the merging of linguistic forms, as do Farsi, Pashtu, and Panjabi. Influences left by the Maurya Dynasty, the Guptas, the Huns, Arabs, Turks, Moghuls, Rajputs, the British, all impacted vast areas of South and Southwest Asia with elements of their traditions and languages. The regions now comprising the provinces of Pakistan have long been a cultural crossroads. These areas were enriched and often exploited by millennia of ethnic intermingling. Many indigenous kingdoms were at times independent political entities in their own right. Contemporary relationships among the subnational ethnic groups in Pakistan are based on ancient competitions and historical interconnections. Standard *Pakistani Studies* textbooks rarely include chapters that discuss the cultures and histories of Balouchis or Pathans or Sindhis.

An observation made by the head of the history department at The University of Balouchistan offers an alternative perspective of Pakistani history, without negating the critique that historical discourse systematically distorts and deletes vast eras of South Asian history nor that the social studies curriculum intentionally divorced Pakistani culture from its Subcontinental roots. The Balouchi history professor pointed out that the official "history of Pakistan does not include the lives of personalities and narration of events which occurred *in*

Pakistan, but is restricted to the leaders and activities of the Muslim League in pre-Partition India." He stated that the history of Pakistan in textbooks not only "ends just as Pakistan comes into being," but the contributions toward anti-colonialism and the creation of Pakistan is "restricted to what happened in Lucknow and Delhi and Aligarh." There is scant mention of Balouchis or Pathans who battled the British for over a century, nor any discussion of the activities of ethnic or regional leaders in what were to become the provinces of the newly formed nation.

From the point of view of a Balouch or Pathan, the "history of Pakistan focuses entirely on events in the Indian Subcontinent," of which culturally and historically they do not attribute a deep connection. Balouchis draw their historical identities from Iran and Central Asia, not from South Asia.[51] Ironically, they are therefore doubly denied a history, both of their ancestors who lived in this area in the ancient pre-Islamic period and the contributions of their ethnic groups to the modern nation-state. When Pakhtun leaders such as Abdul Ghaffar Khan, known as the "Frontier Gandhi," or historical Balouchis, such as the Khan of Kalat are mentioned, their convictions are downplayed or distorted and their activities eclipsed. An irrational paradigm implemented since the days of One Unit[52] makes the assumption that denying cultural differences in the provinces will nullify ethnic affiliations and bring the Sindhis, Pathans, and Balouchis together under the flag of Pakistani nationalism. Islam has been the tool and Panjabi hegemony the rule, in response to which people who live in the provinces have steadily soured to what they perceive as pseudonationalism and Islamabad's economic exploitation and political manipulation of religion, and the ongoing anti-federalism of the center.

Pakistan is a country encompassing several distinct ethnic communities and has faced many challenges on the road to achieving unity within diversity. Pakistan was founded on the principle that Islam, as the great leveler of class and caste, was a sufficient force to tie the Sindhis, the Pathans, and the Balouchi tribes, and also the Bengalis together with the dominant Panjabis to form a cohesive and stable national identity that would supersede regional loyalties and ethnicities.[53] Through the years, this mission to create a strong centrally controlled government has been pursued by various methods including realignment of political associations between its minority groups, usually based more on gains for provincial party bosses than national cohesion and by the use of military coercion, which in the case of the Bengali majority, resulted in the split up of the original country.

In Balouchistan this autocratic response from the central government resulted in a civil war that lasted four years and is almost unknown, and never mentioned in the textbooks. "The Balouch . . . have become conscious of their particularist identity in the face of perceived threats to national and cultural characteristics."[54] Though One Unit was abandoned prior to the elections of 1970, the dismissal of which led to the secessionist war in East Pakistan, even today, the central government operates under the assumption that Pakistan is a unitary cultural and political entity. The Pakistani bureaucracy and military are still grappling with the problems that the contradictions inherent in the Ideology of Pakistan continue to create within the varied ethnocultural landscapes of the nation. The powers at the center, usually more intent at retaining the profitable reins on the government, are inevitably unable to make equitable policies that can reverse decentralized loyalties nor reconcile those tendencies with the imperatives of a highly centralized state apparatus. As Feroz Ahmed in his book *Ethnicity and Politics in Pakistan,* wrote,

> The state and its ideologues have steadfastly refused to recognize the fact that these regions are not merely chunks of territory with different names but areas which were historically inhabited by peoples who had different languages and cultures, and even states of their own. This official and intellectual denial has, no doubt, contributed to the progressive deterioration of inter-group relations, weakened societies cohesiveness, and undermined the state's capacity to forge security and sustain development.[55]

Dr. Anwar Halepota, a psychiatrist at the Civil Hospital in Karachi, discussed the negative impact that narrow interpretations of nationalism and intellectual censorship can have on citizens. He explained,

> Paradoxical double bind denial of the self—cultural denial—leads to identity crises resulting in subsequent intellectual confusion. Students are not only exposed to this, it is hammered into them. Their response is a struggle to make sense.

Though, according to Dr. Halepota, many may seek help from other sources such as the media or teachers, in order "to bring some sense of clarity, and work out an intellectual point of reference within the available framework," there are however, "few resources to help them." Dr. Halepota, who has a strong grounding in his native Sindhi literature and history believes that "It is the strength of the culture and traditions which saves students from the deep psychotic schism to which they are exposed by the educational system. Culture and family will save them." When asked to explain this cultural tradition that can save citizens from alienation, he responded that

> Culture is the traditional interactions of communities. Social harmony can be found at the level of micro-social interactions, which are strong enough to help sustain the nation at a macro-level. This culture of community can be the basis of a healthy cultural synthesis of old social systems and new challenges.

The most alarming challenge, according to Dr. Halepota, is conservative religious fundamentalism. He called it "religious colonization" and said that it "is in disharmony with the culture and traditions" of the ethnic groups who reside in Pakistan. He explained,

This orthodoxy is being imposed but Pakistani people resist, they always reject fundamentalism—one proof is that they have never voted the religious parties into office. Islamic parties always suffer humiliating defeats at the poles. People go for practical slogans, not for religion.

A few years after this interview, during an election allowed by General Musharaff in October 2002, following his bloodless coup in 1999, the Islamic parties won an unprecedented number of votes. They gained control of the Baluochistan legislature as well as NWFP. Many observers blame these unusual election results on two main issues. General Musharraf banned the old political parties in the country such as the Pakistan Peoples Party (PPP), and did not allow them to contest the elections or to hold rallies, claiming as he did that they were corrupt and should not be allowed back in the government. In contrast, he allowed the Islamic parties to participate and they held massive rallies and won elections for the first time in Pakistan's history. Another cause often contributed to the ballot victories of the Islamic fundamentalist parties is the anti-Americanism that was rampant in many quarters of Pakistan following the U.S. bombardment of Afghanistan. Musharraf went so far as to allow an Islamic militant who was in jail to contest an election, and he won. The balance of power between intellectuals like Dr. Halepota and the Islamizing forces of Pakistani society, after the election of 2002 shifted dramatically to the politicized clerics.

Dr. Halepota blamed the rise of fundamentalism in part on the "poor quality of formal education and lack of knowledge about the true nature of Islam, which is tolerance, equality, and justice." He mentioned Shah Latif Bitai, the famous Sindhi poet, as a "good example of someone who studied the Quran and found profound awareness." Dr. Halepota, added, "If only today's Mullahs were able to understand!"

Of particular interest in this regard is a conversation I had with a Sindhi family at their home outside a village in Larkana District, in February 2000. I was told by a middle-aged farmer that these days they are "afraid to go to the mosque," they may be killed, "shot in the back while praying." They are afraid "NOT to go to the mosque," they may be killed for not being outwardly orthodox. He told me "ten years ago people went to the mosque when they wanted to, Eid, Ramzan, Jamaah, but no one forced you to go." He added, "Now Mullahs from Panjab, trained by the Taliban, have come to our village and built a madrassah next to the mosque. Three boys from the village have gone to fight in Kashmir and Chechnya." He added that when the boys leave the madrassah, "Some of them have become quite intolerant. Sindhis have never been intolerant." He lamented, "We never had this situation before, we have always been Sindhi Muslims, now we have to fake our religiosity just to protect our lives. At home, we sing Shah Latif couplets, we are Sufis." Indeed his children chanted some poems written by the famous Sindhi mystic, Shah Latif of Bhit. This gentleman-farmer in Larkana district, who lives with his four brothers and their wives and children in a long serai-type rustic mud home with a thatched roof confided, "our names are Muslim but our chromosomes are Buddhist." He laughed and said that he wouldn't have said that "in the presence of a Pakistani," whom he equates with Panjabis. He didn't consider himself to be "Pakistani," he thinks of himself as a Sindhi. Nor did he think of himself as strictly Muslim, he was a Sufi. However he did say that he had to "hide his real identity" or he would endanger his life, family, and property. There is an intense fear among many people in Pakistan, not just the Westernized middle class, that the Taliban is coming to town. In some places, their arrival is past tense.

Dr. Halepota explained that Sufism, a philosophy familiar to Pakistanis, could help them deal with the turmoil of their nation-state,

> Sufi tradition has been outside the power of kings, Sufism is extremely powerful and traditional wisdom springs from it. It has saved this nation from extreme ideological confusion. Yet, we don't find different Islam in our textbooks. However, the Sufi tradition is deeply embedded in the culture—it is what designs the psyche of the people, the true intellectual and spiritual foundations of the people. Transplants from outside and above do find some place in the intellectual and environmental framework and they do disturb and confuse. But deep down still there are the Sufi tradition, philosophy, and belief system, which would dictate their lives. Sufis don't actively convert, people are attracted to them—there is no fixed set way of Sufism. The historical reality of the land is now at loggerheads with the structural political reality created by the establishment and dictated from above. I have no doubt who will win. History cannot be stopped—the inexorable source of history is relentless, it can't be stopped.

Though the electorate never supported the religious parties until the last election, conservative clerics had gradually exercised an increasingly coercive psychological influence on society. For years the narratives and symbols of the nation have been pushed along this ever-narrowing path. Non-Muslim cultural influences are often blamed for regional allegiances, such as in this discussion in Dr. Mohammed Sarwar's *Pakistani Studies* book,

> At present a particular segment, in the guise of modernization and progressive activity, has taken the unholy task of damaging our cultural heritage. Certain elements aim at the promotion of cultures with the intention to enhance regionalism and provincialism and thereby damage national integration.

Progressive forces and regional cultural affinities are deemed anti-Pakistani and thereby inherently anti-Islamic. The same stance is consistently used when describing the emergence of Bengali irredentism. The Sarwar textbook states "It is in the interest of national solidarity that such aspects of culture should be promoted as reflect affinity among the people of the provinces." This type of discourse denies the impetus and urges of the cultural expressions of the Sindhis, the Pathans, and the Balouchis, instead of valuing them as part of the multicultural whole. Regional cultural tendencies are seen as a threat to the nation, and Islam is employed to ameliorate these dangerously fissiparous ethnic differences.

India has faired somewhat better on the question of subnationalism and through a stable democratic system has achieved a wider degree of integration among diverse cultural groups. However, the topic of religion has consistently caused dilemmas not only for secular or Marxist scholars but also for Hinducentric and Indian Nationalist intellectuals as well. Not all textbooks in India are based on the Nehruvian model of secular socialism. The older, now discontinued textbooks sponsored by NCERT can be contrasted to those published by historians associated with the Indian History and Culture Society (IHCS) who are critical of the NCERT series. IHCS textbooks often include statements such as "the Muslim rule was a period of unmitigated suffering and misery."[56]

In general, historians, such as Romila Thapar, Bipin Chandra, or R. S. Sharma who have long been associated with NCERT textbooks, write from a decidedly noncommunal perspective, preferring to disentangle their historical analyses from religious elements. Other Indian historians are not always free from certain assertions which may appear to be communal in that religion is seen as one of the dominate motivating forces in Subcontinental power relations. The well-known historian, R.C. Majumdar, who began his illustrious career at Dhaka University prior to the partition of the Subcontinent, teaches that religion was an essential element in the composition of India's past and that Hindus and Muslims had always constituted separate communities.[57] In his book, *Glimpses of Bengal in the Nineteenth Century*, Majumdar emphasizes the sharp divide that characterized interreligious relationships.

> A fundamental and basic difference between the two communities was apparent even to the casual observer. Religious and social ideas and institutions counted for more in men's lives in those days than anything else; and in these two respects the two differed as poles asunder.[58] ... It is a strange phenomenon that although the Muslims and Hindus had lived together in Bengal for nearly six hundred years, the average people of each community knew so little of the other's traditions.[59]

These obvious disparities in historical interpretation bring into question the rationale for organizing Area Studies in the United States that focus on South Asia. It also makes the writing of World History textbooks challenging. Was communalism a colonial construct or did Hindus and Muslims always constitute separate communities? This is not a question that can be answered by a closer examination of primary documents. It is a matter of definition.

Stitching Caps and Staging Coups

Of immediate interest in Pakistani textbooks are justifications that condone and even welcome the military's involvement in politics. General Zia-ul Haq, who overthrew Z. A. Bhutto's unpopular but democratically elected regime in 1977, is eulogized because he "took concrete steps in the direction of Islamization," even though he usurped the political process and suspended civilian rule for eleven years. Pakistani textbooks tend to describe martial law as inevitable, stimulated by the rise of "un-Islamic forces" and "corrupt bureaucrats." This same nonchalance toward military coups was evident in the lukewarm reception that greeted General Parvez Musharraf in October 1999, when he overthrew Nawaz Sharif's corrupt elected government. In textbooks, the period of General Ayub Khan, the first military ruler, is described as a necessary alternative to the threat of secular Western values,

> The political leadership did not come up to the expectations and lacked commitment to Islamic objectives. . . . Bureaucratic elite had Western orientation with secular approach to all national issues . . . the result was political instability and chaos paving the way for the intervention of military and the imposition of Martial Law.[60]

The next statement reveals the power of the clergy behind the curriculum committee when the textbook accuses Ayub Khan of imposing "un-Islamic family laws" meant to guarantee equal legal protection for women. The textbook asserts that Ayub's "secular" outlook ultimately brought about his decline. General Zia-ul Haq on the other hand, described as simple and sincere, "patronized religious institutions" and is praised for his efforts toward the Islamization of Pakistani society.

In social studies textbooks there is no mention of important court cases, such as Tamizuddin's legal challenge to the first coup or the mass Movement to Restore Democracy (MRD) at the end of Zia's reign. With little discussion of civil society and less about the destruction of the constitution by the military, Pakistani textbooks often substitute historical analyses for polemics about an idealized Islamic nation.[61] Since there is no consensus on the actual form of an Islamic state, contradictions inherent in the textbooks can cause confusion leading to hostile expressions of nationalism, religious fundamentalism, and/or political disenchantment.

During the past two decades, the Pakistani military has helped to empower a vast cadre of politically motivated, religiously conservative Mujahideen, evidenced by the accelerating crisis in Kashmir, the war like situation in Kargil, airplane hijackings, and the Talebanization of madrassah[62] education, culminating in the recent election of Islamist parties. This continuing move toward Islamization is accentuated against the ominous backdrop of nuclear testing, missile development, failed diplomacy, and sporadic tit-for-tat acrimonious exchanges between India and Pakistan. The social studies curriculum in Pakistan employs a very narrow definition of Islam in the construction of Pakistani nationalism.

Islamization is a controversial term with a variety of interpretations. There are subtle distinctions among usages of words such as Islamization, Islamic nationalism, Islamic Republic, and Islamizing, that represent the manipulation and implementation of religious terminology and symbols as political tools. Both Maududi of the *Jaamat-i-Islami* and Ayatollah Khomeini of Iran saw Islamization as a model for the worldwide community of Islamic Ummah, distinct from Islamic nationalism, which is "essentially a Western, non-Islamic, secular, and territorial concept that emphasizes patriotism and love of one's nation-state, its sacred territory, political institutions and symbols."[63] A more thoroughly Islamized Pakistan, which would finally fulfill the true Shariat-ruled mandate inherent in the creation of an Islamic Republic was how General Zia constructed the meaning of his Islamization campaign, which he propagated and popularized as the inevitable evolution of Pakistani nationalism. Zia institutionalized a kind of paranoia about parading Islamic symbols, which were seen as essential for the survival of the nation-state. Unfortunately some of the strategies that Zia and his fundamentalist mullah supporters appropriated and propagated were based on narrow, medieval interpretations of Islam, which resulted in gender-biased attitudes and policies and militarized exhortations to take up arms for the sake of jihad.

The Ideology of Pakistan is based on Islamic nationalism. Islamization is what Zia called it, but not coincidentally. He was consciously pushing for stricter adherence to external expressions of religion—placating the conservative forces, exerting social control, influencing social norms. Pakistan's ideology of "Islamic nationalism," though an oxymoron according to Maududi, still has a dynamic and powerful hold over the overwhelming majority of Pakistanis. Professor Mir Zohair Husain wrote in a personal communication,

> Just because Zia used the word "Islamization" time and again, doesn't mean that he was successful in his so-called "Islamization" of Pakistani political and economic institutions. While Pakistan's governing elite may have been relatively liberal, pragmatic and secular, the majority of Pakistanis were always devout Muslims, and Pakistani culture was always "Islamic" [and] thus didn't need any further "Islamizing." If Zia's so-called "Islamization" of Pakistani society had actually occurred, Pakistanis would never have elected two relatively liberal, pragmatic, and secular Muslims to run Pakistan four times in 11 years in free and fair elections based on adult franchise—Benazir Bhutto (1988–1990, 1993–1996) and Nawaz Sharif (1990–1993, 1996–1999). General Pervez Musharraf, who usurped power on October 12th, 1999, is also a liberal and pragmatic Muslim, who has said that he admired Mustafa Kemal Ataturk of Turkey [who] is denounced by devout Muslims all over the world for being a secular dictator who tried to Westernize Turkey. Quaid-e-Azam Muhammad Ali Jinnah was not "actually working to establish an Islamic-dominated state." A "Muslim-led government" is by no means the same thing as an "Islamic-dominated state!" Most governments in the Muslim world are led by Muslims, but they are not Islamic regimes based on the Islamic Shariah (like Iran or Afghanistan).

Professor Husain's observation, contrasting the elites with the more "Islamized common" people highlights the irony of Zia's efforts that were in a sense redundant. Though this impetus to Islamize the outward manifestations of social and political institutions was itself a reflection of a worldwide movement toward religious conservatism and fundamentalism within the Islamic community, in real terms, the results of twenty years of Zia's Islamization indoctrination program has given rise to more women in burkas, a generation of Pakistani girls prevented by social conventions from riding bicycles, and militant mullahs preaching political jihad from their Friday pulpits. Though certainly, these expressions are part of the international trend among Muslims toward religious conservatism, Zia latched on to that and used it.

With hyperbole and political and social coercion, the Islamization of Pakistan initiated during the 1980s brought an end to the liberal secular ambience of the 1960s and 1970s, inherited from the sophisticated and educated father of the nation, Quaid-e-Azam, when some ladies still wore saris to weddings and elbow-length sleeves were the norm in a hot climate, and girls still rode bicycles to the market. Middle-aged Pakistani women remember when hijab and traditional headgear was an anomaly, especially flapping dangerously on the back of a motor scooter. Men in Pakistan have also adopted more Islamic expressions in their outward attire.

Prior to the pressures exerted by Zia to Islamize all facets of society, Pakistani men who sported long beards and short pants could be seen on their way to pray at the Mosque, they were respected as either sincere Tabliqi practitioners or elderly gentlemen who had performed Haj. Now, as a friend in Sindh told me, "Most of the men who dress up as mullahs are quacks and crackpots. Every dacoit, shopkeeper, middle class businessman, and rickshaw wala wants to look like a mullah." He added, "Twenty or thirty years ago Pakistani men were not judged by the length of their pants or their beards." Once social and political conventions become codified by conservative religious dictates, it is extremely difficult to break or oppose those newly imposed norms that quickly become sacrosanct and in fact, required of "true believers." External expressions of Islamization, such as traditional Muslim fashion—beards and caps for males, burkas, purdah, or at least long-sleeved clothing for females—are also potent symbols of patriotism, proving one's personal commitment to the Ideology of Pakistani.

Hegemonic Hindustan: Pakistan's Significant Other

In Pakistan, most educational reforms and curriculum policies have been politically and religiously driven, pedagogy being secondary. Denial and erasure are the primary tools of historiography as it is officially practiced in Pakistan. There is little room in the official historical narrative for questions or alternative points of view. *Nazariya Pakistan*, or the Ideology of Pakistan, is devoted to a mono-perspectival religious orientation. There is no other correct way to read the historical record. It is, after all, a capital crime[64] to talk against the ideology of Pakistan.[65] "What is important in the exercise is the faithful transmission, without any criticism or reevaluation, of the particular view of the past which is implicit in the coming to fruition of the 'Pakistan Ideology.'"[66] Rahat Saeed of the Irtiqa Institute of Social Sciences in Karachi explained that school-level history teachers are often aware that what they are teaching in their Pakistan Studies classes is at best contradictory and often quite incorrect. They usually do not attempt to explain "the 'real' history regarding such events as the civil war in 1971, because to do so might jeopardize their jobs," and, as Rahat explains, the teachers are afraid to "corrupt their students with the truth."[67]

As mentioned, in Pakistani textbooks the historical narrative is based on the Two-Nation Theory beginning with the advent of Islam in South Asia, when Mohammed-bin-Qasim arrived in Sindh followed by Mahmud Ghaznavi riding through the Khyber Pass, sixteen times, bringing the Light of Islam to the infidels who "converted en mass" to escape the "evil domination" of the "cruel Brahmins." Reviewing a selection of textbooks published since 1972 in Pakistan will verify the assumption that there are little or no discussions of the ancient cultures that flowered in the land that is now Pakistan, such as Taxila and Mohenjo-Daro. Any mention of Hinduism is inevitably accompanied by derogatory critiques, and none of the greatness of Indic civilization is considered—not even the success of Chandragupta Gupta Maurya, who defeated, or at least frightened the invading army of Alexander the Great at the banks of the Beas River where it flows through the land that is now called Pakistan. These events are deemed meaningless since they are not about Muslim heroes. There is an elision in time between the moment Islam first arrived in Sindh in 712 and the birth of Pakistan on August 14, 1947.

Exclusivist ideologically driven historiography in contemporary Pakistan gives free reign to communal tirades replete with phrases such as "diabolical Hindus" and "Hindu conspiracies." India, as a Hindu-dominated political entity, is a hegemonic threat to Pakistani national sovereignty, whereas Hinduism, as a pseudoreligion, is an effeminate farce, incapable of surviving any interaction with Islam. The contradiction of such a convoluted stance is lost to the propagandist.

This blinkered approach to history was not always the case. Up until 1972, the textbooks had included much more elaborate sections on the history of the Subcontinent, while adopting the colonial frame of periodization—the books described the Hindu Period, the Muslim Period, and the British Period. History textbooks, such as *Indo Pak History, Part 1* published in 1951, included chapters such as "Ramayana and Mahabharata Era," "Aryan Religion and Educational Literature," "Caste System," "Jainism and Buddhism," "Invasions of Iranians and Greeks," "Chandra Gupta Maurya," "Maharaja Ashok," "Maharaja Kaniska," "The Gupta Family," "Maharaja Harish," "New Era of Hinduism," "The Era of Rajputs." Regardless of the tone employed to narrate South Asian history, whether negative or positive, importantly, it was included in the textbooks as relevant to Pakistan's past.

This South Asian orientation was prevalent until after the breakup of the country in 1971. These early textbooks quite naturally also included numerous chapters on the history of Islam beginning with the life of the Prophet (PBUH) and the rise of the Muslim Ummah, tracing Pakistani history from Mecca to Lahore. The many references to Indian kingdoms and traditions found in older Pakistani textbooks indicate that the social studies curriculum was not always estranged from South Asian history and culture. A textbook published in 1970, for use at a military academy in Kakul, had a chapter titled, "Mahatma Gandhi, Man of Peace," which tells the students that Gandhi died for Pakistan, since he had been killed by a Hindu radical who thought he had betrayed India by permitting the creation of Pakistan. The textbook states that after Partition, Gandhi insisted that Pakistan be given its fair share of the exchequer. Since he was assassinated by a Hindu who was bitter about the communally adjudicated bifurcation of the country, Pakistani textbooks could claim that "Gandhi died for Pakistan."[68]

Beginning with Zulfikar Ali Bhutto and accelerating under the Islamized tutelage of General Zia-ul Haq, not only has all non-Islamic history of the Subcontinent been discarded, but it has been vilified and mocked and transformed into the evil other, a measure of what Pakistan is not. Z. A. Bhutto's influence on the textbooks was profound—he blamed India for the breakup of the country. Though his mother was a Hindu, he vehemently launched an anti-Indian campaign with vituperative anti-Hindu rhetoric, swearing that his countrymen would "eat grass" in order to compete with India's nuclear program and vowing to fight a "thousand years war" for Kashmir. Politically weak, he needed to play the hate-the-Hindus-card to shore up his popularity. The legacy of this orchestrated hatred is still the basis of Pakistani historical narratives where Gandhi, regardless of his contribution to the decolonization of the Subcontinent, is now only referred to as a "conniving bania"[69] and certainly never called Mahatma. In fact, in today's Pakistani social studies narratives, the colonial enemy was not the British, but the Hindus.

Z. A. Bhutto, in a precarious political position, governing a drastically diminished territory, strove to win the support of the religious sectors of the population and had the textbooks altered to placate these factions. An integrated Pakistan, one strong Islamic nation that could overcome separatist movements and prevent another splitting such as the creation of Bangladesh, was the mandate. To appease the conservative clerics, such policies as the declaration that Ahamadis[70] were "non-Muslims" were enacted under Bhutto. Textbooks laid even greater stress on the Islamic perspective of historical events. Islamiyat was made a required subject up until grade eight. The use of the phrase, Ideology of Pakistan had already been inserted into social studies textbooks during Bhutto's first term, and as mentioned previously, pre-Islamic South Asian history was obliterated. Despite all this, Bhutto gets very little credit for Islamization, one textbook calling his efforts "too little, too late."

The military coup that ended Bhutto's second term and eventually his life, brought his protégé General Zia-ul Haq to power. Islamization began in full measure. Non-Muslims, such as Hindus in rural Sindh, were stripped of many of their rights and made to vote in separate electorates. Blasphemy laws were often used selectively against non-Muslims. The phrase, Ideology of Pakistan, was installed with vigor and the textbooks were rewritten by committee to reassert the Islamic orientations of Pakistani nationalism, according to General Zia's sociopolitical decrees. It has now been over a decade since Zia was assassinated yet, the textbooks he caused to be authorized have survived four democratically elected governments, and the propagandistic tone of the historical narrative is still taught as absolute truth to the youth of Pakistan. Zia is depicted as benevolent and religious-minded, a discourse that remains in the textbooks published through the 1990s during the two tenures of his protégé, Nawaz Sharif. Benazir Bhutto was too preoccupied with remaining in power to concern herself about the revision of curriculum, even concerning the dismal representation of her father in textbooks. Once a historical character or event is divinely sanctioned and anointed with religious significance, altering that discourse is difficult, almost apostasy.

From their government-issued textbooks, students are taught that Hindus are backwards, superstitious, they burn their widows and wives, and that Brahmins are inherently cruel, and if given a chance, would assert their power over the weak, especially Muslims and Shuddras, depriving them of education by pouring molten lead in their ears.[71] In their social studies classes, students are taught that Islam brought peace, equality, and justice to the Subcontinent and only through Islam could the sinister ways of Hindus be held in check. In Pakistani textbooks "Hindu" rarely appears in a sentence without adjectives such as politically astute, sly, or manipulative.

The Goal: Complete Islamization

Discourses about Islam and its relationship to the Ideology of Pakistan comprise the majority of *Pakistani Studies* textbooks that delve at length on how Islam can create a fair and just nation,

> In the eyes of a Muslim all human beings are equal and there is no distinction based on race or colour. . . . The rich or poor [are] all equal before law. A virtuous and pious man has precedence over others before Allah.[72]

This *Pakistani Studies* textbook goes on to say, "Namaz [prayer] prevents a Muslim from indulging in immoral and indecent acts." And regarding issues of justice, the 1999 edition of this Pakistan Studies textbook, which is in wide usage in Pakistan states,

> On official level (sic) all the officers and officials must perform their duties justly, i.e., they should be honest, impartial and devoted. They should keep in view betterment of common people and should not act in a manner, which may infringe the rights of others or may cause inconvenience to others.

How does this discourse tally with the tales that the students have heard about corruption and the hassles their parents have endured simply to pay a bill or collect a refund? Several students in Pakistan complained that they felt cheated and pessimistic when they read these things. They were angry because they could not rectify their cognitive dissonance of what they hear about elected officials and wealthy landholders and industrialists buying off court cases lodged against them or simply not charged for known crimes, with statements from their textbooks such as,

> Every one should be equal before law and the law should be applied without any distinction or discrimination. . . . Islam does not approve that certain individuals may be considered above law.

A textbook published by the Punjab Textbook Board states, "The Holy Prophet (PBUH) says that a nation which deviates from justice *invites its doom and destruction*" (emphasis added).[73] With such a huge disparity between the ideal and the real, there is a great deal of fatalism apparent among the educated citizens and the school-going youths concerning the state of the nation in Pakistan. Further compounding the students' distress and distancing them from either their religion or their nation-state, or both, are contradictory statements made in this *Pakistani Studies* book that "the enforcement of Islamic principles. does not approve dictatorship or the rule of man over man." Compared with the reality unfolding a few paragraphs later when the student is told uncritically that,

> General Muhammad Ayub Khan captured power and abrogated the constitution of 1956 . . . dissolved the assemblies and ran the affairs of the country under Martial Law without any constitution.[74]

In Muhammad, Sarwar's *Pakistani Studies* a whole chapter is dedicated to "Islamization of Pakistan" with subtitles, "Islamization under Zia," "Hindrances to Islamization," and "Complete Islamization Is Our Goal." Other themes and events in the history and culture of Pakistan are judged vis-à-vis their relationship and support of complete Islamization. Within this rhetoric are found dire warnings that Islam should be applied severely so that it can guard against degenerate Western influences, yet a few pages later the text encourages the students to embrace Western technological innovations in order to modernize the country. One part of the book complains that Muslims in British India lost out on economic opportunities because conservative religious forces rejected Western education yet a few pages later the authors are telling the students to use Islam to fend off the influences of Western education, eulogizing the efforts of conservative clerics who are the last hope of preventing the degeneration of the country through their desire to implement the Sharia Law. This seems to be schizophrenic reasoning, but may reflect the inherent contradiction of British pedagogical constructs underlying and undermining postcolonial Islamized interpretations.

The Sarwar textbook claims that Islam sees no differences and promotes unity among peoples while it also discriminates between Muslims and nonbelievers. On page 120 the author states,

> The Islamic state, of course, discriminates between Muslim citizens and religious minorities and preserves their separate entity. Islam does not conceal the realities in the guise of artificialities or hypocrisy. By recognizing their distinct entity, Islamic state affords better protection to its religious minorities. Despite the fact that the role of certain religious minorities, especially the Hindus in East Pakistan, had not been praiseworthy, Pakistan ensured full protection to their rights under the Constitution. Rather the Hindu Community enjoyed privileged position in East Pakistan by virtue of its effective control over the economy and the media. It is to be noted that the Hindu representatives in the 1st Constituent Assembly of Pakistan employed delaying tactics in Constitution-making.

That this claim is exaggerated can be seen in the recent book by Allen McGrath, *The Destruction of Democracy in Pakistan*, in which the author, a lawyer, analyzes the efforts at constitution making in the first decade after independence before Iskandar Mizra dissolved the National Assembly. In the McGrath book the productive role D. N. Dutt, a Hindu from East Pakistan played in constitution making is mentioned. Yet, in *Pakistani Studies* textbooks, anti-Hindu rhetoric, and the vilification of the Hindu community of East Pakistan are the standard fare.

In this particular version of Pakistani history, which is the official version, General Zia-ul Haq is praised as someone who "took concrete steps in the direction of Islamization." He is often portrayed as very pious and perhaps stitching caps alongside Aurangzeb. Though Zulfikar Ali Bhutto is generally criticized in the textbooks, General Zia escapes most criticism though he was the most autocratic of the four military rulers who have usurped the political process in Pakistan. Each time that martial law was declared in Pakistan, and the constitution aborted, placed in abeyance, or otherwise raped, textbooks describe it as a necessary repercussion responding to the rise of decadent secular values. Dr. Sarwar's textbook describes martial law as an inevitable solution stimulated by un-Islamic forces,

> During the period under Zia's regime, social life developed a leaning towards simplicity. Due respect and reverence to religious people was accorded. The government patronized the religious institutions and liberally donated funds.[75]

This textbook and many like it, claim that there is a "network of conspiracies and intrigues" which is threatening the "Muslim world in the guise of elimination of militancy and fundamentalism." In this treatment Pakistan, under the guidance of General Zia, takes credit for the fall of the Soviet Union and lays claim to have created a situation in the modern world where Islamic revolutions can flourish and the vacuum left by the fall of the USSR will "be filled by the world of Islam." Sarwar continues, "The Western world has full perception of this phenomena, [which] accounts for the development of reactionary trends in that civilization." Concluding this section under the subheading "Global Changes," the author seems to be preparing for Samuel Huntington's *Clash of Civilizations* when he writes,

> The Muslim world has full capabilities to face the Western challenges provided Muslims are equipped with self-awareness and channelize their collective efforts for the well-being of the Muslim Ummah. All evidences substantiate Muslim optimism indicating that the next century will glorify Islamic revolution with Pakistan performing a pivotal role.[76]

Pakistani Studies textbooks are full of inherent contradictions. On one page the text brags about the modern banking system and on another page complains that interest, *riba*, is unIslamic. There is also a certain amount of self-loathing written into the *Pakistani Studies* textbooks, the politicians are depicted as inept and corrupt and the industrialists are described as pursuing "personal benefit even at the cost of national interest."

Bouncing between the poles of conspiracy theory and threat from within, the textbooks portray Pakistan as a victim of Western ideological hegemony, threatened by the perpetual Machiavellian intentions of India's military and espionage machine, together with the internal failure of its politicians to effectively govern the country, coupled with the fact that the economy is in the hands of a totally corrupt class of elite business interests who have only enriched themselves at the cost of the development of the nation. Ironically, in textbooks intended to create patriotism and pride in the nation, the country is ridiculed and despised. All of these failures of the state and internal and international conspiracies could, according to the rhetoric in the textbooks, be countered by the application of more strictly Islamic practices. In July 1999, I spoke to several well-placed individuals who told me that they would welcome a Taliban-type government in Pakistan so that the country could "finally achieve its birth-right as a truly Islamic, corruption-free nation." This is certainly not a majority opinion among the middle classes, however there is a large segment of society who thinks along these lines and they cast their votes in the October 2002 elections.

Most of the intellectuals I have met in Pakistan are alarmed about the "Talibanization of the nation." I was told time and again "the CIA created the Taliban Frankenstein in Pakistan's backyard, then walked away, leaving the monster behind." Some Pakistanis, inspired by the politicized sermons of Mullah elites, vociferously call for a "Taliban-type system" and are willing to die to Islamize the nation. This may be especially true among the poor, whose only access to education is in a crowded madrassa where they learn that Sunni Islam is poised to take over the world of kafirs (nonbelievers) and apostates. These economically and emotionally deprived young men have been taught that a Taliban-type system could overcome their poverty, their powerlessness, and despair. Caught between conspiracies, corruption, and the Holy Quran, they see no alternatives.

When textbooks and clerics cry conspiracy and the majority of newspapers, particularly the Urdu Press, misinform the people and sensationalize the issues, the tendency for Pakistanis to feel betrayed and persecuted is not surprising. During the 1971 war, newspapers in Pakistan told very little about the violent military crackdown in Dhaka nor did they keep the people informed of the deteriorating strategic situation. The role of the *Mukti Bahini*[77] was practically unknown in the western wing of the country, and when defeat finally came, it was a devastating and unexpected shock that could only be explained by the treachery of Indira Gandhi, who is often quoted as saying, "We have sunk the Two-Nation Theory in the Bay of Bengal." India remains a hyperbolic threat to Pakistan's existence.

In the thirty years since the "fall of Dhaka" the government-controlled curriculum still does not include a historically circumspect version of the causes of the civil war that dismembered the nation. It is no wonder that during and in the aftermath of the Kargil crisis in the summer of 1999, newspapers often ran stories referring to the occupation of the heights above Kargil as "revenge for 1971." There is a chronic shortage of objective information available to the majority of Pakistani citizens that can adequately explain the actual events that led to the three wars with India. Kashmir in 1948, the war with India in 1965, and the Bangladesh War of Independence have become national metaphors[78] for betrayal within and a reminder of the constant threat looming from Hindu India. The split-up of the nation and the creation of Bangladesh remains a potent symbol of Pakistan's disempowerment and a constant reminder of what will happen if the Muslim Ummah does not remain vigilant.

During the warlike situation in the summer of 1999 at the Line of Control near Kargil, the Pakistani government claimed that the Mujahideen were not physically supported by Pakistan, that they were indigenous Kashmiri freedom fighters. However, the presence of satellite television, the internet, and newspapers, which are now, more connected to international media sources, offered the possibility of broader exposure than during the two previous wars fought over Kashmir. Perhaps there is at least one positive outcome of the tragic Kargil crisis where hundreds of young men lost their lives; in the aftermath there was an outpouring of newspaper and magazine articles in Pakistan that attempted to analyze the brinkmanship from various angles. Such critical reflexivity is essential in a civil society. Although some of the essays in Pakistani newspapers prophetically called for the military to take over the government in the wake of Nawaz Sharif's sell out to the imperialist Clinton, which of course happened the following year, most of the discussions were more circumspect and many authors looked at the Kargil debacle through a lens of history, trying to understand the cause of Pakistan's repeated failures arising from military brinkmanship. Many of the observations made after Kargil, such as the inadequacy of Pakistan's international diplomatic missions, are interestingly, also cited in *Pakistani Studies* textbooks regarding India's perceived manipulation of world opinion during the 1971 war and Pakistan's inability to counter it.

Pakistani textbooks are particularly prone to historical narratives manipulated by omission, according to Avril Powell, professor of history at the University of London. History by erasure can have its long-term negative repercussions. Another example of this is the manner in which the Indo-Pak War of 1965 is discussed in Pakistani textbooks. In standard narrations of the 1965 war manufactured for students and the general public, there is no mention of Operation Gibraltar, even after four decades. In fact, several university-level history professors whom I interviewed claimed never to have heard of Operation Gibraltar and the repercussions of that ill-planned military adventurism which resulted in India's moves toward Lahore. In Pakistani textbooks the story is told that "the Indian army, unprovoked, inexplicably attacked Lahore" and that "one Pakistani jawan (soldier) equals ten Indian soldiers," who, upon seeing the fierce Pakistanis, "drop their banduks (rifles) and run away." Many people in Pakistan still think like this, and several mentioned this assumed cowardice of the Indian army in discussions with me while the fighting was raging in Kargil. The nation is elated by the valiant victories on the battlefield, as reported in the newspapers, then shocked and dismayed when their country is humiliated at the negotiating table. Because they were not fully informed about the adventurism of their military leaders, they can only feel betrayed that somehow Pakistani politicians once again "grabbed diplomatic defeat from the jaws of military victory."

Operation Gibraltar, the recent debacle in Kargil, and especially the tragic lessons that could have been learned from the Bangladesh War are products of the same myopic processes. The Kargil crisis was a legacy of the lack of information that citizens have had about the real history of their country. The Kashmiri conflict has left a trail of denied incursions and undeclared wars. In 1948 the Pakistani army took an active role in the military action in Kashmir, and numerous historical accounts, such as Hodson's *The Great Divide*, offer evidence that Jinnah was ready "to 'call the whole thing off' if 'India would withdraw' its forces."[79] In a letter to Mountbattan in late December 1948, Nehru wrote:

> the resources of Pakistan are being employed . . . [and] the invasion of Kashmir is not an accidental affair resulting from the fanaticism or exuberance of the tribesmen, but a well-organized business with the backing of the state.

Nehru added ominously, "The present objective is Kashmir. The next declared objective is Patiala, East Punjab and Delhi. 'On to Delhi' is the cry all over West Punjab."[80]

It is relevant to note in this context, an episode from a book by Akbar S. Ahmed in which he tells of a personal conversation in Dhaka with General Niazi, head of the Pakistani forces in East Bengal, who claimed that he was planning to "cross into India and march up the Ganges and capture Delhi and thus link up with Pakistan." General Niazi told Ahmed that "This will be the corridor that will link East with West Pakistan. It was a corridor that the Quaid-e-Azam demanded and I will obtain it by force of arms." This way of thinking can still be seen among those who were battling the Indian army in Kargil. In an interview published in *The News* in June 1999, a commander of one group of Mujahideen told the reporter that their plan was first to take "Kargil, then Srinagar, then march victorious into Delhi." In January 2001, an article in the Pakistani newspaper, the *DAWN*, in reference to the BJP's ceasefire in Kashmir and the bomb attack on the Red Fort in Delhi a few weeks earlier stated, "Mujahideen groups . . . have stepped up their armed campaign—stretching from the heart of the Indian capital to the heart of the matter, in Kashmir."

As exuberant Pashto tribesmen swarm over Delhi and sinister Hindus lay siege to Lahore, rumors and wild imaginings have far more power than what in reality is half a century of hostile stalemates. The social studies curriculum is just one vehicle through which Pakistan must manufacture adequate paranoia to sustain a passionate insecurity portraying South Asian Muslims as a beleaguered community in need of constant vigilance to retain its special identity. In this particularistic worldview, Muslims were denied their divine right to rule over the Indian Subcontinent and in the final analysis, the trusting Muslims were betrayed in the bargain, robbed of Kashmir and handed a "Moth-eaten Pakistan."

Pakistani textbooks have a particular problem when defining geographical space. The terms "South Asia" and "Subcontinent" have partially helped to solve this problem of the geohistorical identity of the area formally known as British India. However, it is quite difficult for Pakistani textbook writers to ignore the land now known as India when they discuss Islamic heroes and Muslim monuments in the Subcontinent. This reticence to recognize anything of importance in India, which is almost always referred to as "Bharat" in both English and Urdu versions of the textbooks, creates a difficult dilemma for historians writing about the Moghul Dynasties. It is interesting to note that M. A. Jinnah strongly protested the Congress's appropriation of the appellation "India," but his arguments were dismissed by Mountbattan. Because Pakistani textbook writers are constrained by the imperative to represent all facts and events in the historical record of South Asia so as to prove the inevitability of the Two-Nation Theory, there are, by necessity of this agenda, numerous misrepresentations. Geography also falls prey to this ideological orientation, as can be seen in this quote from one of the many textbooks titled, *Pakistani Studies,*

> During the 12th century the shape of Pakistan was more or less the same as it is today. . . . Under the Khiljis, Pakistan moved further south-ward to include a greater part of Central India and the Deccan. In retrospect it may be said that during the 16th century "Hindustan" disappeared and was completely absorbed in "Pakistan."[81]

That social studies textbooks in Pakistan have long been victimized by distorted politics can be seen by the following example. In 1953, prior to Ayub Khan's period, the second half of the seventh grade *Geography and Civics* textbook,[82] published by the West Pakistan Textbook Board, was devoted to a discussion of various political systems, and featured chapters titled "Democracy," "Theocracy," "Military Dictatorship," and "Federalism." In a subsequent edition of this seventh grade *Geography and Civics* textbook[83] published in 1962, four years after Ayub Khan's military government had taken control of the country, the discussions of comparative political systems had been eliminated, and instead, chapters such as "What It Means to Be a Good Pakistani," and "Standing in Queue" are included. Perceived political imperatives shaped by a pervasive distrust of the Pakistani people have motivated previous manipulations of the textbooks.

Another recent example of alterations made in textbooks to conform the narrative to the current political jargon can be seen by comparing two editions of the textbook *Pakistani Studies for Secondary Classes*, published by the Punjab Textbook Board. First, the 1997 edition states on page 206–7,

> India is very advanced in its nuclear energy programme and has performed an atomic test in 1974. To divert world attention from its nuclear plans, Bharat launched a propaganda campaign against Pakistan to the effect that Pakistan was manufacturing nuclear weapons. Pakistan categorically contradicted these baseless allegations and proposed that both the countries should adopt such limitations with mutual consent as may be acceptable at international level, putting an end to the possibility of proliferation of nuclear arms in South Asia. *Bharat is not prepared to accept any restriction in this respect and desires that Pakistan should give up its peaceful nuclear energy programme. Obviously this is an unrealistic demand.* (emphasis added)

After the nuclear tests in May of 1998, pages 206–7 of this textbook were changed in the 1999 imprint and the substituted comments added in a different font:

> India is very advanced in its nuclear energy programme and has performed an atomic test in 1974. To divert world attention from its nuclear plans, Bharat launched a propaganda campaign against Pakistan to the effect that Pakistan was manufacturing nuclear weapons. Pakistan categorically contradicted these baseless allegations and proposed non-proliferation of nuclear arms in South Asia. *On 11th, 13th May, 1998, India detonated five nuclear explosions and threatened the strategic and security balance in the region. Pakistan was com-*

pelled to respond in the same language and it conducted its six nuclear explosions on 28th and 30th May of 1998 at Chagi. (emphasis added)

The day following the nuclear tests, public servants in Pakistan, without their consent, were docked a day's pay to help offset the cost of exploding nuclear devices. Subsequently, Yome Takhbeer Day is celebrated in Pakistan on May 28. The revised curriculum guide suggests that school children draw posters and march in parades to mark the date of Pakistan's nuclearization.

If war begins in people's minds, as the UN Charter suggests, then our minds are prepared for war while we are students. By the time young people become policy-makers, the templates of hostility may be deeply embedded in their worldviews. Textbooks can teach students about international cooperation and respect for other cultures, or they can serve as a source of contentiousness—poisoning the diplomatic climate and heightening the chances of war. Notions of militarized nationalism inculcated through the curriculum subvert efforts at international cooperation thereby diminishing the inherent conflict management capacity in South Asia.

Kashmir: A Vehicle for the Creation and Transmission of Nationalism

India and Pakistan have fought three wars over Kashmir, embroiling them in a vicious cycle of armed hostilities persisting for over fifty years—the heated rhetoric increased dramatically during the last decade. Kashmir's strategic location and each nation's self-image of its own meaning and worth endow the Kashmir issue with tremendous political and religious symbolism. Kashmir is integral to the self-perceived notions of statehood for both nations.

Kashmir is tied to the ideals of India's founding fathers—that a modern nation should not be established on the basis of religion but on political and economic considerations. India knows very well the value of their Kashmiri real estate in both philosophical and monetary terms. Kashmir symbolizes India's Himalayan heaven—Shangri-la, idyllic houseboats surrounded by lotus blossoms on Dal Lake, yellow fields of flowering mustard seeds, purple fields of valuable saffron, towering snow peaks, the abode of Amarnath, the famous ice lingum. Kashmir is a scenic treasure, the crown of India. Kashimiriyat was a philosophy wherein Hindus and Muslims had lived together peacefully for centuries. Kashmir is symbolic of *Bharatvarsha*, the primordial land of the Hindus—a limb of the body of Mother India saved from Pakistani occupation during her dismemberment. Though tied to India through metaphor and memory, Kashmir is anchored in modern India's identity and territorial integrity in the twentieth-century context of the nation-state. It's also a matter of maps. Losing Kashmir would be the geographical equivalent of shaving off Mother India's beautiful hair, a custom practiced by widows, symbolizing loss and death.

For Pakistan, Kashmir is perhaps even more essential to its nationhood—the "K" in Pakistan *stands for Kashmir*. Without Kashmir, Pakistan's mandate remains unfulfilled, much less the pronunciation of its name, invented by Chaudhry Rehmat Ali, a student living in London during the 1930s.[84] Kashmir as a symbol is integral to the very meaning and existence of Pakistan. Even in the days of united Pakistan, before textbooks became virulently anti-Indian, they mourned the loss of the Valley of Kashmir and blamed a Mountbattan/Nehru conspiracy and a "toothless resolution from the United Nations Security Council" for the illegal occupation of territory that, according to the guidelines drawn up to partition British India, should "rightfully have acceded to Pakistan." The betrayals of Kashmir fit neatly into the historical narratives in which Pakistanis are portrayed as a beleaguered community, struggling against injustice.

In his newspaper article, Mushirul Hasan mocks the self-pitying tone with which many Pakistani historians write,

> With the debris of the constructive effort of centuries around them, the Muslims of the subcontinent stood alone. They were weak, disorganised, and backward, hardly equipped for a great struggle, standing on the crossroads of destiny without knowing in which direction safety lay and yet determined to fight for their right of existence and freedom.[85]

About many issues, Pakistanis may feel insecure, but they feel historically vindicated and politically justified vis-à-vis their position on Kashmir. As one young historian in Lahore told me, "Our position on Kashmir is perfect, flawless. Kashmir is a contiguous territory with a majority Muslim population, India is clearly the aggressor in Kashmir. Their position is not supported by international opinion or protocol." Many Pakistanis feel quite attached to the issue and very emotional about Kashmir. Many others think that Pakistan has squandered vast opportunities for economic, political, and educational development in the desire to liberate Srinagar. They feel cheated. There is a shared ominous realization that the Kashmir issue has brought militarized Islamic zealots into the society, even into areas of rural Sindh where Shah Latif's Sufi ballads shape the philosophies of the people. One Sindhi journalist told me, concerning the weaponization of religious groups in Pakistan, "the ISI[86] thought they could buy guns that only faced north."

In the 1953 *History of Indo-Pakistan Part II for Class VII* published in Urdu, Kashmir is only mentioned once in the textbook, without any reference to contemporary problems,

> Till the 14th century, Rajput Rajas ruled Kashmir. At the end of the century one of the ministers, Sikandar Mirza occupied it. The area had always been free. Sikandar and Sultan Zain-ul-Abidin were the famous kings of that area. In 1586, Akbar included Kashmir into his Empire.

Since most textbooks during the 1950s were based on British models which approached historical materials from a chronological perspective designed to include the long expanse of South Asian history beginning with Mohen-jo Daro and Aryan civilization, there were few passages in this early textbook dedicated to the justification of Pakistan's existence. The textbooks however gradually became more Islamized and nationalized, though not localized. The first manifestations of this were the commentaries about unequal distribution of resources and the violence of partition, typified by this excerpt from a 1962 social studies textbook for grade seven,

> Pakistan had to start every thing from the base, which caused many difficulties. Sectarian violence[87] was continuing. There was a flood of caravans of immigrants from India. India had taken over Kashmir by force. The economy of the nation was unstable.[88]

This is the early version of a rhetorical style that remains central to the narration of the nation found in the Pakistani social studies curriculum. During the last few decades, the themes of victimization and justification have been amplified in both textbooks and the popular media. Abandoning the struggle for Kashmir, for many Pakistanis, means forsaking the very meaning of their beloved nation. For a half century, propaganda about Kashmir has been produced by both the government-controlled sources of information and the independent press, images of the Indian army oppressing Kashmiris dominate the television news.

Omission of Transmission: The Emergence of Bangladesh

One of the more remarkable aspects of textbooks in Pakistan is their ability to completely eliminate cause and effect regarding the creation of Bangladesh. There is usually only a passing mention of the general elections called by Yahya Khan who is uniformly seen as a bad leader, a heavy drinking womanizer. There is nothing about the cancellation of the National Assembly, little about the military crackdown in Dhaka, and less about the misfortunes of the Pakistani Army. Bangladesh is blamed on Indian cunning and incipient Bengali irredentism.

"Eras and events deemed either irrelevant, hostile or inconvenient to the fulfillment of the Pakistan Movement are omitted." In contemporary Pakistan it is not surprising that the Vedic Age and the Gupta Age would not be emphasized, what is startling is "the complete omission from some textbooks of any reference to East Bengal [or East Pakistan] and the creation of Bangladesh."[89] When the civil war is mentioned, it is simply explained as a Hindu conspiracy, as in this extract from *An Introduction to Pakistani Studies*, published in 1999,

> Since independence, the leadership of East Pakistan has been in the hands of [separatists, who] in collaboration with the Hindu teachers, polluted the political air, and spread poisonous propaganda among the young students of East

Pakistan. Bangladesh, in fact, was the sequel of that poisonous propaganda which the separatist elements and pro-Hindu teachers had been spreading in the educational institutions of East Pakistan. [90]

In most *Pakistani Studies* textbooks there is usually no mention of the Six-Point Plan of the Awami League in East Pakistan, nor the cancellation of the national elections in 1971. This one short and ill-informed paragraph about the emergence of Bangladesh is all that Pakistani students learn from their textbooks about the breakup of East and West Pakistan. Students are told that India, the evil enemy, manipulated the East Pakistanis, enlisting their Hindu minority, and split the motherland by unprovoked military action. Ironically, though textbooks in Pakistan blame the breakup of the country on Hindus living in the eastern wing, Bangladeshi textbooks, and official narratives about the liberation war, do not even mention the contribution made by Hindus to the independence movement. Hindus are blamed in the Pakistani textbooks and ignored in the Bangladeshi version of events.

Many textbooks published under the title, *Pakistani Studies*, argue that ideology had been insufficiently infused into the citizens—this being the root cause of the "debacle of 1971." For example, the textbook, *Pakistani Studies* by Sarwar, published for students preparing for the B.A. and B.Com. exams, explains on page 14 that

Invariably, charismatic leadership swept the polls through their clever moves and techniques employed as election strategy. The political scene was characterized with the diffusion of alien ideologies, especially during the 1970s. As a result, Pakistan had to face the tragedy of the separation of its east wing. Secessionist tendencies could be overcome by tightening the grip of the ideological bond but it was not paid due heed.

Even in books purporting to be more objective and scholarly, such as, *Jinnah, Pakistan and Islamic Identity: The Search for Saladin*, the author though appearing to be sympathetic to the Bengalis and regretting the racism dealt out to them during their twenty-four years under West Pakistani domination, still does not mask his inherent bias, as can be seen in the following quote in which he relates a conversation he had with General Yaqub Khan, who summed up the situation he faced before the military crackdown

Pakistan is like a Ming vase, priceless, and delicate, he said. Mujib-ur-Rehman, leading the Bengali nationalist party the Awami League and later president of Bangladesh, is like a fly sitting on it. We have to smack the fly but make sure the vase does not break [said Yaqub]. Only a few months later his colleagues would use a hammer to swat the fly; they would smash the vase and the fly would be unharmed.

Bangladesh's most famous hero of the liberation struggle, Bongobandhu Sheikh Mujibur Rahman, the father of the nation, is unapologetically reduced to an insect in this purportedly sympathetic Pakistani account, circa 1997.

In the entire narrative as presented in *Search for Saladin*, there is only one passing mention of the general elections called by Yahya Khan, but nothing about the cancellation of the election results, nothing about Bhutto's political machinations. Akbar S. Ahmed ends his discussion of Bangladesh with numerous excerpts from newspapers about crime and violence in Dhaka and statements from Bengalis who complain about the Research and Analysis Wing (RAW) of the Indian intelligence agency influence and the failure of the state as if to say that the problems of East Pakistan were not solved by the creation of Bangladesh. Ironically, Bangladesh in some ways seems to fair even worse in Pakistani textbooks and historical discourses than does India, where at least there is a discussion, albeit, negative.

Bangladeshi textbooks not only fail to mention the contributions of "pro-Hindu teachers" in the creation of their country, but acknowledgment of India's military support was omitted from Bangladeshi textbooks after the 1975 assassination of Sheikh Mujibur Rahman. During the seventeen years of military rule, the role of the freedom fighters and their slogan, "Joy Bangla" (Long-live Bangladesh) was banned from the textbooks and popular media, replaced by "Bangladesh Zindabad," the Urdu translation. Unlike textbooks published immediately after the war which discussed political and economic exploitation and genocide in erstwhile East Pakistan, in textbooks published under the military regimes of Bangladesh, who were seeking to normalize relations with their Islamic neighbors, Pakistan is not mentioned explicitly as the enemy—references are simply to an anonymous "enemy army." Many Bangladeshis still harbor resentments against the Pakistani military, but there may be generations of young adults who are partially "unaware that Pakistan was actually 'the enemy,'" and may mistakenly believe that "the Bangladesh *army* fought the *Indian* army."[91] When Sheikh Hasina became prime minister in 1996, textbooks were again remodified to include the "Muktijudha" (Freedom Fighters) and the contributions of her father, Sheikh Mujib. When in October 2002, the Bangladesh Nationalist Party (BNP) returned Begum Khalida Zia to power, the additions made to textbooks during the six years of Awami government were immediately expunged. This brings to light the assertion that the rewriting of social studies textbooks is not particular to Pakistan, but rather a very common practice.

Concluding Comments: Investigating the Politics of Curriculum Reform

In the countries of the Subcontinent, as in most nations, education is viewed as the penultimate social panacea. Claims are ubiquitously made that if properly designed and regulated, education will solve the problems of society and save the nation from an accelerating descent down the road to ruin upon which the citizens, and especially the youth seem to be sliding. Such ideas drive the pervasive machine of educational reform. Education is far more than personal enrichment and skill development; it is the cure-all for a nation's economic and moral woes.

Politicians use education as a rallying cry. Curriculum committees are appointed to transform schools and the contents of textbooks, usually to modernize them and prepare students for the future, and sometimes to return to traditional values, saving the children from "degenerate cultural influences." Education policy may encourage social change or may conversely take the syllabus "back to the basics" to recapture the past glories of bygone eras or guarantee the status quo. These agendas may exist simultaneously, since social paradigms are constantly changing, driven by class conflict and social, religious, and economic cross-purposes. Unfortunately, if educational reform is based on narrow interpretations of religious dogma or the perpetuation of unequal power relations, the society can atrophy. If education can change a nation's ethos, if curriculum is designed toward basic human values that support individual human rights and international goodwill, it is more likely that the generations will prosper intellectually.

In today's Pakistan, I have met several educators, themselves raised on biased, myopic textbooks, but who now see the need to recast the underlying ideologically bound and moribund rhetoric. Before the 9/11 shift of focus in Pakistani society there was a movement on the progressive front and educators were meeting to discuss "Vision 2000," a curriculum review that in part was working to tone down the jihadi rhetoric in the *Pakistani Studies* textbooks. Now that the fundamentalists have gained political validation, these forward-looking education specialists may find less support for their efforts to develop textbooks, which place value on peace and international cooperation. Nonetheless, transforming the inherently belligerent orientation of Pakistani social sciences would contribute to the goal of constructively managing antagonisms in South Asia. A reevaluation and modification of curriculum policies and educational documents that perpetuate hostile paradigms may help to contribute to the conversation of reconciliation essential for conflict resolution and lasting peace, leading to increased prosperity in South Asia. On the other hand, representatives of the fundamentalist faction, that gained positions of power during Zia's time when Deeni-Madrassa schools were made equivalent with national universities, still occupy their positions, such as vice-chancellors and professors, explicitly involved in pedagogy and curriculum design, and in shaping the minds of the Pakistani youth. Now that the clerics have gained a level of political power that they have never before enjoyed, this standoff between the secular intellectuals and the religious forces that once seemed static and not easily resolved, may have tilted in the direction of fundamentalism. Earlier efforts among liberal scholars to rewrite Pakistani history from a less biased perspective will have to undoubtedly be abandoned until the political climate changes.

Investigations into the rhetoric of educational reform can offer constructive insights into curriculum policies through which nations transmit their aspirations for the future. Those seeking peace and justice need relevant information to deal with sources of conflict. Historical perspectives of educational policy can help to shine light on contemporary issues.

Nuclear testing and missile development in the Subcontinent have brought five decades of intermittent animosity and militarization into sharp focus. The expenses and instability associated with hostilities in South Asia have contributed to the economic deprivation of hundreds of millions of citizens. The need for mutual understanding calls for a broader investigation into the sources of antagonism, including the impact of educational policy in the creation of patriotic discourse and political culture.

Notes

1. Mushtaq, Najum, "Ideological Crossroads," *The New International*, June 10, 2001, www.jang-group.com/thenews/jun2001-daily/10-06-2001/oped/o3.htm.

2. "Islamization" is the word that is used in the English editions of *Pakistan Studies* textbooks and in UGC curriculum documents to describe the imperatives of Pakistani Islamic nationalism institutionalized under General Zia-ul-Haq. See also Tamara Sonn, *After "Fundamentalism": Distinguishing between Islamism and Political Islam*.

3. There is no value judgment in this. This is simply the way that social studies textbooks tend to be written within nation-states, any other approach, critical of the nation, would be condemned as traitorous and treacherous.

4. The phonetic spelling of the name of this large linguistic and cultural area that straddles the border between India and Pakistan is "Panjab" meaning "five waters." The British spelled it as "Punjab" which has been retained in most English language transliterations in Pakistan. Here I have used Panjab, unless "Punjab" appeared in the original.

5. Yvette Claire Rosser, "Is the Taliban Coming to Town?" *The Friday Times*, March 13, 2001, Lahore, Pakistan.

6. Known as ninth "standard" in Pakistan.

7. *University Grants Commission Directive* (Islamabad: Mutalliyah-i-Pakistan, Alama Iqbal Open University, 1983), xi.

8. Pervez Hoodbhoy and A. H. Nayyar, "Rewriting the History of Pakistan," in *Islam, Politics, and the State*, Asghar Khan, ed. (London: Zed Press, 1985), 164.

9. Hoodbhoy, "Rewriting the History of Pakistan," 165.

10. Hoodbhoy, "Rewriting the History of Pakistan," 176.

11. Satish Chandra, *Medieval India, A History Textbook for Class XI* (New Delhi: NCERT, 1990).

12. *Social Studies for Class VI* (Jamshoro: Sindh Textbooks Board, April 1997).

13. *Social Studies for Class VI*, Chapter 7.

14. Personal interviews in Sindh, July 1997.

15. This style of narrative is the norm in Pakistani textbooks dealing with bin-Qasim and Mahmud Ghaznavi.

16. This rhetoric is such a pervasive narrative tool in *Pakistan Studies* texts, that there is no need for multiple citations. An economic or nonreligious explanation is the exception in Pakistan.

17. *Our World, for Class IV* (Directorate of Education Punjab, New Curriculum, Malik Din Mohammad and Sons, no date), translated from Urdu by Zahra Jafri.

18. J. Husain, *The Illustrated History of Pakistan* (Karachi: OUP, 1981–1983), 26.

19. Chandra, *Medieval India*, 205.

20. Romila Thapar, *Medieval India: History Textbook for Class VII* (New Delhi: NCERT, 1988), 25–26.

21. Manoj Raghuvanshi the host of Zee Television's program, *Aap ki Adalat*, in *Eminent Historians*, Arun Shourie (New Delhi: HarperCollins 1998), 63.

22. From a personal interview, June 1997.

23. Avril Powell, "Perceptions of the South Asian Past: Ideology, Nationalism and School History Textbooks," in *The Transmission of Knowledge in South Asia, Essays in Education, Religion, History, and Politics*, Nigel Crook, ed. (Delhi: Oxford University Press, 1996), 217.

24. From an interview with a member of the RSS (Rashtriya Swayamsevak Sangh), Chennai, July 2000.

25. National Curriculum History Working Group, "Relationship of History to the Rest of the School Curriculum," *Final Report* (London, 1990), 183.

26. Powell, "Perceptions of the South Asian Past," 222.

27. Powell, "Perceptions of the South Asian Past," 205.

28. Thapar, *Medieval India*, 94.

29. Mubarak Ali (Khan), "Akbar in Pakistani Textbooks," in *Pioneer*, November 13, 1992, under the title, "Akbar in Pakistan: Historians Malign Him as Anti-Islam, Says Mubarak Ali," *ICHR*, New Delhi, October 15-17, 1992.

30. *Social Studies for Class VI* (Lahore: Punjab Textbook Board, 1996), 114.

31. *Pakistani Studies for Class IX–X* (Lahore: Punjab Textbook Board, 1997), 18.

32. *Pakistani Studies for Secondary Classes* (Lahore: Punjab Textbook Board, 1997).

33. Stanley A. Wolpert, *A New History of India,* 3rd ed. (New York: Oxford University Press, 1989), 125.

34. "Akbar" means "great" in Arabic, therefore "Akbar the Great" actually translates as "Great the Great."

35. M. Ikram Rabbani and Monawwar Ali Sayyid, *An Introduction to Pakistani Studies, for Intermediate/Senior Cambridge Classes* (Lahore: The Caravan Book House, 1992).

36. Mubarak Ali, "Akbar in Pakistani Textbooks," 2–3.

37. I. H. Qureshi, *The Muslim Community of the Indo-Pakistan Subcontinent (610–1947)* 2nd ed. (Karachi: The Bureau of Composition, Compilation and Translation, University of Karachi, 1977).

38. I. H. Qureshi, *Akbar, The Architect of the Mughul Empire* (Karachi: Ma'aaref, Ltd., 1978), 155.

39. Muhammad Hashim Khafi Khan, ca. 1663–ca. 1731. Khafi Khan's History of Alamgir: being an English translation of the relevant portions of Muntakhab al-lubab, with notes and an introduction (Karachi: 1975).

40. From a personal interview in New Delhi with K. S. Lal, a scholar of Medieval Indian history.

41. Mushirul Hasan, "The Historic Divide," *The Indian Express*, Saturday, February 20, 1999.

42. Hasan, "The Historic Divide."
43. M. A. Zafar, *Pakistani Studies for Secondary Education* (Lahore, 1986), 7.
44. Husain, *Illustrated History of Pakistan*, 105.
45. This 1975 version was the third edition of this textbook originally published in 1968: *Social Studies, History & Civics, Class VII*, 3rd ed. (Lahore: Punjab Textbook Board, February 1975, Circular # C-D/Education/65-54-1, March 9, 1968).
46. Lawrence Ziring, *Pakistan in the Twentieth Century: A Political History* (Karachi: Oxford University Press, 1997), 291–93.
47. Chandra, *Medieval* India, 151–2.
48. Powell, "Perceptions of the South Asian Past," 96.
49. Powell, "Perceptions of the South Asian Past," 219.
50. Powell, "Perceptions of the South Asian Past," 221.
51. From an interview in April 2000 with Balouchi historian, Prof. Agha Mir (Noori) Naseer Khan, in Quetta, Pakistan, who told me that "Balouchis are less fundamentalist than are Pathans and Afghans."
52. Ziring, *Pakistan in the Twentieth Century*, 163, 177. *West Pakistan As One Unit* (Karachi: Government of Pakistan, 1954).
53. Imtiaz Alam, "Of Punjabi and Punjabiyat," *The News International* (Pakistan), April 20, 2001.
54. Mahmud S. Ali, *The Fearful State* (London: Zed Press, 1993), 120.
55. Feroz Ahmed, *Ethnicity and Politics in Pakistan* (Karachi: Oxford University Press, 1998).
56. Quoted in Powell, "Perceptions of the South Asian Past," 223.
57. Ironically, this echoes the Pakistani version of historical interpretation and the inevitability of the Two-Nation Theory.
58. It has also been conversely argued that for centuries in Bengal, Hindus and Muslims had lived together quite seamlessly and continued to operate within the same social system. When the census of 1881 revealed a Muslim majority in Bengal, it came as a surprise to the colonial census takers and to the local inhabitants—Hindu and Muslim—because there had been a continuity of culture among the social groups, until forced by colonial classifications to declare their religious differences.
59. R. C. Majumdar, *Glimpses of Bengal in the Nineteenth Century* (Calcutta: Firma K. L. Mukhopadhyay, 1960), 5–6.
60. Muhammad Sarwar, *Pakistani Studies* (Lahore: Ilim Kitab Khana, 1997).
61. Hoodbhoy, "Rewriting the History of Pakistan," 166.
62. Religious schools attached to a masjid or mosque.
63. Thanks to Mir Zohair Husain, Department of Political Science, University of South Alabama, Mobile, for constructive comments regarding Zia's use of the term "Islamization."
64. Though General Zia enacted the law that made it illegal to criticize the Ideology of Pakistan, this crime was made a *capital offense* by Nawaz Sharif.
65. During Martial Law, one well-known case was lodged by the state against Jam Saqi, a Sindh nationalist who was accused of criticizing the Ideology of Pakistan. During the trial the prosecution witnesses could not agree on a definition of the term. Benazir Bhutto was a witness for the defense. Jam Saqi was acquitted.
66. Hoodbhoy, "Rewriting the History of Pakistan," 165.
67. From an interview, August 1999, Karachi.
68. Kh. A. Haye, *First Steps in Our History* (Lahore: Feroz Sons Ltd., 1971).
69. Refers to a Gujarati of the merchant class.

70. Ziring, *Pakistan in the Twentieth Century*, 477.
71. *Social Studies Grade VII* (Jamshoro: Sindh Textbook Board, 1997).
72. Rabbani, *Introduction to Pakistani Studies*, 3.
73. Hassan Askri Rizvi, Javed Iqbal, and Ghulam Abid Khan, *Pakistani Studies for Secondary Classes* (Qamer, Lahore: Punjab Textbook Board, 1999), 9–13.
74. Rizvi, *Pakistani Studies for Secondary Classes*, 65.
75. Sarwar, *Pakistani Studies*, 136.
76. Sarwar, *Pakistani Studies*, 146.
77. The Mukti Bahini (Liberation Army) were anti-Pakistani guerilla soldiers from East Bengal, supported and supplied by India. They spearheaded a nine-month civil war which began when Pakistani troops staged a military crackdown on March 26, 1971, and massacred thousands of Bengalis/East Pakistanis, including hundreds of students at Dhaka University. On December 16, 1971, Indian troops liberated Dhaka and the independent country of Bangladesh was created.
78. For example, a headline that ran in the Islamabad edition of the newspaper, *The News*, in June 1999, said, "Nawaz Sharif's Policies are Turning Sindh into Another Bangladesh."
79. H. V. Hodson, *The Great Divide, Britain-India-Pakistan* (Karachi: Oxford University Press, 1997), 459.
80. Hodson, *Great Divide*, 467.
81. M. A. Zafar, *Pakistani Studies for Secondary Education.* (Lahore: 1986), 4–7.
82. *Geography and Civics,Class VII* (Lahore: West Pakistan Textbook Board, 1953).
83. *Geography and Civics,Class VII* (Lahore: West Pakistan Textbook Board, 1962).
84. The name, Pakistan has two meanings: Pak = pure in Arabic + stan = land—"Land of the Pure." It is also an acronym: P = Pakhtun, A = Afghan, K = Kashmir, S = Sindh, and the "tan" stands for "Balouchistan." Bengal was not included.
85. Hasan, "The Historic Divide."
86. Pakistan's intelligence agency.
87. Sectarian in this context referring to Hindu/Muslim violence.
88. *Social Studies* (History Portion), seventh grade (Lahore, Pakistan: Education Department, 1st ed., February 1962).
89. Powell, "Perceptions of the South Asian Past," 222.
90. Rabbani, *Introduction to Pakistani Studies*, 319.
91. Based on interviews with Bangladeshi students.

Bibliography

Agadjanian, Alexander. "Revising Pandora's Gifts: Religious and National Identities in Post-Soviet Societies." *Europe-Asia Studies* 53, no. 3 (September 2001).

———. "The Public Religion in Russia and the Search for National Ideology." *Journal for the Scientific Study of Religion* 40, no. 3 (September 2001).

Agnivesh, S., and V. Thampu. "Islam and Modernity: The Contradiction of Holy Wars." *Statesman*, Calcutta, 6–7 December 2001.

Ahmed, Akbar S. *Islam Today: A Short Introduction to the Muslim World*. London: I. B. Tauris Publishers, 1998.

———. *Jinnah, Pakistan and Islamic Identity: The Search for Saladin*. Karachi: Oxford University Press, 1977.

Ahmed, Feroz. *Ethnicity and Politics in Pakistan*. Karachi: Oxford University Press, 1999.

Alam, Sardar Fakhre, Rashid Aziz Khan, and Hamid Ali Mirza. *General Elections Report, Vol. II: Comparative Statistics for General Elections, 1988, 1990, 1993 & 1997*. Islamabad: Printing Corporation of Pakistan Press, n.d., vi. JUI-F: Jamaat-i Ulama-I-Islam—afFazlur Rehman Group.

Ali, Mahmud S. *The Fearful State*. London: Zed Books, Inc., 1993.

Ali, Mubarak (Khan). "Akbar in Pakistani Textbooks." Paper presented at a seminar on Akbar and his age, held at the ICHR, New Delhi, 15–17 October 1992.

———. *Historian's Dispute*. Lahore: Progressive Publishers, 1992.

———. *History on Trial*. Lahore: Fiction Books, 1999.

Ali, Syed Ameer. *The Spirit of Islam: A History of the Evolution and Ideals of Islam*. London: Christophers, 1922.

Alivizados, N. "A New Role for the Greek Church?" *Journal of Modern Greek Studies* 17, no. 1 (1999).
Al-Jawzi, Bandali. *Min Ta'rikh al-Harakat al-Fikriyyah fi'l-Islam.* Jerusalem, 1928.
Almond, G., E. Sivan, and R. S. Appleby. "Fundamentalism: Genus and Species." In *Fundamentalisms Comprehended*, vol. 5. Edited by M. E. Marty and R. S. Appleby. Chicago: University of Chicago Press, 1995.
Anderson, John Ward. "Iranian Village Creates Model of Democracy." *Washington Post*, 2 September 2001.
Ansari, S. "Islam." In *Understanding Contemporary Society*. Edited by G. Browning, A. Halcli, and F. Webster. London: Sage, 2000.
Anwar, Mian Muhammad. *Pakistan Studies Volume I—The History and Cultural Heritage of Pakistan.* Lahore: White Rose Publishers, 1998.
Appignanesi, Lis, and Sara Maitland, eds. *The Rushdie File.* Syracuse, N.Y.: Syracuse University Press, 1990.
Apple, Michael. *Ideology and Curriculum.* New York: Routledge, 1993.
Arnold, Michael. "Guardian of the Torah." *Jerusalem Post*, 31 March 2000.
Artz, Lee Wigle, and Mark A. Pollock. "Limiting the Options: Anti-Arab Images in the U.S. Media Coverage of the Persian Gulf Crisis." In *The U.S. Media and the Middle East: Image and Perception.* Edited by Yahya R. Kamalipour. Westport, Conn.: Praeger, 1997.
Asa-El, Amotsa. "On Jewish Catholicism." *Jerusalem Post*, 14 March 1997.
Asaria, Iqbal. "Media Proves Mightier than the Sword and Penetrates Islamic Defenses." *Crescent International*, no. 4 (May 1–15, 1982).
Avishai, Bernard. *The Tragedy of Zionism: Revolution and Democracy in the Land of Israel.* New York: Farrar, Straus, Giroux, 1985.
Aziz, Khursheed Kamal. *The Murder of History: A Critique of History Textbooks Used in Pakistan.* Lahore, Pakistan: Vanguard Books, 1993.
Banerjee, Sikata. *Warriors in Politics: Hindu Nationalism, Violence, and the Shiv Sena in India.* Boulder, Colo.: Westview Press, 1999.
Barker, Ernest, trans., ed. *The Politics of Aristotle.* New York: Oxford University Press, 1974.
Barnett, Richard. *North India between Empires: Awadh, the Mughals and the British, 1720-1801.* Berkeley: University of California Press, 1980.
Basu, Amrita. "The Dialectics of Hindu Nationalism." In *The Success of India's Democracy.* Edited by Atul Kohli. New York: Cambridge University Press, 2001.
Baudrillard, J. *Simulations I.* New York: Semiotext(e), 1983.
Bell, D. "The Social Framework of Information Society." In *The Microelectronics Revolution.* Edited by T. Forrester. Oxford: Basil Blackwell, 1980.
Beyer, P. *Religion and Globalization.* London: Sage, 1994.
Bhatt, Chettan. *Liberation and Purity: Race, New Religious Movements, and the Ethics of Postmodernity.* London and Bristol, Pa.: UCL Press, 1997.

Bhattacharya, S. *Paddhatir Panchali*, translated from Bengali, *The Parable of Methodology*. Calcutta: Dey's Publishing, 2002.
Birnbaum, Ervin. "The Religious-Secular Confrontation: A Lesson for Israel." *Nativ* [Hebrew] 12, no. 6 (November 1999).
Blakemore, M., and R. Longhorn. "Communicating Information about the World Trade Centre Disaster." www.firstmonday.dk/issues612/blakemore/index.html (9 September 2002).
Boustany, Nora. "Presenting a Moderate Face in Pakistan." *Washington Post*, 19 July, 2000.
Bresheeth, Haim. "The New World Order." In *The Gulf War and the New World Order*. Edited by Haim Bresheeth and Nira Yuval-Davis. London: Zed Books, 1991.
Burns, Gene. *The Frontiers of Catholicism: The Politics of Ideology in a Liberal World*. Berkeley: University of California Press, 1992.
Byrnes, Timothy A. "The Challenge of Pluralism: The Catholic Church in Democratic Poland." Edited by Ted G. Jelen and Clyde Wilcox. *Religion and Politics in Comparative Perspective: The One and the Many*. New York: Cambridge University Press, forthcoming.
Carter, Stephen L. *The Culture of Disbelief: How American Law and Politics Trivialize Religious Devotion*. New York: Basic Books, 1993.
Caspi, Arie. "Les religieux plutot victimes que beneficiares du systeme educatif." *Courrier International* (27 January–2 February 2000).
Cazanova, J. *Public Religions in the Modern World*. Chicago: University of Chicago Press, 1994.
Chakrabarti, Dilip K. *Colonial Indology: Sociopolitics of the Ancient Indian Past*. New Delhi: Munshiram Manoharlal, 1997.
Chakravarty, Dipesh. *Provincializing Europe: Postcolonial Thought and Historical Differences*. Princeton: Princeton University Press, 2000.
Chandra, Satish. *Medieval India, A History Textbook for Class XI*. New Delhi: NCERT, 1990.
Chatterjee, Partha, *The Nation and Its Fragments—Colonial and Postcolonial Histories*. Princeton: Princeton University Press, 1993.
Clark, V. *Why Angels Fall? A Portrait of Orthodox Europe from Byzantium to Kosovo*. London: Macmillan, 2000.
Collins Cobuild English Dictionary for Advanced Learners. Glasgow: HarperCollins, 2001.
Commager, Henry Steele. *The Nature and the Study of History*. N.Y.: Charles Merril Books, 1965.
Coreno, T. "Fundamentalism as Class Culture." *Sociology of Religion* 63, no. 3 (2002): 335–60.
Cottam, Richard W. "Inside Revolutionary Iran." *Middle East Journal* 43, no. 2 (Spring 1989).
Crossette, Barbara. "Muslims Storm U.S. Mission in Pakistan." *New York Times*, 13 February 1989.

Cumings, B. "Some Thoughts Subsequent to September 11." www.ssrc.org/sept11/essays/cumings_text_only.htm (14 July 2002).
DaCosta, Y. "The Spatial Origins of the Early Cape Muslims, and the Diffusion of Islam to the Cape Colony." *Journal for Islamic Studies* 10 (1990).
Davids, Achmat. *The Mosques of the Bo-Kaap.* Athlone: South African Institute of Arabic and Islamic Research, 1980.
———. *The History of the Tana Baru.* Cape Town: Committee for the Preservation of the Tana Baru, 1985.
Dayan, Arie. "Israel: Entre ultras de tous bords, un fosse toujours plus large." *Courrier International*, no. 493 (13–19 April 2000).
Derfner, Larry. "The Shas Dilemma." *Jerusalem Post*, 28 May 1999.
Dettman, Paul. *India Changes Course: Golden Jubilee to Millennium.* London: Praeger, 2001.
Dharampal. *The Beautiful Tree: Indigenous Indian Education in the Eighteenth Century.* New Delhi: Sita Ram Goel, 1983.
Dillon, Michele. "Cultural Differences in the Abortion Discourse of the Catholic Church: Evidence from Four Countries." *Sociology of Religion* 47 (1996).
Don-Yehiya, Eliezer. "The Solution of the 'Status Quo' in the Realm of Religion and State in Israel." *Medinah u-Mimshal beYahasim Benleumiyim* 1, no. 1 (Summer 1971).
———. "Religiosity and Ethnicity in Israeli Politics: The Religious Parties and the Elections to the 12th Knesset." *Medinah u-Mimshal beYahasim Benleumiyim* 32 (1990).
Dorman, William A., and Ehsan Omeed. "Reporting Iran the Shah's Way." *Columbia Press Review* (January–February 1979).
Dorman, William A., and Mansour Farhang. *The U.S. Press and Iran: Foreign Policy and the Journalism of Deference.* Berkeley and Los Angeles: University of California Press, 1987.
Edsall, Thomas B. "The Shifting Sands of America's Political Parties." *Washington Post Weekly Edition*, 9–15 April 2001.
Efty, Alex. "Khomeini Aimed his 'Verses' Attack to Stop Liberal Trends." *Birmingham New*, 26 February 1989.
Eickelman, D. F. "Bin Laden, The Arab 'Street,' and the Middle East's Democratic Deficit." *Current History* (January 2002).
Eisenstadt, S. N. "Fundamentalism, Phenomenology and Comparative Dimensions." In *Fundamentalisms Comprehended.* Edited by M. E. Marty and R. S. Appleby. Chicago: Chicago University Press, 1994.
Eisenstadt, S. M. *Fundamentalism, Sectarianism, and Revolution: The Jacobin Dimension of Modernity.* Cambridge: Cambridge University Press, 1999.
Embree, Ainslie T. "The Function of the Rashtriya Swayamsevak Sangh: To Define the Hindu Nation." In *Fundamentalisms Comprehended.* Edited by Marty and Appleby. Chicago: University of Chicago Press, 1994.

Entman, Robert M. "Framing U.S. Coverage of International News: Contrasts in Narratives of the KAL and Iran Air Incidents." *Journal of Communication* 41, no. 4 (Autumn 1991).

Esack, Farid. *Qur'an, Liberation, and Pluralism.* Oxford: Oneworld, 1997.

Esposito, John L. *The Islamic Threat: Myth or Reality?* 3rd ed. New York: Oxford University Press, 1999.

Esposito, John L., and John O. Voll. *Islam and Democracy.* New York: Oxford University Press, 1996.

Etzioni, Amital. "A Proud American Moment." *Christian Science Monitor*, 11 October, 2001.

Evans, Richard J. *In Defence of History.* London: Granta Books, 1997.

Fado, David. "The Struggle between Hindu and Secular Nationalism in India." www.utexas.edu/depts/das/ html/south.asia/sagar/fall (1994).

Farish Noor. "How 'Secularism' Became a Dirty Word in Malaysia." msanews.mynet.net/ (4 September 2000).

Finke, Roger, and Patricia Wittberg. "Organizational Revival from Within: Explaining Revivalism and Reform in the Roman Catholic Church." *Journal for the Scientific Study of Religion* 39 (2000).

Finke, Roger, and Rodney Stark. *The Churching of America, 1776-1990.* New Brunswick, N.J.: Rutgers University Press, 1992.

Flood, G. *Beyond Phenomenology: Rethinking the Study of Religion.* London and New York: Castell, 1999.

Foote, Donna. "At Stake: The Freedom to Imagine." *Newsweek* February 27, 1989.

Ford, Peter. "Listening for Islam's Silent Majority." *Christian Science Monitor*, November 5, 2001.

———. "Xenophobia Follows U.S. Terror." *Christian Science Monitor*, 11 October, 2001.

Fox, Richard G. "Gandhian Socialism and Hindu Nationalism: Cultural Domination in the World System." *Journal of Commonwealth and Comparative Politics* (November 1987).

——— ed. *Nationalist Ideologies and the Production of National Cultures.* Washington, D.C.: American Anthropological Association, 1990.

Freitag, Sandria. Cited in *Making India Hindu: Religion, Community, and the Politics of Democracy in India.* Edited by David Ludden. Delhi: Oxford University Press, 1996.

Fukuyama, F. "Their Target: The Modern World," *Newsweek* (December–January, 2001–2002).

Gangadharan, K. K. *Sociology of Revivalism: A Study of Indianization, Sanskritization and Golwalkarism.* New Delhi: Kalamkar Prakashan, 1970.

Georgescu-Roegan. *The Entropy Law and the Economic Process.* Cambridge, Mass.: Harvard University Press, 1971.

Gergen, K. J. *An Introduction to Social Construction.* London: Sage, 1999.

Ghosh, A. *A World of Difference.* Calcutta: Centre for Studies in Social Sciences, 2002.
Ghosh, Deepshikha. "Ram Temple Issue Helped BJP's Rise to Power: Advani." www.rediff.com.news/2001 /oct/21bjp1.htm (21 October 2001).
Ghosh, Oroon K. *How India Won Freedom.* Delhi: Ajanta Publications, 1989.
Gilderhus, Mark T. *History and Historians: A Historiographical Introduction.* Prentice Hall, 1987, 1992.
Glendon, Mary Ann. *Rights Talk.* New York: The Free Press, 1991.
Golan, Matti. *Shimon Peres: A Biography.* New York: St. Martin's Press, 1982.
Gold, Daniel. "Rational Action and Uncontrolled Violence: Explaining Hindu Communalism." *Religion* 21 (1991).
Golwalkar, M. S. *Bunch of Thoughts.* Bangalore, India: Jagaran Prakashan, 1980.
Graham, B. D. *Hindu Nationalism and Indian Politics.* Cambridge: Cambridge University Press, 1990.
Grief, Howard, "Labor and Shas—On Party Corruption and Electoral Fraud." *Nativ* [Hebrew] 6, no. 5 (September 1993).
Groen, B. "Nationalism and Reconciliation: Orthodoxy in the Balkans." *Religion, State, and Society* 26, no. 2 (1998).
Gurau, A. *"The Policies of Heresy in Romania: The Influence of the Orthodox Church's Nationalist Ideology on the Regulation of Proselytism."* Paper presented at the annual meeting of the Society for the Scientific Study of Religion, Houston, October 2000.
Haddad Y. Y. "Sayyid Qutb." in *Fi Zilal al-Qur'an, Sayyid Qutb.* Beirut: Dar al-Shuruq, 1973–1974, 79.
———. "Sayyid Qutb: Ideologue of Islamic Revival." In *Voices of Islamic Resurgence.* Edited by J. L. Esposito. New York: Oxford University Press, 1983.
Haddad, Yvonne Yazbeck. *Contemporary Islam and the Challenge of History.* Albany: State University of New York Press, 1982.
Halas, E. "Rola Kosciola rzymskokatolickiego w procesie integracji europejskiej." *Spoleczenstwo Polskie w perspektywie czlonkostwa w unii europejskiej.* Edited by J. Muchy. Warzawa: Wydawnictwo IfiS PAN, 1999.
Hallaq, Wael B. *Islamic Legal Theories.* New York: Cambridge University Press, 1997.
Hamilton, Alexander, James Madison, and John Jay. *The Federalist: Or the New Constitution.* New York: E. F. Dutton & Co., Inc., 1948.
Hansen, Thomas Blom. "Recuperating Masculinity: Hindu Nationalism, Violence and the Exorcism of the Muslim Other." *Critique of Anthropolgy* 16, no. 2 (1996).
———. *The Saffron Wave: Democracy and Hindu Nationalism in Modern India.* Princeton: Princeton University Press, 1999.
Hardgrave, R. *India, Government and Politics.* Austin: HBJ Publishers, 1996.

Harvey, D. "From Fordism to Flexible Accumulation." In *Readings in Contemporary Political Sociology*. Edited by K. Nash. Malden, Mass.: Blackwell, 2000.
———. *The Condition of Postmodernity*. Oxford: Basil Blackwell, 1989.
Hashim, R. *Educational Dualism in Malaysia*. Kuala Lumpur: Oxford University Press, 1996.
Hefner, R. "Public Islam and the Problem of Democratization." *Sociology of Religion* 62, no. 4 (2001): 491–514.
Heidegger, M. "The Question concerning Technology." *The Question Concerning Technology and Other Essays*. New York: Harper, 1977.
Heuze, Gerad. "Shiv Sena and National Hinduism." *Economic and Political Weekly* (10 October 1992).
Hobsbawm, Eric J. *On History*. London: Weidenfeld & Nicolson, 1997.
Hodson, H. V. *The Great Divide, Britain-India-Pakistan*. Karachi: Oxford University Press, 1969, 1985, 1997 Jubilee Series.
Honig, Sarah. "Shas Issues Ultimatum on Joint Coalition." *Jerusalem Post*, September 25, 1994.
Hoodbhoy, Pervez. *Islam and Science: Religious Orthodoxy and the Battle for Rationality*. London: Zed Books, 1991.
Hoodbhoy, Pervez and Nayyar, A. H. "Rewriting the History of Pakistan." *Islam, Politics, and the State*. Edited by Asghar Khan. London: Zed Press, 1985.
Horowitz, Dan, and Moshe Lissak. *Trouble in Utopia: The Overburdened Polity of Israel* [Hebrew]. Tel Aviv: Am Oved, 1990.
Hughes, John. "Authors, Death Threats, and Islam." *Christian Science Monitor*, 22 February 1989.
Hunter, Shireen T. *Iran after Khomeini*. Washington, D.C.: CSIS, 1991.
Hussain, J. *A History of the Peoples of Pakistan*. Karachi: OUP, 1997.
Iannaccone, Laurence R. "The Consequences of Religious Market Structure." *Rationality and Society* 3 (1991).
Ibrahim, Youssef M. "Khomeini Assails Western Response to Rushdie Affair." *New York Times*, 22 February 1989.
Inayatullah, Dr. *State and Democracy in Pakistan*. Lahore: Vanguard, 1997.
Indo-Pak History, Part 1 (Both for boys and girls, class 6, translated from Urdu by Zahra Jafri), 3rd ed. Lahore: Sher Ghulam Ali and Sons Press Ltd., 1951.
Jaffrelot, Christophe. *The Hindu Nationalist Movement in India*. New York: Columbia University Press, 1998.
Jalal, Ayesha. *Democracy and Authoritarianism in South Asia*. Delhi: Cambridge University Press, 1995.
Jelen, Ted G. *To Serve God and Mammon: Church-State Relations in American Politics*. Boulder, Colo.: Westview Press, 2000.
Jelen, Ted G., and Clyde Wilcox. "Context and Conscience: The Catholic Church as an Agent of Political Socialization in Western Europe." *Journal for the Scientific Study of Religion* 37 (1998).

Jenkins, Keith. *Re-Thinking History*. London: Routledge, 1991.
Jensen, Lene Arnett. "Moral Divisions Within Countries Between Orthodoxy and Progressivism: India and the Unites States." *Journal for the Scientific Study of Religion* 37, no. 1 (March 1998).
Johnston, H. "Religious Nationalism: Six Propositions from the Eastern Europe and the Former Soviet Union." In *Religion and Politics in Comparative Perspective. Revival of Religious Fundamentalism in East and West*. Edited by B. Misztal and A. Shupe. London: Praeger, 1992.
Kakar, Sudhir. *The Colors of Violence: Cultural Identities, Religion, and Conflict*. Chicago: Chicago University Press, 1990.
Kanashkin, Dmitry. "Politichnyi sens okkultnoi pandemii v Ukraine." Visti z Ukrainy, no. 45. Yelensky: Kiev Patriarchy, 1994.
Kanter, R. M. *Commitment and Community: Communes and Utopias in Sociological Perspective*. Cambridge: Harvard University Press, 1972.
Kazi, Aftab. *Ethnicity and Education in Nation-Building: The Case of Pakistan*. Lanham, Md.: University Press of America, 1987.
Keddie, Nikki R. "The New Religious Politics: Where, When, and Why Do Fundamentalism Appear?" *Comparative Studies in Society and History* 40, no. 4 (1998).
Keinon, Herb. "Elections Again." *Jerusalem Post*, June 16, 2000.
Kelkar, B. K. *Pandit Deendayal Upadhyaya: Ideology and Perception: Political Thought*. New Delhi: Suruchi Prakashan, 1988.
Kellner, Douglas. *The Persian Gulf TV War*. Boulder, Colo.: Westview Press, 1992.
Kephart, W. M. *Extraordinary Groups: An Examination of Unconventional Lifestyles*. New York: St. Martin's Press, 1987.
Kermani, N. "Roots of Terror: Suicide, Matyrdom, Self-redemption and Islam." www.opendemocracy.net/forum/document_details.asp?catD=110&DocIDF =1106 (23 February 2002).
Khatami, Mohammad. *Hope and Challenge: The Iranian President Speaks*. Binghamton, N.Y.: Institute of Global Cultural Studies, Binghamton University, 1997.
———. *Islam, Liberty and Development*. Binghamton, N.Y.: Institute of Global Cultural Studies, Binghamton University, 1998.
———. www.undp.org/missions/iran/new.html (9 December 1997).
Khomeini, Imam. *Islam and Revolution: Writings and Declarations of Imam Khomeini*. Translated and annotated by H. Algar. London: KPI, 1985.
Kiefer, Francine, and Ann Scott Tyson. "In War of Words, U.S. Lags Behind." *Christian Science Monitor*, 17 October 2001.
Kirill, Metropolitan of Smolensk and Kaliningrad, "Gospel and Culture." *Proselytism and Orthodoxy in Russia: A New War for Souls*. Edited by J. Witte and M. Bourdeau. New York: Orbis Books, 1999.
Kumar, Krishna. *Political Agenda of Education: A Study of Colonialist and Nationalist Ideas*. New Delhi: Sage Publications, 1991.

Lal, Jayanta K. *Hindutva: The Emergence of the Right.* Madras: Earthworm Books Ltd., 1995.
Laqueur, W. *The New Terrorism.* New York: Oxford University Press, 1999.
Larson, Gerald James. *India's Agony Over Religion.* Albany: State University of New York.
Lash, S. *Critique of Information.* London: Sage, 2002.
Lash, S. and J. Urry. *Economies of Signs and Space.* London: Sage, 1994.
———. *The End of Organized Capitalism.* Cambridge: Polity Press, 1987.
Lawrence, B. *Defenders of God: The Fundamentalist Revolt against the Modern Age.* San Francisco: Harper & Row, 1989.
Leege, David C. "Religion and Politics in Theoretical Perspective." In *Rediscovering the Religious Factor in American Politics.* Edited by David C. Leege and Lyman A. Kellstedt. Armonk, N.Y.: M. E. Sharpe, 1993.
Leonard, K. "American Muslims before and after September 11, 2001." *Economic and Political Weekly,* 15 June, 2002.
Llewellyn, J. E. *The Legacy of Women's Uplift in India: Contemporary Women Leaders in the Arya Samaj.* New Delhi: Sage Publications, 1998.
Louw, E. P. *The Media and Cultural Production.* London: Sage, 2001.
Madan, T. N. *Modern Myths, Locked Minds: Secularism and Fundamentalism in India.* Delhi: Oxford University Press, 1997.
———. "Secularism in its Place." *Journal of Asian Studies* 46 (November 1987).
Mahajan, V. D. *Constitutional Development and the National Movement in India.* New Delhi: S. Chand & Company Ltd., 1986.
Makovsky, David. "Deri's Diplomatic Debut." *Jerusalem Post,* 21 July, 1989.
Makrides, V., and D. Uffelmann. "Studying Eastern Orthodox Anti-Westernism: the Need for a Comparative Research Agenda." In *Orthodox Christianity and Contemporary Europe.* Edited by J. Sutton and W. van den Bercken. Leuven: Peeter Publishers, forthcoming.
Martin D. *A General Theory of Secularization.* New York: Harper & Row, 1978.
Marty, M. E., and R. S. Appleby. *Accounting for Fundamentalisms: The Dynamic Character of Movements.* Chicago: University of Chicago Press, 1994.
Mawdudi, Abu'l A'la. *Islamic Law and Constitution.* Translated by Khurshid Ahmad. Lahore: Islamic Publications, 1967.
———. *Purdah and the Status of Woman in Islam.* Lahore: Islamic Publications, 1993.
Mazhar, F. *Crusade, Jihad O Sreni Sangram* (Crusade, Jihad and Class Struggle), *Chintaa* (in Bengali), October 9–13, 2001.
Mazrui, Ali. *The Satanic Verses or a Satanic Novel? The Moral Dilemmas of the Rushdie Affair.* Greenpoint, N.Y.: Committee of Muslim Scholars and Leaders of North America, 1989.
McGrath, Allen. *The Destruction of Democracy in Pakistan.* Karachi: Oxford University Press, 1998.

McKean, Lise Diane. "Towards a Political Spirituality: Hindu Religious Organizations and Indian Nationalism." (Ph.D. dissertation, University of Sydney, 1992).

Medzini, Meron. *The Proud Jewess: Golda Meir and the Vision of Israel* [Hebrew]. Jerusalem: Edanim, 1990.

Meer, Fatima, *Portrait of Indian South Africans*. Durban: Avon House, 1969.

Mele, C. "Cyberspace and Disadvantaged Communities: The Internet as a Tool for Collective Action." In *Communities in Cyberspace*. Edited by M. A. Smith and P. Kollocks. London: Routledge, 1999.

Menon, V. P. *The Story of the Integration of the Indian States*. Bombay: Orient Longmans, 1961.

Michalak, Laurence. "Cruel and Unusual: Negative Images of Arabs in American Popular Culture." *ADC Issues* (January 1984).

Michel, P. *Politics and Religion in Eastern Europe*. Cambridge, Mass.: Polity Press, 1990.

Miller, S. "Religion and Politics in Poland: The Abortion Issue." *Canadian Slavonic Papers* 39, no. 1–2 (1997).

Milstein, Uri. "Ideological Views of the Israeli Political Parties in Religion-State Relations." *Medinah u-Mimshal beYahasim Benleumiyim* (Spring 1975).

Mishra, Pankaj. "Death in Kashmir." *New York Review* (21 September 2000).

Mitra, Subrata Kumar. "Desecularising the State: Religion and Politics in India after Independence." *Comparative Studies in Society and History* 33 (October 1991).

Mitsuo, N., S. Siddique, and O. F. Bajunid. *Islam and Civil Society in Southeast Asia*. Singapore: Institute of Southeast Asian Studies, 2001.

Mody, Nawab B. "The Press in India: The Shah Bano Judgement and its Aftermath." *Asian Survey* 28, no. 8 (August 1987).

Monshipouri, Mahmood. "The Islamic World's Reaction to the Satanic Verses: Cultural Relativism Revisited." *Journal of Third World Studies* 3, no. 1 (spring 1991).

Mucha, J. "Religious Revival Movement in Changing Poland. From Opposition to Participation in the Systemic Transformations." *Polish Sociological Review*, no. 2 (1993).

Mukherji, Nirmal, and Ashis Banerji. "Neo-nationalism Symposium: The Hindus and Their Isms." *Seminar*. New Delhi (1985).

Munson, Jr., H. *Faith and Power in Morocco*. New Haven: Yale University Press, 1993.

Nagata, J. "Beyond Theology: Toward an Anthropology of 'Fundamentalism.'" *American Anthropologist* 103, no. 2 (2001): 481–98.

Nandy, Ashis. "The Politics of Secularism and the Recovery of Religious Tolerance." In *Mirrors of Violence: Communities, Riots and Survivors in South Asia*. Edited by Veena Das. Delhi: Oxford University Press, 1990.

Neuhaus, Richard John. *The Naked Public Square: Religion and Democracy in America*. Grand Rapids, Mich.: Eerdmans, 1984.

Nisbet, Robert. *The Quest for Community: A Study in the Ethics of Order and Freedom.* New York: Oxford University Press, 1953.
Offe, C. *Disorganized Capitalism: Contemporary Transformations of Work and Politics.* Cambridge, Mass.: Polity Press, 1985.
Osman, Fathi. "Ayatullah Khomeini: A Genuine 'Alim-Leader' in the Contemporary World." *The Minaret* 10, no. 3 (Summer 1989).
Oureshi, I.H. *Akbar. The Architect of the Mughul Empire.* Karachi: Ma'aaref Ltd., 1978.
———. *A Short History of Pakistan, Books One to Four.* Karachi: The University of Karachi, 1992.
Pace, E. "The Crash of the Sacred Canopy in Polish Society: A Systems Theory Approach." *Religion and Politics in Eastern and Central Europe: Traditions and Transitions.* Edited by W. Swatos, Jr. London: Praeger, 1994.
Padmanavan, Arvind, and Liz Mahew. "Differing Views: Cultural Regeneration or Cultural Regression." *India Abroad*, 17 March 2000.
Pakistani Studies for Secondary Classes. Lahore: Punjab Textbook Board, 1st ed., 1999.
Palkhivala, N. A. *We, the People: India, the Largest Democracy.* Bombay: Strand Book Stall, 1984.
Pantic, D. "Internet the Globalizer, and the Impossibility of the Impossibility of the Global Dialogue," www.firstmonday.dk/issues/issue71/pantic/index.html (9 September 2002).
Parenti, Michael. *Make-Believe Media: The Politics of Entertainment.* New York: St. Martin's Press, 1992.
Pettigrew, Joyce. "In Search of a New Kingdom of Lahore." *Pacific Affairs* 60, no. 1 (Spring 1987).
Ping, H. "September 11: A Challenge to Whom?" www.ssrc.org/september11/essays/huang_text_only.htm (14 July 2002).
Powell, Avril. "Perceptions of the South Asian Past: Ideology, Nationalism and School History Textbooks." In *The Transmission of Knowledge in South Asia, Essays in Education, Religion, History, and Politics.* Edited by Nigel Crook. Delhi: Oxford University Press, 1996.
Qutb Syed. *Islam: The True Religion.* Translated by Rafi Ahmed Fidai. Karachi: International Islamic Publishers, 1981.
Qutb Sayyid. *Maarakat al-Islam wa'l-Rasmaliyyah.* Beirut: Dar al-Shuruq, 1975.
———. *Milestones.* Indianapolis, Ind.: American Trust Publications, 1990.
———. *This Religion of Islam (hadha'd-din).* Kuwait: International Islamic Federation of Student Organizations, 1988.
Rabbani, M. Ikram, and Monawwar Ali Sayyid. *An Introduction to Pakistani Studies, for Intermediate/Senior Cambridge Classes.* Lahore: The Caravan Book House, 1992 and 1999 editions.
Ramet, S. *Nihil Obstat: Religions, Politics and Social Change in East Central Europe and Russia.* Durham, N.C.: Duke University Press, 1998.

Ramet, S. *Whose Democracy? Nationalism, Religion, and the Doctrine of Collective Rights in the Post-1989 Eastern Europe.* Lanham, Md.: Rowman & Littlefield Publishers, 1987.

Rao, B. Shiva, et al., eds. *The Framing of India's Constitution: Select Documents II.* New Delhi: The Indian Institute of Public Administration, 1967.

Rao, P. R. K. "Science and Technology as an Ideology." *Seminar* (January 1982).

Ravitzky, Aviezer. *Freedom Inscribed: Diverse Voices of the Jewish Religious Thought* [Hebrew]. Tel Aviv: Am Oved, 1999.

Raychaudhury, Tapan. *Europe Reconsidered.* Delhi: Oxford University Press, 1988.

Reed, Ralph. *Politically Incorrect: The Emerging Faith Factor in American Politics.* Dallas: Word, 1994.

Reichley, A. James. *Religion in American Public Life.* Washington, D.C.: Brookings, 1985.

Richard P. Mitchell. "The Society of the Muslim Brothers." Ph. D. dissertation, Princeton University, 1960.

Riesebrot, M. Pious. *Passion: The Emergence of Modern Fundamentalism in the United States and Iran.* Berkeley: University of California Press, 1993.

Rizvi, Hassan Askri, Javed Iqbal, and Ghulam Abid Khan. *Pakistani Studies for Secondary Classes.* Lahore: Punjab Textbook Board, 1999.

Robertson, R., and J. Chirico. "Humanity, Globalization, and Worldwide Religious Resurgence: A Theoretical Exploration." *Sociological Analysis* 46, no. 3 (1985).

Robertson, R., and R. Garrett. "Religion and Globalization: An Introduction." In *Religion and Global Order.* Edited by R. Robertson and W. Garrett. New York: Paragon House Publishers, 1991.

Roudometoff, V. *Nationalism, Globalization and Orthodoxy: The Social Origin of Ethnic Conflict in the Balkans.* London: Greenwood Press, 2001.

Roy, A. "The Algebra of Infinite Justice." *Guardian*, 29 September 2001.

Rubinstein, Amnon. *The Zionist Dream Revisited: From Herzl to Gush Emunim and Back.* New York: Schoken, 1984.

Sabine, George H. *A History of Political Thought.* London: George G. Harrap & Co., Ltd., 1937.

Sabri, Sahibzada Masud-ul-Hassan Khan. *The Constitution of Pakistan, 1973.* Lahore: Publishers Emporium, 1994.

Saha, Santosh C. and Thomas K. Carr. *Religious Fundamentalism in Developing Countries.* West Port, Conn.: Greenwood Press, 2001.

———. *Religious Fundamentalism and Public Policy: Global Perspectives.* New York: The Edwin Mellen Press, 2003.

Said, Edward W. *Covering Islam: How the Media and the Experts Determine How We See the Rest of the World.* New York: Pantheon Books, 1981.

———. "The Clash of Ignorance," www.zmag.org/saidclash.htm (6 May 2002).

———. "Inside Islam." *Harpers* (January 1981).

———. "Islam Rising." *Columbia Journalism Review* (March/April 1980).
———. *Orientalism.* New York: Pantheon Books, 1978.
Saigol, Rubina. *Education, Critical Perspectives.* Lahore: ASR Publications, 1993.
Sandler, Shmuel. "Rabin and the Religious Parties: The Limits of Power Sharing." In *Israel Under Rabin.* Edited by Robert O. Freedman. Boulder, Colo.: Westview Press, 1995.
Sarkar, Tanika. "Educating the Children of the Hindu Rashtra: Notes on RSS Schools." *South Asia Bulletin* 14, no. 2 (1994).
Sarwar, Muhammad. *Pakistani Studies.* Lahore: Ilim Kitab Khana, 1997.
Shah, Mehtab Ali. *Foreign Policy of Pakistan: Ethnic Impacts on Diplomacy.* London: I. B. Tauris, 1997.
Shaheed, Syed Qutb. *Islam, the True Religion.* Translated by Rafi Ahmad Fidai. Karachi: International Islamic Publishers, 1981.
Shaheen, Jack G. *Reel Bad Arabs: How Hollywood Vilifies a People.* New York: Olive Branch Press, 2001.
Shaheen, Jack G. *The TV Arab.* Bowling Green, Wis.: Bowling Green State University Popular Press, 1984.
Shamir, Michal, and Asher Arian. "Ethnic Voting in the 1981 Elections." *Medinah u-Mimshal beYahasim Benleumiyim* [Hebrew] 19-20, no. 7 (Spring 1982).
Shapiro, Haim. "The Collapse of Haredi Hegemony." *Jerusalem Post* 27 April 1990.
Shapiro, Yonathan. *An Elite Without Successors: Generations of Political Leaders in Israel* [Hebrew] Tel Aviv: Sifriyat Poalim, 1984.
———. *Chosen to Command: The Road to Power of the Herut Party—A Socio-Political Interpretation* [Hebrew] Tel Aviv: Am Oved, 1989.
Sharan, Shlomo. "Why Separation of Religion from the State is Inappropriate for Israel." *Nativ* [Hebrew] 12, no. 6 (November 1999).
Sharma, Arvind. *Hindu Scriptual Value System and the Economic Development of India.* New Delhi: Heritage, 1980.
Shaw, Martin, and Roy Carr-Hill. "Public Opinion and Media Coverage in Britain." In *Triumph of the Image: The Media's War in the Persian Gulf—A Global Perspective.* Edited by Hamid Mowlana, George Gerbner, and Herbert I. Schiller. Boulder, Colo.: Westview Press, 1992.
Sheleg, Yair. *The New Religious Jews: Recent Developments Among Observant Jews in Israel* [Hebrew]. Jerusalem: Keter, 2000.
Silverstone, R. *Why Study the Media.* London: Sage, 2000.
Simpson, J. "Globalization and Religion: Themes and Prospects." In *Religion and Global Order.* Edited by R. Robertson and W. Garrett. New York: Paragon House Publishers, 1991.
Singh, B. P. *India's Culture: The State, the Arts and Beyond.* Delhi: Oxford University Press, 1998.

Sinha, D. *Communicating Development in the New World Order: A Critical Analysis*. New Delhi: Kanishka, 1999.

———. "On Reworking the Global Information Order in the 21st Century— Past Lessons, Future Strategy." *Indian Journal of Political Science* 62, no. 3 (2001).

Social Studies (History & Civics) Class VI. Lahore: Punjab Textbook Board, January 1975.

Sonn, Tamara. *Interpreting Islam: Bandali Jawzi's Islamic Intellectual History*. New York: Oxford University Press, 1996.

———. "Islamic Studies in South Africa." *American Journal of Islamic Social Sciences* 11, no. 2 (Summer 1994).

Stonier, T. *The Wealth of Information: A Profile of the Post-Industrial Economy*. London: Thames Methuen, 1983.

Szawiel, T. "Religion and the Church in the New Democracy." *Polish Sociological Review*, no. 4 (2000).

Talbot, Ian. *Freedom's Cry: The Popular Dimension in the Pakistan Movement and Partition Experience in North-West India*. Karachi: OUP, 1996.

Tamadonfar, Mehran. "Islam, Law, and Political Control in Contemporary Iran." *Journal for the Scientific Study of Religion* 40 (2000).

Tefft, Sheila. "Muslims Debate Rushdie Uproar." *Christian Science Monitor*, 27 February 1989.

Thapar, Romila. *Medieval India: History Textbook for Class VII*. New Delhi: NCERT, 1988.

Tummala, Krishna K. "India's Federalism Under Stress." *Asian Survey* 38, no. 6 (June 1992).

———. "Religion and Politics in India," *Asian Journal of Political Science* 1, no. 2 (December 1993).

———. "The Indian Administrator in the New Millennium." *Asian Journal of Political Science* 9, no. 1 (June 2001).

———. "The Indian Union and the Emergency Powers." *International Journal of Political Science* 17, no. 4 (October 1996).

———. "Policy of Preference: Lessons from India, the United States and South Africa." *Public Administration Review (PAR)* 59, no. 6 (November–December 1999).

———. "Religion and Politics in India." *Asian Journal of Political Science* 1, no. 2 (December 1993).

University Grants Commission. *Mutalliyah-i-Pakistan*. Islamabad: Alama Iqbal Open University, 1983.

Van der Veer, Peter. "'God Must be Liberated!' A Hindu Liberation Movement in Ayodhya." *Modern Asian Studies* 21, no. 2 (April 1987).

Varshney, Ashutosh. "Contesting Meanings: India's National Identity: Hindu Nationalism and Politics of Anxiety." *Daedalus* 122, no. 3 (Summer 1993).

Varshney, Ashutosh. *Democracy, Development and the Countryside: Urban-Rural Struggles in India*. Cambridge: Cambridge University Press, 1995.

Viorst, Milton. *In the Shadow of the Prophet.* Boulder, Colo.: Westview, 2001.
Voltaire. *The Portable Voltaire.* Edited by Ben Ray Redman. New York: Viking Press, 1961.
Watt, William Montgomery. *Muslim-Christian Encounters: Perceptions and Misperceptions.* New York: Routledge, 1991.
Wilcox, Clyde. *God's Warriors: The Christian Right in Twentieth Century America.* Baltimore: Johns Hopkins University Press, 1992.
Witte, J., and M. Bourdeaux, eds. *Proselytism and Orthodoxy in Russia: The New War for Souls.* Maryknoll, N.Y.: Orbis Books, 1999.
Wolpert, Stanley A. *A New History of India,* 3rd ed. New York: Oxford University Press, 1989.
Yelensky, V. "Proselytism, Missionerstvo i bor'ba vokrug identichnosti ukrainskogo obshchestva," *Religiia i obshchestvo.* Bulletin by *Liudina i svit* magazine and Ukraine-American Bureau of Human Rights, no. 15 (2002).
―――. "Mezhpravoslavnyi konflikt v Ukraine (1990 gody)." *Religiia i obshchestvo.* Bulletin by *Liudina i svit* magazine and Ukraine-American Bureau of Human Rights, no. 12 (2001).
―――. "Religioznye obshchiny Ukrainy v tsyfrakh: poslednie izmenenia," *Religiia i obshchestvo,* Bulletin by *Liudina i svit* magazine and Ukraine-American Bureau of Human Rights, no. 15 (2002).
Yudelman, Michal. "A Festival of Political Correctness," *Jerusalem Post,* 2 May 1997.
Zamert, Zvi. "On the Unbearable Lightness of Blaming Ben-Gurion and the 'Religiose.'" *Medinah u-Mimshal beYahasim Benleumiyim,* vols. 41–42 (Summer 1997).
Zia, Mian, ed. *Making Enemies, Creating Conflict: Pakistan's Crisis of State and Society.* Lahore: Mashal, 1997.
Ziring, Lawrence. *Pakistan in the Twentieth Century, A Political History.* Karachi: Oxford University Press, 1997.
Zohar, Michael Bar. *Facing a Cruel Mirror: Israel's Moment of Truth* [Hebrew]. Tel Aviv: Yediot Aharonot, 1990.

Index

Abbasid Dynasty, 270
Aceh (Indonesia), 68
Act of terrorism, 184
Action-reaction syndrome, 180
adherence to orthodoxy, 55
Advani, L. K., 134, 147, 215, 219, 220, 223, 226, 227
Afghan warlords, 21
Afghani ethnic groups, 246
Afghani society, 268
Afghanistan war, 120
Afghanistan, 2, 16, 21, 22, 40, 96, 119, 120, 174, 181, 185, 187, 199, 200, 202, 208, 218, 227, 271, 282, 286; ..Taliban, 2, 16, 96, 119, 120, 208, 218, 185, 200, 201, 268, 282, 293, 294
African National Congress (ANC), 110
African Traditional Religions, 113
African-Americans: social and political equality, 41
Akali Dal Party, 218
Akbar the Great (Emperor), 5, 275
Akhil Bharatiya Vidyarthi Parishad, 145
Ala Mawdudi, Abdul, 101
Al-Aqsa Mosque in Jerusalem, 247
Ali, Syed Ameer, 97
Al-Jazeera, 185, 200, 201

All India Muslim Personal Law Board (AIMPL), 223
Allahabad High Court, 216, 223
Allende, Salvador, 193
al-Queda, 11, 14, 19–22
American hostages, 174, 188, 190
American Jew, 174, 249
Anderson, Benedict, 131
Anti-American demonstrations, 120
anti-modernism, 48, 49
anti-modernist extremes, 76
Anti-religious stance, 131
Anti-Semitism, 177
Arab world, 95
Arab-Israeli conflict, 177, 182
Archeological Survey of India, 221
Arthashastra, 148
Arya Samaj, 73, 128, 133, 135, 138, 153
Ashoka Maurya (Emperor), 275
authoritarian Muslim regimes, 174
authoritarian state, 63
Ayodhya Mandir-Musjid affair, 153
Ayub Khan (General), 277, 285, 291, 297

Baathists of Syria, 94
Babar (Emperor), 145, 214, 271, 272, 276

Babri Masjid, 214
Bahai, 85
Bahujana Samajwadi Party, 225
Bajrang Dal Party, 136, 139, 216, 217, 220, 226, 227
Balinese Hindus, 65
Balkanization of Protestant evangelicalism, 36
Baltic states, 179
Bangladesh, 300
Barak's peace initiative, 246
Baudrillardian vision of simulation, 20
Bay of Bengal, 294
Bazargan, Mehdi, 186
Begin, Menachem, 237, 248
Benizri, Shlomo, 252, 257
Bhagavat Gita, 142
Bhakti, 277
Bharatiya Jana Sangh (BJS), 212
Bharatiya Janata Party (BJP), 3,5, 127–129, 135–152, 155, 159, 160, 207–209, 211–217, 219–229, 274, 278, 296; Overseas Friends of the BJP, 144
Bhatt, Chetan, 132
Bhutto, Zulfikar Ali, 116, 117, 278, 285, 286, 289, 290, 292, 302
Bin Laden, Osama, 9, 10, 15, 16, 19–22, 24, 119, 181, 185, 199–201
Bitai, Shah Latif, 282
Black-white diabolical enemy, 180, 185
Bosnians, 177
Brahmanical paradigm, 132
Brahmo Samaj Society, 135, 138
Brahmo Samaj, 135, 138
Branch Davidians, 181
bridge-building exercise, 20
British national curriculum reforms, 274
Buddhists, 63, 65, 209
Bush, George W., 9, 10, 21, 24, 41, 185, 190, 196, 199, 200, 202

Cable News Network (CNN), 180, 182, 184, 185
camouflage jacket, 19
canonical territory, 77, 78
Carter, Jimmy, 186, 195, 202
caste hierarchy, 128, 157, 158

Catholic Church, 40, 41, 76
Catholic Irish Republican Army, 178
Catholic structural internationalism, 79
Central Intelligence Agency (CIA), 16, 178, 250, 294
Chandragupta Mauya (Emperor), 288
Chechnya, 16, 174, 179, 201, 282
China: 20th century, 60; Confucian corpus, 50; Confucian writings, 50, 60; Confucian writings and commentaries, 60; Confucianism, 50, 62; cultural revolution, 49, 50; Little red book, 50; Maoism, 49; Maoist, 52
Chinese-dominated city-state, 60
Christian antiabortion zealots, 178
Christian Byzantine Empire, 172
Christian Church propaganda, 172
Christian community, 82
Christian evangelical groups, 62
Christian missionaries in the North Eastern Frontier Agency, 218
Christian Orthodox tradition, 80
Christian personalism and tolerance, 82
Christian Right in the United States, 30, 34
Christian Right, 30, 34, 41
Christian terrorists, 177, 178
Christianity and Islam, 61, 62, 145
Civil Islam, 67
Civil Rights movement, 114
clash of civilizations, 4, 127, 158, 185
clash of ignorance, 17, 23
clash of worldviews, 17
classical ancient *oecumene*, 72
CNN, 180, 182, 184, 185
coalition *dharma*, 223, 227
cognitive consistency, 179, 180, 183, 185
Cold War paradigm, 175, 187
collections, believers, 51, 53, 65
colonialist stereotypes, 19
commonsensical epistemology, 22
communal exclusiveness, 113
communal tinder box, 224
communication order, 12
communist ideologies, 74, 76
communitarian values, 63
community building, 131

Index

comparative science of politics, 29
complexity of Islam, 175
comprehensive social justice, 99
conceptualization of information, 12
configurations of power, 10
confluence of cultures, 279
confrontation between traditional religion and modernity, 35, 36
Confucianism, 31, 38, 50, 62
consensual view of traditional society, 129
conservative Christian worldview, 175
conservative political movements, 32
contemporary humanity, 35
contract theory, 133
corporate social organization, 129
Council of Islamic Ideology, 117
coverage of Islam, 178, 183, 184, 196, 201
creation of the national religion, 77
cross-national concept, 32
cross-national laws of political behavior, 29
Crusades, 172
Culture: colonialism, 127; crust of modernity, 15; disconnect, 18; homogeneous population, 58; imperialism, 185, 189; nationalism, 127, 137, 138, 146, 158, 159, 219; of violence, 16; parochial, 202; pollutants, 158; relativism, 12, 84; revivalism, 48, 156; strategies, 129, 158, 160; understandings, 23; uniformity, 132, 135

Dayan, Shlomo, 245, 250, 251
Death before Dishonor, 183
Deccan Education Society, 135
Declaration on Religious Rights and Responsibilities, 113
decline of natural communities, 130
Deen-I-Ilahi, 277
Delhi Sultanate, 272
demonizing the West, 20
Deri, Aryeh, 236, 241, 242, 244–246, 248–258
developing practical programs, 96
Dharma yudha, 222

dialectical relationship, 73
Diktats of the sacred Book, 15
dilemma of the BJP leadership, 160
dismantling of communist regimes, 74
diversification of higher education, 56
doctrinal viewpoints, 175
downfall of modernity, 16
Dravida Munnetra Kazagam Party, 135
Dumont, Louis, 130

East and Southeast Asia, 60
East Pakistan, 116, 280, 292, 300, 301, 302
Eastern European religions, 85
Eastern Orthodox Churches, 74, 75, 84
Eastern Orthodox cultural area, 71
Eastern Orthodox identity, 80
Eastern Orthodox, 71, 74, 75, 77, 80, 84
Eastern Slav, 77
economic reforms, 94, 128
ecumenism, 37, 75, 84
egalitarian, 57, 112, 158
emancipatory potential, 23
empowerment through political Islam, 114
End of History, 18
endemically Orthodox, 78
Enlightenment Project, 10
enlightenment, 5, 81, 10, 149, 172, 228
Esfandiar, Ali, 109
ethnic nationalism, 127
ethnocentric chills, 188
ethno-nationalism, 48, 77
ethno-religious conflict, 61
European model, 94
European Renaissance, 172
European state-building, 133
evolution of secular pluralist, 57
exclusive sectarian identities, 110
extra-territorial forces, 13

Falkland Islands war, 197
Falwell, Jerry, 32
fanatics, 175, 178, 179, 181, 193
Fatwa, 15
Federal Shariah Court, 117
Federalist papers, 208
feelings of downtrodden, 176

Fellowship of Christian Nationalists, 76
feudal patriarchy, 152
First Amendment freedoms, 195
First Conference of the Sephardi Federation, 239
Friedman, Menachem, 248
Frontier Gandhi, 280
Fukuyama, Francis, 18
Fundamentalism: capture of institutions, 58; conceptualization, 47; consequences, 51; definition, 48; fundamentalist-cultural knowledge, 63; governing institutions, 57; ideology, 57; kinds of, 10, 11, 14; non-Muslim population, 67; partial institutionalization, 59; prime principles, 58, 59, 60, 63, 64, 65; social stability, 61, 63
Fundamentalism Project, 10

Gandhi, Indira, 155, 212, 214, 218, 219, 221, 270, 294
Gandhi, Rajiv, 143, 219
Gandhian *Rama Rajya*, 229
Gandhism, 140
geostrategic interests, 174
Ghaznavi, Mahmud, 271, 272, 273, 275, 277, 288
Glasnost, 76
glimpses of Bengal, 284
global capitalism, 36
global character, 11
Global Information Order (GIO), 9–23
global Islamism, 13, 115, 180, 185
globalist, 83
Golan Heights, 250
Golden Temple in Amritsar, 218
Goldstein, Baruch, 181
Golkar Party, 67
Golwalkar, Madhav Sadashiv, 135
good traditions, 107
Goren, Chief Rabbi Shlomo, 246
Granth Sahib, 38
Great Satan, 185, 187
Greek Catholics, 75, 77
Green peril, 171, 172
Grenada, 193, 202
ground for radicalization, 94, 121

group identity, 48
Gulf War, 21, 174, 184, 196–198
Gurion, Ben, 243, 246
Gujarat, 229; fiasco, 209

Haifa University, 245
Haj, 287
Halacha, 240, 241, 246, 247, 249
Hamas, 2, 177, 178
Harem-keeping oil-rich shaykhs, 178
Hasina, Sheikh, 302
Hatorah, Degel, 235, 246
Hebrew Scriptures, 35, 240
Hebrew, 35, 82, 240, 244
hedonism and greed, 106
Hefner, Robert, 65, 67
heterodoxy, 134
Hezbollah, 177, 178
high modernity, 18
Hill and Knowlton media blitz, 196
Hindu: agenda, 228; cosmology, 213; cultural renaissance, 134; deities, 225; fundamentalists, 3, 5, 37, 127, 178, 226, 228
Hindu Mahasabha Party, 127, 133, 142, 153, 211, 212
Hindu Marriage and Divorce Act, 151
Hindu nationalists, 129, 219, 227, 274
Hindu Rajas, 272
Hindu Rashtra, 132, 133, 160, 211
Hindu state, 130, 132, 136, 140, 159, 211, 226
Hindu Widow Remarriage Act, 151
Hindu women, 128, 149, 150–155
Hindu-centric historians, 273
Hindu-Muslim conflicts, 271
Hindutva, 3, 4, 131, 138–148, 152, 156, 211, 212, 219, 221, 227
Hippocratic oath, 117
Historical narratives, 268, 289, 295, 299
Historical societies and groups, 56
Histories of Balouchis, 279
holiest cities, 201
Hollywood, 182, 183
holocaust, 177, 246
Holy Agenda, 16
Holy Land, 172, 174
Holy Prophet, 102, 291

Index 329

Homogenization, 65, 133
human rights, 30, 61, 62, 82, 93, 178, 185, 187, 193, 254, 303
humane and tolerant world, 23
Huntington, Samuel P., 30, 127, 158, 175, 176, 179, 181, 185, 201, 293
Husain, Maqbool Fida, 136
Hussain, Zakir, 228
Hussein, Saddam, 181, 190, 198, 201

Identity crisis, 127
ideological institutions, 51, 53
Ideological validation, 277
Ikhwan al-Muslimin, 97
Ilaiah, Kancha, 139
imagining India, 159
immigration, 56, 59
incidents of terrorism, 174
inclusive community, 80
India: 1980 general elections, 212; anosticism, 158; anti-religious stance, 131; caste hierarchy, 128, 157, 158; child marriages, 133; civil society, 141, 150; coalition politics, 220; communal party, 212, 222; communal riots, 224; community building, 131; community-in-the-making, 160; consensual view of traditional society, 129; Constituent Assembly, 209, 210; corporate social organization, 129; cultural colonialism, 127; cultural essences, 143; cultural nationalism, 127, 137, 138, 146, 158, 159; cultural strategies, 129, 158, 160; cultural uniformity, 132, 135; decline of natural communities, 130; *Dharma*, 222, 223, 227; *dharmik*, 223; divide and rule, 209; Emergency Powers, 216, 217; English education, 141; ethnic nationalism, 127; Godra riots, 224; Hindu Education, 147; homogenization, 133; human resources development, 146; identity crisis, 127; Little Traditions, 132; Mandal Commission, 215; Muslim collaboration, 214; National education, 142; national stewardship, 132; national values, 146; neo-Buddhist influences, 136; nostalgic view, 129; primacy of moral education, 143; quasi-military discipline, 137; religious consciousness, 130; religious discord, 133; religious politics, 209; representative principle, 208; Secular democracy, 208; secular system of education, 146; secularists, 130, 146; social regressions, 128; spiritual development, 128, 153; Supreme Court, 216, 217; traditional family structure, 151; traditional syncretism, 158; tyranny of the majority, 210; Western-style nation, 148
Indian Council of Social Science Research, 146
Indian History and Cultural Society, 146
Indian National Congress (INC), 211
Indian nationalist intellectuals, 284
Indian Nationalist Movement, 266
Indonesia, 2, 31, 47, 60, 64–68, 94, 145, 159
Indonesian constitution, 64
Information and communication technology, 12
Information Society, 13
institutional implications, 47, 50
intellectual balkanization, 42
intense ideological struggle, 173
interfaith services, 113
International fundamentalism, 134
International Information Order (IIO), 11, 12
inter-religious pluralism, 112
Investigative assignments, 20
Iran: 1980 Iraqi invasion, 190; anger, 189; hostage crisis, 174; Islamic Revolution of 1979, 107; Islamist Iran, 96; militants, 188; political correctness, 194; repressive act, 193; students, 188, 189; western media misperceptions of, 189

Iranian hostage, 174, 180
Iranian Revolution, 186, 187–189, 195
Iran-Iraq War, 189–191
Iraqi conscripts, 183
Islam: anchor of, 174; antipathy to, 187; contemporary movements, 93, 121; identity, 94; intellectual freedom, 108; intellectuals, 65, 67, 277; Islamic consciousness, 96; Islamic government, 100; Islamic law, 94–96, 100, 102, 117, 118, 119; Islamist discourse, 95, 96, 97; Islamist reformers, 103; law, 94–96, 100, 102, 117–119; love of plunder, 272; Militant Islam, 14, 15, 17, 22, 180, 181, 195; motivational phase, 97; organizational style, 95; political Islam, 95–97, 110, 112, 114, 115, 120, 121; radical changes, 95; reformist, 96, 116, 120; reforms, 116; Revolutionary political Islam, 172; symbols, 94; Twentieth-century thought, 94; unbiased view, 184; vilification of, 185, 189
Islamic ascendancy in South Asia, 274
Islamic fundamentalism, 3, 19, 172, 177
Islamic invaders, 274
Islamic militants, 16, 19, 134, 175
Islamic nationalism, 266, 286, 266
Islamic rage, 174
Islamic Republic of Iran, 52
Islamic Republic, 52, 104, 278, 286
Islamic resistance organizations, 111
Islamic Revolution, 174, 195
Islamic Summit Conference, 105
Islamic terrorists, 176, 177
Islamic threat, 172, 174, 176, 180
Islamism, 3, 17, 95–97, 103, 105, 114, 115, 118–121, 180
Islamist groups, 96, 117
Islamization, 208
Islamized State, 268
Israel: Ashkenazi (European) establishment, 235, 236, 239, 240, 243, 244; Ashkenazi religious yeshiva men, 236; Commando raids, 177; conflict between Yosef and Schach, 246; cultural revolution, 240, 248, 252, 255, 256; Defense Forces, 239; El HaMa'ayan's extracurricular activities, 242; Emunim, Gush, 247; ethnic parties, 235, 237, 255; Gesher party, 245; Homeland, 177; Kach party, 250; Keshet charity organization, 245; Knesset, 32; Labor party, 236, 241, 243, 248–250; Labor Zionism, 236, 237, 238; Labor-Meretz coalition, 250; Labor-Shas relations, 251; Lithuanian religious leaders, 241; Mapai, 237, 238, 247, 256; Meretz party, 243, 246, 250–254, 257; Mossad, 178; National Religious Party, 235; National Unity Government, 249, 253; opposition to clericalism, 238; oriental (Sephardi) descent, 235; overall peace agreement, 249; preemptive strikes, 177; religious Mizrahi faction, 243; Russian immigrants, 245, 252; secular segments of society, 235, 258; Shas institutions, 244; Shas Knesset, 245, 246, 251; Shas school system, 251; Shas, 32, 235–258; Shinui (Change) party, 238; Welfare party, 243; Women's Network chairman, 254; Zionist ideology, 238, 243
Israeli Olympic athletes, 182

Jamaat-i Islami, 4, 95, 101, 103, 110, 119
Jana Sangh Party, 127, 129, 133, 136, 137, 142–145, 146, 147, 154, 156, 157, 212
Janata Party, 152, 207, 208, 212, 215, 274
Japan: *Aum Shinrikyo*, 181; Shinto, 31, 37, 38
Jerusalem Post, 250, 254, 258
Jesus Christ, 82
Jewish nation, 82, 238

Index

Jewish people, 36, 38, 82, 97, 113, 119, 172, 174, 177, 178, 181, 182, 184, 236–258
Jewish terrorists, 177
Jewish threat, 174
Jihad, 4, 15, 20, 24
Jonathan Pollard Affair, 174
Jones, Rev. Jim, 181
Joshi, Murali Manohar, 212, 220
Judaic studies, 241, 245
Judaic theology of covenants, 72

Kahane, Rabbi Meir, 181, 247, 250
Kakar, Sudhir, 137
KAL disaster, 191
Kalam, A. P. J. Abdul, 228
Kali (or Durga), 149
Kanchi Kamakoti Sankaracharya Jayendra Saraswati, 221
Kar sevaks, 215, 216
Kargil, 218
Kargil, 285, 294, 295, 296
Kashmir conflict, 120
Kaur, Raj Kumari Amrit, 210, 229
Kellner, Douglas, 196
Khalisthan, 214, 218
Khan, Abudul Ghaffar, 280
Khatami, Mohammad, 96, 104, 105, 208
Khomeini, Ayatollah, 32, 40, 96, 103–105, 181, 186, 187, 190–195, 202, 208, 286
King Hussein, 180
King Ravana, 140
Kishore, Acharya Girija, 225, 228
Knesset, 235, 237, 238, 241, 245, 246, 249–257
Kosovar independence, 179
Kosovo, 16, 179; Genocide, 179; Muslims of, 177
Kumar, Shanta, 217

Larger-scale society, 54
Larijani, Mohammad Javad, 115
late modern, 15, 18, 20, 83
Law of God, 102
Lebanon, 32, 174, 190, 250
LeFebre movement in France, 32
Leftist academics, 147

Leftist Christianity, 62
Levy, Yair, 244, 245
Lewis, Bernard, 175
LeYom, Yom, 243
liberal secular, 14, 79, 287
Likud Party, 235–239, 243–252, 254–258
Line of Control, 294
Lithuanian yeshivas, 238, 248
Lok Sabha, 215, 216, 220, 225

Madan, T. N., 38, 131
Mahabharata, 138, 142, 147, 288
Mahashiva ratri, 221
Mahila Morcha, 149
Majlis-i shura, 104
Mandela, Nelson, 114
Manicheanism, 80
Manifest destiny, 128
Mao Zedong, 50
Marg Darshan Mandal, 155
marginalization of religion, 79
Marx, Karl, 106, 173
Marxist scholars, 284
Marxist-Leninist corpus, 50
mediaeval Christianity, 72
Medieval anti-Muslim propaganda, 176
Meir, Golda, 239
Millenarianism, 48
Minorities Sub-committee, 210
Minto-Marley reforms (1909), 218
modern evil, 19
modern Jacobin movements, 49
modern rationalist idea, 130
modern science, 56
modern western scholars, 175
modernist Islamists, 186, 195
Mody, Narendra, 224
monotheist scripturalism, 131
Mookerji, Shyam Prasad, 142, 212
Moscow Jubilee Bishops Council, 79
Moscow Patriarchate, 77
Mossadeq, Muhammad, 193
Mother India, 145, 298
Movement to Restore Democracy, 285
Mubarak, Hosni, 180, 275, 276
Mughul glory, 275
Muhammad-bin-Qasim, 269–272
Muharram, 103

Mujahidin, 96
Mukti Bahini, 294
Musharraf, Pervez (General), 118, 282, 285, 286
Muslim: frustration, 174; Islam is the solution, 95, 99
Muslim Brotherhood, 2, 95, 97, 99, 101, 103, 110
Muslim conviction, 179
Muslim economic and political power, 173
Muslim elites, 156
Muslim festival of Bakr-id, 214
Muslim perceptions of the West, 184
Muslim personal law, 213
Muslim polygamists, 155
Muslim threat, 174
Muslim *Ummah*, 289, 293, 294
Muslim women, 154, 155
Muslim world, 17, 93–97, 105, 106, 109, 111, 112, 121, 172–176, 179, 180–189, 192–195, 197–201, 272, 286, 293
Mutual derision and distrust, 191

Nai Talim, 142
Nandy, Ashis, 131, 159
Nasserites, 94
Nation before community, 62
National Consultative Assembly, 104
National Council of Educational Research and Training (NCERT), 221, 272–275, 284
National Democratic Alliance (NDA), 208, 219–228
National Human Rights Commission (NHRC), 224
National ideology and national institutions, 65
national stewardship, 132
Native Americans, 182
Nativist party, 138
Nawab Salimullah, 218
Negative images of Islam, 176, 178
Nehru, Jawaharlal, 5, 131, 141, 146, 211, 212, 227, 295, 296, 299
New Age movements, 85
New International Information Order (NIIO), 12

New Jewish identity, 236
new social order, 127
New Testament, 82
New universal taxonomy, 73, 85
New World Information and Communication Order, 12
non-Christian state, 80
non-Muslim cultural influences, 283
non-Muslim Indonesians, 65
non-western settings, 42
North American Christian variety, 38
Northern Alliance in Afghanistan, 21
nostalgic view, 129

oil-rich Muslim nations, 185
Oklahoma City bombing, 176
Old Calendarist movement, 75
Omar, Mullah, 16, 22
Operation Enduring Freedom, 21
Operation Gibraltar, 279, 295
Operation Infinite Justice, 21
option of syncretism, 37
orientalist prejudice, 176
Orientalist theory, 130
Orthodox monasticism, 75
orthodox traditions, 76
Orthodox versus New Religious Movements, 75
Orthodox versus Roman Catholics and Uniates, 75
Other fundamentalism, 9, 10, 14, 18
Ottomans, 172

Pak-India War, 278
Pakistan: beleaguered community, 296, 299; chronological perspective, 300; complete Islamization, 290, 291; corrupt bureaucrats, 285; destruction of democracy, 292; historical narrative, 278; history textbooks, 265; hostile paradigms, 303; ideology, 267, 268, 269, 271, 281, 286, 287, 289, 290; influences of Western education, 292; Islamic parties, 282; Islamization campaign, 268, 286; Islamization under Zia, 291; Light of Islam, 288; military dictatorship, 297; missile

development, 285, 304; National Centre for Educational Research and Training, 273; nationalism, 265, 280, 285, 286, 290; patriotic discourse, 267, 304; polarization in society, 120; political mandates, 266; religious minorities, 292; rhetoric of educational reform, 304; selective history, 266; Sindh Textbook Board, 270; Sindhi Muslims, 282; social harmony, 281; social studies curriculum, 271, 278, 300; Social Studies textbooks, 265; Talibanization, 294; Talibanization of Madrassah, 285; unIslamic forces, 285, 292
Pakistan Movement, 269, 271, 300
Pakistan studies for secondary classes, 275, 297
Pakistani Studies, 266–269, 271, 272, 275, 276, 279, 283, 288, 290–295, 297, 300, 301
Palestine Liberation Organization (PLO), 177, 187
Palestinian Arabs, 177
Palestinian Authority, 177, 178
Pancasila, 2, 64, 66, 67
Parochial caprices, 180
Particularistic and primordial, 49
particularistic disposition, 84
particularistic expression, 74
particularistic ideologies, 72
Patel, Vallabhai, 211
Patriarch of Constantinople, 78
Patriarchal agenda, 48
Patriarchalism, 48
Patriotic Americans, 188
Peacock Throne, 188
Pearl, Daniel, 14, 16
Peasant *Samooborona* party, 76
Pentagon, 19, 171, 174, 179, 191, 199, 200
Pentecostal movements, 31
people of the book, 38
People's Action Party (PAP), 60
persecuted Muslims, 176
Peter the Great, 188
pluralist institutional complexes, 53
pluralist national polity, 68

pluralist society, 57
pluralist systems, 47
Polish civil society, 40
political consequences of religion, 30
Political marginalization, 93
political minority, 32
political role of religion, 30
political socialization, 176
populist cultural ideology, 159
Post-Cold War era, 71
potentially intolerant religious socialization, 61
Practical Islamism, 94, 110
Prasad, Rajendra, 211
Prayer Society, 138
precision bombing, 22
Preferential treatment of minorities, 213
Pre-modern West, 106
Prism of the Cold War, 173
process the dialectic of overture and compression, 75
Prophet Muhammad, 97, 102, 103, 107, 109, 172
prophetic character of religion, 42
Proselytism, 78
prosperous and westernized society, 61
Protestant Christianity, 47
Protestant embracing strategies, 85
Protestant fundamentalism, 39
Protestant missionaries, 78
Protestant Ulster Defense Association, 178
pro-western secularists, 174
psychologists, 52
Pundits, 218
Punjab Textbook Board, 291, 297

Qatari government, 185
Quaid-e-Azam, 269, 286, 287, 296
Quran and hadith, 65
Qutb, Sayyid, 99, 100, 112

racist violence, 199
radical demagogues, 186
radical Islamists, 174
Rafsanjani, Hashemi, 105
Rahman, Sheikh Mujibur, 302

Ram janmabhumi issue, 209, 211, 213–217, 219, 222, 226
Ram Janmabhumi Mukti Yajna, 214
Ram Janmabhumi Seva Committee, 214
Ram Katha Park, 222
Ram Rajya Parshad (RRP), 128
Rama-Bhakti, 139
Ramanandi sadhus, 214
Ramarajya, 140
Ramayana, 142, 147, 148, 288
Rashtra Sevika Samity, 149
Rashtriya Swayamsevak Sangh (RSS), 3, 4, 32, 34, 38, 127, 129, 135–138, 142–160, 211–214, 217, 219–222, 226, 227
Rath yatra, 215
Raza, Rahi Masoom, 228
reductionist perceptions, 175
Reform and Conservative rabbis, 251
relativist or fallibilist position, 22
relativization of personal identity, 72
Religious adventurism, 277
Religious Authority, 37
religious based political movement, 38
religious consciousness, 130
religious discord, 133
religious identity, 10, 84, 110, 112, 113, 139
Religious intellectuals, 108
Religious Knowledge (RK), 61, 62
religious nationalism, 85, 131
religious pluralism, 74, 76, 113, 135, 254
religious responses to global culture, 73
religious resurgence, 72
religious symbolic capital, 76
religious universalism, 76
Restoration of Muslim pride, 104
Revivalist Educational Philosophy, 141
Revolutionary Islamism, 171, 172, 179, 183, 196
Right of canonical law, 77
rise of communism, 173
Roman Catholicism, 31, 36, 37, 78
Rushdie, Salman, 191–195
Russian Church, 79, 82
Russian linguistic flavor, 80

Sabbath, 240, 247
Sadat, Anwar Muhammad, 174
Said, Edward, 19, 181
Sanatan Dharma Sabha, 144
Sangh pariwar, 211
Sarada Act, 210
Saraswati Bandana, 144
Saraswati, 134, 138, 144, 221
satanic overtones, 192
Satellite television, 294
Sati, 152
Savarkar, Vinayak Damodhar, 132
Schach, Rabbi Eliezer, 238
Scheduled Castes and Tribes, 213
Science: enterprise, 57; society, 57; visions, 57
Search for Saladin, 301, 302
secular and liberal worldview, 175
secular nationalists, 65, 66
secular philosophies, 94
secular pro-Western nationalists, 173
secular Western nation-states, 173
secularists, 37, 64, 130, 146, 195
secularization, 10, 30, 130, 174, 180, 188, 195
self-aggrandizement of the godless human being, 81
Sephardi: girls, 239; Jewry, 244; Knesset members, 238; music, 244; population, 245
Sephardi Judaism, 238, 244
Sephardim, 235–248, 251, 253–257
Sepoy Mutiny of 1857, 224, 271
September 11, 2001, 1, 3, 9, 10, 14–17, 20, 21, 24, 119, 172, 174, 180, 181, 185, 199, 223, 303
Serbian bishop, 75
Serbian ethnic identity, 75
Serbs, 177, 178
Shah of Iran, 40, 103, 210, 275, 276, 277, 282, 299
Shah, K. T., 210
Shakers, 48
Shas: critics of, 252; institutions, 244; Knesset, 245, 246, 251; Labor-Shas relations, 251; school system, 251
Shamir, Yitzhak, 239, 246
shared space, 10, 11, 14, 23

Index

Sharif, Nawaz, 118, 120, 285, 286, 290, 295
Shaykhs, 178, 182
Shekawat, Bhairon Singh, 217
Shindler, Alexander, 249
Shiv Sena Party, 128, 129, 135, 136, 138, 141, 149, 226, 228
Sikh community, 214
Singapore, 47, 60, 61, 62, 63, 64, 67, 68, 148; regime, 63; society, 60, 63
Singh, Dara, 220
Singh, Kalyan, 152, 216, 217, 222
Singhal, Ashok, 215, 222
Sishu Mandir, 145
small community, 54
social justice, 62, 64, 98, 103, 105, 108, 111, 112, 115, 116, 128, 140
social organization and governance, 56, 57
social studies curriculum, 267, 271, 278, 279, 285, 289, 296, 300
socialization and social control, 54
social-justice movements, 62
social-psychological consequences, 55
societal hegemony, 37
society for some basic principles, 58
Somnath Temple, 271
South Africa, 110–114, 121, 192; apartheid, 112, 113; Muslim communities, 110; Muslims, 110, 112, 114; Political Islamists, 112; spectrum, 111
South Asia Studies, 274
Soviet Communism, 172
Soviet expansion, 174
Spatial and temporal borders, 78
Spatial and temporal privileges, 77
spiritual development, 128, 153
stereotypical images, 18, 19
Stern Gang, 177
strapped reality, 18
Subaltern studies, 130
Sub-continent: indigenous kingdoms, 279; Muslim community, 276; world history textbooks, 284
Suez Canal, 98
Sufism, 136, 283
Sukarno, 64, 65, 66

Sunni Umayyads, 103
support for Israel, 201
surveillance technology, 21
Swayamsevak, 157
Symbolic *puja*, 223
synergy with Creator, 80
Syntegrationist energies, 277
Syrian Jewish community, 249

tactical flirting, 17
Taliban, 2, 16, 96, 119, 120, 185, 200, 201, 208, 218, 268, 282, 293, 294
Talmudic text, 240
Tami, 244, 250
technocratic capitalist system, 63
technological advances, 15, 30
technological superiority, 173
teleological idea of uniform progress, 84
temporal duty, 16
territorial concessions to the Palestinians, 252, 253
Thakre, Kashbhau, 219
Third World cultural identity, 95
tolerance of other creeds, 61
top-down system of control, 54
Tora, 241, 253
Tower of Babel, 81
traditionalist, 93, 211, 212
trajectory of modernity, 15
Transmission of Nationalism, 298
Treta yuga, 213
Two-Nation Theory, 267, 276, 277, 294

U.S. military presence in Saudi Arabia, 199
ubiquitous anti-globalization, 79
ultimate universal truth, 72
ultimate universalism, 82
Ummah, 49, 286, 289, 293, 294
Union of Torah Observant Sephardim, 239
universal discourse of late Modernity, 84
universal identity, 31
universal order, 72
universal psychological factors, 178
universal socialization, 51, 53

universalism, 72, 73, 76, 79, 81, 82, 83, 85
universalistic framework, 61
University Grants Commission (UGC), 221, 268
University of Balouchistan, 279
Upanishads, 142
Urdu, 154, 155, 156, 157, 213, 267, 279, 294, 296, 299, 302
US-led Western policies, 22

Values of Brahmanism, 213
Varshney, Ashutosh, 134
Vedic Age, 38, 129, 158, 221, 300
Vedic virtues, 129
Vietnamese Buddhism, 31
Vishva Hindu Parishad (VHP), 3, 127–129, 135, 136, 139, 140, 143–145, 153, 155, 212, 214–217, 220–226, 228; International Secretary General, 222
Voltaire, 172

West and Islam, 18
Westcentric terms, 10, 17
western denominations, 78
western fear of Islam, 173
western interest, 174
western mass media, 171, 174, 176–178, 180–182, 184, 186–188, 190, 191, 194, 196, 198, 201
western media: anti-Islamic bias, 176; Cinema stereotypes, 182; dehumanization of Muslims, 183; Domestic priorities, 174; Double standard in terminology, 177; malice in mass media, 178; Media war, 196; Muslim bashing, 199; national interests, 179; Negative perceptions of Islam, 175; perception of, 172, 179; Realm of ideas, 173; Us-versus-them mentality, 179
western policy makers, 185, 186, 196, 202
western reports, 197
western stereotypes, 179, 198
western way of life, 172, 174
Western world, 79, 106, 136, 175, 176, 182, 198, 293
westernization, 132, 142, 154, 180, 195
Western-modeled approaches, 95
World Conference on Religion and Peace, 113
World Information and Communication Order (WICO), 11, 12
World Trade Center, 171, 174, 179, 199, 200
Worldview, 10, 79, 105, 132, 176, 179, 181, 187, 191, 192, 202, 268
Worldwide conspiracy of Islam, 175
Worldwide Muslim community, 104

Yadav, Mulayam Singh, 215, 225
Yisrael, Agudat, 235, 238, 243, 246, 248, 254
Yosef, Rabbi Ovadia, 236, 240

Zia-ul Haq, 208, 266–268, 277, 284, 285, 289, 290, 292; Islamization, 218
Zionist ideology, 238, 243
Zionist movement, 243, 254
Zionist religious camp, 250
Zionists, 177
Zoroaster, 97

About the Contributors

Jacob Abadi is Professor of Middle Eastern History at the United States Air Force Academy in Colorado Springs. His books include *Britain's Withdrawal from the Middle East: The Economic and Strategic Imperatives, 1947–1971* (Princeton, N.J.: Kingston Press, 1982); and *Israel's Leadership: From Utopia to Crisis* (Westport, Conn.: Greenwood Press, 1993). Professor Abadi has also written numerous articles on topics dealings with modern Middle Eastern history.

Alexander Agadjanian is Professor of the Department of Religious Studies, Arizona State University, Tempe, Arizona. He has published a book and a number of articles on religion, one of which has appeared in the *Journal of the Scientific Study of Religion*.

Zohair Husain is Associate Professor of Political Science at the University of South Alabama. His publications include, *Global Islamic Politics* (New York: Longman, 2003). He is currently completing two manuscripts: "Prominent Islamic Revivalist in the Muslim World," and "A Chronological History of Islam and the Muslim World."

Ted G. Jelen is Chairman of Political Science Department, University of Nevada at Las Vegas and the current Editor of *Journal of the Scientific Study of Religion*. He published many books including *To Serve God and Mammon: Church State Relations in American Politics* (Boulder, Colo.: Westview Press, 2000); *The Political World of the Clergy* (Westport, Conn.: Praeger, 1993); and *The Political Mobilization of Religious Beliefs* (New York: Praeger, 1991). His numerous articles have appeared in *American Politics Quarterly; Journal of*

Politics; The Public Perspective; International Journal of Public Opinion Research; Social Science Journal; Review of Religious Research, Sociology of Religion; and *Journal for the Scientific Study of Religion.* His chapters have appeared in monographs, such as *Religion and Liberal Democracy: An American Perspective and the Encyclopedia of Women in American Politics.* He is on the Editorial Board of *Women and Politics; Social Science Quarterly;* and *Review of Religious Research.*

Graeme Stuart Lang is Associate Professor, Department of Applied Social Studies, City University of Hong Kong where he teaches science, technology, religion, and society in Asia. His publications appeared in *Sociology of Religion; International Migration Review; Applied Sociology; Organization and Environment;* and other international journals. He has also coauthored a book on Chinese popular religion, *The Rise of a Refuge God: Hong Kong's Tai Sin*, with Lars Ragvald (New York: Oxford University Press, 1993). His current research includes a study of temples and temple reconstruction in China, and a comparative study of syncretistic sects in East and Southeast Asia.

Anthony J. Parel was educated at Harvard and is currently professor Emeritus of Political Science at the University of Calgary. He has also taught at the University of British Columbia and Concordia University, Montreal, and is now a member of Claire Hall, Cambridge, England. His publications include *The Machiavellian Cosmos* (New Haven: Yale University Press, 1992). He is also editor of several books including: *Gandhi, Freedom and Self-Rule* (Waterloo, Ont., Canada: Wilfrid Laurier University Press, 1979); *Comparative Political Philosophy: Studies Under Upas Tree* (Newbury Park, CA: Sage, 1992), coedited with Ronald C. Keith; *Ideology, Philosophy and Politics* (Waterloo, Ont., Canada: Wilfrid Laurier University Press, 1983); *The Political Calculus: Essays on Machiavelli's Philosophy* (Toronto: University of Toronto Press, 1972); *Theories of Property: Aristotle to the Present* (Waterloo, Ont., Canada: Wilfrid Laurier University Press, 1979), coedited with Thomas Flanagan; *Comparative Political Philosophy* (Newbury Park, CA: Sage Publications, 1992), coedited with Ronald C. Keith.

David M. Rosenbaum is Commissioning Editor with Blackwell Publishing in Ames, Iowa. He is also a freelance writer.

Yvette Claire Rosser is Founding Member of Peace Works, a group of educators in the Austin School District, Texas, and dedicated to promoting peace and justice in public schools. She has published essays and articles in *Asia Review; South Asian Graduate Research Journal; Hindu Diaspora; Global Perspectives; Journal of the Midwest History of Education Society; Education about Asia;* as well as several newspaper articles in the *Friday Times* and *The Hindu*. Her Master's thesis in Asia Studies investigated stereotypes in the representation of India and U.S. World History textbooks and her Ph.D. dissertation in Curriculum and Instruction looked at textbooks in India, Pakistan, and Bangladesh as sites for the creation of nationalism.

Santosh C. Saha is a History professor at Mount Union College in Ohio. He previously taught Asian and African history in colleges and universities in India, Africa, and the United States. Dr. Saha was Editor-in-Chief of the *Cuttington Research Journal* in Liberia. He is the author of several books including *Dictionary of Human Rights Advocacy Organizations in Africa* (Westport, Conn.: Greenwood Press, 1999), *Culture in Liberia: An Afrocentric View of the Cultural Interaction between the Indigenous Liberians and the Americo-Liberians* (Lewiston, N.Y.: Edwin Mellen Press, 1998), and *Indo-U.S. Relations, 1947–1989: A Guide to Information Sources* (New York: Peter Lang, 1990). His articles have appeared in several journals including *International Journal of African Historical Studies*; *Journal of Negro History*; *Journal of Asian History*; *Pakistan Historical Journal*; *Indian Journal of Asian Affairs*; and *Canadian Journal of African Studies*. Currently he is on the editorial board of the *Indian Journal of Asian Affairs*.

Dipankar Sinha is Reader in Political Science in University of Calcutta, India. Earlier he worked as Lecturer in Political Science in Kalyani University and Scottish Church College, Calcutta, as Visiting Faculty in Burdwan University, and as Guest Lecturer in Rabindra Bharati University. Sinha is also on the editorial board of *Ekak Matra*, a Bengali literary journal. Sinha's writings focus on the development-communication linkage, in both global and local contexts, in postcolonial societies, including India. His first book was *Communicating Development in the New World Order* (New Delhi: Kanishka, 1999). His latest book is *Media Culture* (in Bengali) (Calcutta: Dey's Publishing, 2003). His current research explores the role of communication in globalization. As part of his interest in situating the Information Society in the "Third World" reality Sinha is currently also working on a project on *Citizen Empowerment through E-governance in West Bengal*. He also contributes regularly to academic journals of India and abroad and national newspapers.

Tamara Sonn is the William R. Kenan Distinguished Professor of Humanities in the Department of Religion at the College of William and Mary. She has written and lectured widely on the Muslim world. Her books include: *Comparing Religions through Law: A Sourcebook for Judaism and Islam*, with Jacob Neusner and Jonathan Brockopp (New York: Routledge, 2000); *Comparing Religions through Law: Judaism and Islam*, with Jacob Neuser (New York: Routledge, 1999) (Voted "One of the Best Books of the 1990s" by the *Journal of Law and Religion*); *Interpreting Islam: Bandali Jawzi's Islamic Intellectual History* (New York: Oxford University Press, 1996) (Choice "Books of the Year" award); *Islam and the Question of Minorities* (Atlanta, Ga.: Scholars Press, 1996);

Between Qur'an and Crown: The Challenge of Political Legitimacy in the Arab World (Boulder, Colo. and London: Westview Press, 1990); *The State and Islam: The Challenge of Political Legitimacy in the Muslim World* (Lahore: Pakistan Book Corporation, 1991).

Krishna K. Tummala is Professor and Director, Graduate Program in Public Administration at Kansas State University. He specializes in Comparative Administration, Personal Management, and Public Budgeting. His books include *Public Administration in India*. He edited *Public Administration and Policy*, for UNESCO as part of their effort in bringing out a multivolume *Encyclopedia of Life Support Systems*. He made presentations at numerous international and national Political Science and Public Administration conferences. Recently he edited *Comparative Bureaucratic Systems* (New York: Lexington Books, 2003). He received the first prize in an international essay contest on "Reservations in the Indian Public Service," held by the Indian Institute of Public Administration, government of India. He was given the "Public Administrator of the Year, 2001," award by the Kansas Chapter of ASPA. He currently serves as a member of the National Council of ASPA, and the Executive Council of the National Association of Schools of Public Affairs and Administration (NASPAA).

Vivienne Wee is Associate Professor in the Department of Applied Social Studies and Programme Coordinator of the Southeast Asia Research Centre, City University of Hong Kong. She formerly taught at The Chinese University of Hong Kong and the National University of Singapore. She was also previously Executive Director of the Centre for Environment, Gender, and Development (ENGENDER)—a regional development organization. Trained as an anthropologist, she has wide-ranging interests in religion and ideology, nation-state evolution, ethnicity and ethnonationalism, gender and development. She has done field research in almost every country in Southeast Asia. Her special expertise is in the remaking of the Malay world in Riau, Indonesia. In the field of religion, she has done ethnographic research in Singapore, Malaysia, Indonesia, and Hong Kong on Buddhism, Chinese religion, Islam, and secularism. She has published extensively in international journals and books. She recently edited a special issue of the journal *The Pacific Review*, vol. 15, no. 4: "Exploring the new fault-lines in Southeast Asia." She is currently editing a volume titled *Political Fragmentation in Southeast Asia: Alternative Nations in the Making* (New York: Routledge; City University of Hong Kong Southeast Asia Series, forthcoming).